The Orations of Demosthenes

Williamson

to

Henry W. Haynes.

P. D. Williamson
to
Henry N. Haynes.

THE

ORATIONS

OF

DEMOSTHENES.

PRONOUNCED TO

EXCITE THE ATHENIANS AGAINST PHILIP, KING OF MACEDON;

AND ON

OCCASIONS OF PUBLIC DELIBERATION.

TRANSLATED BY

THOMAS LELAND, D. D.

FELLOW OF TRINITY COLLEGE, DUBLIN.

———

COMPLETE IN ONE VOLUME.

———

New-York:

WILLIAM BURGESS, 97 FULTON-STREET.

———

1832.

PREFACE.

To animate a people renowned for justice, humanity, and valour, yet in many instances degenerate and corrupted; to warn them of the dangers of luxury, treachery, and bribery; of the ambition and perfidy of a powerful foreign enemy; to recall the glory of their ancestors to their thoughts; and to inspire them with resolution, vigour, and unanimity; to correct abuses, to restore discipline, to revive and enforce the generous sentiments of patriotism and public spirit :—these were the great purposes for which the following Orations were originally pronounced. The subject therefore may possibly recommend them to a British reader, even under the disadvantages of a translation, by no means worthy of the famous original. His candour may pardon them; or sometimes, perhaps, they may escape him, if he suffers his imagination to be possessed with that enthusiasm which our orator is, of all others, most capable of inspiring; and will, for a while, interest himself in the cause of Athens.

To the history of Greece, I must suppose he is no stranger. Yet, though it may not inform him, his memory may possibly be assisted, by a summary review of the affairs and interests of that country; particularly of those divisions, which had a long time subsisted between its principal states, and on which Philip justly grounded his hopes of success, in his attempts upon their liberties.

These states were Lacedemon, Athens, and Thebes.

The first, famous for her ancient kings, had acquired new splendour under the reign of Lycurgus. The wisdom of the constitution which he established, and the exact obedience paid to his laws, preserved the state from those domestic divisions which prevailed in other places; and the remarkable temperance of Sparta, the severity of her discipline, her public spirit, and concern for the liberty and happiness of other communities, made her long revered as the parent of Greece. Her constitution, however, was not without its faults. Her government savoured of the humour of her inhabitants, who extended the same harsh severity to their allies, which they used toward each other. Besides, they were devoted to arms; and their constitution required continual wars for the preservation of it. This made their government distasteful, and favoured the ambition of the Athenians, their rivals, who, though a more ancient people, had, for many years (through their weakness or disorders) lived without any thought of command.

Athens was originally governed by kings: the last of whom sacrificed his life to the good of his country; and, upon his death, the Athenians took occasion to abolish the royalty, and instituted their perpetual archons, which were changed to decennial, and afterward to an annual, magistracy. The state, however, was not completely settled, until Solon, by his wise laws, restored the love of labour and husbandry, opened a way for commerce, taught his countrymen to enrich themselves, and found means to subdue their licentiousness by the rules of justice, order, and discipline. Athens, thus reformed, was in a fair way of growing great and illustrious, when one of the citizens found means to seize the supreme power. The struggles of the Athenians for liberty, against the successors of this man, was one occasion of the Persian war; the glorious exploits of which are too well known to need a recital. The victories of Marathon, Salamis, and Platæa, the chief honour of which the Athenians assumed to themselves, determined the character of that people, inspired them with the highest notions of glory and honour, and at last prompted them to set up for sovereign umpires of Greece. Sparta was willing to resign to them the command of the sea; but they would be absolute in all. And as they had delivered Greece from the oppression of the barbarians, they thought themselves entitled to oppress her in their turn. They called themselves protectors of the Grecian cities, but behaved like their lords; till at last, Sparta, urged by the complaints of several states against the violence of Athens, began the famous Peloponnesian war, which was carried on with various success twenty-seven years. The unhappy expedition of the Athenians into Sicily, first shook their power: and the victory of Lysander at Ægos-Potamos, entirely overthrew it.

By this event, however, Greece only changed her masters. Sparta resumed the superiority; but her new reign lasted only thirty years. The Spartans were possessed with such a prejudice in favour of their own form of government, that they attempted to abolish democracy every where; and while they imposed their thirty tyrants upon Athens, established a government of ten, in other states, composed of men devoted to their interest. Thus they became more absolute, but at the same time more odious. Their prosperity made them presume too much upon their strength. Their forces were lent to support the pretensions of the younger Cyrus. Their king, Agesilaus, was sent into Persia; where the Great King could not put a stop to his progress, but by bribing the Greeks, and by that means raising up enemies against Sparta.

The Greeks readily hearkened to his solicitations. The Athenians, at the head of the malcontents, resolved to hazard every thing for liberty; and without reflecting on their late miserable condition, presumed to affront that state which had reduced them to it. They knew so well to make a right use of the oversight the Spartans had committed, in provoking the great king, that, joining their force with the Persian fleet, they defeated them, and rebuilt their walls: nor did they lay down their arms, till the Lacedemonians were obliged, by a solemn treaty, to restore the Grecian cities to their liberty. For although the Lacedemonians pretended a voluntary generosity in this affair, yet it appeared, by the consequence, that fear only had obliged them to it; as they took an opportunity, some time after, to oppress Thebes, though expressly comprehended in the treaty. This raised the states of Greece against them. The Athenians (who always harboured the most inveterate hatred and jealousy of them, and had lately been particularly provoked by an attempt of one of their generals to seize their port) set themselves once more at the head of the confederacy, and took upon themselves the whole expense of the war; in which their arms were crowned with victories by sea and land, at Corinth, Naxos, Corcyra, and Leucas. Thus were the Spartans obliged to renew the treaty, and the cities of Greece again restored to an entire independency.—These bold efforts of the Athenians to reduce the Spartan power, and to regain their former sovereignty, are frequently extolled in the following Orations, as the glorious effects of their concern for the liberties of Greece.

And now the peace was just concluded, and the Greeks had the fairest prospect of enjoying it, when, on a sudden, the Thebans started up, and asserted their claim to sovereign power.

Thebes had, from the earliest ages, been ranked amongst the most considerable states. The natural slowness and heaviness of the inhabitants had, however, prevented them from aiming at any pre-eminence. In the Persian war, they even had the baseness to join with the barbarians. And in order to screen themselves from the resentment of the Athenians on this account, they afterward attached themselves to Lacedemon: and continued firm, through the whole course of the Peloponnesian war. They shifted sides, however, some time after, and had some contests with the Lacedemonians. The seizing of their citadel, and the recovery of it out of the hands of the Lacedemonians by Pelopidas, had created a mutual hatred between these two states. And the Thebans, naturally hardy and robust, and grown experienced since the Peloponnesian war (from which time their arms had been constantly exercised,) now at length began to entertain thoughts of commanding. They refused to accede to the treaty negotiated by the Athenians, unless they were acknowledged chief of Bœotia. This refusal not only exposed them to the resentment of the king of Persia (who was at that time particularly concerned that the Greeks should be at peace,) but raised Athens, Sparta, and indeed all Greece against them. The Lacedemonians declared war; and thinking them an easy victory, now that they were deserted by their allies, marched their forces a considerable way into the Theban territory. Now it was, that Epaminondas first shone out in all his lustre. He put himself at the head of the Thebans, and met the enemy at Leuctra, where he gave them a total overthrow. He then marched into Peloponnesus, and had well-nigh made himself master of the city of Sparta; relieved some people who had been oppressed by the Spartans; and by his justice and magnanimity, his extensive abilities, and zealous concern for his country, promised to raise the Thebans to the most exalted degree of power and dignity; when, in another engagement with the Lacedemonians at Mantinea, he fell, as it were, in the arms of victory.

The death of Epaminondas, and the peace which ensued, slackened the zeal of the principal powers of Greece, and rendered them too secure. The Athenians, particularly (when they saw the fortune of Lacedemon at the lowest ebb, and that, on the part of Thebes, they were freed from all apprehensions by the death of the general, the soul of all their counsels and designs,) were now no longer upon their guard, but abandoned themselves to ease and pleasure. Festivals and public entertainments engaged their attention, and a violent passion for the stage banished all thoughts of business and glory. Poets, players, singers, and dancers, were received with that esteem and applause, which were due to the commanders who fought their battles. They were rewarded extravagantly, and their performances exhibited with a magnificence scarcely to be conceived. The treasures which should have maintained their armies, were applied to purchase seats in their theatres. Instead of that spirit and vigour which they exerted against the Persian, they were possessed with indolence and effeminacy; they had no farther concern about the affairs of war, than just to keep a few foreign troops in pay: in short, treachery, corruption, and degeneracy, overspread the state.

But while they were sinking into this condition, they found themselves unexpectedly engaged with a very formidable enemy, Philip, king of the Macedonians, a people hitherto obscure, and in a manner barbarous; but now, by the courage, activity, and consummate policy of their monarch, ready to lay the foundation of a most extensive empire.

Philip had been sent early into Thebes as an hostage, where he was so happy as to improve his natural abilities, by the instructions of Epaminondas. The news of his brother Perdiccas being slain in a battle with the Illyrians, determined him to fly to the relief of his country; he eluded the vigilance of his guards, and escaped privately to Macedon; where, taking advantage of the people's consternation for the loss of their king, and of the dangers they apprehended from an infant reign, he first got himself declared protector to his nephew, and soon after king in his stead: and indeed the present condition of the Macedonians required a prince of his abilities. The Illyrians, flushed with their late victory, were preparing to march against them: the Pæonians harassed them with perpetual incursions; and, at the same time, Pausanias and Argæus, two of the royal blood, pretended to the crown: the one supported by Thrace, the other by Athens.

Under these circumstances, Philip's first care was to gain the affections of his people, to raise their spirits, to train and exercise them, and to reform their military discipline. And now he began to discover those abilities, which afterward raised him to such a height of power, and which were not to be expected in a prince of the age of twenty-two years.

The chief motive of the Athenians, in supporting the pretensions of Argæus, was the hopes of getting possession of Amphipolis, a city bordering on Macedon, which they had long claimed as their colony. It had sometimes been in their hands, sometimes subjected to Lacedemon, according to the different changes of fortune of these states. After the peace of Antalcidas, the Greeks acknowledged the pretensions of the Athenians; and it was resolved, that they should be put in possession of this city at the common charge. Probably the people of Amphipolis refused to submit to their old masters: for the Athenians were obliged to despatch Iphicrates thither with forces. But the kings of Macedon now began to dispute it with them. Perdiccas made himself master of it; and Philip would very gladly have kept it in his own hands; but this could not be done without weakening his army, and incensing the Athenians, whom his present circumstances required him rather to make his friends: on the other hand, he could not think of suffering them to possess it, as it was the key to that side of his dominions. He therefore took a middle course, and declared it a free city; thereby leaving the inhabitants to throw off their dependence on their masters, and making it appear to be their own act. At the same time he disarms the Pæonians by the force of presents and promises, and then turns his arms against the Athenians, who had marched to the assistance of Argæus. A battle ensued, in which Philip was victorious. By the death of Argæus, who fell in the action, he was freed from that dispute; and by his respectful care of the Athenians, when he had them in his power, he so far gained upon that people, that they concluded a peace with him. He now found himself strong enough to break with the Pæonians, whom he subdued; and having gained a complete victory over the Illyrians, he obliged them to restore all their conquests in Macedon. He also shut up the entrance of his kingdom against Pausanias; but having provided for the security of it, in the next place he thought of making it more powerful and flourishing.

The reunion of Amphipolis he considered as the principal means to this end; and therefore, under pretence of punishing some wrongs, which he alleged against that city, he laid siege to it. The moment they perceived their danger, the people of Amphipolis sent two of their citizens to Athens, to solicit succours: but, in order to prevent any opposition on the part of the Athenians, Philip gave them the strongest assurances, that his sole design was to put them in possession of it, the moment it was in his power: they therefore suffered him to make a conquest of it. But, instead of performing his promise, he proceeded to take from them Pydna and Potidæa, with which he purchased the friendship of the Olynthians, whom it concerned him at that time to oblige. The golden mines of Crenides fell next into his hands, and contributed greatly to his successes.

The Athenians could not but be alarmed at the progress of this prince. His vigilance and activity, his policy and insincerity, now began to appear dangerous; and councils were held to deliberate upon the measures proper to be taken. But, although the Athenians were possessed with delicacy and sensibility, and entertained magnificent ideas of virtue and its duties, yet they wanted application, constancy, and perseverance. The good qualities which had long been the boast of that people, were now disappearing, while their faults increased. Hence it was, that they easily suffered themselves to be lulled into a false security. Besides, they had enough of difficulty to support their jurisdiction in other parts, and to bear up against a considerable revolt of their allies.

This revolt produced the war called the social war; which lasted three years, and was succeeded by the Phocian or sacred war, so called, because begun from a motive of religion. The Phocians had ploughed up some ground adjoining to the temple of Apollo at Delphos, which their neighbours exclaimed against as sacrilege, and was so judged by the council of Amphictyons, that venerable assembly composed of representatives from the principal states of Greece, who sat twice every year at Delphos and Thermopylæ. They laid a heavy fine upon them; but, instead of submitting to the sentence, the Phocians alleged, that the care and patronage of the temple belonged anciently to them; and, encouraged by Philomelus, one of their principal citizens, took up arms to assert their claim. The several states of Greece took part in this quarrel, as their interests and inclinations directed. Athens and Sparta, with some other of the Peloponnesians, declared for the Phocians. The Thebans were their principal opposers; and were assisted by the Thessalians, Locrians, and other neighbouring states. At first, Philomelus had some success; but, in the second year of the war, the Thebans gave him a signal defeat, and he himself was killed in the pursuit.

In the mean time, Philip took no part in this war. He was well pleased that the parties should exhaust their strength; and also had an opportunity of securing and extending his frontier without interruption, by taking in such places as were either convenient or troublesome to him. Of this latter kind was the city of Methone, which, after some resistance, he took and, demolished, annexing its lands to Macedon. During the siege, he was in imminent danger of his life, having lost one of his eyes by an arrow. But it was not long before Philip had a fair opportunity of engaging as a party in the Phocian war. The Thessalians, a people susceptible of all impressions, and incapable of preserving any, equally forgetful of benefits and injuries, ever ready to submit to tyrants, and to implore the assistance of their neighbours to free them from slavery—had some time since been governed by Alexander of Pheræ, the most detestable tyrant ever known in Greece. He was despatched by Tisiphonus, Lycophron, and Pitholaus, who seized the government, and became equally intolerable. So that the nobility of Thessaly, with the Aleuadæ, descendants from Hercules, at their head, declared against them, and implored the assistance of Philip. This prince willingly sacrificed the hopes of extending his conquests in Thrace to the honour of assisting the Aleuadæ, who were of the same race with him; and of imitating Pelopidas in giving liberty to Thessaly. He had also long wished to have the Macedonians considered as a Grecian people; and, as he thought no opportunity could be so honourable and favourable, as to effect an interest of the affairs of Thessaly, he readily marched against the tyrants, and soon divested them of all their authority.

But Philip's apparent danger from the wound which he received at Methone, imboldened Lycophron to resume the sovereign power. The Phocians (who, after the death of Philomelus, had renewed the war with all imaginable vigour under Onomarchus) espoused the cause of this tyrant, who had engaged the Thessalians to observe a neutrality; and they, in return, supported him with all their power. Philip, therefore, now became involved in the general quarrel. At first, the Phocian general gained some advantages over him: but he afterward had such success, as enlarged his views, and inspired him with new hopes and expectations. He thought of nothing less than the conquest of Greece: and under pretence of marching against the Phocians, made a bold attempt to seize the famous pass at Thermopylæ, which he justly called the key of Greece. This roused the Athenians from their lethargy. At the first news of his march they flew to the pass, and prevented his design; as he did not think it prudent to force his way. We may reasonably look on his retreat from Thermopylæ as the era of Philip's hatred to the Athenians. He saw that they were the only people of Greece capable of defeating his projects, or of giving him uneasiness in his own kingdom: he therefore provided himself, with much diligence, a fleet composed of light ships, which might disturb their trade, and, at the same time, enrich his subjects by bringing in prizes. He also increased his army, and projected the destruction of the Athenian colonies in Thrace. At the same time, he practised very successfully at Athens itself; and, by large appointments, secured some eminent orators, to charm the people with delusive hopes of peace, or to frighten them with expensive estimates, while they pretended a zeal for the defence of the state.

In a democratical government, like that of Athens, ELOQUENCE was the sure means of recommending its possessor to the attention and regard of his fellow-citizens, and of raising him to all public honours and advantages. The gradual improvements of literature had introduced and perfected the arts of moving and persuading; and perhaps the disorders of the state contributed to make them more important, called forth a greater number of public speakers, and opened a larger field for their abilities. Many of those orators, who, about that time, took the lead in the Athenian assemblies, are lost to posterity. The characters, however, of the most eminent have been transmitted, or may be collected from the writings of antiquity.

Demades, by his birth and education, seemed destined to meanness and obscurity; but as the Athenian assembly admitted persons of all ranks and occupations to speak their sentiments, his powers soon recommended him to his countrymen, and raised him from the low condition of a common mariner, to the administration and direction of public affairs. His private life was stained with those brutal excesses, which frequently attend the want of early culture, and an intercourse with the inferior and least refined part of mankind. His conduct, as a leader and minister, was not actuated by the principles of delicate honour and integrity; and his eloquence seems to have received a tincture from his original condition. He appears to have been a strong, bold, and what we call a blunt speaker, whose manner, rude and daring, and sometimes bordering on extravagance, had oftentimes a greater effect than the more corrected style of other speakers, who confined themselves within the bounds of decorum and good-breeding.

Hyperides, on the contrary, was blessed with all the graces of refinement: harmonious, elegant, and polite, with a well-bred festivity, a delicate irony; excellent in panegyric, and of great natural abilities for affecting the passions; yet his eloquence seems rather to have been pleasing than persuasive. He is said to have been not so well fitted for a popular assembly, and for political debates, as for private causes, and addressing a few select judges; and even here, when he pleaded the cause of a woman for whom he had the tenderest passion, he was obliged to call the charms of his mistress to the assistance of his eloquence, and was more indebted to these for his success than to his own powers.

Lycurgus had all the advantages which birth and education could afford for forming an orator. He was the hearer of Plato, and the scholar of Isocrates. He seems to have been particularly affected by the charms of poetry and the polite arts; nor was he less remarkable for diligence and attention; yet his influence in the assembly seems, like that of Phocion, to have arisen rather from a respect to his character, and the general opinion of his virtue and integrity, than from his abilities as a speaker.

Æschines was an orator, whose style was full, diffusive, and sonorous. He was a stranger to the glowing expressions and daring figures of Demosthenes, which he treats with contempt and ridicule. But, though more simple, he is less affecting; and, by being less contracted, has not so much strength and energy. Or, as Quintilian expresses it, *carnis plus habet, lacertorum minus*. But, if we would view his abilities to the greatest advantage, we must not compare them with those of his rival. Then will his figures appear to want neither beauty nor grandeur. His easy and natural manner will then be thought highly pleasing; and a just attention will discover a good degree of force and energy in his style, which, at first, appears only flowing and harmonious.

But all the several excellences of his countrymen and contemporaries were at least equalled by Demosthenes. [1.] His own, no age or nation could attain to. From him, critics have formed their rules; and all the masters in his own art have thought it an honour to imitate him. To enlarge upon his character, would be to resume a subject already exhausted by every critic, both ancient and modern. Let it be sufficient to say, that energy and majesty are his peculiar excellencies. From the gravity of Thucydides, the pomp and dignity of Plato, the ease and elegance, the neatness and simplicity of the Attic writers, he formed a style and manner admirably fitted to his own temper and genius, as well as that of his hearers. His own determined him to the more forcible methods of severity, astonishing and terrifying, rather than the gentle and insinuating arts of persuasion; nor did the circumstances and dispositions of his countrymen admit of any but violent impressions. As many of those to whom he addressed himself were men of low rank and occupations, his images and expressions are sometimes familiar. As others of them were themselves eminent in speaking, and could readily see through all the common artifices of oratory, these he affects to despise; appears only solicitous to be understood; yet, as it were without design, raises the utmost admiration and delight; such delight as arises from the clearness of evidence, and the fulness of conviction. And, as all, even the lower part of his hearers, were acquainted with the beauties of poetry and the force of harmony, he could not admit of any thing rude or negligent, but with the strictest attention laboured those compositions which appear so natural and unadorned. They have their ornaments, but these are austere and manly, and such as are consistent with freedom and sincerity. A full and regular series of diffusive reasoning would have been intolerable in an Athenian assembly. He often contents himself with an imperfect hint: a sentence, a word, even his silence, is sometimes pregnant with meaning. And this quickness and vehemence flattered a people who valued themselves on their acuteness and penetration. The impetuous torrent that in a moment bears down all before it, the repeated flashes of lightning, which spread universal terror, and which the strongest eye dares not encounter, are the images by which the nature of his eloquence hath been expressed.

As a statesman and as a citizen, his conduct was no less remarkable. If the fire of his eloquence seems sometimes abated, his judgment and accuracy and political abilties are then conspicuous. The bravery with which he opposed the passions and prejudices of his countrymen, and the general integrity of his character (to which Philip himself bare witness) are deserving of the highest honour; and, whatever weakness he betrayed in his military conduct, his death must be acknowledged truly heroic.

The reader will observe, that the Oration entitled, On the Halonesus, is not admitted into the following collection. Some critics ascribe it to Hegesippus, [2.] an Athenian orator of inferior character. But, however this may be, it is certainly entirely different from those compositions of Demosthenes which are confessedly genuine. That he really wrote an oration so entitled, [3.] the authority of the ancient writers confirm, I think, sufficiently. But one would be tempted to believe, that the passages which they have quoted, had been taken up by some old scholiast, and inserted in a performance of his own.

As to the translation now offered to the public, the author has no doubt but that it will meet with all due indulgence from the ingenious and judicious reader. His sentence must determine its fate, and to him it is implicitly submitted.

[1.] Nihil Lysiæ subtilitate cedit; nihil argutiis et acumine Hyperidi; nihil lenitate Æschini et splendore verborum. *Cic. de Orat.*

[2.] In the oration on the Halonesus, the speaker takes notice of his having been the manager of a prosecution against Calippus, on account of an illegal motion made by this man in the assembly, relative to the boundaries of Cardia. Hegesippus was the person who conducted this prosecution; and this circumstance Libanius mentions as having (together with the difference of style) induced the critics to ascribe this oration, not to Demosthenes, but to Hegesippus. To this we may add another circumstance of the like nature. The speaker observes that he went on an embassy to Macedon, in order to obtain an explanation and amendment of some articles in the treaty concluded between Philip and the Athenians. Hegesippus was at the head of this embassy: nor was Demosthenes at all concerned in it, as appears from the oration of this latter (Περι της Παραπρ.)

[3.] Æschines, in his oration on the Embassy, mentions two particulars in that of Demosthenes on the Halonesus, neither of which are found in the oration now extant. The first is, that Demosthenes treated Philip's ambassadors with great severity, and insisted that they were really sent as spies. The other, that he recommended to the Athenians by no means to submit their disputes with Philip to the decision of an umpire; for that no one impartial meditating state could be found through Greece, so totally were the minds of all men corrupted by the Macedonian.

CONTENTS.

ORATIONS OF DEMOSTHENES.

THE FIRST ORATION AGAINST PHILIP:

PRONOUNCED IN THE ARCHONSHIP OF ARISTODEMUS, IN THE FIRST YEAR OF THE
HUNDRED AND SEVENTH OLYMPIAD, AND THE NINTH OF PHILIP'S REIGN.

INTRODUCTION.

WE have seen Philip opposed in his design of passing into Greece through Thermopylæ, and obliged to retire. The danger they had thus escaped deeply affected the Athenians. So daring an attempt, which was, in effect, declaring his purposes, filled them with astonishment; and the view of a power, which every day received new accessions, drove them even to despair. Yet the aversion to public business was still predominant. They forgot that Philip might renew his attempt, and thought they had provided sufficiently for their security, by posting a body of troops at the entrance of Attica, under the command of Menelaus, a foreigner. They then proceeded to convene an assembly of the people, in order to consider what measures were to be taken to check the progress of Philip; on which occasion Demosthenes, for the first time, appeared against that prince, and displayed those abilities which proved the greatest obstacle to his designs.

At Athens, the whole power and management of affairs were placed in the people. It was their prerogative to receive appeals from the courts of justice, to abrogate and enact laws, to make what alterations in the state they judged convenient: in short, all matters, public or private, foreign or domestic, civil, military, or religious, were determined by them.

Whenever there was occasion to deliberate, the people assembled early in the morning, sometimes in the forum or public place, sometimes in a place called Pnyx, but most frequently in the theatre of Bacchus. A few days before each assembly, there was a Πρόγραμμα or placard fixed on the statues of some illustrious men erected in the city, to give notice of the subject to be debated. As they refused admittance into the assembly to all persons who had not attained the necessary age, so they obliged all others to attend. The Lexiarchs stretched out a cord dyed with scarlet, and by it pushed the people toward the place of meeting. Such as received the stain were fined; the more diligent had a small pecuniary reward. These Lexiarchs were the keepers of the register, in which were enrolled the names of such citizens as had a right of voting. And all had this right who were of age, and not excluded by a personal fault. Undutiful children, cowards, brutal debauchees, prodigals, debtors to the public, were all excluded. Until the time of Cecrops, women had a right of suffrage, which they were said to have lost on account of their partiality to Minerva, in her dispute with Neptune about giving a name to the city.

In ordinary cases, all matters were first deliberated in the senate of five hundred, composed of fifty senators chosen out of each of the ten tribes. Each tribe had its turn of presiding, and the fifty senators in office were called Prytanes. And according to the number of the tribes, the Attic year was divided into ten parts, the four first containing thirty-six, the other thirty-five days; in order to make the Lunar year complete, which, according to their calculation, contained three hundred and fifty-four days. During each of these divisions, ten of the fifty Prytanes governed for a week, and were called Proëdri: and of these he, who in the course of the week presided for one day, was called the Epistate; three of the Proëdri being excluded from this office.

The Prytanes assembled the people; the Proëdri declared the occasion; and the Epistate demanded their voices. This was the case in the ordinary assemblies: the extraordinary were convened as well by the generals as the Prytanes; and sometimes the people met of their own accord, without waiting the formalities.

The assembly was opened by a sacrifice; and the place was sprinkled with the blood of the victim.—Then an imprecation was pronounced, conceived in these terms: "May the gods pursue that man to destruction, with all his race, who shall act, speak, or contrive, any thing against this state !". This ceremony being finished, the Proëdri declared the occasion of the assembly, and reported the opinion of the senate. If any doubt arose, a herald by commission from the Epistate, with a loud voice, invited any citizen, first of those above the age of fifty, to speak his opinion; and then the rest according to their ages. This right of precedence had been granted by a law of Solon, and the order of speaking determined entirely by the difference of years. In the time of Demosthenes, this law was not in force. It is said to have been repealed about fifty

2

years before the date of this oration. Yet the custom still continued, out of respect to the reasonable and decent purpose for which the law was originally enacted. When a speaker had delivered his sentiments, he generally called on an officer appointed for that purpose, to read his motion, and propound it in form. He then sat down, or resumed his discourse, and enforced his motion by additional arguments : and sometimes the speech was introduced by his motion thus propounded. When all the speakers had ended, the people gave their opinion, by stretching out their hands to him whose proposal pleased them most. And Xenophon reports, that, night having come on when the people were engaged in an important debate, they were obliged to defer their determination till next day, for fear of confusion, when their hands were to be raised.

"Porrexerunt manus," saith Cicero (pro Flacco,) "et Psephisma natum est." And, to constitute this Psephisma or decree, six thousand citizens at least were required. When it was drawn up, the name of its author, or that person whose opinion had prevailed, was prefixed : whence, in speaking of it, they called it his decree. The date of it contained the name of the Archon, that of the day and month, and that of the tribe then presiding. The business being over, the Prytanes dismissed the assembly.

The reader who chooses to be more minutely informed in the customs, and manner of procedure in the public assemblies of Athens, may consult the Archæologia of Archbishop Potter, Sigonius, or the Concionatrices of Aristophanes.

PHILIPPIC THE FIRST.

Aristodemo, Archon—A. R. Philip. 9—
Olympiad. 107. An. 1.

HAD we been convened, Athenians ! on some new subject of debate, I had waited until most of the usual persons had declared their opinions. If I had approved of any thing proposed by them, I should have continued silent : if not, I had then attempted to speak my sentiments.

But since those very points on which these speakers have oftentimes been heard already, are at this time to be considered : though I have arisen first, [1.] I presume I may expect your pardon ; for if they on former occasions had advised the necessary measures, ye would not have found it needful to consult at present.

First, then, Athenians ! these our affairs must not be thought desperate ; no, though their situation seems entirely deplorable. For the most shocking circumstance of all our past conduct is really the most favourable to our future expectations. And what is this ? That our own total indolence hath been the cause of all our present difficulties. For were we thus distressed, in spite of every vigorous effort which the honour of our state demanded, there were then no hope of a recovery.

In the next place, reflect (you who have been informed by others, and you who can yourselves remember,) how great a power [2.] the Lacedemonians not long since possessed : and with what resolution, with what dignity, you disdained to act unworthy of the state, but maintained the war against them for the rights of Greece. Why do I mention these things ? That ye may know, that ye may see, Athenians ! that if duly vigilant, ye cannot have any thing to fear ; that if once remiss, not any thing can happen agreeable to your desires ; witness the then powerful arms of Lacedemon, which a just attention to your interests enabled you to vanquish ; and this man's late insolent attempt, which our insensibility to all our great concerns hath made the cause of this confusion.

If there be a man in this assembly who thinks that we must find a formidable enemy in Philip, while he views, on one hand, the numerous armies [3.] which attend him ; and, on the other, the weakness of the state thus despoiled of its dominions ;·he thinks justly. Yet, let him reflect on this : there was a time, Athenians ! when we possessed Pydna, and Potidæa, and Methone, and all that country round : when many of those states, now subjected to him, were free and independent, and more inclined to our alliance than to his. Had then Philip reasoned in the same manner— "How shall I dare to attack the Athenians, whose garrisons command my territory while

---

[1.] Though I have arisen first, &c.] Demosthenes was at that time but thirty years old, which made it necessary for him to apologize for his zeal in rising before the other speakers ; and the ingenious turn which he gives it, not only prevents any unfavourable impression on the minds of his hearers, but engages their affection, and excites their attention, by the tacit promise of better counsel than they had hitherto received. *Tourreil.*

[2.] How great a power, &c.] It has been already observed in the preface to these orations, that Demosthenes takes many occasions of extolling the efforts of Athens to reduce the Spartan power, and to regain that sovereignty which they lost by the victory of Lysander at Ægos-Potamos. These efforts he every where

represents as high instances of magnanimity and public spirit : though revenge and jealousy had no less share in them. The victories which the Athenians gained over Sparta at Corinth, Naxos, &c. and which he here alludes to, happened about twenty-four years before the date of this oration : so that he might well appeal to the memories of many persons present.

[3.] The numerous armies, &c.] The number of Philip's forces at that time amounted to twenty thousand foot and three thousand horse : a great army compared with those of the Greeks. At their march to Marathon, the Athenians could not assemble more than ten thousand forces. *Tourreil.*

I am destitute of all assistance!"—he would not have engaged in those enterprises which are now crowned with success; nor could he have raised himself to this pitch of greatness. No, Athenians! he knew this well, that all these places are but prizes, [1.] laid between the combatants, and ready for the conqueror: that the dominions of the absent devolve naturally to those who are in the field; the possessions of the supine to the active and intrepid. Animated by these sentiments, he overturns whole countries; he holds all people in subjection: some, as by the right of conquest; others, under the title of allies and confederates: for all are willing to confederate with those whom they see prepared and resolved to exert themselves as they ought.

And if you, my countrymen! will now at length be persuaded to entertain the like sentiments: if each of you, renouncing all evasions, will be ready to approve himself a useful citizen, to the utmost that his station and abilities demand: if the rich will be ready to contribute, and the young to take the field: in one word, if you will be yourselves, and banish those vain hopes which every single person entertains,—that while so many others are engaged in public business, his service will not be required; you then (if heaven so pleases) shall regain your dominions, recall those opportunities your supineness hath neglected, and chastise the insolence of this man. For you are not to imagine, that, like a god, he is to enjoy his present greatness for ever fixed and unchangeable. No, Athenians! there are who hate him, who fear him, who envy him, even among those seemingly the most attached to his cause. These are passions common to mankind; nor must we think that his friends only are exempted from them. It is true, they lie concealed at present, as our indolence deprives them of all resource. But let us shake off this indolence! for you see how we are situated; you see the outrageous arrogance of this man, who does not leave it to your choice whether you shall act, or remain quiet; but braves you with his menaces; and talks (as we are informed) [2.] in a strain of the highest extravagance: and is not able to rest satisfied with his present acquisitions, but is ever in pursuit of farther conquests; and while we sit down inactive and irresolute, encloses us on all sides with his toils.

When, therefore, O my countrymen! when will you exert your vigour? When roused by some event? When forced by some necessity? What then are we to think of our present condition? To freemen, the disgrace attending on misconduct, is, in my opinion, the most urgent necessity. Or say, is it your sole ambition to wander through the public places, each inquiring of the other, "What new advices?" Can any thing be more new, than that a man of Macedon should conquer the Athenians, and give law to Greece?—" Is Philip dead?" [3.]—" No, but in great danger."—How are you concerned in those rumours? Suppose he should meet some fatal stroke: you would soon raise up another Philip, if your interests are thus regarded. For it is not to his own strength that he so much owes his elevation, as to our supineness. And should some accident [4.] affect him, should Fortune, who hath ever been more careful of the state, than we ourselves, now repeat her favours; (and may she thus crown them!)—be assured of this, that by being on the spot, ready to take advantage of the confusion, you will every where be absolute masters; but in your present disposition, even if a favourable juncture should pre-

[1.] But prizes, &c.] His hearers were of all others most devoted to public games and entertainments, and must therefore have b en particularly sensible of the beauty of this image.
[2.] And talks (as we are informed,) &c.] The success which had hitherto attended Philip's arms, must naturally have inspired him with those designs which he afterward executed against the Athenians: and resentment of their late opposition at Thermopylæ might have made him less careful to conceal them, at least in his own court. This the orator represents as arrogant and extravagant menaces: not that a man who had so just a conception of the weakness of the Athenian politics, and the vigour and abilities of their enemy, could really believe such designs extravagant and romantic. But it was part of his address sometimes to avoid shocking the national vanity of his countrymen. After all their losses, and amidst all their indolence, they could not entertain a thought so mortifying, as that the conquerors of Persia and the Arbiters of Greece could ever see their liberty essentially affected, or their power and glory entirely wrested from them, by a king of Macedon.

[3.] Is Philip dead, &c.] These rumours and inquiries of the Athenians were occasioned by the wound Philip received at Methone, the year before, and which was followed by a dangerous fit of sickness.—Longinus quotes this whole passage as a beautiful instance of those pathetic figures, which give life, and force, and energy, to an oration. Tourreil.
The English reader will find the remark in Sect. 18 of Mr. Smith's translation.
[4.] Some accident, &c.]—If he should die. This is plainly the sense of it: but it must be expressed covertly, as Demosthenes has done, not to transgress against that decorum which Cicero says this orator made his first rule. For there were certain things. which the ancients presumed not to express but in terms obscure and gentle; that they might not pronounce what were called verba male ominata. They did not dare to say to any person, "If you should be killed; If you should die:" they concealed as much as possible the melancholy and odious idea of an approaching, or even of a distant, death. The Greeks said εἴ τι πάθοι· the Romans, si quid humanitus contingat. Oliret.

sent you with Amphipolis, [1.] you could not take possession of it, while this suspense prevails in your designs and in your councils.

And now, as to the necessity of a general vigour and alacrity, of this you must be fully persuaded: this point therefore I shall urge no farther. But the nature of the armament, which, I think, will extricate you from the present difficulties, the numbers to be raised, the subsidies required for their support, and all the other necessaries: how they may (in my opinion) be best and most expeditiously provided; these things I shall endeavour to explain.—But here I make this request, Athenians! that you would not be precipitate, but suspend your judgment till you have heard me fully. And if, at first, I seem to propose a new kind of arrangement, let it not be thought that I am delaying your affairs. For it is not they who cry out instantly! This moment! whose counsels suit the present juncture (as it is not possible to repel violences already committed, by any occasional detachment,) but he who will show you, of what kind that armament must be, how great, and how supported, which may subsist until we yield to peace, or till our enemies sink beneath our arms; for thus only can we be secured from future dangers.—These things, I think, I can point out: not that I would prevent any other person from declaring his opinion.—Thus far am I engaged: how I can acquit myself, will immediately appear: to your judgments I appeal.

First, then, Athenians! I say that you should fit out fifty ships of war: and then resolve, that on the first emergency you will embark yourselves. To these I insist that you must add transport and other necessary vessels sufficient for half our horse. Thus far we should be provided against those sudden excursions from his own kingdom, to Thermopylæ, to the Chersonesus, [2.] to Olynthus, [3.] to whatever places he thinks proper. For of this he should

---

[1.] Present you with Amphipolis, &c.] They had nothing more at heart than the recovery of this city. So that the author here gives the last and most heightening stroke to his description of their indolence. *Tourreil.*

And at the same time, by artfully hinting at such an event, as possible, he rouses their attention, and enlivens their hopes and expectations.

The Italian commentator illustrates this passage in the following manner: "Monet orator, quod, quamvis occidat ejusdem (scil. Amphipolis) compotes fieri, ipsis tamen non satis id fore ad turbandas res Macedonicas; cum aliis tot locis quæ memoravimus, privati, ad tantam rerum molem parum opis habere possint, ex una duntaxat civitate." Accordingly, the passage before us hath been rendered to this effect: If some favourable conjuncture should deliver up Amphipolis to you, &c. you could not receive the least benefit from the possession, with respect to Macedon. The assertion of the orator, as expressed in the present translation, hath been pronounced extraordinary, and the argument inconclusive. The substance, therefore, of the present argument, I shall here endeavour to collect: You are all earnest to be informed whether Philip be dead or no. But, unless you change your measures, his death or life can make no difference, or prove of any consequence. Indeed, if some accident should take him off, nothing more would be necessary to give the full advantage of the confusion which such an event must occasion, than to appear on the frontier of Macedon with a powerful force. This would make you absolute masters of the country. But in your present circumstances, what would it avail, even if such a favourable incident, as that of Philip's death, should give you an opportunity of recovering Amphipolis? So important an acquisition (which would in a great measure enable you to command all Macedon) must still be lost: unless you had your forces ready you could not take possession of it. Whether there be any thing unreasonable in this assertion, or impertinent in this argument, must be submitted to the reader. With deference to this judgment, I must declare, that it appears to me to have rather more force, and to set the fatal consequence of the indolence and irresolution of the Athenians in a stronger light, than the other interpretation; whose propriety may be at once determined, by comparing the passage with the sentence immediately preceding. In that the orator declares, that in case of Philip's death, the Athenians had no more to do, but to appear on the frontier of Macedon, in order to gain the absolute disposal of the affairs of that kingdom: 'Ισθ' ὅτι πλησίον μὲν ὄντες, ἅπασιν ἂν τοῖς πράγμασι τεταραγμένοις, ἐπιστάντες, ὅπως βούλεσθε διοικήσαισθε. We must, therefore, be at some pains to clear Demosthenes of the suspicion of inconsistency, if the very next sentence be understood as containing a declaration, That although the Athenians should not only appear upon the border of Macedon, but there possess themselves of a post of the utmost consequence, still they could derive no advantage from their acquisition, far from having the whole kingdom at their disposal. What seems to have tempted the Italian commentator to suggest this interpretation is, the expression, διδόντων ὑμῖν τῶν καιρῶν 'Αμφίπολιν, if some conjunctures should give you Amphipolis, which he takes in a literal sense. But the genius of spirited eloquence, and of our orator in particular, fully warrants us to regard it only as a lively figure, and to understand no more by giving up than affording a favourable opportunity of gaining.

[2.] To the Chersonesus.] The year before, Cersobleptes, unable to defend this country against Philip, had put the Athenians in possession of it. Cardia, one of the chief cities, refused to acknowledge these new sovereigns, and had recourse to the protection of Philip, who, under pretence of supporting them, carried his arms into the Chersonesus. *Tourreil.*

[3.] To Olynthus.] Philip had already com-

necessarily be persuaded, that possibly you may break out from this immoderate indolence, and fly to some scene of action: as you did to Euboea, [1.] and formerly, as we are told, to Haliartus, [2.] and but now, to Thermopylae. But although we should not act with all this vigour, (which yet I must regard as our indispensable duty) still the measures I propose will have their use; as his fears may keep him quiet, when he knows we are prepared, (and

this he will know, for there are too many [3.] among ourselves, who inform him of every thing;) or if he should despise our armament, his security may prove fatal to him; as it will be absolutely in our power, at the first favourable juncture, to make a descent upon his own coasts.

These, then, are the resolutions I propose, —these the provisions it will become you to make. And I pronounce it still necessary to

---

mitted some acts of hostility against this state, but had not as yet formed the siege of Olynthus, or taken any measures tending to it: for in such a case Demosthenes would not have touched so lightly upon an enterprise, which he afterward dwells upon so often and with so much force. *Tourrei*

[1.] To Euboea, &c.] Mons. Tourreil translates this passage thus: Et qu'il risque de retrouver en vous ces mêmes Athéniens, qu'il rencontra sur son chemin en Eubée, &c. (for which there is no warrant in the original:) and taking for granted that all the expeditions here mentioned were made against Philip, he endeavours to settle the date of this to Euboea by conjecture. But it does not appear from history that Philip carried his arms into that island, before his attempt on Thermopylae. In the three succeeding Olynthiac orations, there is not the least mention of such a thing, though there is a particular recital of his expeditions in the third, and though afterward the orator inveighs loudly against his hostile attempts in Euboea. I apprehend, therefore, that the expedition hinted at in this place was that which the Athenians made about seven years before in favour of the Euboeans against Thebes; when in five days they brought an army into Euboea, and in thirty obliged the Thebans to come to terms, and evacuate the island (according to Æschines.)—Demosthenes mentions this in other places; particularly about the end of the oration on the state of the Chersonesus; where he quotes part of the speech made by Timotheus to encourage the Athenians to this expedition.

In the above note, I have endeavoured to suggest some reasons why the expeditions here alluded to, could not have been made against Philip. But it hath been affirmed that, if this were so, it would be almost impertinent in our orator to mention them. That as facts, they must be found spiritless, if taken in a general sense, and, as arguments, inconclusive. The translator can, with sincerity, declare, that if any representation of his tends, in the least, to depreciate the value of the great original, he readily gives it up as utterly erroneous and indefensible. But at the same time, he must observe, that if it be a fault to make use of such facts and such arguments, it is a fault which Demosthenes has frequently committed. Thus he speaks of the vigorous opposition of his countrymen to the Lacedemonians; of their marching against the Corinthians and Megareans; of their expelling the Thebans from Euboea, &c. In the second Philippic oration, he tells his countrymen, that the Ma-

cedonian must regard them as the great and strenuous defenders of Greece; because he must be informed of the spirit which their ancestors discovered in the days of his predecessor Alexander. If we are not to allow the orator to reason, from the conduct of his contemporaries, on former occasions, to the conduct which they ought to pursue, or which may be expected from them in their contest with Philip, what shall we say of an argument deduced from their ancestors in the heroic age of Athens? The truth seems to be, that although the facts supposed to be alluded to in this passage, had been passed over by historians (which I cannot admit;) yet, we are not from hence to conclude, that they had no weight or importance in the Athenian assembly. We are not to judge of the light in which they appeared there, from the obscurity into which distance of time and place may have now cast them. The reasons of this are obvious.

[2.] To Haliartus.] Tourreil refers this to some action which he supposes might have happened in Boeotia in the course of the Phocian war, and in which the Athenians might have had their share of the honour. But from the text, it should seem that the event alluded to must have happened at some considerable distance of time, and have descended to the orator by tradition.—About forty years before this oration, when Thebes and Sparta began to quarrel, Lysander, the Spartan general, threatened the Thebans with a very dangerous war, and began with laying siege to this city of Haliartus. The Thebans applied for aid to the Athenians, which they readily granted (though the Thebans had just before pressed for the utter demolition of their state,) and obliged Pausanias to raise the siege, after Lysander had been killed. I apprehend that this is the expedition here alluded to. It was the more remarkable, as the Athenian power was then at the lowest ebb. You, Athenians! says Demosthenes in his oration on the Crown, at a time when the Lacedemonians had the absolute command both at sea and land; when Attica was quite encompassed with their commanders and their garrisons; when Euboea, Tanagra, all Boeotia, Megara, Ægina, Cleone, and the other islands, were in their possession; when the state had not one ship, not one wall, —ye marched out to Haliartus, &c.

[3.] Too many, &c.] He glances particularly at Aristodemus and Neoptolemus. As to Æschines, he had not been with Philip six years after. *Tourreil.*

raise some other forces which may harass him with perpetual incursions. Talk not of your ten thousands, or twenty thousands, of foreigners; of those armies which [1.] appear so magnificent on paper; but let them be the natural forces of the state; and if you choose a single person, if a number, if this particular man, or whomever you appoint as general, let them be entirely under his guidance and authority. I also move you, that subsistence be provided for them. But as to the quality, the numbers, the maintenance of this body; how are these points to be settled?—I now proceed to speak of each of them distinctly.

The body of infantry, therefore,—but here give me leave to warn you of an error, which hath often proved injurious to you. Think not that your preparations never can be too magnificent: great and terrible in your decrees; in execution, weak and contemptible. Let your preparations, let your supplies, at first be moderate; and add to these, if you find them not sufficient.—I say, then, that the whole body of infantry should be two thousand: of these, that five hundred should be Athenians, of such an age as you shall think proper, and with a stated time for service; not long, but such as that others may have their turn of duty. Let the rest be formed of foreigners. To those you are to add two hundred horse, fifty of them at least Athenians, to serve in the same manner as the foot. For these you are to provide transports.—And now, what farther preparations? —Ten light galleys. For, as he hath a naval power, [2.] we must be provided with light vessels, that our troops may have a secure convoy.

But whence are these forces to be subsisted?

This I shall explain, when I have first given my reasons, why I think such numbers sufficient, and why I have advised that we should serve in person. As to the numbers, Athenians! my reason is this: it is not at present in our power to provide a force able to meet him in the open field; but we must harass him by depredations: thus the war must be carried on at first. We therefore cannot think of raising a prodigious army (for such we have neither pay nor provisions,) nor must our forces be absolutely mean. And I have proposed that citizens should join in the service, and help to man our fleet; because I am informed, that some time since the state maintained a body of auxiliaries at Corinth [3.] which Polystratus commanded, [4.] and Iphicrates, and Chabrias, and some others; that you yourselves served with them: and that the united efforts of these auxiliary and domestic forces gained a considerable victory over the Lacedemonians. But ever since our armies have been formed of foreigners alone, their victories have been over our allies and confederates; while our enemies have arisen to an extravagance of power. And these armies, with scarcely the slightest attention to the service of the state, sail off to fight for Artabazus, [5.] or any other person; and their general follows them: nor should we wonder at it; for he cannot command, who cannot pay his soldiers. What then do I recommend? that you should take away all pretences both from generals and from soldiers, by a regular payment of the army, and by incorporating domestic forces with the auxiliaries, to be, as it were, inspectors into the conduct of the commanders. For at present our manner of acting is even ridiculous.

[1.] Those armies which, &c.] In the Greek it is ἐπιστολιμαίους δυνάμεις.—Instead of enumerating the various senses in which the commentators interpret this expression, I shall copy an observation on it by the Abbé D'Olivet, whose interpretation I have followed:—I have, without any refinement, chosen a plain expression, which seems to hit the thought of Demosthenes directly, and to paint strongly the bitter ridicule of the passage. It was usual for the Athenians, upon any emergency, to write to all quarters to demand soldiers. They were answered, that in such a place such a number would be provided: from another place, so many more might be expected. But in the end it appeared, that these were by no means so many effective men. There were great abatements to be made from the numbers promised: and we find besides, from this oration, that these foreigners were not paid at all, or ill-paid; so that these grand armies were nowhere complete, but in the letters written to demand them on one part, and to promise them on the other. If I am not mistaken, this is what Demosthenes calls δυνάμεις ἐπιστολιμαίους, armies which exist only in letters.

[2.] As he hath a naval power.] In consequence of his engagements with the Thessalians, he commanded their ports and ships.

[3.] At Corinth.] This was in the same war which he alludes to in the beginning of the oration (Sect. 2.) Corinth was appointed as the place of general rendezvous for the Greeks when confederated against Sparta.

[4.] Which Polystratus commanded.] Instead of Polystratus, which is a name little known in history, Monsieur Tourreil proposes to read Callistratus, who, according to Xenophon and Diodorus, was colleague to Iphicrates and Chabrias in the war of Corcyra. But, as Mr. Mounteney has observed, Polystratus is again mentioned by Demosthenes, together with Iphicrates, in the oration on the Immunities; so that it is probable this is the true reading.

[5.] To fight for Artabazus.] He here alludes to an affair which had happened some time before, and had occasioned great commotion. The Athenians had sent Chares at the head of a powerful force to reduce Byzantium, Cos, and Chios, which had revolted from them. But this general, when he had a prospect of success in that enterprise, suffered himself to be corrupted by Artabazus, a rebellious satrap of Asia, and assisted him against an army of seventy thousand men. Chares received a reward proportioned to the service; but this action raised the indignation of the Athenians, as

If a man should ask, "Are you at peace, Athenians?" the answer would immediately be, "By no means! we are at war with Philip. [1.] Have not we chosen the usual generals and officers, [2.] both of horse and foot?" And of what use are all these, except the single person whom you send to the field? the rest attend your priests in their processions. So that, as if you formed so many men of clay, you make your officers for show, and not for service. My countrymen! should not all these generals have been chosen from your own body; all these several officers from your own body, that our force might be really Athenian? and yet, for an expedition in favour of Lemnos, [3.] the general must be a citizen, while troops engaged in defence of our own territories are commanded by Menelaus. [4.] I say not this to detract from his merit; but to whomsoever this command had been intrusted, surely he should have derived it from your voices. [5.]

Perhaps you are fully [6.] sensible of these truths, but would rather hear me upon another point,—that of the supplies; what we are to raise, and from what funds. To this I now proceed.—The sum therefore necessary for the maintenance of these forces, that the soldiers may be supplied with grain, is somewhat above ninety talents. [7.] To the ten galleys forty talents, that each vessel have a monthly allowance of twenty minæ. To the two thousand foot, the same sum, that each soldier may receive ten drachmæ a month for corn. To the two hundred horse, for a monthly allowance of thirty drachmæ each, twelve talents. And let it not be thought a small convenience, that the soldiers are supplied with grain: for I am clearly satisfied that if such a provision be made, the war itself will supply them with every thing else, so as to complete their appointment, and this without any injury to the Greeks or allies: and I myself am ready to sail with them, and to answer for the consequence with my life, should it prove otherwise. From what funds the sum which I propose may be supplied, shall now be explained. * * * *

[Here the secretary of the assembly reads a scheme for raising the supplies, and proposes it to the people in form, in the name of the orator.]

These are the supplies, [8.] Athenians! in our power to raise. And when you come to

---

he had not only deserted the cause of the republic, but also incensed the king of Persia. Demosthenes, however, here shifts the blame from Chares to his soldiers, who refused to obey him (or rather to the people, who took no care to provide for their pay.) Tourreil.

[1.] We are at war with Philip.] So the orator affects to speak. Though I apprehend it does not appear from history that they were at that time directly at war with him. They had indeed joined with the Phocians, and Philip was at the head of the opposite confederacy. Thus far they were engaged against each other, though neither of them as principals in the quarrel. The Athenians, indeed, might have made some attempts to recover Amphipolis; they certainly made some ineffectual preparations to relieve Potidæa and Methone; and after Philip's attempt on Thermopylæ, did station some forces upon their frontiers to oppose him, in case he renewed his attack. But still the war was not declared in form.—But of this I shall speak more hereafter.

[2.] The usual officers.] In the text they are mentioned particularly. Ten taxiarchs (στραρχγοι, or generals,) and phylarchs, and two hipparchs. Each of the ten tribes chose a new general every year, and each of these (originally, when all went to the field) had the command for one day in his turn. Philip was very pleasant on this number of commanders. I never, said he, could find but one general (meaning Parmenio,) but the Athenians can get ten every year. Anciently, the people, upon extraordinary occasions, chose a polemarch, to determine, when the opinions of the generals were equally divided. The taxiarch commanded the infantry, the phylarch the cavalry, of his tribe. The whole body of horse was divided into two corps, each of which was commanded by a general of horse or hipparch. Tourreil.

[3.] In favour of Lemnos.] When, in the social war, the revolters invaded it with a fleet of a hundred sail. Tourreil.

[4.] By Menelaus.] Monsieur Tourreil says, that this Menelaus was the brother of Philip, by another marriage. But though Philip and his brother were not on good terms, yet it is not likely that the Athenians would have trusted one so nearly allied to their enemy. Olivet.

[5.] From your voices.] The regular method of choosing all officers. However, the choice was sometimes left to the commander-in-chief. Tourreil.

[6.] Perhaps you are fully, &c.] it is not impossible but that the people might have been struck with the freedom and candour of the orator, and given some marks of their approbation.

[7.] Ninety talents.] The Attic talent is computed by Tourreil equal to 187l. 10s.; by Prideaux, to 188l. 6s.; by Arbuthnot, to 193l. 15s. It contained sixty minæ, and each mina, one hundred drachmæ. By the computation of the orator it appears that the provisions he recommends to be supplied were to last one year. Mounteney.

[8.] These are the supplies, &c.] Dionysius of Halicarnassus gives us the rest of this oration as a sixth Philippic, pronounced in the archonship of Themistocles. But it appears to me, as well as to the other interpreters, a natural conclusion of the first Philippic; and therefore I could not prevail upon myself to separate them. Tourreil.

The scholiast is of the same opinion, and flatly accuses Dionysius of a mistake. Mr. Mounteney has expressed greater deference for this critic. He supposes that this second

give your voices, determine upon some effectual provision, [1.] that you may oppose Philip, not by decrees and letters only, but by actions. And in my opinion, your plan of operation, and every thing relating to your armament, will be much more happily adjusted, if the situation of the country which is to be the scene of action be taken into the account; and if you reflect, that the winds and seasons have greatly contributed to the rapidity of Philip's conquests; that he watches the blowing of the Etesians, [2.] and the severity of the winter, and forms his sieges when it is impossible for us to bring up our forces. It is your part then to consider this, and not to carry on the war by occasional detachments, (they will ever arrive too late,) but by a regular army constantly kept up. And for winter-quarters you may command Lemnos, and Thassus, and Sciathus, and the adjacent islands, in which there are ports and provisions, and all things necessary for the soldiery in abundance. As to the season of the year in which we may land our forces with the greatest ease, and be in no danger from the winds, either upon the coast to which we are bound, or at the entrance of those harbours where we may put in for provisions—this will be easily discovered. In what manner and at what time our forces are to act, their general will determine, according to the junctures of affairs. What you are to perform, on your part, is contained in the decree I have now proposed. And if you will be persuaded, Athenians! first, to raise these supplies which I have recommended, then to proceed to your other preparations, your infantry, navy, and cavalry; and lastly, to confine your forces, by a law, to that service which is appointed to them; reserving the care and distribution of their money to yourselves, and strictly examining into the conduct of the general; then your time will be no longer wasted in continual debates upon the same subject, and scarcely to any purpose; then you will deprive him of the most considerable of his revenues. For his arms are now supported, by seizing and making prizes of those who pass the seas. But is this all?—No.—You shall also be secure from his attempts: not as when some time since [3.] he fell on Lem-

part is not that which Dionysius quotes; but that there was another oration, since lost, which began with the same words; for he observes, that the former part is plainly imperfect of itself, and the two parts are joined in all the copies and manuscripts, and that naturally and consistently.

I must confess (with all submission to these authorities,) that although I could not presume to separate them, yet I am not quite satisfied that these two parts are one oration. In the first place, I cannot think that the first Philippic would end abruptly, if this second part was away: for we find in the first part, all that the orator proposes to speak to in the beginning; and it concludes (not unlike a speech in parliament) with a motion in form, for such and such subsidies to be raised, for the maintenance of such and such forces. And as to the manner in which the second part begins, supposing it a distinct oration, we cannot object to that; as Dionysius quotes an oration beginning exactly in the same manner : (see his letter to Ammæus.)—It might also be observed, that in the beginning of the oration, having for some time exhorted the Athenians to change their conduct, and act with vigour, Demosthenes says expressly that he intends to speak no more on that subject; and yet this second part is entirely taken up with it; and lastly, there are some passages in the second part which I suspect do not agree to the particular time when the first oration against Philip was pronounced) and I imagine that some editors were sensible of this, by their placing the Olynthiac orations before this, which is called the first Philippic:) these passages I shall take notice of as they occur.

As to any similitude between the two parts, I apprehend that is no more than what runs through all these orations, and may be accounted for from the similitude of the subject, without joining them.—But if this second part be really a distinct oration, spoken after the destruction of Olynthus (for this city was taken the year before the archonship of Themistocles,) how comes it that this event is not mentioned in it?—It had just then thrown the Athenians into the greatest consternation; and as it was the orator's business to encourage them, possibly he might have kept it out of view on purpose. Though perhaps he does hint at it obscurely, and as far as was consistent with prudence, as I shall observe by and by.

[1.] Effectual provision.] In Greek it is—ἃ ἂν ὑμῖν ἀρέσκῃ χειροτονήσατε—choose those things which may be agreeable to you. I own I do not see how their entering into the resolution they liked best, would of consequence enable them to oppose Philip effectually. Perhaps it might be of disservice, for in other places the orator is ever cautioning them against following the bent of their inclinations.—If we should make a very small alteration in the text, and for ἀρέσκῃ read ἀρκέσῃ, those things which may be sufficient for your purposes, I apprehend the sense would be better and more agreeable to Demosthenes. I have taken the liberty to translate after this reading.

[2.] Of the Etesians.] Winds which blew regularly every year at the rising of the dog-star; when the Greeks were obliged to retire from action, on account of the excessive heats; and which, as they blew from the north, of consequence opposed any attempt of invading Macedon, or sending any forces to those parts which were the seat of Philip's wars at first.

[3.] Not as when some time since, &c.] If this be really a part of the first Philippic, these hostilities must have preceded the attempt on Thermopylæ (else the orator could not have distinguished them into those which happened some time ago, and that committed lately.)

nos and Imbrus, and carried away your citizens in chains: not as when he surprised your vessels at Gerastus, and spoiled them of an unspeakable quantity of riches: not as when lately he made a descent on the coast of Marathon, and carried off our sacred galley [1.] while you could neither oppose these insults, nor detach your forces at such junctures as were thought convenient.

And now, Athenians! what is the reason (think ye,) that the public festivals [2.] in honour of Minerva and of Bacchus are always celebrated at the appointed time, whether the direction of them falls to the lot of men of eminence, or of persons less distinguished (festivals which cost more treasure than is usually expended upon a whole navy; and more numbers and greater preparations, than any one perhaps ever cost:) while your expeditions have been all too late, as that to Methone, that to Pegasæ, that to Potidæa? The reason is this: every thing relating to the former is ascertained by law; and every one of you knows long before, who is to conduct [3.] the

several entertainments in each tribe; what he is to receive, when, and from whom, and what to perform. Not one of these things is left uncertain, not one undetermined. But in affairs of war, and warlike preparations, there is no order, no certainty, no regulation. So that, when any accident alarms us, first we appoint our trierarchs; [4.] then we allow them the exchange; then the supplies are considered. These points once settled, we resolve to man our fleet with strangers, [5.] and foreigners; then find it necessary to supply their place ourselves. In the midst of these delays, what we are sailing to defend, the enemy is already master of: for the time of action we spend in preparing: and the junctures of affairs will not wait our slow and irresolute measures. These forces too, which we think may be depended on, until the new levies are raised, when put to the proof, plainly discover their insufficiency. By these means, hath he arrived to such a pitch of insolence as to send a letter to the Eubœans, [6.] conceived in such terms as these.

Now I cannot tell how to reconcile such open acts of hostility, with the other parts of Philip's conduct at that time. There was a peace subsisting between him and the Athenians, which he affected to observe; and so far does he appear from making any open and professed attack upon them, that in the taking of Potidæa and Pydna, he would not act as principal, but as ally to the Olynthians; and, when these cities were taken, dismissed the Athenian garrisons with all imaginable respect and honour; and upon all occasions courted and cajoled the Athenians. This then is one of those passages which I suspect do not agree to the particular time when the first Philippic was spoken. But if we suppose that this, which I call the second part, is really the oration which Dionysius quotes (and which was spoken to engage the Athenians to defend the islanders and the cities of the Hellespont against the attempts of Philip,) then all the difficulty vanishes. The hostilities here mentioned agree very well to a time of open war. Now Diodorus Siculus informs us, that it was after Olynthus was taken, that the Athenians declared war against Philip in form; and we find that, immediately upon this, he attacked them and their tributary states with such fury, that they were soon glad to sue for peace.

[1.] Our sacred galley.] There were two of these appropriated to religious ceremonies (and all extraordinary emergencies and occasions of the state,) the Paralian and Salaminian. Harpocration understands here the Paralion. *Tourreil.*

[2.] Festivals, &c.] For the Panathenæa and Dionysia (as these festivals are called in the original,) I refer the reader to Potter, and other writers on the antiquities of Greece.

[3.] To conduct, &c.] In the original it is, who is the chorægus (that is, the citizen who provided the music, of which each tribe had a band,) and the gymnasiarch (he who presided over the wrestlers, and provided what was necessary for that entertainment.)

[4.] We appoint our trierarchs.] The rich citizens, who were obliged not only to command, but to equip a vessel of war, at their own expense (either severally or jointly) for the service of the public. As this was an office of great expense, it was allowed to any one who was nominated, to point out some citizen richer than himself, and to desire he might be substituted in his place, provided he was willing to exchange fortunes with that citizen, and then to take upon him the office of trierarch. This is what Demosthenes calls allowing the exchange, (which in its nature must have occasioned confusion and delay.)

For a fuller account of these trierarchs, &c. I refer the reader to Potter's Archæol.

[5.] We resolve to man our fleet with strangers.] Μετοικοι, which I translate strangers, were those foreigners who were permitted to sojourn at Athens, on certain conditions.

The whole passage is an exact description of the proceedings of the Athenians in defence of Olynthus, and of the event. I had it in view, when I observed that possibly we might find some obscure allusions to that affair.

[5.] A letter to the Eubœans, &c.] This letter has not descended to us. It is probable from the context, that he expressed in it a contempt for the Athenian power, and insisted how little dependence the Eubœans could have on that state. And if this be so, it confirms an observation, which I made before (see a preceding note) viz. that the Athenians had as yet given Philip no remarkable opposition in Eubœa.——The letter must have been written when Philip began to raise commotions in that island, in order to make himself master of it. I am induced to think, both from history and Demosthenes, that he did not make any attempts of this kind so early as the first Philippic, and therefore that this is no part of that oration.

3

†

[*** *The Letter is read.*]

What hath now been read, is for the most part true, Athenians! too true! but perhaps not very agreeable in the recital. But if, by suppressing things ungrateful to the ear, the things themselves could be prevented, then the sole concern of a public speaker should be to please. If, on the contrary, these unseasonably pleasing speeches be really injurious, it is shameful, Athenians! to deceive yourselves, and, by deferring the consideration of every thing disagreeable, never once to move until it be too late; and not to apprehend that they who conduct a war with prudence, are not to follow, but to direct events; to direct them with the same absolute authority with which a general leads on his forces: that the course of affairs may be determined by them, and not determine their measures. But you, Athenians, although possessed of the greatest power [1.] of all kinds, ships, infantry, cavalry, and treasure; yet, to this day, have never employed any of them seasonably, but are ever last in the field. Just as barbarians [2.] engage at boxing, so you make war with Philip: for, when one of these receives a blow, that blow engages him; if struck in another part, to that part his hands are shifted: but to ward off the blow, or to watch his antagonist—for this, he hath neither skill nor spirit. Even so, if you hear that Philip is in the Chersonesus, you resolve to send forces thither; if in Thermopylæ, thither; if in any other place, you hurry up and down, you follow his standard. But no useful scheme for carrying on the war, no wise provisions, [3.] are ever thought of, until you hear of some enterprise in execution, or already crowned with success. This might formerly have been pardonable, but now is the very critical moment, when it can by no means be admitted.

It seems to me, Athenians! that some divinity, who, from a regard to Athens, looks down upon our conduct with indignation, hath inspired Philip with this restless ambition. For,

were he to sit down in the quiet enjoyment of his conquests and acquisitions, without proceeding to any new attempts, there are men among you, who, I think, would be unmoved at those transactions, [4.] which have branded our state with the odious marks of infamy, cowardice, and all that is base. But as he still pursues his conquests, as he is still extending his ambitious views, possibly, he may at last call you forth, unless you have renounced the name of Athenians. To me it is astonishing, that none of you look back to the beginning [5.] of this war, and consider that we engaged in it to chastise the insolence of Philip; but that now it is become a defensive war, to secure us from his attempts. And that he will ever be repeating these attempts is manifest, unless some power rises to oppose him. But if we wait in expectation of this, if we send out armaments composed of empty galleys, and those hopes with which some speaker may have flattered you; can you then think your interests well secured? Shall we not embark? Shall we not sail, with at least a part of our domestic force, now, since we have not hitherto? But where shall we make our descent? —Let us but engage in the enterprise, and the war itself, Athenians! will show us where he is weakest. But if we sit at home, listening to the mutual invectives and accusations of our orators; we cannot expect, no, not the least success, in any one particular. Wherever a part of our city is detached, although the whole be not present, the favour of the gods and the kindness of fortune attend to fight upon our side; but when we send out a general, and an insignificant decree, and the hopes of our speakers, misfortune and disappointment must ensue. Such expeditions are to our enemies a sport, but strike our allies with deadly apprehensions. For it is not, it is not possible for any one man to perform every thing you desire. He may promise, and harangue, and accuse this or that person; but to such proceedings we owe the ruin of our af-

---

[1.] *Possessed of the greatest power, &c.*] They could then command three hundred ships of war, and those capable of engaging a navy of double that number; they had twenty thousand foot, and two thousand eight hundred horse; and their revenue amounted to above twelve hundred talents. *Tourreil* and *Mounteney.*

[2.] *As barbarians, &c.*] The learned reader will find a beautiful passage in Aulus Gellius, (l. 3. c. 27.) where, on the contrary, a man of true prudence, who engages in the business and dangers of the world, is compared to a skilful boxer, who is ever attentive to defend himself and annoy his adversary. *Tourreil.*

[3.] *No wise provisions, &c.*] I have followed the reading which Mr. Mounteney adopts Περι των πραγμάτων, &c. instead of χρημάτων.

[4.] *At those transactions, &c.*] The taking of Pydna, and Potidæa, and Amphipolis, may warrant what the orator here says. Yet I should choose to apply it to their suffering

Olynthus, by their misconduct, to fall under the power of Philip.

[5.] *Look back to the beginning, &c.*] I shall trouble the reader but with one argument more, in favour of my suspicion, that this is no part of the first Philippic. The passage I now quote, I cannot think, is applicable to the transactions of the Athenians and Philip, before his attempt on Thermopylæ: when (from the time of Argæus's death) they acted against each other only indirectly, and instead of punishing Philip, the Athenians could not even prevail upon themselves to defend those dominions which they claimed as their own. But it is a very exact description of what happened after their declaration of war against Philip, which succeeded the taking of Olynthus: for this declaration was made from a sense of the danger of Philip's growing power, a resentment of his infractions, and a resolution to reduce him: and yet they were quickly obliged to defend themselves against farther attempts.

fairs. For when a general, who commanded a wretched collection of unpaid foreigners, hath been defeated; when there are persons here, who, in arraigning his conduct, dare to advance false oods, and when you lightly engage in any determination, just from their suggestions; what must be the consequence? How then shall these abuses be removed?—By offering yourselves, Athenians! to execute the commands of your general, to be witnesses of his conduct in the field, and his judges at your return; so as not only to hear how your affairs are transacted, but to inspect them. But now, so shamefully are we degenerated, that each of our commanders is twice or thrice called before you, to answer for his life, though not one of them dared to hazard that life, by once engaging his enemy. No: they choose the death of robbers and pilferers, rather than to fall as becomes them. Such malefactors should die by the sentence of the law. Generals should meet their fate bravely in the field.

Then, as to your own conduct—Some wander about, crying, Philip hath joined with the Lacedemonians, and they are concerting the destruction of Thebes, and the dissolution [1.] of some free states. Others assure us he hath sent an embassy to the King: [2.] others, that he is fortifying places in Illyria. [3.] Thus we all go about framing our several tales. I do believe indeed, Athenians! he is intoxicated with his greatness, and does entertain his imagination with many such visionary prospects, as he sees no power rising to oppose him, and is elated with his success. But I cannot be persuaded that he hath so taken his measures,

that the weakest among us know what he is next to do (for it is the weakest among us who spread these rumours.)—Let us disregard them: let us be persuaded of this; that he is our enemy, that he hath spoiled us of our dominions, that we have long been subject to his insolence, that whatever we expected to be done for us by others, hath proved against us, that all the resource left is in ourselves, that if we are not inclined to carry our arms abroad, we may be forced to engage here—let us be persuaded of this, and then we shall come to a proper determination, then shall we be freed from those idle tales. For we are not to be solicitous to know what particular events will happen; we need but be convinced nothing good can happen, unless you grant the due attention to affairs, and be ready to act as becomes Athenians.

I, on my part, have never upon any occasion chosen to court your favour, by speaking any thing but what I was convinced would serve you. And on this occasion I have freely declared my sentiments, without art, and without reserve. It would have pleased me indeed, that as it is for your advantage to have your true interest laid before you, so I might be assured that he who layeth it before you, would share the advantage: for then I had spoken with greater alacrity. However uncertain as is the consequence with respect to me, I yet determined to speak, because I was convinced that these measures, if pursued, must have their use. And, of all those opinions which are offered to your acceptance, may that be chosen which will best advance the general weal!

[1.] The dissolution, &c.] Whenever the Lacedemonians had power, they were always for establishing oligarchies, as has been observed in the preface to these orations.

[2.] To the King.] So the King of Persia was called. The intent of this embassy was supposed to be to make such demands as must

produce a war with the Persian, which Isocrates had exhorted him to very early.

[3.] He is fortifying places in Illyria.] Possibly these rumours were spread by Philip's friends, to persuade the Athenians that his views and schemes were removed to a great distance from Athens.

THE FIRST OLYNTHIAC ORATION:

PRONOUNCED FOUR YEARS AFTER THE FIRST PHILIPPIC, IN THE ARCHONSHIP OF CALLI-
MACHUS, THE FOURTH YEAR OF THE HUNDRED AND SEVENTH OLYMPIAD,
AND THE TWELFTH OF PHILIP'S REIGN.

INTRODUCTION.

THE former oration doth not appear to have any considerable effect. Philip had his creatures in the Athenian assembly, who probably recommended less vigorous measures, and were but too favourably heard. In the mean time, this prince pursued his ambitious designs. When he found himself shut out of Greece, he turned his arms to such remote parts as he might reduce without alarming the states of Greece: and at the same time he revenged himself upon the Athenians, by mak-

ing himself master of some places which they laid claim to. At length his success emboldened him to declare those intentions which he had long entertained secretly against the Olynthians.

Olynthus (a city of Thrace, possessed by Greeks originally from Chalcis,—a town of Euboea, and colony of Athens) commanded a large tract called the Chalcidian region, in which there were thirty-two cities. It had arisen by degrees to such a pitch of grandeur, as to have frequent and remarkable contests both with Athens and Lacedemon. Nor did the Olynthians show great regard to the friendship of Philip when he first came to the throne, and was taking all measures to secure the possession of it ; for they did not scruple to receive two of his brothers by another marriage, who had fled to avoid the effects of his jealousy, and endeavoured to conclude an alliance with Athens against him, which he, by secret practices, found means to defeat. But as he was yet scarcely secure upon his throne, instead of expressing his resentment, he courted, or rather purchased, the alliance of the Olynthians, by the cession of Anthemus, a city which the kings of Macedon had long disputed with them; and afterward by that of Pydna and Potidæa, which their joint forces had besieged and taken from the Athenians. But the Olynthians could not be influenced by gratitude toward such a benefactor. The rapid progress of his arms, and his glaring acts of perfidy, alarmed them exceedingly. He had already made some inroads on their territories, and now began to act against them with less reserve. They therefore despatched ambassadors to Athens, to propose an alliance, and request assistance against a power which they were equally concerned to oppose.

Philip affected the highest resentment at this step, alleged their mutual engagements to adhere to each other in war and peace, inveighed against their harbouring his brothers, whom he called the conspirators ; and under pretence of punishing their infractions, pursued his hostilities with double vigour, made himself master of some of their cities, and threatened the capital with a siege.

In the mean time, the Olynthians pressed the Athenians for immediate succours. Their ambassadors opened their commission in an assembly of the people, who had the right either to agree to, or to reject, their demand. As the importance of the occasion increased the number of speakers, the elder orators had debated the affair before Demosthenes arose. In the following oration, therefore, he speaks as to a people already informed, urges the necessity of joining with the Olynthians, and confirms his opinion by powerful arguments; lays open the designs and practices of Philip, and labours to remove their dreadful apprehensions of his power. He concludes with recommending to them to reform abuses, to restore ancient discipline, and to put an end to all domestic dissensions.

<hr>

THE

FIRST OLYNTHIAC ORATION. [1.]

Callimach. Archon.—A. R. Philip. 12.—
Olympiad. 107. *An.* 4.

IN many instances (Athenians!) have the gods, in my opinion, manifestly declared their favour to this state ; nor is it least observable in this present juncture. For, that an enemy should arise against Philip, on the very confines of his kingdom, of no inconsiderable power, and, what is of most importance, so determined upon the war, that they consider any accommodation with him, first as insidious, next, as the downfal of their country: this seems no less than the gracious interposition of heaven itself. It must, therefore, be our care, (Athenians,) that we ourselves may not frustrate this goodness. For it must reflect disgrace, nay, the foulest infamy, upon us, if we appear to have thrown away not those states and territories only which we once commanded, but those alliances and favourable incidents which fortune hath provided for us.

To begin on this occasion with a display of Philip's power, or to press you to exert your vigour by motives, drawn from hence, is, in my opinion, quite improper. And why? Because whatever may be offered on such a subject, sets him in an honourable view, but seems to me as a reproach to our conduct. For the higher his exploits have arisen above his former estimation, the more must the world admire him ; while your disgrace hath been the greater, the more your conduct hath proved unworthy of your state. These things therefore I shall pass over. He, indeed, who examines justly, must find the source of his greatness here, not in himself. But the services he hath here received, from those whose public administration hath been devoted to his interest; those services which you must punish, I do not think it seasonable to display. There are other points of more moment for you all to hear, and which must excite the greatest abhorrence of him in every reasonable mind.— These I shall lay before you.

And now, should I call him perjured and perfidious, and not point out the instances of this his guilt, it might be deemed the mere virulence of malice, and with justice. Nor will it engage too much of your attention to hear him fully and clearly convicted, from a full and clear detail of all his actions. And this I think useful upon two accounts; first, that he may appear, as he really is, treacherous and false ; and then, that they who are struck with terror, as if Philip was something more than human, may see that he has exhausted all those artifices to which he owes his present elevation, and that his affairs are now ready to decline. For I myself (Athenians!) should think Philip really to be dreaded and admired, if I saw him raised by honourable means. But I find, upon reflection, that at the time when certain persons drove out the Olynthians from this assembly, when desirous of conferring with you, he began with abusing our simplicity by his promise of surrendering Amphipolis, and

[1.] I have disposed the Olynthiac orations in the order pointed out by Dionysius of Halicarnassus. And it plainly appears that this should precede the others; for in this, Demosthenes solicits the immediate conclusion of an alliance with Olynthus ; in the others, executing the secret article [1.] of his treaty, then so much spoken of: that, after this, he courted the friendship of the Olynthians by seizing Potidæa, where we were rightful sovereigns, despoiling us his former allies, and giving them possession; that, but just now, he gained the Thessalians, by promising to give up Magnesia; [2.] and for their ease, to take the whole conduct of the Phocian war upon himself. In a word, there are no people who ever made the least use of him, but have suffered by his subtlety; his present greatness being wholly owing to his deceiving those who were unacquainted with him, and making them the instruments of his success. As these states therefore raised him, while each imagined he was promoting some interest of theirs; these states must also reduce him to his former meanness, as it now appears that his own private interest was the end of all his actions.

Thus then, Athenians! is Philip circumstanced. If not, let the man stand forth who can prove to me, I should have said to this assembly, that I have asserted these things falsely; or that they whom he hath deceived in former instances, will confide in him for the future; or that the Thessalians, who have been so basely, so undeservedly enslaved, [3.] would not gladly embrace their freedom.—If there be any one among you who acknowledges all this, yet thinks that Philip will support his power, as he hath secured places of strength, convenient ports, and other like advantages, he is deceived. For when forces [4.] join in harmony and affection, and one common interest unites the confederating powers, then they share the toils with alacrity, they endure the distresses, they persevere. But when extravagant ambition, and lawless power (as in his case,) have aggrandized a single person; the first pretence, the slightest accident, over-

throws him, and all his greatness is dashed at once to the ground. For it is not, no, Athenians! it is not possible to found a lasting power upon injustice, perjury, and treachery. These may perhaps succeed for once, and borrow for a while, from hope, a gay and flourishing appearance. But time betrays their weakness, and they fall into ruin of themselves. For as in structures of every kind, the lower parts should have the greatest firmness, so the grounds and principles of actions should be just and true. But these advantages are not found in the actions of Philip.

I say then, that you should despatch succours to the Olynthians (and the more honourably and expeditiously this is proposed to be done, the more agreeably to my sentiments;) and send an embassy to the Thessalians, to inform some, and to enliven that spirit already raised in others (for it hath actually been resolved to demand the restitution of Pegasæ, [5.] and to assert their claim to Magnesia.) And let it be your care, Athenians! that our ambassadors may not depend only upon words, but give them some action to display, by taking the field in a manner worthy of the state, and engaging in the war with vigour. For words, if not accompanied by actions, must ever appear vain and contemptible, and particularly when they come from us, whose prompt abilities, and well-known eminence in speaking, make us to be always heard with the greater suspicion.

Would you indeed regain attention and confidence, your measures must be greatly changed, your conduct totally reformed; your fortunes, your persons, must appear devoted to the common cause; your utmost efforts must be exerted. If you will act thus, as your honour and your interest require; then, Athe-

---

he supposes the alliance already concluded, and insists only on the necessity of effectually fulfilling their engagements.

[1.] The secret article, &c.] When Philip had declared Amphipolis a free city, the Athenians, who were desirous of recovering it, sent ambassadors to Philip to solicit his assistance for that purpose; and on this condition promised to make him master of Pydna. But lest the people of Pydna, who were averse to Philip's government, should take the alarm, the whole negotiation was transacted secretly in the senate, without being referred, as usual, to the assembly of the people. This account Ulpian and Suidas cite from Theopompus.

[2.] Magnesia.] He had made himself master of this city when he marched into Thessaly against the tyrants. The Thessalians remonstrated against this proceeding, but suffered themselves to be amused by his assurances that he would give it up; while he really determined to keep possession of it. Tourreil.

[3.] Enslaved.] When Philip had dispossessed the tyrants of Thessaly, he began to set himself up in their place; but not by open force. He was so complete a master of dis-

simulation, appeared so gentle, so affable, so humane, so amiable, even to the conquered, that the Thessalians gave themselves up to him with an entire confidence; which he knew how to take the advantage of. Tourreil.

[4.] For when forces, &c.] I need not take notice to the learned reader, how highly this passage is ornamented in the original, by the beauty of the metaphors, the grandeur of the composition, and the fineness of the sentiment. The word ἀνεχαίτισε, by which he expresses the downfal of Philip, I apprehend, is not to be rendered into our, or perhaps any other language. It gives us the idea of a generous steed, tossing its mane, impatient of the bit, and casting his rider to the ground; which at once expresses the subjection of the states conquered by Philip, their impatience of his government, their bold effort to regain their liberty, and the downfal of their master. The change of tenses (ἀνεχαίτισε καὶ διέλυσεν) adds greatly to the force and beauty; it seems as if the destruction of Philip was too quick for words.

[5.] Pegasæ.] A city of Thessaly, which he had made himself master of five years before.

nians! you will not only discover the weakness and insincerity of the confederates of Philip, but the ruinous condition of his own kingdom will also be laid open. The power and sovereignty of Macedon may have some weight indeed, when joined with others. Thus, when you marched against the Olynthians under the conduct of Timotheus, it proved a useful ally; when united with the Olynthians against Potidæa, it added something to their force; just now, when the Thessalians were in the midst of disorder, sedition, and confusion, it aided them against the family of their tyrants (and in every case, any, even a small accession of strength, is, in my opinion, of considerable effect.) But of itself, unsupported, it is infirm, it is totally distempered ; for, by all those glaring exploits which have given him this apparent greatness, his wars, his expeditions, he hath rendered it yet weaker than it was naturally. For you are not to imagine that the inclinations of his subjects are the same with those of Philip. He thirsts for glory; this is his object, this he eagerly pursues, through toils and dangers of every kind, despising safety and life, when compared with the honour of achieving such actions as no other prince of Macedon could ever boast of. But his subjects have no part in this ambition. Harassed by those various excursions he is ever making, they groan under perpetual calamity: torn from their business and their families, and without opportunity to dispose of that pittance which their toils have earned ; as all commerce is shut out from the coasts of Macedon by the war.

Hence, one may perceive how his subjects in general are affected to Philip. But then his auxiliaries, and the soldiers of his phalanx, [1.] have the character of wonderful forces, completely trained to war. And yet I can affirm, upon the credit of a person from that country, incapable of falsehood, that they have no such superiority. For, as he assures me, if any man of experience in military affairs should be found among them, he dismisses all such, from an ambition of having every great action ascribed wholly to himself (for, besides his other passions, the man hath this ambition in the highest degree.) And if any person from a sense of decency, or other virtuous principle, betrays a dislike of his daily intemperance, and riotings, and obscenities, [2.]

he loses all favour and regard; so that none are left about him but wretches who subsist on rapine and flattery, and who, when heated with wine, do not scruple to descend to such instances of revelry, as it would shock you to repeat. Nor can the truth of this be doubted; for they whom we all conspired to drive from hence, as infamous and abandoned, Callias the public servant, [3.] and others of the same stamp; buffoons, composers of lewd songs, in which they ridicule their companions; these are the persons whom he entertains and caresses. And these things, Athenians! trifling as they may appear to some, are to men of just discernment great indications of the weakness both of his mind and fortune. At present, his successes cast a shade over them; for prosperity hath great power to veil such baseness from observation. But let his arms meet with the least disgrace, and all his actions will be exposed. This is a truth, of which he himself, Athenians! will, in my opinion, soon convince you, if the gods favour us, and you exert your vigour. For, as in our bodies, while a man is in health, he feels no effect of any inward weakness; but when disease attacks him, every thing becomes sensible, in the vessels, in the joints, or in whatever other part his frame may be disordered; so in states and monarchies, while they carry on a war abroad, their defects escape the general eye; but when once it approaches their own territory, then they are all detected.

If here be any one among you, who, from Philip's good fortune, concludes that he must prove a formidable enemy; such reasoning is not unworthy a man of prudence. Fortune hath great influence, nay, the whole influence, in all human affairs; but then, were I to choose, I should prefer the fortune of Athens (if you yourselves will assert your own cause with the least degree of vigour,) to this man's fortune. For we have many better reasons to depend upon the favour of heaven than this man. But our present state is, in my opinion, a state of total inactivity; and he who will not exert his own strength, cannot apply for aid, either to his friends or to the gods. It is not then surprising, that he, who is himself ever amidst the dangers and labours of the field; who is every where; whom no opportunity escapes; to whom no season is unfavourable; should be

---

[1.] The soldiers of his phalanx.] In the original, πεζέταιροι, fellow-soldiers. A term invented for the encouragement of this body, and to reconcile them to all the severities of their duty. Such kind of familiarities cost but little, and are often of considerable service to a prince. *Tourreil.*

[2.] Obscenities.] In the original, κορδακισμούς. Certain lascivious dances, so called from the name of a satyr, said to have invented them. Theophrastus mentions it as a part of the character of a man utterly abandoned, that when inflamed by wine he is even capable of dancing the Chordax. *Tourreil.*

In this description of the dissolute manners of Philip and his court, one would imagine that the orator had aggravated a little; yet we have the whole description still more heightened in history. The learned reader will find it in Athenæus, Book 6. *Tourreil.*

[3.] The public servant.] One of those public slaves who attended the Athenian generals in the field. They chose slaves for this business, that if there was occasion for their evidence on any public inquiry into the conduct of the war, they might be put to the torture, from which free citizens were exempted. *Ulpian.*

superior to you, who are wholly engaged in contriving delays, and framing decrees, and inquiring after news. I am not surprised at this, for the contrary must have been surprising; if we, who never act, in any single instance, as becomes a state engaged in war, should conquer him, who, in every instance, acts with an indefatigable vigilance. This indeed surprises me, that you, who [I.] fought the cause of Greece against Lacedemon, and generously declined all the many favourable opportunities of aggrandizing yourselves; who, to secure their property to others, parted with your own by your own contributions, and bravely exposed yourselves in battle, should now decline the service of the field, and delay the necessary supplies, when called to the defence of your own rights: that you, in whom Greece in general, and each particular state, hath often found protection, should sit down quiet spectators of your own private wrongs: This, I say, surprises me: and one thing more; that not a man among you can reflect how long a time we have been at war with Philip, and in what measures this time hath all been wasted. You are not to be informed, that, in delaying, in hoping that others would assert our cause, in accusing each other, in impeaching, then again entertaining hopes in such measures as are now pursued, that time hath been entirely wasted. And are you so devoid of apprehension, as to imagine, when our state hath been reduced from greatness to wretchedness, that the very same conduct will raise us from wretchedness to greatness? No! this is not reasonable, it is not natural; for it is much easier to defend, than to acquire dominions. But now, the war hath left us nothing to defend: we must acquire. And to this work you yourselves alone are equal.

This, then, is my opinion. You should raise supplies; you should take the field with alacrity. Prosecutions should be all suspended until you have recovered your affairs; let each man's sentence be determined by his actions: honour those who have deserved applause; let the iniquitous meet their punishment: let there be no pretences, no deficiencies on your part; for you cannot bring the actions of others to a severe scrutiny, unless you have first been careful of your own duty. What indeed can be the reason, think ye, that every man whom ye have sent out at the head of an army, hath deserted your service, and sought out some private expedition (if we must speak ingenuously of these our generals also?) The reason is this: When engaged in the service of the state, the prize for which they fight is yours. Thus, should Amphipolis be now taken, you instantly possess yourselves of it: the commanders have all the danger, the rewards they do not share. But in their private enterprises the dangers are less; the acquisitions are all shared by the generals and soldiers; as were Lampsacus, Sigœum, [2.] and those vessels which they plundered. Thus are they all determined by their private interest. And when you turn your eyes to the wretched state of your affairs, you bring your generals to a trial; you grant them leave to speak; you hear the necessities they plead, and then acquit them. Nothing then remains for us, but to be distracted with endless contests and divisions (some urging these, some those measures,) and to feed the public calamity. For in former times, Athenians, you divided into classes, [3.] to raise supplies. Now, the business of these classes is to govern; each hath an orator at its head, and a general, who is his creature; the THREE HUNDRED are assistants to these, and the rest of you divide, some to this, some to that party. You must leave the power of speaking, of advising, and of acting, open to every citizen. But if you suffer some persons to issue out their mandates, as with a royal authority; [4.] if one set of men be forced to fit out ships, to raise supplies, to take

---

[1.] See note on Philip. I. page 13.

[2.] Lampsacus, Sigœum, &c.] Chares received these two cities of Asia Minor, from the Satrap Artabazus, in return for his service (see note on Ph. I. p. 14.) This general, instead of employing the fleet he had been intrusted with, for the recovery of Amphipolis, according to his instructions, joined with some pirates, and committed considerable outrages in the Ægean Sea. He was accused of this at his return, but escaped, by flying from public justice, until his faction grew powerful enough to reinstate him in his former command. *Tourreil.*

[3.] Classes, &c. [Συμμορίαι.] Each of the ten tribes elected one hundred and twenty of the richer citizens, out of their own body, who were obliged to perform the public duties, and to raise supplies for the exigencies of the state out of their private fortunes. The twelve hundred persons thus chosen, were divided into two parts, and each of these into ten classes, called συμμορίαι. These were again subdivided into two parts, according to the estates of those who composed them. And thus, out of the ten first classes were appointed the THREE HUNDRED, that is, such a number of the wealthy citizens, who were on all occasions to supply the commonwealth with money; and with the rest of the twelve hundred to perform all extraordinary duties in their turns. It seems, however, that in the time of Demosthenes, these classes sought pretences to avoid their duty, and contended for the power of throwing the whole weight of public business on each other.

[4.] As with a royal, &c.] Eubulus, Aristophon, Hyperides, and Lycurgus, governed every thing with an absolute power, in the assemblies; the conduct of military affairs was entirely engrossed by Diopithes, Menestheus, Leosthenes, and Chares. Thus the administration of affairs was shared among a few men as it were by lot; so that the popular government degenerated into an oligarchy. See Plutar. in Phocion.

up arms; while others are only to make decrees against them, without any charge, any employment besides; it is not possible, that any thing can be effected seasonably and successfully: for the injured party ever will desert you; and then your sole resource will be to make them feel your resentment instead of your enemies.

To sum up all, my sentiments are these: —That every man should contribute in proportion to his fortune; that all should take the field in their turns, until all have served; that whosoever appears in this place should be allowed to speak; and that when you give your voices, your true interest only should determine you, not the authority of this or the other speaker. Pursue this course, and then your applause will not be lavished on some orator, the moment he concludes; you yourselves will share it hereafter, when you find how greatly you have advanced the interests of your state.

THE SECOND OLYNTHIAC ORATION:

PRONOUNCED IN THE SAME YEAR.

INTRODUCTION.

To remove the impression made on the minds of the Athenians by the preceding oration, Demades and other popular leaders in the interest of Philip rose up, and opposed the propositions of Demosthenes with all their eloquence. Their opposition, however, proved ineffectual; for the assembly decreed, that relief should be sent to the Olynthians: and thirty galleys and two thousand forces were accordingly despatched under the command of Chares. But these succours, consisting entirely of mercenaries, and commanded by a general of no great reputation, could not be of considerable service; and were besides suspected, and scarcely less dreaded, by the Olynthians than the Macedonians themselves. In the mean time the progress of Philip's arms could meet with little interruption. He reduced several places in the region of Chalcis; rased the fortress of Zeira; and having twice defeated the Olynthians in the field, at last shut them up in their city. In this emergency, they again applied to the Athenians, and pressed for fresh and effectual succours. In the following oration, Demosthenes endeavours to support this petition; and to prove, that both the honour and the interest of the Athenians demanded their immediate compliance. As the expense of the armament was the great point of difficulty, he recommends the abrogation of such laws as prevented the proper settlement of the funds necessary for carrying on a war of such importance—the nature of these laws will come immediately to be explained.

It appears, from the beginning of this oration, that other speakers had arisen before Demosthenes, and inveighed loudly against Philip. Full of the national prejudices, or disposed to flatter the Athenians in their notions of the dignity and importance of their state, they breathed nothing but indignation against the enemy, and possibly with some contempt of his present enterprises, proposed to the Athenians to correct his arrogance, by an invasion of his own kingdom. Demosthenes, on the contrary, insists on the necessity of self-defence: endeavours to rouse his hearers from their security, by the terror of impending danger; and affects to consider the defence of Olynthus as the last and only means of preserving the very being of Athens.

OLYNTHIAC THE SECOND.

Callimach. Archon.—A. R. Philip. 12.— Olympiad. 107. An. 4.

I AM by no means affected in the same manner, Athenians! when I review the state of our affairs, and when I attend to those speakers, who have now declared their sentiments. They insist, that we should punish Philip; but our affairs, situated as they now appear, warn us to guard against the dangers with which we ourselves are threatened. Thus far, therefore, I must differ from these speakers, that I apprehend they have not proposed the proper object for your attention. There was a time indeed, I know it well, when the state could have possessed her own dominions in security, and sent out her armies to inflict chastisement on Philip. I myself have seen that time, when we enjoyed such power. But now, I am persuaded we should confine ourselves to the protection of our allies. When this is once effected, then we may consider the punishment his outrages have merited. But till the first great point be well secured, it is weakness to debate about our more remote concernments.

And now, Athenians! if ever we stood in need of mature deliberation and counsel, the present juncture calls aloud for them. To point out the course to be pursued on this emergency, I do not think the greatest difficulty: but I am in doubt in what manner to propose my sentiments; for all that I have observed, and all that I have heard, convinces me, that most of your misfortunes have proceeded from a want of inclination to pursue the necessary measures! not from ignorance of them.—Let me entreat you, that, if I now speak with an unusual boldness, ye may bear it: considering only, whether I speak truth, and with a sincere intention to advance your future interests: for you now see, that by some orators, who study but to gain your favour, our affairs have been reduced to the extremity of distress.

I think it necessary, in the first place, to recall some late transactions to your thoughts. You may remember, Athenians! that, about three or four years since, you received advice that Philip was in Thrace, and had laid siege to the fortress of Heræa. It was then the month of November. [1.] Great commotions and debates arose: It was resolved to send out forty galleys; that all citizens under the age of five-and-forty [2.] should themselves embark; and that sixty talents should be raised. Thus it was agreed; that year passed away; then came in the months July, [3.] August, September. In this last month, with great difficulty, when the mysteries had first been celebrated, you sent out Charidemus, [4.] with just ten vessels unmanned, and five talents of silver. For when reports came of the sickness and the death of Philip (both of these were affirmed,) you laid aside your intended armament, imagining, that at such a juncture there was no need of succours. And yet this was the very critical moment; for had they been despatched with the same alacrity with which they were granted, Philip would not have then escaped, to become that formidable enemy he now appears.

But what was then done cannot be amended. Now we have the opportunity of another war: that war, I mean, which hath induced me to bring these transactions into view, that you may not once more fall into the same errors. How then shall we improve this opportunity? This is the only question. For if you are not resolved to assist with all the force you can command, you are really serving under Philip, you are fighting on his side. The Olynthians are a people whose power was thought considerable. Thus were the circumstances of affairs: Philip could not confide in them; they looked with equal suspicion upon Philip. We and they then entered into mutual engagements of peace and alliance: this was a grievous embarrassment to Philip, that we should have a powerful state confederated with us, spies upon the incidents of his fortune. It was agreed that we should by all means engage this people in a war with him. And now, what we all so earnestly desired is effected; the manner is of no moment. What then remains for us, Athenians! but to send immediate and effectual succours, I cannot see. For besides disgrace that must attend us, if any of our interests are supinely disregarded, I have no small apprehensions of the consequence (the Thebans, [5.] affected as they are toward us, and the Phocians exhausted of their treasures,) if Philip be left at full liberty to lead his armies into these territories, when his present enterprises are accomplished. If any one among you can be so far immersed in indolence, as to suffer this, he must choose to be witness of the misery of his own country, rather than to hear of that which strangers suffer; and to seek assistance for himself, when it is now in his power to grant assistance to others. That this must be the consequence, if we do not exert ourselves on the present occasion, there can scarcely remain the least doubt among us.

But as to the necessity of sending succours, this, it may be said, we are agreed in; this is our resolution. But how shall we be enabled? that is the point to be explained.—Be not surprised, Athenians! if my sentiments on this occasion seem repugnant to the general sense of this assembly.—Appoint magistrates for [6.] the inspection of your laws: not in order to enact any new laws; you have already a sufficient number; but to repeal those whose ill effects you now experience. I mean the laws

---

[1.] Of November.] The reducing the Attic months to the Julian hath occasioned some dispute among the learned. As I thought it best to make use of Roman names in the translation, I have followed the reduction of Scaliger.

[2.] Under the age of five-and-forty, &c.] This expresses their zeal, and their apprehensions of the danger: for by the laws of Athens a citizen was exempted from military service at the age of forty, except on some very urgent occasions.

[3.] July, &c.] That is, the first months of the next year; for the reader is to observe, that the Attic year commenced on that new moon, whose full moon immediately succeeded the summer solstice.

[4.] Charidemus.] That is, the worst of all your generals: a foreigner, a soldier of fortune, who had sometimes fought against you, sometimes betrayed your cause, and who, on many occasions, had proved himself unworthy of the confidence you reposed in him.—Monsieur Tourreil translates this passage thus: "Ce fut en ce dernier mois, qu' IMMEDIATEMENT après la célébration des mystères, vous DEPESCHATES d'ici Charidème," &c. Here there are two unfortunate words which ex-press haste and expedition: whereas the description in the original labours on in the slowest and heaviest manner possible. Every single word marks out the tediousness or the meanness of their armament.

[5.] The Thebans, &c.] They had a mortal hatred to the Athenians, as they had favoured Lacedemon after the battles of Leuctra and Mantinea, and had lately taken part with the Phocians against them, in the sacred war. [And even before these times, at the conclusion of the Peloponnesian war, the Thebans strenuously contended for the utter extirpation of Athens.] *Tourreil.*

[6.] Magistrates for, &c.] In the original νομοθέτας. So were those citizens called, who were intrusted by the people with the regulation of their laws. They were chosen by lot, to the number of 1001, that their votes might not be equal. Every citizen, at certain times, and in certain assemblies, had usually a right to complain of any law. The president of the assembly proposed the complaint to the people: five advocates were allowed to plead in defence of the law; and after hearing them, the people referred the affair to the Nomothetæ.

4

†

relating to the theatrical funds [1.] (thus openly I declare it) and some about the soldiery. [2.] By the first, the soldier's pay goes as theatrical expenses to the useless and inactive ; the others screen those from justice who decline the service of the field, and thus damp the ardour of those disposed to serve us. When you have repealed these, and rendered it consistent with safety to advise you justly, then seek for some person to propose that decree, which [3.] you all are sensible the common good requires. But till this be done, expect not that any man will urge your true interest, when, for urging your true interest, you repay him with destruction. Ye will never find such zeal, especially since the consequence can be only this ; he who offers his opinion, and moves for your concurrence, suffers some unmerited calamity ; but your affairs are not in the least advanced ; nay, this additional inconvenience must arise, that for the future it will appear more dangerous to advise you than even at present ; and the authors of these laws should also be the authors of their repeal. For it is not just that the public favour should be bestowed on them who, in framing these laws, have greatly injured the community ; and that the odium should fall on him whose freedom and sincerity are of important service to us all.—Until these regulations be made, you are not to think any man so great, that he may violate these laws with impunity ; or so devoid of reason, as to plunge himself into open and foreseen destruction.

And be not ignorant of this, Athenians ! t a decree is of no signification, unless atten with resolution and alacrity to execute it. I were decrees of themselves sufficient to eng you to perform your duty ; could they e execute the things which they enact ; so m would not have been made to so little, or ther to no good purpose ; nor would the in lence of Philip have had so long a date. if decrees can punish, he hath long since all their fury. But they have no such pow for though proposing and resolving be firs order ; yet, in force and efficacy, action is perior. Let this then be your principal cern ; the others you cannot want : for have men among you capable of advising, you are of all people most acute in apprehe ing : now, let your interest direct you, an will be in your power to be as remarkable acting. What season indeed, what opportu do you wait for, more favourable than the sent ? or when will you exert your vig if not now, my countrymen ? Hath not man seized all those places that were ou should he become master of this country too, must we not sink into the lowest stat infamy ? Are not they whom we have mised to assist, whenever they are engage war, now attacked themselves ? Is he not enemy ? is he not in possession of our d nions ? is he not a barbarian ? [5.] is he every base thing words can express ? It are insensible to all this, if we almost aid designs :—Heavens ! can we then ask to wl

---

[1.] The theatrical funds, &c.] The Athenians, as well as the other Greeks, were ever passionately fond of the entertainments of the theatre. Disputes for places soon became remarkably inconvenient, and called for a regulation. The magistrates therefore ordered that a small price should be paid for places, to reimburse the builders of the theatre, which as yet knew not that magnificence which riches and luxury afterward introduced. This purchasing of places began to be complained of by the poorer citizens ; and therefore Pericles, out of a pretended zeal for their interest, proposed, that a sum of money (which had been deposited in the treasury, after the war of Egina, when they had made a thirty years' peace with Lacedemon, and was intended as a public resource in case of any invasion of Attica) should be distributed among the citizens, to defray the expense of their entertainments in time of peace only. The proposal and the restriction were both agreed to. But as all indulgences of this kind degenerate, sooner or later, into licentiousness, the people began to consider this distribution as their unalienable property. And the very year of the Olynthiac orations, Eubulus, a popular leader of a party opposite to Demosthenes, prevailed to have a law passed, which forbade any man, upon pain of death, to make a motion, or proposal of a decree, for restoring what was now called the theatrical funds, to the military, or any other public service. This is the law which Demosthenes here attacks.

[2.] About the soldiery.] The laws of S exacted personal service from every citi with the utmost rigour. Those which the tor complains of, must have been made w the state began to be corrupted.

[3.] That decree, which, &c.] A decre the alienation of the theatrical funds. W Eubulus's law was in force, such a de could not be proposed. The usefulness necessity of it, however, the orator vent to insinuate ; for the penalty was not un stood as extending to a man's barely decla his sentiments, provided he did not make motion in form. In the latter part of this ora he seems to propose another method of av ing the ill consequences of the law of Eubu and that is, that the theatrical distribut should be still continued ; but that all t who were in public offices, and who us received their several salaries and app ments, should now serve the state withou or reward. The name only of these dist tions would have then remained.

[4.] Of this country, &c.] That is, the c try of Chalcis, where Philip took two-thirty cities, before he laid siege to Olynt Tourreil.

[5.] A barbarian ?] This was the ter reproach which the Greeks applied t other nations : nor were the Macedonian cepted. In the time of Xerxes, Alexa king of Macedon could not be admitted the Olympic games, until he had proved descent to be originally from Argos.

the consequences are owing? Yes, I know full well, we never will impute them to ourselves. Just as in the dangers of the field: not one of these who fly will accuse himself; he will rather blame the general, or his fellow-soldiers: yet every single [1.] man that fled was accessary to the defeat: he who blames others might have maintained his own post; and had every man maintained his, success must have ensued. Thus then, in the present case, is there a man whose counsel seems liable to objection? let the next rise, and not inveigh against him, but declare his own opinion. Doth another offer some more salutary counsel? pursue it, in the name of Heaven! But then it is not pleasing.—This is not the fault of the speaker, unless in that he hath [2.] neglected to express his affection in prayers and wishes. To pray is easy, Athenians! and in one petition may be collected as many instances of good fortune as we please. To determine justly, when affairs are to be considered, is not so easy. But what is most useful, should ever be preferred to that which is agreeable, where both cannot be obtained.

But, if there be a man who will leave us the theatrical funds, and propose other subsidies for the service of the war, are we not rather to attend to him? I grant it, Athenians! if that man can be found. But I should account it wonderful, if it ever did, if it ever can happen to any man on earth, that, while he lavishes his present possessions on unnecessary occasions, some future funds should be procured, to supply his real necessities. But such proposals find a powerful advocate in the breast of every hearer. So that nothing is so easy as to deceive one's self: for what we wish, that we readily believe: but such expectations are oftentimes inconsistent with our affairs. On this occasion, therefore, let your affairs direct you; then will you be enabled to take the field; then will you have your full pay. And men, whose judgments are well directed, and whose souls are great, could not support the infamy which must attend them, if obliged to desert any of the operations of a war, from the want of money: they could not, after snatching up their arms and marching against the Corinthians [3.] and Megareans, [4.] suffer Philip to enslave the states of Greece, through the want of provisions for their forces.—I say not this wantonly, to raise the resentment of some among you.

---

when he came over from the Persian camp, to give the Greeks notice of the motions of Mardonius, he justified his perfidy by his ancient descent from Greece; which he needed not to have had recourse to, if Macedon had not then been considered as a part of the barbarian world. *Tourreil.*

[1.] Yet every single, &c.] The orator did not foresee, that in ten years after, he himself would be guilty of this very crime; branded with the name of infamy, for casting away his shield at the battle of Chæronea, and have nothing to oppose to the reproaches of his enemies, but a weak and trifling pleasantry. *Tourreil.*

[2.] Unless in that he hath, &c.] This passage, which is translated pretty exactly from the original, seems, at first view, to have something of a forced and unnatural air. Indeed it is not possible for us to perceive fully and clearly the strength and propriety of every part of these orations. To this it would be requisite to know the temper and disposition of the hearers, at that particular time when each of them was delivered: and also to have before us every thing said by other speakers in the debate. In many places, we find very plain allusions to the speeches of other orators. And it is not unreasonable to think, that there are other more obscure ones which escape our observation. If we suppose, for instance, that in the present debate, before Demosthenes arose, some other speaker had amused the people with flattering hopes, with professions of zeal and affection, with passionate exclamations, and prayers to the gods for such and such instances of public success; while at the same time he neglected to point out such measures as were fit to be pursued, or perhaps recommended pernicious measures;—upon such a supposition, I say, this passage, considered as an indirect reproof of such a speaker, will perhaps appear to have sufficient force and propriety.

[3.] The Corinthians.] This alludes to an expedition that the Athenians had made about an age before. Some time after the Persian war, when the Greeks began to quarrel among themselves, Corinth and Megara had some dispute about their boundaries. The better to support their quarrel, the Megareans quitted the Lacedemonians, and entered into an alliance with Athens. But as this state was then engaged both in Egypt and Egina, the Corinthians imagined they would not be able to give any assistance; and therefore invaded the territories of Megara. But the Athenians came immediately to the assistance of their allies, although they were obliged to commit the defence of their city to their old men and boys; and the Corinthians were repulsed. *Tourreil.*

[4.] And Megareans.] This war happened twelve years after that mentioned in the preceding note. The Megareans, after having put an Athenian garrison to the sword, that was stationed in their territory, joined with Lacedemon, and even with Corinth, their mortal enemy, against whom the Athenians had espoused their quarrel. The state, incensed at the ingratitude of their revolt, determined to reduce them to reason. They issued out a mandate, directing the Megareans to abstain from cultivating a piece of ground consecrated to Ceres and Proserpine; and on their refusing to comply, published an edict, to exclude them from all commerce in Attica; and bound their generals by an oath to invade their territories once every year. *Tourreil.*

No; I am not so unhappily perverse, as to study to be hated, when no good purpose can be answered by it : but it is my opinion, that every honest speaker should prefer the interest of the state to the favour of his hearers. This (I am assured, and perhaps you need not be informed) was the principle which actuated the public conduct of those of our ancestors who spoke in this assembly : (men, whom the present set of orators are ever ready to applaud, but whose example they by no means imitate :) such were Aristides, Nicias, the former Demosthenes, and Pericles. But since we have had speakers, who, before their public appearance, ask you : What do you desire ? what shall I propose ? how can I oblige you ? the interest of our country hath been sacrificed to momentary pleasure and popular favour. Thus have we been distressed; thus have these men risen to greatness, and you sunk into disgrace.

And here let me entreat your attention to a summary account of the conduct of your ancestors, and of your own. I shall mention but a few things, and these well known; for if you would pursue the way to happiness, you need not look abroad for leaders; our own countrymen point it out. These our ancestors, therefore, whom the orators never courted, never treated with that indulgence with which you are flattered, held the sovereignty of Greece, with general consent, five-and-forty years; [1.] deposited above a thousand talents in our public treasury; kept the king of this country in that subjection which a barbarian owes to Greeks ; erected monuments of many and illustrious actions, which they themselves achieved, by land and sea : in a word, are the only persons who have transmitted to posterity such glory as is superior to envy.—Thus great do they appear in the affairs of Greece. —Let us now view them within the city, both in their public and private conduct. And, first, the edifices which their administrations have given us, their decorations of our temples, and the offerings deposited by them, are so numerous and so magnificent, that all the efforts of posterity cannot exceed them. Then, in private life, so exemplary was their moderation, their adherence to the ancient man-

ners so scrupulously exact, that if any of you ever discovered the house of Aristides, or Miltiades, or any of the illustrious men of those times, he must know that it was not distinguished by the least extraordinary splendour. For they did not so conduct the public business as to aggrandize themselves ; their sole great object was to exalt the state. And thus by their faithful attachment to Greece, by their piety to the gods, and by that equality which they maintained among themselves, they were raised (and no wonder) to the summit of prosperity.

Such was the state of Athens at that time, when the men I have mentioned were in power. But what is your condition, under these indulgent ministers who now direct us ? Is it the same, or nearly the same ?—Other things I shall pass over, though I might expatiate on them. Let it only be observed, that we are now, as you all see, left without competitors ; the Lacedemonians lost; [2.] the Thebans engaged [3.] at home; and not one of all the other states of consequence sufficient to dispute the sovereignty with us. Yet, at a time when we might have enjoyed our own dominions in security, and been the umpires in all disputes abroad, our territories have been wrested from us ; we have expended above one thousand five hundred talents to no purpose ; the allies [4.] which we gained in war have been lost in time of peace ; and to this degree of power have we raised an enemy against ourselves. (For let the man stand forth, who can show whence Philip hath derived his greatness, if not from us.)

Well ! if these affairs have but an unfavourable aspect, yet those within the city are much more flourishing than ever.—Where are the proofs of this ? The walls which have been whitened ?—the ways we have repaired ?—the supplies of water ; and such trifles ? —Turn your eyes to the men, of whose administrations these are the fruits. Some of whom, from the lowest state of poverty, have arisen suddenly to affluence ; some from meanness to renown : others have made their own private houses much more magnificent than the public edifices. Just as the state hath fallen, their private fortunes have been raised.

[1.] Five-and-forty years.] In Wolfius's edition, it is sixty-five. But this reading is found in other copies, and is confirmed by the parallel passage in the oration on Regulating the Commonwealth. The orator computes from the death of Pausanias, when the supreme command was given to the Athenians, to the beginning of the Peloponnesian war. Add to this twenty-seven years of that war, during which time the Athenians maintained their power, though not with consent; and the whole will be seventy-two years complete and part of the seventy-third year. Agreeably to this last calculation, Demosthenes says, in the third Philippic, that the Athenians commanded in Greece seventy-three years. These two accounts are thus easily reconciled, by distinguishing the times of the voluntary and the involuntary obedience of the Greeks. *Tourreil.*

[2.] The Lacedemonians lost.] The battles of Leuctra and Mantinea had entirely destroyed their power. *Tourreil.*

[3.] Engaged, &c.] In the Phocian war.

[4.] The allies, &c.] Ulpian and Wolfius understand this of the peace, by which the Athenians consented that the people of Chios, Rhodes, and Byzantium, and other revolters, should all continue free. But it seems more natural to apply it to some prior events ; as the taking of Pydna and Potidæa, and other cities of Thrace, that were then subject to Athens, and which Philip made himself master of, after he had concluded a peace with the Athenians, in the second year of his reign. *Tourreil.*

And what cause can we assign for this? How is it that our affairs were once so flourishing, and now in such disorder? Because, formerly, the people dared to take up arms themselves; were themselves masters of those in employment; disposers themselves of all emoluments; so that every citizen thought himself happy to derive honours and authority, and all advantages whatever, from the people. But now, on the contrary, favours are all dispensed, affairs all transacted, by the ministers; while you, quite enervated, robbed of your riches, your allies, stand in the mean rank of servants and assistants: happy if these men grant you the theatrical appointments, and send you scraps of the public meal. [1.] And, what is of all most sordid, you hold yourselves obliged to them for that which is your own: while they confine you within these walls, lead you on gently to their purposes, and sooth and tame you to obedience. Nor is it possible, that they, who are engaged in low and grovelling pursuits, can entertain great and generous sentiments. No! Such as their employments are, so must their dispositions prove.—And now, I call heaven to witness, that it will not surprise me, if I suffer more, by mentioning this your condition, than they who have involved you in it! Freedom of speech you do not allow on all occasions: and that you have now admitted it, excites my wonder.

But if you will at length be prevailed on to change your conduct: if you will take the field, and act worthy of Athenians; if these redundant sums which you receive at home be applied to the advancement of your affairs abroad; perhaps, my countrymen! perhaps some instance of consummate good fortune may attend you, and ye may become so happy as to despise those pittances, which are like the morsels that a physician allows his patient. For these do not restore his vigour, but just keep him from dying. So, your distributions cannot serve any valuable purpose, but are just sufficient to divert your attention from all other things, and thus increase the indolence of every one among you.

But I shall be asked, What then! is it your opinion, that these sums should pay our army? —And besides this, that the state should be regulated in such a manner, that every one may have his share of public business, and approve himself a useful citizen, on what occasion soever his aid may be required? Is it in his power to live in peace? He will live here with greater dignity, while these supplies prevent him from being tempted by indigence to any thing dishonourable. Is he called forth by an emergency like the present? Let him discharge that sacred duty which he owes to his country, by applying these sums to his support in the field. Is there a man among you past the age of service? Let him, by inspecting and conducting the public business, regularly merit his share of the distributions which he now receives, without any duty enjoined, or any return made to the community. And thus, with scarcely any alteration, either of abolishing or innovating, all irregularities are removed, and the state completely settled, by appointing one general regulation, which shall entitle our citizens to receive, and at the same time oblige them to take arms, to administer justice, to act in all cases as their time of life and our affairs require. But it never hath, nor could it have, been moved by me, that the rewards of the diligent and active should be bestowed on the useless citizen; or that you should sit here, supine, languid, and irresolute, listening to the exploits of some general's foreign troops (for thus it is at present.)—Not that I would reflect on him who serves you in any instance. But you yourselves, Athenians! should perform those services for which you heap honours upon others; and not recede from that illustrious rank of virtue, the price of all the glorious toils of your ancestors, and by them bequeathed to you.

Thus have I laid before you the chief points in which I think you interested. It is your part to embrace that opinion which the welfare of the state in general, and that of every single member, recommends to your acceptance.

[1.] Of the public meal.] Demetrius Phalereus records a saying of Demades, in ridicule of the custom of distributing victuals to the people. *The state,* said he, *is now become a feeble old woman, that sits at home in her slippers, and sups up her ptisan.*

THE THIRD OLYNTHIAC ORATION.

PRONOUNCED IN THE SAME YEAR.

INTRODUCTION.

The preceding oration had no farther effect upon the Athenians, than to prevail on them to send orders to Charidemus, who commanded for them at the Hellespont, to make an attempt to relieve Olynthus. He accordingly led some forces into Chalcis, which, in conjunction with the forces of Olynthus, ravaged Pallene, a peninsula of Macedon, toward Thrace, and Bottia, a country on the confines of Chalcis, which, among other towns, contained Pella, the capital of Macedon.

But these attempts could not divert Philip from his resolution of reducing Olynthus, which he had now publicly avowed. The

Olynthians, therefore, found it necessary to have once more recourse to Athens; and to request, that they would send troops, composed of citizens, animated with a sincere ardour for their interest, their own glory, and the common cause.

Demosthenes, in the following oration, insists on the importance of saving Olynthus; alarms his hearers with the apprehension of a war, which actually threatened Attica, and even the capital; urges the necessity of personal service; and returns to his charge of the misapplication of the public money, but in such a manner as showeth that his former remonstrances had not the desired effect.

OLYNTHIAC THE THIRD.

Callimach. Archon.—A. R. Philip. 12.— Olympiad. 107. An. 4.

I AM persuaded, Athenians! that you would account it less valuable to possess the greatest riches, [1.] than to have the true interest of the state, on this emergency, clearly laid before you. It is your part, therefore, readily and cheerfully to attend to all who are disposed to offer their opinions. For your regards need not to be confined to those whose counsels are the effect of premeditation: [2.] it is your good fortune to have men among you, who can at once suggest many points of moment. From opinions, therefore, of every kind, you may easily choose that most conducive to your interest.

And now, Athenians! the present juncture calls upon us: we almost hear its voice, declaring loudly that you yourselves must engage in these affairs, if you have the least attention to your own security. You entertain I know not what sentiments on this occasion: my opinion is, that the reinforcements should be instantly decreed; that they should be raised with all possible expedition; that so our succours may be sent from this city, and all former inconveniences be avoided; and that you should send ambassadors to notify these things, and to secure our interests by their presence. For as he is a man of consummate policy, complete in the art of turning every incident to his own advantage, there is the utmost rea-

son to fear, that partly by concessions where they may be seasonable, partly by menaces (and his menaces may [3.] be believed,) and partly by rendering us and our absence suspected,— he may tear from us something of the last importance, and force it into his own service.

Those very circumstances, however, which contribute to the power of Philip, are happily the most favourable to us. For that uncontrolled command with which he governs all transactions, public and secret; his entire direction of his army, as their leader, their sovereign, and their treasurer; and his diligence, in giving life to every part of it by his presence; these things greatly contribute to carrying on a war with expedition and success, but are powerful obstacles to that accommodation which he would gladly make with the Olynthians. For the Olynthians see plainly that they do not now fight for glory, or for part of their territory, but to defend their state from dissolution and slavery. They know how he rewarded those traitors of Amphipolis, who made him master of that city, and those of Pydna, who opened their gates to him. In a word, free states, I think, must ever look with suspicion on an absolute monarchy, but a neighbouring monarchy most double their apprehensions.

Convinced of what hath now been offered, and possessed with every other just and worthy sentiment, you must exert your spirit, you must apply to the war, now, if ever; your fortunes, your persons, your whole powers, are now demanded. There is no excuse, no pretence left, for declining the preformance of your duty. For that which you were all ever urging loudly, that the Olynthians should be engaged in a war with Philip, hath now happened of itself; and this in a manner most agreeable to our interest. For if they had entered into this war at our persuasion, they must have been precarious allies, without steadiness or resolution; but as their private injuries have made them enemies to Philip, it is probable that enmity will be lasting, both on account of what they fear, and what they have already suffered. My countrymen! let not so favourable an opportunity escape you: do not repeat that error which hath been so often fatal to you. For when, at our return from assisting the Eubœans, [4.] Hierax and Stra-

[1.] The greatest riches.] Ulpian finds out a particular propriety in this exordium. He observes, that, as the orator intends to recommend to them to give up their theatrical appointments, he prepares them for it by this observation; and, while he is endeavouring to persuade them to a just disregard of money, appears as if he only spoke their sentiments.

[2.] Premeditation.] Monsieur Tourreil admires the greatness of mind of Demosthenes, who, though he gloried in the pains and labours his orations cost him, was yet superior to that low and malignant passion, which oftentimes prompts us to decry those talents which we do not possess. I suspect, however, that

this passage was occasioned by some particular circumstance in the debate. Perhaps some speaker, who opposed Demosthenes, might have urged his opinion somewhat dogmatically, as the result of mature reflection and deliberation.

[3.] His menaces may, &c.] Although his promises could by no means be relied on.

[4.] The Eubœans.] This refers to the expedition in favour of the Eubœans against the Thebans, which is mentioned in the note on Philip. 1. page 14. The Athenians prepared for this expedition in three days, according to Demosthenes; in five, according to Æschines. And their success was as sudden as their preparation.

tocles, citizens of Amphipolis, mounted this gallery, [1.] and pressed you to send out your navy, and to take their city under your protection, had we discovered that resolution in our own cause, which we exerted for the safety of Eubœa, then had Amphipolis been yours, and all those difficulties had been avoided, in which you have been since involved. Again, when we received advice of the sieges of Pydna, Potidæa, Methone, Pegasæ, and other places (for I would not detain you with a particular recital,) had we ourselves marched with a due spirit and alacrity to the relief of the first of these cities, we should now find much more compliance, much more humility, in Philip. But by still neglecting the present, and imagining our future interests will not demand our care, we have aggrandized our enemy, we have raised him to a degree of eminence greater than any king of Macedon had ever yet enjoyed—Now we have another opportunity. That which the Olynthians, of themselves, present to the state: one no less considerable than any of the former.

And in my opinion, Athenians! if a man were to bring the dealings of the gods toward us to a fair account, though many things might appear not quite agreeable to our wishes, yet he would acknowledge that we had been highly favoured by them; and with great reason: for that many places had been lost in the course of war is truly to be charged to our own weak conduct. But that the difficulties arisen from hence have not long affected us, and that an alliance now presents itself to remove them, if we are disposed to make the just use of it; this I cannot but ascribe to the divine goodness. But the same thing happens in this case as in the use of riches. If a man be careful to save those he hath acquired, he readily acknowledges the kindness of fortune; but if by his imprudence they be once lost, with them he also loses the sense of gratitude. So in political affairs, they who neglect to improve their opportunities, forget the favours which the gods had bestowed; for it is the ultimate event which generally determines

men's judgment of every thing precedent. And therefore all affairs hereafter should engage your strictest care, that, by correcting our errors, we may wipe off the inglorious stain of past actions. But should we be deaf to these men too, and should he be suffered to subvert Olynthus,—say, what can prevent him from marching his forces into whatever territory he pleases?

Is there not a man among you, Athenians! who reflects by what steps Philip, from a beginning so inconsiderable, hath mounted to this height of power? First, he took Amphipolis: then he became master of Pydna; then Potidæa fell; then Methone: then came his inroad into Thessaly: after this, having disposed affairs at Pheræ, at Pegasæ, at Magnesia, entirely as he pleased, he marched into Thrace. [2.] Here, while engaged in expelling some, and establishing other princes, he fell sick. Again recovering, he never turned a moment from his course to ease and indulgence, but instantly attacked the Olynthians. His expeditions against the Illyrians, the Pæonians, against Arymbas, [3.] I pass all over.—But I may be asked, why this recital now?—That you may know and see your own error, in ever neglecting some part of your affairs, as if beneath your regard: and that active spirit with which Philip pursueth his designs: which ever fires him; and which never can permit him to rest satisfied with those things he hath already accomplished. If then he determines firmly and invariably to pursue his conquests; and if we are obstinately resolved against every vigorous and effectual measure; think, what consequences may we expect! in the name of Heaven, can any man be so weak, as not to know, that by neglecting this war, we are transferring it from that country to our own? and should this happen, I fear, Athenians! that as they who inconsiderately borrow money upon high interest, after a short-lived affluence are deprived of their own fortunes; so we, by this continued indolence, by consulting only our ease and pleasure, may be reduced to the grievous necessity of

---

[1.] This gallery.] In the original, τὸ τοῦτο BH˜MA. That eminence where all the public speakers were placed, and from whence the people were addressed on all occasions.

[2.] Into Thrace. Here, while engaged, &c.] Thrace was inhabited by an infinite number of different people, whose names Herodotus hath transmitted. And he observes, that could they have united under a single chief, or connected themselves by interest or sentiment, they would have formed a body infinitely superior to all their neighbours. After Teres, the Thracians had divers kings. This prince had two sons, Sitalces and Sparadocus, among whose descendants various contests arose; till, after a series of usurpations and revolutions, Seuthes recovered part of the territory of his father, Mæsades, and transmitted the succession peaceably to Cotis the father of Cersobleptes (as Demosthenes says, not his brother, as Diodorus.) At the death of Cotis, the di-

visions recommenced; and the place of one king, Thrace had three, Cersobleptes, Berisades, and Amadocus; Cersobleptes dispossessed the other two, and was himself dethroned by Philip. Frotinus reports, that Alexander, when he had conquered Thrace, brought the princes of that country with him in his expedition into Asia, to prevent their raising any commotions in his absence; a proof that Philip and Alexander had established several petty kings in Thrace who were vassals to Macedon.

[3.] Arymbas.] He was the son of Alcetas, king of Epirus, and brother to Neoptolemus, whose daughter Olympias Philip married. About three years before the date of this oration, the death of their father produced a dispute between the brothers about the succession: Arymbas was the lawful heir; yet Philip obliged him, by force of arms, to divide the kingdom with Neoptolemus; and not contented with this, at the death of Arymbas he

engaging in affairs the most shocking and dis-agreeable, and of exposing ourselves in the defence of this our native territory.

To censure, some one may tell me, is easy, and in the power of every man : but the true counsellor should point out that conduct which the present exigence demands.—Sensible as I am, Athenians ! that, when your expectations have in any instance been disappointed, your resentment frequently falls not on those who merit it, but on him who hath spoken last ; yet I cannot, from a regard to my own safety, suppress what I deem of moment to lay before you. I say, then, this occasion calls for a two-fold armament. First, we are to defend the cities of the Olynthians ; and for this purpose to detach a body of forces ; in the next place, in order to infest his kingdom, we are to send out our navy manned with other levies. If you neglect either of these, I fear your expedition will be fruitless. For if you content yourselves with infesting his dominions, this he will endure, until he is master of Olynthus ; and then he can with ease repel the invasion : or, if you only send succours to the Olynthians, where he sees his own kingdom free from danger, he will apply with constancy and vigilance to the war, and at length weary out the besieged to a submission. Your levies, therefore, must be considerable enough to serve both purposes.—These are my sentiments with respect to our armament.

And now as to the expense of these preparations. You are already provided for the payment of your forces better than any other people. This provision is distributed among yourselves in the manner most agreeable ; but if you restore it to the army, the supplies will be complete without any addition : if not, an addition will be necessary ; or the whole, rather, will remain to be raised. How then, I may be asked, do you move for a decree to apply those funds to the military service ? By no means ! it is my opinion, indeed, that an army must be raised ; that this money really belongs to the army ; and that the same regulation which entitles our citizens to receive, should oblige them also to act. At present you expend the sums on entertainments, without regard to your affairs.

It remains, then, that a general contribution be raised : a great one, if a great one be required : a small one, if such may be sufficient. Money must be found : without it nothing can be effected : various schemes are proposed by various persons ; do you make that choice which you think most advantageous ; and while you have an opportunity, exert yourselves in the care of your interests.

It is worthy [1.] your attention to consider how the affairs of Philip are at this time circumstanced. For they are by no means so well disposed, so very flourishing, as an inattentive observer would pronounce. Nor would he have engaged in this war at all, had he thought he should have been obliged to maintain it. He hoped that the moment he appeared, all things would fall before him. But these hopes are vain. And this disappointment, in the first place, troubles and dispirits him. Then the Thessalians alarm him : a people remarkable for their perfidy [2.] on all occasions, and to all persons. And just as they have ever proved, even so he finds them now. For they have resolved in council to demand the restitution of Pegasæ, and have opposed his attempt to fortify Magnesia : and I am informed, that for the future he is to be excluded from their ports and markets, as these conveniences belong to the states of Thessaly, and are not to be intercepted by Philip. And should he be deprived of such a fund of wealth, he must be greatly straitened to support his foreign troops. Besides this, we must suppose that the Pæonians and the Illyrians, and all the others, would prefer freedom and independence to a state of slavery. They are not accustomed to subjection ; and the insolence of this man, it is said, knows no bounds ; nor is this improbable, for great and unexpected success is apt to hurry weak minds into extravagances. Hence it often proves much more difficult to maintain acquisitions, than to acquire. It is your part, therefore, to regard the time of his distress as your most favourable opportunity : improve it to the utmost ; send out your embassies : take the field yourselves, and excite a general ardour abroad ; ever considering how readily Philip would attack us, if he were favoured by any incident

---

found means, by his intrigues and menaces, to prevail on the Epirots to banish his son, and to constitute Alexander, the son of Neoptolemus, sole monarch. *Tourreil.*

[1.] It is worthy, &c.] Hitherto the orator has painted Philip in all his terrors. He is politic, and vigilant, and intrepid ; he has risen gradually to the highest pitch of power ; and is now ready to appear before the walls of Athens, if he is not instantly opposed. But lest this description should dispirit the Athenians, he is now represented in a quite different manner. His power is by no means real and solid ; his allies are prepared to revolt ; his kingdom is threatened with war and desolation ; and he is just ready to be crushed by the very first effort that is made to distress him. But as it was necessary that the danger to

which they were exposed should make the deepest impression upon the mind of his hearers, he returns to his former description, and concludes with the dreadful image of a formidable enemy, ravaging their territory, and shutting them up within their walls.

[2.] Their perfidy.] This people had a bad character from the earliest times, so as to become even proverbial ; and Greece, and Athens particularly, had experienced their want of faith on very important occasions. They invited Xerxes into Greece, and were not ashamed to join Mardonius after the battle of Salamis, and to serve him as guides in his invasion of Attica ; and in the heat of the battle between Athens and Sparta, they on a sudden deserted their allies, the Athenians, and joined the enemy. See Thucyd. Book I.

like this, if a war had broken out on our borders. And would it not be shameful to want the resolution to bring that distress on him, which had it been equally in his power, he certainly would have made you feel.

This too demands your attention, Athenians! that you are now to determine whether it be most expedient to carry the war into his country, or to fight him here. If Olynthus be defended, Macedon will be the seat of war: you may harass his kingdom, and enjoy your own territories free from apprehensions. But should that nation be subdued by Philip, who will oppose his marching hither? Will the Thebans? Let it not be thought severe, when I affirm that they will join readily in the invasion. [1.] Will the Phocians? a people scarcely able [2.] to defend their own country, without your assistance. Will any others? [3.] But, Sir, cries some one, he would make no such attempt.—This would be the greatest of absurdities; not to execute those threats, when he hath full power, which, now when they appear so idle and extravagant, he yet dares to utter. And I think you are not yet to learn how great would be the difference between our engaging him here, and there. Were we to be only thirty

days abroad, and to draw all the necessaries of the camp from our own lands, even were there no enemy to ravage them, the damage would, in my opinion, amount to more than the whole expense of the late war. [4.] Add then the presence of an enemy, and how greatly must the calamity be increased? but, farther, add the infamy: and to those who judge rightly, no distress can be more grievous than the scandal of misconduct.

It is incumbent, therefore, upon us all (justly influenced by these considerations,) to unite vigorously in the common cause, and repel the danger that threatens this territory. Let the rich exert themselves on this occasion; that, by contributing a small portion of their affluence, they may secure the peaceful possession of the rest. Let those who are of the age for military duty; that by learning the art of war in Philip's dominions, they may become formidable defenders of their native land. Let our orators; that they may safely submit their conduct to the public inspection. For your judgment of their administrations will ever be determined by the event of things. And may we all contribute to render that favourable!

[1.] Join readily in the invasion.] The reason of Thebes's hatred to Athens have been already assigned. See note on Olynth. II. p. 67.

[2.] Scarcely able, &c.] The Phocians were at this time reduced to a very low state, by a continued series of ill success in the sacred war. Philomelus' and Onomarchus had perished; Phayllus and Phalecus, their successors, had been frequently defeated; and the Thebans were continually gaining advantages over them. *Tourreil.*

[3.] Will any others?] He avoids all mention of the Thessalians; because he had just showed that they were ill-affected to Philip, and therefore might be supposed willing to join with the Athenians.

[4.] Of the late war.] That is, their expedition into Thrace, in order to recover Amphipolis, which, according to the calculation of Æschines, cost them 1500 talents. *Tourreil.*

THE ORATION ON THE PEACE.

PRONOUNCED IN THE ARCHONSHIP OF ARCHIAS, THREE YEARS AFTER THE OLYNTHIAC ORATIONS.

INTRODUCTION.

THE Athenians sent those succours to Olynthus, which were recommended in the preceding oration. But they could not defend that state against its domestic enemies: for the year following, two of its citizens, Lasthenes and Euthycrates, betrayed the city to Philip. He razed it, threw part of the inhabitants in chains, sold another part, and distinguished the two traitors only by the cruelty of their death. His two brothers, who had been harboured in Olynthus, he also sacrificed to his jealousy and revenge.

These events, no less than the repeated instances of Demosthenes, prevailed on the Athenians to declare war against Philip in form. Hitherto he had kept some measures with them, and had sought various pretences for

glossing over his hostilities; but now he fell with the utmost fury upon all their tributary states, and obliged Demosthenes to appear once more in the assembly, to persuade the Athenians to defend the Islanders, and their colonies which lay upon the Hellespont. But scarcely had the war been declared, when the vigour of their enemy, and their own fickleness and indolence, made them weary of it. Ctesiphon and Phrynon were sent to sound Philip's dispositions toward a separate peace. This was as he could wish. The Phocian war was at present the object of his views: and his arts had just regained the Thessalians over to the confederacy, who had been prevailed on to stand neuter. To the Athenian ministers, therefore, he made such professions, that Demosthenes and nine others were sent to negotiate the peace; who proceeded as far as they were authorized, and returned with Antipater, Parmenio, and Eurylochus, on the part of Philip. Ambassadors were sent soon after, from Athens, with full powers to conclude the treaty. In the first of these embassies, Demosthenes had met with some Athenian prisoners in Macedon, whom he promised to redeem at his own expense, and took this opportunity to perform it, while his colleagues, in the mean time, were to proceed with all expedition, in order to conclude with Philip. Three months elapsed, however, before they came to an audience with the king, who was all this time making himself master of those places in Thrace, which the Athenians claimed as their right. At last the terms of the treaty were agreed to; but by affected delays, and by corrupting the ambassadors, he found means to defer the execution of it, until he had advanced his troops into Thessaly, in order to proceed against the Phocians. He then concluded the peace; and on their return, the ambassadors who had conducted the treaty (and Æschines in particular) expatiated upon his candour and sincerity. They declared (at the very time when he was giving Thebes the most solemn assurances that he would exterminate the Phocians,) that his sole views were to screen this people from the fury of their enemies, and to control the insolence of the Thebans. They also vouched for his performing several things in favour of the state, not formally stipulated in the treaty. Thus were the Athenians amused, and Philip suffered to pass the straits of Thermopylæ, and to pursue his march into Phocis.

His reputation and approach struck such a terror into the Phocians, that although they received a reinforcement of a thousand Spartans, they yet sent to treat, or refuse to submit. He allowed Phalecus with eight thousand mercenaries to retire into Peleponnesus: but the rest, who were inhabitants of Phocis, were left at his mercy. The disposal of these he referred

to the Amphictyons, from an affected rega: to the authority of an assembly composed the representatives of the states of Greec They thundered out the severest decrees agair this wretched people. Among other things, was enacted, that they should lose their se in the Amphictyonic council, and that t double voice which they had enjoyed in should be transferred to Philip; who, by t same resolution, gained the superintenden of the Pythian games, which the Corinthia forfeited by taking part with the Phocians.

The Athenians had not been present at P lip's election into this council; and probal to avoid all opposition he had assembled or such Amphictyons as were devoted to his terest. He thought it proper, however, to se circular letters to the absent states, invit them to assemble at Delphos, and to ratify election.

Athens, among others, received the inv tion: and as Philip's ambitious designs co be no longer concealed, many were for viol measures. The proposal raised a fermen the assembly; which seems to have breat nothing but indignation and opposition. this occasion, Demosthenes thought it his d to moderate their heat; and, in the follow oration, endeavours to prevent their being trayed into any rash and imprudent measu

---

THE ORATION ON THE PEACE. [

Archia, Archon.—A. R. Philip. 15. Ol; *piad.* 108. *An.* 3.

ATHENIANS! I see that this debate mu attended with many difficulties and great motion: not only because many of our inte are already given up, and therefore unn sary to be now laid before you; but becat

[1.] I shall here take the liberty to transcribe a remark from the authors of the Universal History.

Libanius and Photius had taken pains to prove that the oration to which we refer above ought not to be ascribed to Demosthenes. We might well enough defend ourselves, by alleging, that it has been generally esteemed his, and, as such, has constantly maintained its place in his works. This would be sufficient for our purpose, but in truth, the arguments on which the opposite sentiment is built, are so easily overturned, that we might be justly blamed for neglecting so favourable an occasion of setting this point in a true light. Demosthenes (say those who will not allow this oration to be his,) charged Æschines with betraying his country, on account of his recommending warmly a peace with Philip; they cannot therefore think, that Demosthenes would run openly into those measures which he had so lately and so warmly decried: or that he, who on every other occasion singly opposed Philip, and ran all hazard to bring him into odium with the people, should now be

single on the other side, and attempt to the disposition of the Athenians, in favo peace and Philip. These objectors forget Demosthenes was a patriot as well as an or that he did not pursue Philip with implac hatred, because he was king of Macedo n because he thought him both willing and to obstruct the designs of Athens, and ev reduce her, from that splendid pre-emin which she now held in Greece, to the ordi rank of a state, in name free but in trut pendent upon him; this was the moti Demosthenes' heat on other occasions; the motive to his coolness now was the alliance between Philip and the other Gr states, which rendered it a thing impracti for Athens to contend with him and 1 alone. Besides, as he rightly observes i harangue, it would have been ridiculo those who refused to enter into an equa for rich cities and fertile provinces, to rushed suddenly into an unequal contest an empty title, or, as he emphatically ex sees it, 'to take away the shadow of De from him who was master of Delphos

is impossible to agree on such expedients as may secure what yet remain; but that a variety of clashing opinions must divide the assembly. Then, to advise, is naturally a difficult and distressing part. But you, Athenians! have rendered it yet more distressing: for all other people naturally seek counsel while affairs are yet depending; you deliberate, when the event hath made it too late. Hence hath it happened, through the whole course of my observation, that the man who arraigns your conduct is heard with esteem, and his sentiments approved; yet have your affairs ever miscarried, and the objects of your deliberation have all been lost. But although this be too true, still I am persuaded (and from this persuasion I arose to speak,) that if you will put an end to tumult and opposition, and grant me that attention which becomes those who are consulting for their country, and upon so important an occasion; I have some points to urge, some measures to propose, which may serve our present interests, and repair our past miscarriages.

Sensible as I am, Athenians! that to expatiate on those counsels one hath formerly given, and to speak of one's self, is the most successful artifice of those who dare to practise such artifice; yet to me it is so odious, so detestable, that although I see it necessary, yet I loathe it. However, it will assist your judgment, I presume, on this occasion, if you recall to mind something of what I formerly have mentioned. —You may remember, that during the disorders of Euboea, when certain persons persuaded you to assist Plutarchus, [1.] and to undertake an inglorious and expensive war, I was the first, the only one, who rose up to oppose it, and scarcely escaped their fury, who, for a trifling gain, were urging you to many highly pernicious measures. In a little time, when the load

of infamy had fallen upon you, and that you had suffered such treatment as no people ever received from those they had assisted, you were all made sensible of the iniquity of your seducers, and the justness and integrity of my counsels. Again, when I saw Neoptolemus the player [2.] (in that full security which his profession gave him) involving the state in the greatest distress, and in all his public conduct devoted to Philip; I appeared, and warned you of the danger; and this from no secret motive, no private enmity, [3.] no officious baseness, as the event itself discovered. But it is not the defenders of Neoptolemus that I accuse (for he was not depending on a single one,) but you yourselves: for had you been spectators in the theatre, not engaged in affairs of the highest and most intimate concernment to the public, you could not have heard him with more indulgence, nor me with more resentment. And now you all know, that he who then went over to the enemy, pretending to collect some debts that he might bring them hither (as he said,) to enable him to serve the state; that he who was perpetually inveighing against the cruelty of accusing a man for thus transferring his effects from that country hither; the moment that a peace freed him from all apprehensions, converted that estate [4.] into money, which he acquired here, and brought it off with him to Philip.

These two instances which I have produced, show with what fidelity and truth I spoke on those occasions. I shall mention one, and but one more, and then proceed to the point now to be debated. .When we had received the solemn ratification of the treaty, and that the embassy returned home; when certain persons assured you, that Thespia and Platæa were to be repeopled: [5.] that, if Philip became master of the Phocians, he would spare them:

We therefore acknowledge this to be the oration of Demosthenes, because he was worthy of it.

It is scarcely worth while to take notice of a small mistake in this remark. Libanius does not deny that Demosthenes was the author of this oration. He allows it to have been written by him, but is of opinion that he never ventured to pronounce it.

[1.] To assist Plutarchus.] Philip had long regarded Euboea as very proper, by its situation, to favour the designs he meditated against Greece. He therefore took pains to form a party in the island, and fomented divisions and factions in the several states of which it was composed. Plutarch, the governor of Eretria, one of the principal cities of Euboea, applied to the Athenians for assistance against some attempts of Philip, and obtained it; but afterward (having probably been gained over to Philip's party) he took up arms against the very auxiliaries he had invited. But this perfidy did not disconcert Phocion, who commanded them. He gained a victory over the Macedonians, and drove Plutarch out of Eretria. Phocion was afterward recalled, and Molossus,

his successor in this war, was defeated and taken prisoner by Philip.

[2.] Neoptolemus the player.] This Neoptolemus was also a great tragic poet, though the orator only mentions the less honourable distinction. Not that the profession of a player was held in disesteem in Greece. Players were the favourites of princes, and were raised to the highest employments in the state. This very man was nominated, the year before, one of the ten ambassadors that were to conclude the peace with Philip. Tourreil.

[3.] No private enmity, &c.] Probably this is a repetition of the very words of Neoptolemus's party.

[4.] That estate.] The text has it, οὐσίαν φανεράν. The Athenians distinguished two sorts of goods or estates: apparent, by which they understood lands: and not apparent, that is, money, slaves, moveables, &c.

[5.] That Thespia and Platæa were to be repeopled.] Thespia had been razed by the Thebans, under Epaminondas. Platæa had been twice destroyed by them; once, when Archidamus, king of Sparta, obliged the Platæans to surrender at discretion, in the fifth

that Thebes was to submit to his regulation: [1.] that Oropus[2.] was to be ours; that Euboea should be given up [3.] to us as an equivalent for Amphipolis; with other such insidious promises, which in spite of interest, of justice, and of honour, drove you to abandon Phocis; I never attempted to deceive you; I was not silent; no, you must remember I declared that I knew of none, that I expected none of these things: but thought that whoever mentioned them could scarcely be serious.

And these instances of my superior foresight I do by no means ascribe to any extraordinary penetration; I speak it not from boasting or arrogance; nor do I pretend to any superiority but what arises from these two causes: The first is fortune, which I find more powerful than all the policy and wisdom of man; the other, that perfect disinterestedness with which my judgments are ever formed; so that no man can hold out any advantage to my view, to influence my public conduct. Hence it is, that on all occasions of debate, your true interest strikes my eye directly. But when a bribe is, as it were, cast into one scale, it then preponderates, and forces down the judgment with it; so that it is not possible that a person, thus influenced, can ever offer good and salutary counsel.

And now, to give my sentiments on the present occasion:—Whether subsidies, or alliances, or whatever schemes are concerting for the public good, one point must be secured; the continuance of the present peace. Not that it is so very excellent, or so worthy of you; but, of what kind soever it may be it were more for the interest of your affairs that it had never been concluded, than that now, when it is concluded, you should infringe it; for we have suffered ourselves to be deprived of many advantages, which would have given our arms much more security and strength.

In the next place, we must be careful not to drive those to extremities, who are now assembled, and call themselves the council of Amphictyons; nor to afford them a pretence for a general war against us. Were we again engaged with Philip for Amphipolis, or any such private matter of dispute, in which neither Thessalians, nor Argians, nor Thebans, were concerned; in my opinion none of these would join against us; and, least of all,—let me be heard out without interruption,—the Thebans: not that they wish well to us, or would not willingly recommend themselves to Philip: but they are perfectly sensible (however mean their understandings may be thought,) that were they to engage in a war with you, the evils would all fall on them; [4.] the advantages others would lie ready to intercept. They would therefore never be betrayed in such a quarrel, unless the cause were general. In like manner, another war with the Thebans for Oropus, or any such private cause, could not, I think, distress us: for there are those who would ei her join with us or them, to repel an invasion, but in offensive measures would concur with neither. This is the true nature, the very spirit of alliances. There are none so much attached to us or Thebes as to desire that we should maintain our own power and triumph over our competitor. To be secure, they would all wish us for their own sakes; but that either of us should reduce the other to subjection, and so be enabled to give law to them, not one would bear.

Where then lies the danger? What are you to guard against? that general pretence for uniting against us, which the war, now in agitation may afford the states. For if the Argians, [5.] and the Messenians, and the Megalopolitans, and such other of the Peloponnesians, as are in the same interest, should make it a cause of quarrel, that we have sought a treaty with the Lacedemonians, and seem to have favoured their designs: [6.] if the The-

---

year of the Peloponnesian war. The Thebans, who were then joined with Lacedemon, insisted that they should be exterminated. The treaty of Antalcidas restored them: but this did not last long; for three years before the the battle of Leuctra, the Thebans reduced them to their former wretched state, because they refused to join with them against the Lacedemonians. *Tourreil.*

[1.] That Thebes was to submit to his regulation.] In the Greek it is διοικεῖν, 'administraturam.' Philip made use of this soft expression, to persuade the Athenians that he would reduce the Thebans to reason, and put it out of their power to undertake any act of outrage or injustice; and at the same time to avoid alarming the Thebans, or alienating them from his party. Wolfius thinks that διοικεῖν is put for διοικίζειν, and translates it 'dissipaturum,' that he would exterminate the Thebans. But I cannot think that he would have expressed himself in a manner ⬤harsh, and so likely to make the Thebans his enemies. *Tourreil.*

[2.] That Oropus, &c.] This city had been taken from the Athenians, the third year of the 103d Olympiad, by Themision, the tyrant of Eretria, and afterward put into the hands of the Thebans. Their mutual pretensions to this city had oftentimes embroiled these two states. *Tourreil.*

[3.] Euboea should be given up, &c.] For he had by this time gained a great authority in that island, and stationed his garrisons in most of its cities.

[4.] The evils would all fall on them, &c.] Sparta only waited for this rupture, to assert its power once more. And from Philip's former conduct it appeared very plainly, that he knew how to avail himself of such a quarrel.

[5.] For if the Argians, &c.] When the Spartan power was broken by Thebes, these people, who had been dependent on Sparta, asserted their freedom. This occasioned some contests which still subsisted, and in which the Spartans were favoured by Athens. *Tourreil.*

[6.] To have favoured their designs, &c.] The designs of the Lacedemonians, of reducing these people to their former subjection.—

bans, incensed as they are said to be at present, should become yet more incensed at our harbouring their exiles, [1.] and taking every occasion of declaring ourselves implacably averse to them; if the Thessalians should resent our reception of the fugitive Phocians, and Philip our opposing his admission into the council of Amphictyons; I fear, that, to revenge these private quarrels, they may use the authority of this council, to give sanction to a general war against us; and, in the violence of resentment, forget even their own interest, as it happened in the Phocian war. You are not ignorant that the Thebans and Philip, and the Thessalians, although they had by no means the same views, have yet all concurred in the same scheme of conduct. The Thebans, for instance, were not able to hinder Philip from passing, and becoming master of Thermopylæ, nor from coming in after all their toils, and depriving them of the glory; (for as to possessions, [2.] and the acquisition of territories, the Thebans have succeeded happily; but in point of honour and reputation they have suffered most shamefully.) If Philip did not pass, they were to expect nothing; it was highly disagreeable to them; yet, for the sake of Orchomenus and Coronea, [3.] which they greatly desired, but were not able to take, they chose to endure all this. And yet there are persons who dare to assert that Philip did not surrender these cities to the Thebans freely, but was compelled. Away with such pretences! I am satisfied that this was equally his concern with the gaining the Straits, the glory of the war, the honour of deciding it, and the direction of the Pythian games; and these were the greatest objects of his most earnest wishes. As to the Thessalians, they neither desired to see the Thebans aggrandized, nor Philip (for in their power they saw danger to themselves;) but two things they greatly desired, a seat in the council [4.] of Amphictyons, and the wealth of Delphos; and thence they were induced to join in the confederacy. Thus you may observe that private interest oftentimes engages men in measures quite opposite to their inclinations. And therefore it is your part to proceed with the utmost caution.

What then! saith some one, shall these apprehensions make us yield to his demands? is this your motion? Not at all! I only mean to show you, how you may maintain your dignity, avoid a war, and approve your moderation and justice to the world. As to those violent men who think we should brave all dangers, I wish them to consider this. We allow the Thebans to possess Oropus: were we asked the motive, we should answer, To avoid a war. In like manner, by the present treaty, we yield Amphipolis to Philip; we suffer the Cardians to be distinguished [5.] from the other inhabitants of the Chersonesus; the king of Caria [6.] to possess Chios, and Cos, and Rhodes: and the Byzantines [7.] to cruise for prizes; and this, because we think that peace and tranquillity will produce more advantages than violence and contests about these points. And if thus directed in our conduct toward each particular state, and where our interest is highly and intimately concerned, it would be perfect weakness and absurdity to provoke the resentment of them all for a shadow. [8.]

Tourreil translates ἐκδέχεσθαι, to approve. Suidas renders it stronger—to forward, to promote; ἐκδέχεσθαι, 'significat aliquid ab altero accipere, quod ipse deinde tractandum suscipias.' Wolfius applies ἐκείνοις to the Argians, &c. and translates the passage thus, 'propter acta quædam sua impedita.' But I have chosen the other interpretation as the most natural.

[1.] At our harbouring their exiles.] Many of the cities of Bœotia favoured the Phocians in the sacred war. But when this war was ended, and the Thebans became masters of those cities, they treated the inhabitants with great cruelty, and obliged them to take shelter at Athens.

[2.] As to possessions, &c.] All Phocis was given up to them immediately after the war.

[3.] Orchomenus and Coronea, &c.] The Phocians had taken these two cities from them the year before.

[4.] A seat in the council, &c.] Of which they had been deprived by the Phocians making themselves masters of Delphos where this council assembled.

[5.] We suffer the Cardians to be distinguished, &c.] This is explained in the introduction to the oration on the state of the Chersonesus.

[6.] The king of Caria.] Mausolus, king of that country, had assisted these islands against Athens, in the social war; and when, at the conclusion of this war, the Athenians were obliged to declare them free and independent, their ally made himself master of them. Upon the death of Mausolus, his wife Artemisia maintained his dominion in these new-conquered islands. She survived her husband but two years, and was succeeded by her brother Hidrieus, who reigned in Caria at the time that this oration was pronounced. *Tourreil.*

[7.] And the Byzantines, &c.] These people had also revolted from the Athenians, and joined with the islanders in the social war:—How far, or on what pretence, they were suffered to commit those outrages upon the seas, does not appear. *Tourreil.*

[8.] For a shadow.] In the Greek, Περι της ἐν Δελφοῖς σκιᾶς, for a shadow in Delphos. That is, for an empty title of Amphictyon, or of a protector of the temple of Delphos.

THE SEVENTH ORATION AGAINST PHILIP.

Commonly called the Second.

PRONOUNCED IN THE ARCHONSHIP OF LYCISCUS, TWO YEARS AFTER THE ORATION
ON THE PEACE.

INTRODUCTION.

The Greeks thought it proper to confirm, or at least not to oppose Philip's admission into the council of Amphictyons, where he immediately assumed a despotic power. In every enterprise he armed himself with one of their decrees, and, under pretence of executing them, made a merit of oppressing several states of Greece.

The Thebans opened him an entrance into Peloponnesus, where, from their inveterate hatred to the Lacedemonians, they were constantly fomenting divisions. They solicited Philip to join with them, the Messenians, and the Argians, to reduce the power of Lacedemon, which, without any right but that of the strongest, had erected itself into a kind of sovereignty, to the prejudice of the neighbouring states. Philip willingly listened to an overture which agreed so well with his own views. He proposed, or rather dictated a decree, to the Amphictyons, that the Lacedemonians should suffer Argos and Messene to enjoy an absolute independence; and, under the pretence of supporting their authority, at the same time marched a great body of forces toward those parts.

The Lacedemonians, justly alarmed, applied to Athens for succour; and strongly urged, by their ambassadors, the conclusion of a league, which was necessary for their common safety. All the powers interested in crossing this league used their utmost diligence to that end. Philip, by his ministers, represented to the Athenians, that they could not with justice declare against him; and that if he had not come to a rupture with the Thebans, he had in this done nothing contrary to his treaty with Athens. And this indeed was true, with respect to the public articles of the peace, whatever private assurances he might have given their ambassadors. The representatives of Thebes, Argos, and Messene, pressed the Athenians on their part,

and reproached them with having already too much favoured the Lacedemonians, those enemies of Thebes, and tyrants of Peloponnesus. The strength of those remonstrances somewhat staggered the Athenians. They were unwilling to break with Philip; and then, on the other hand, could not but see danger to themselves in the ruin of Lacedemon. They were therefore in doubt what answer to give to the Lacedemonian ambassadors: on which occasion Demosthenes pronounced the following oration.

PHILIPPIC THE SECOND.

Lycisco Archon.—A. R. Philip. 17.—Olympiad. 109. An. I.

Athenians! When the hostile attempts of Philip, and those outrageous violations of the peace, which he is perpetually committing, are at any time the subject of our debates, the speeches on your side I find humane and just; [1.] and that the sentiments of those who inveigh against Philip never fail of approbation; but as to the necessary measures; to speak out plainly, not one hath been pursued, nor any thing effected even to reward the attention to these harangues. Nay, to such circumstances is our state reduced that the more fully and evidently a man proves that Philip is acting contrary to his treaty, and harbouring designs against Greece, the greater is his difficulty in pointing out your duty.

The reason is this. They who aspire to an extravagant degree of power, are to be opposed by force and action, not by speeches: and yet, in the first place, we public speakers are unwilling to recommend or to propose any thing to this purpose, from the fear of your displeasure; but confine ourselves to general representations of the grievous, of the outrage-

---

[1.] Humane and just.] An opposition to the growing power of Macedon, the orator ever affects to consider as the cause of liberty, of justice, and of Greece. The interest of the nation, that is, of the whole assemblage of the Grecian states, was, professedly, the first great object of regard to every member of every community. This was their most extensive affection. The distinction of Greek and Barbarian precluded the rest of mankind from a just share in their philanthropy. At least it was not generally considered as a duty, to extend their benevolence farther than the boundaries of their nation. These included all that were really considered of the same kind. And

hence it is, as I conceive, that the love of their countrymen was called by the most extensive term, the love of mankind. The word therefore, in the original φιλανθρώπους, which is rendered ' humane,' the translator understood as expressive of a regard to the general welfare of Greece. Nor was it owing to any design of concealing his ignorance, that this explanation was not originally allowed a place in the notes on this oration. What is, or is imagined to be clear to us, we are apt to flatter ourselves must, at first glance, appear to others exactly in the same light. Just as we sometimes suppose that the difficulty we ourselves cannot conquer, is, in itself, absolutely insuperable.

ous nature of his conduct, and the like. Then, you who attend, are better qualified than Philip, either to plead the justice of your cause, or to apprehend it, when enforced by others; but as to any effectual opposition to his present designs, in this you are entirely inactive. You see then the consequence, the necessary, the natural consequence; each of you excels in that which hath engaged your time and application: he, in acting; you in speaking. And if, on this occasion, it be sufficient that we speak with a superior force of truth and justice, this may be done with the utmost ease: but if we are to consider how to rectify our present disorders, how to guard against the danger of plunging inadvertently into still greater; against the progress of a power which may at last bear down all opposition; then must our debates proceed in a different manner; and all they who speak, and all you who attend, must prefer the best and most salutary measures to the easiest and most agreeable.

First, then, Athenians! if there be a man who feels no apprehensions at the view of Philip's power, and the extent of his conquests; who imagines that these portend no danger to the state, or that his designs are not all aimed against you; I am amazed! and must entreat the attention of you all, while I explain those reasons briefly, which induce me to entertain different expectations, and to regard Philip as our real enemy; that if I appear to have looked forward with the more penetrating eye, you may join with me; if they, who are thus secure and confident in this man, you may yield to their direction.

In the first place, therefore, I consider the acquisitions made by Philip when the peace was just concluded; Thermopylæ, and the command of Phocis. What use did he make of these?—He chose to serve the interest of Thebes, not that of Athens. And why? As ambition is his great passion, universal empire the sole object of his views; not peace, not tranquillity, not any just purpose; he knew this well, that neither our constitution nor our principles would admit him to prevail upon you (by any thing he could promise, by any

thing he could do,) to sacrifice one state of Greece to your private interest: but that, as you have the due regard to justice, as you have an abhorrence of the least stain upon your honour, and as you have that quick discernment which nothing can escape; the moment his attempt was made, you would oppose him with the same vigour as if you yourselves had been immediately attacked. The Thebans, he supposed (and the event confirmed his opinion,) would, for the sake of any private advantage, suffer him to act toward others as he pleased; and, far from opposing or impeding his designs, would be ready at his command to fight upon his side. From the same persuasion he now heaps his favours upon the Messenians and Argians. And this reflects the greatest lustre upon you, my countrymen! for by these proceedings you are declared the only invariable assertors of the rights of Greece; the only persons, whom no private attachment, no views of interest, can seduce from their affection to the Greeks.

And that it is with reason he entertains these sentiments of you, and sentiments so different of the Thebans and the Argians; he may be convinced, not from the present only, but from a review of former times. For he must have been informed, I presume, he cannot but have heard, that your ancestors, when, by submitting to the King, they might have purchased the sovereignty of Greece, not only scorned to listen, when Alexander, [1.] this man's ancestor, was made the messenger of such terms, but chose to abandon their city, encountered every possible difficulty; and, after all this, performed such exploits, as men are ever eager to recite, yet with the just force and dignity no man ever could express: and therefore it becomes me to be silent on this subject: for in reality their actions are superior to the power of words. As to the ancestors of the Thebans and the Argians, the one, he knows, fought for the Barbarian; the others did not oppose him. [2.] He knew then that both these people would attend but to their private interest, without the least regard to the common cause of Greece: should he choose you for

---

[1.] When Alexander, &c.] The reader may find the history here alluded to in the eighth and ninth books of Herodotus. The expressions in the original are as contemptuous as possible, ὁ τούτου: or as some editions have it, ὁ τούτων Πρόγονος, the ancestor of these wretches the Macedonians; and then, not Πρόσβυς, ambassador, but ΚΗΡΥΞ, herald or crier, the slave or menial officer of his master Mardonius. Avec le titre d'ambassadeur (as Tourreil translates it) suggests the honourable idea which Demosthenes takes such pains to keep out of view.

[2.] The one, he knows, fought for the Barbarian; the others did not oppose him.] The readiness with which the Thebans granted earth and water, the tokens of submission, to the Persian, the regret with which they joined Leonidas at Thermopylæ, their joining openly

with Xerxes, when his arms had the appearance of success, and other circumstances confirmed by the united testimony of historians, all warrant the assertion of Demosthenes. The Argians were engaged to a neutrality, by an artifice of the Persians, who pretended to derive their descent from Perseus, the son of Acrisius, one of the kings of Argos. This pretence, how gross soever, was sufficient for a people who chose to be deceived; and would not reflect that this monarchy had not the title of Persian till the reign of Cyrus. Their infidelity to the cause of Greece they concealed under the veil of ambition; for they professed themselves ready to concur in the common defence, provided that they were admitted to an equal share of the command with Lacedæmon: which proposal was rejected, as they desired. *Tourreil.*

allies, you would serve him so far only as justice would permit; but if he attached himself to them, he gained assistants in all the schemes of his ambition. This it is that then determined him, this it is that now determines him, to their side rather than to yours; not that he sees they have a greater naval force [1.] than we; or that, having gained the sovereignty in the inland countries, he declines the command of the seas, and the advantages of commerce; or that he hath forgotten those pretences, those promises which obtained him the peace.

But I may be told, It is true, he did act thus; but not from ambition, or from any of those motives of which I accuse him; but as he thought the cause of Thebes more just than ours. [2.]—This of all pretences he cannot now allege. Can he, who commands the Lacedemonians [3.] to quit their claim to Messene, pretend that, in giving up Orchomenus and Coronea to the Thebans, he acted from regard to justice? But now comes his last subterfuge. He was compelled; and yielded these places quite against his inclinations, being encompassed by the Thessalian horse and Theban infantry. Fine pretence!—Just so, they cry, he is to entertain suspicions of the Thebans: and some spread rumours of their own framing, that he is to fortify Elatea. [4.] Yes! these things are yet to be, and so will they remain, in my opinion; but his attack on Lacedemon, in conjunction with the Thebans and Argians, is not yet to be made. No! he is actually detaching forces; supplying money; and is himself expected at the head of a formidable army. The Lacedemonians, therefore, the enemies of Thebes, he now infests. And will he then restore the Phocians, whom he hath but just now ruined? Who can believe this? I, for my part, can never think, if Philip had been forced into those former measures, or if he had now abandoned the Thebans, that he would make this continued opposition to their ene-

mies. No! his present measures prove that all his past conduct was the effect of choice: and from all his actions it appears, that all his actions are directly levelled against this state. And there is in some sort a necessity for this. Consider: he aims at empire, and from you alone he expects opposition. He hath long loaded us with injuries; and of this he himself is most intimately conscious; for those of our possessions which he hath reduced to his service, he uses as a barrier to his other territories: so that if he should give up Amphipolis and Potidæa, he would not think himself secure even in Macedon. He is therefore sensible, that he entertains designs against you, and that you perceive them. Then, as he thinks highly of your wisdom, he concludes that you must hold him in that abhorrence which he merits: hence is he alarmed; expecting to feel some effects of your resentment (if you have any favourable opportunity,) unless he prevents you by his attack. Hence is his vigilance awakened; his arm raised against the state: he courts some of the Thebans, and such of the Peloponnesians as have the same views with him; whom he deems too mercenary to regard any thing but present interest, and too perversely stupid to foresee any consequences. And yet persons of but moderate discernment may have some manifest examples to alarm them, which I had occasion to [5.] mention to the Messenians, and to the Argians. Perhaps it may be proper to repeat them here.

'Messenians!' said I, 'how highly (think ye) would the Olynthians have been offended, if any man had spoken against Philip at that time when he gave them up Anthemus, [6.] a city which the former kings of Macedon had ever claimed? when he drove out the Athenian colony, and gave them Potidæa? when he took all our resentment on himself, and left them to enjoy our dominions? Did they expect to have

---

[1.] A greater naval force, &c.] Athens, as a maritime power, was superior to all the other Greeks. At the battle of Salamis, of the three hundred vessels which composed the Grecian fleet, two hundred were Athenian. Three hundred ships sailed from the port of Athens upon the expedition of Sicily; and their fleet was afterward increased to four hundred.

[2.] The cause of Thebes more just than ours.] The union of Philip with the Thebans had a very plausible colour: that to espousing the cause of Apollo, and punishing the sacrilegious profaners of his temple. It was not convenient to display this at large, and therefore he cuts it short by one vague expression. For the art of an orator appears no less in suppressing such things as may prove unfavourable to his design, than in dwelling on those points which may assist it. *Tourreil.*

[3.] Can he, who commands the Lacedemonians, &c.] Because the pretensions of each were of the same nature. Lacedemon assumed the supreme power in Peloponnesus. Thebes affected the like power in Bœotia.

[4.] To fortify Elatea.] This was the most considerable city in Phocis; and, by its situation, very well fitted to keep the Thebans in awe. So that some years after, when Philip perceived that the Thebans were growing cool to him, his first step was to take possession of Elatea. *Tourreil.*

[5.] Which I had occasion to, &c.] When Philip first began to interest himself in the disputes between these states and Lacedemon, the Athenians sent an embassy, to endeavour to weaken his interest in Peloponnesus, and to dissuade the Messenians and Argians from accepting of his interposition. On this occasion it was, that Demosthenes made the oration from which he now quotes this passage.

[6.] Anthemus.] This city of Macedon had been possessed by the ancestors of Philip from the earliest ages; for we learn from Herodotus, (B. 5.) that about two hundred years before, Amyntas made an offer of Anthemus to Hippias, the son of Pisistratus. *Tourreil.*

suffered thus? had it been foretold, would they have believed it? Yet, after a short enjoyment of the territories of others, they have been for ever despoiled of their own, by this man. Inglorious has been their fall, not conquered only, but betrayed and sold by one another. For those intimate correspondences with tyrants ever portend mischief to free states. Turn your eyes,' said I, 'to the Thessalians! think ye, that when he first expelled their tyrants, when he then gave them up Nicæa [1.] and Magnesia, that they expected ever to have been subjected to those governors [2.] now imposed on them? or that the man who restored them to their seat in the Amphictyonic council, would have deprived them of their own proper revenues? yet that such was the event, the world can testify. In like manner, you now behold Philip lavishing his gifts and promises upon you. If you are wise, you will pray that he may never appear to have deceived and abused you. Various are the contrivances for the defence and security of cities; as battlements, and walls, and trenches, and other kind of fortifications; all which are the effects of labour, and attended with continual expense. But there is one common bulwark, with which men of prudence are naturally provided, the guard and security of all people, particularly of free states, against the assault of tyrants. What is this? Distrust. Of this be mindful: to this adhere: preserve this carefully, and no calamity can affect you.—What is it you seek? said I, 'Liberty? And do ye not perceive that nothing can be more adverse to this than the very titles of Philip? every monarch, every tyrant, is an enemy to liberty, and the opposer of laws. Will ye not then be careful, lest, while ye seek to be freed from war, ye find yourselves his slaves?'

But although they heard these things, and loudly expressed their approbation; though the like points were frequently urged by the ambassadors while I was present, and probably were afterward repeated, yet still they have no less dependence on the friendship and the promises of Philip. But it is not strange that the Messenians and some of the Peloponnesians should act contrary to the dictates of nature, reason, and reflection. Even you, who are

yourselves fully sensible, and constantly reminded by your public speakers, that there are designs forming against you, that the toils of your enemies are surrounding you; will, I fear, be plunged by your supineness into all those dangers that threaten you: so prevalent is 'the pleasure and indulgence of a moment over all your future interests.—But as to the course necessary to be pursued, prudence requires, that this be debated hereafter among yourselves. At present, I shall propose such an answer to these ministers, as may be worthy of your concurrence . . . .[3.]

It would be just, Athenians! to call the men before you, who gave those promises which induced you to conclude the peace. For neither would I have undertaken the embassy, nor would you (I am convinced) have laid down your arms, had it been suspected that Philip would have acted thus, when he had obtained a peace. No! the assurances he then gave were quite different from his present actions. There are others also to be summoned. Who are these?—The men, who, at my return from the second embassy, (sent for the ratification of the treaty,) when I saw the state abused, and warned you of your danger, and testified the truth, and opposed with all my power the giving up Thermopylæ and Phocis;—the men, I say, who then cried out that I, the water-drinker, was morose and peevish: but that Philip, if permitted to pass, would act agreeably to your desires; would fortify Thespia and Platæa; restrain the insolence of Thebes; cut through the Chersonesus [4.] at his own expense; and give you up Eubœa and Oropus as an equivalent for Amphipolis.—That all this was positively affirmed, you cannot, I am sure, forget, though not remarkable for remembering injuries. And to complete the disgrace, you have engaged your posterity to the same treaty, in full dependence on those promises; so entirely have you been seduced.

And now, to what purpose do I mention this? and why do I desire that these men should appear?—I call the gods to witness, that without the least evasion I shall boldly declare the truth!—Not that, by breaking out into invectives, [5.] I may expose myself to the like treatment, and once more give my old enemies

---

[1.] Nicea.] This city of Locris had been given up to Philip, by Phalecus, at the conclusion of the sacred war. *Tourreil.*

[2.] Those governors, &c.] The tyranny said to have been imposed by Philip on the Thessalians is, in the original of this passage, called a government of ten: yet, in the third Philippic, it is styled a tetrarchy, or government of four. Hence there are grounds to presume, that an error has crept into the ancient copies. Unless it be supposed that Philip divided the country of Thessaly into four districts, and over each of those established ten governors; if, by such a supposition, the authority of the copies may be preserved.

[3.] Though none of our editors take notice of it, in this place the proper officer must

have proposed the orator's motion in form. Unless we suppose, that this oration has descended to us imperfect: for as the text now stands, there is a manifest want of connexion between this sentence and what follows. *Olivet.*

[4.] Cut through the Chersonesus, &c.] When Cersobleptes had given up the Chersonesus to the Athenians, it became perpetually exposed to the incursions of Thrace. The only way of putting a stop to them was to cut through the Isthmus (for the Thracians had no ships.) And this Philip promised to do in favour of the Athenians and their colonies. *Tourreil.*

[5.] Not that, by breaking out into invectives.] Wolfius, whom the translator here folan opportunity of receiving Philip's gold; nor yet that I may indulge an impertinent vanity of haranguing. But I apprehend the time must come, when Philip's actions will give you more concern than at present. His designs, I see, are ripening: I wish my apprehensions may not prove just; but I fear that time is not far off. And when it will no longer be in your power to disregard events; when neither mine, nor any other person's information, but your own knowledge, your own senses, will assure you of the impending danger; then will your severest resentment break forth. And as your ambassadors have concealed certain things, influenced (as they themselves are conscious) by corruption; I fear that they who endeavour to restore what these men have ruined, may feel the weight of your displeasure: for there are some, I find, who generally point their anger not at the deserving objects, but those most immediately at their mercy.

While our affairs, therefore, remain not absolutely desperate; while it is yet in our power to debate; give me leave to remind you all of one thing, though none can be ignorant of it. —Who was the man that persuaded you to

give up Phocis and Thermopylæ? which once gained, he also gained free access for his troops to Attica and to Peloponnesus; and obliged us to turn our thoughts from the rights of Greece, from all foreign interests, to a defensive war, in these very territories; whose approach must be severely felt by every one of us: and that very day gave birth to it: for had we not been then deceived, the state could have nothing to apprehend. His naval power could not have been great enough to attempt Attica by sea, nor could he have passed by land through Thermopylæ and Phocis. But he must have either confined himself within the bounds of justice, and lived in a due observance of his treaty, or have instantly been involved in a war, equal to that which obliged him to sue for peace.

Thus much may be sufficient to recall past actions to your view. May all the gods forbid, that the event should confirm my suspicions! for I by no means desire that any man should meet even the deserved punishment of his crimes, when the whole community is in danger of being involved in his destruction.

---

lows, hath been severely censured for this interpretation by the Italian commentator, who renders the former part of the sentence thus: Eos non ideo vocari velim, ut qui olim convitiis dehonestatus fui, æque nunc mihi a vobis famam conciliem.—παρ ὑμῖν ought not to be rendered a vobis, but apud vos: or as the translator, who follows Lucchesini's authority, has justly explained it in his note, in your presence. But my objection to this interpretation does not arise from grammatical nicety, but from a regard to the context, the surest comment. If Demosthenes, instead of the disgraceful treatment he formerly received, both from the partisans of Macedon and from the people, was now to be received with applause, and to triumph over his opposers, how could these have another opportunity of receiving Philip's gold? Such wages were only paid when earned. They were bestowed, not on ineffectual efforts, but real services; and these

his friends could not perform, if disgraced and discouraged by the assembly. The whole sentiment of the orator, as translated by Wolfius, is this; 'I do not wish that these men may appear, in order to indulge my indignation and resentment against them, that so they may retort my accusations with double virulence, (as was the case when we first returned from our embassy,) and thus, by once more gaining your favour, and triumphing over me, they may have an opportunity of boasting their services to Philip, and obtaining their reward.' The passage manifestly alludes to the transactions of the assembly, when the ten ambassadors returned, who had been sent to treat with Philip about a peace: and which are particularly described by Demosthenes, in his oration on the embassy. And we may safely appeal to the reader who consults that oration, as to the propriety of the present interpretation.

THE ORATION ON THE STATE OF THE CHERSONESUS:

PRONOUNCED IN THE ARCHONSHIP OF SOSIGENES, TWO YEARS AFTER THE SECOND PHILIPPIC.

INTRODUCTION.

IN the foregoing oration, the vehemence of Demosthenes determined the Athenians to oppose the attempts of Philip; and his representations to the Argians and Messenians inspired them with suspicion, and at length detached them from all connexions with Macedon. When Philip therefore found his practices in Peloponnesus unsuccessful, he began to turn

his thoughts to other enterprises; to pursue his conquests in Thrace, and cross the Athenian interest in the Chersonesus. This peninsula had, with some little interruption, been for many years in the hands of the Athenians. Cotys, as king of the country, had lately wrested it from them, and left it in succession to his son Cersobleptes. But he, being unable to support himself against the power of Philip, resigned it again to the Athenians; and they, according to custom, sent in a colony, which the inhabitants received, and freely shared their lands and habitations with their new guests. The people of Cardia, the principal city, however, still asserted their independence; and when Diopithes, the commander of the Athenian colony, would have reduced them by force of arms, had recourse to Philip, who immediately detached a body of forces to their support. Diopithes considered this proceeding as an act of hostility against Athens; and without waiting for instructions from his state, raised a considerable force; and while Philip was engaged in war in the inland parts of Thrace, entered the maritime parts (which were his territories) with fire and sword, and brought off a great booty, which he lodged safe in the Chersonesus. Philip was not at leisure to repel this insult: he therefore contented himself with complaining by letters to the Athenians of this conduct of their general. The pensioners which he had at Athens immediately exerted themselves for their master. They inveighed loudly against Diopithes, accused him of violating the peace which then subsisted between them and Philip, of involving the state in war, of exaction, rapine, and piracy; and pressed for his being recalled.

Demosthenes, judging that at such a juncture the public interest was connected with that of Diopithes, undertakes his defence in the following oration; throws the whole blame of the exactions and piracies he is accused of, upon the Athenians themselves; turns their attention to Philip and his hostilities; and concludes, that whoever opposes or distresses him in any manner does a service to the state; and that, instead of disavowing what Diopithes had done, or directing him to dismiss his army, they should reinforce him, and show the king of Macedon, they know how to protect their territories, and to maintain the dignity of their country, as well as their ancestors.

It appears, from the beginning of this oration, that before Demosthenes arose, the affair had been violently contested in the assembly. Possibly the heat of opposition added to the natural fire of the orator. For the style of the oration is (in my opinion) remarkably animated: and we find an extraordinary degree of severity and indignation breaking out in every part of it.

THE

ORATION ON THE STATE OF THE CHERSONESUS.

Sosigene Archon—A. R. Philip. 19— *Olympiad.* 109. *An.* 3.

It were to be wished, Athenians! that they

who speak in public would never suffer hatred or affection to influence their counsels; but in all that they propose, be directed by unbiassed reason; particularly when affairs of state, and those of highest moment, are the object of our attention. But since there are persons, whose speeches are partly dictated by a spirit of contention, party by other like motives; it is your duty, Athenians! to exert that power which your numbers give you: and in all your resolutions, and in all your actions, to consider only the interest of your country.

Our present concernment is about the affairs of the Chersonesus, and Philip's expedition into Thrace, which hath now engaged him eleven months: but most of our orators insist upon the actions and designs of Diopithes. As to crimes objected to those men, whom our laws can punish when we please; I, for my part, think it quite indifferent, whether they be considered now, or at some other time; nor is this a point to be violently contested, by me or any other speaker. But when Philip, the enemy of our country, is now actually hovering about the Hellespont [1.] with a numerous army, and making attempts on our dominions, which if one moment neglected, the loss may be irreparable; here, our attention is instantly demanded; we should resolve, we should prepare with all possible expedition, and not run from our main concern, in the midst of foreign clamours and accusations.

I have frequently been surprised at assertions made in public; but never more, than when I lately heard it affirmed in the senate, [2.] that there are but two expedients to be proposed: either absolutely to declare war, or to continue in peace. The point is this: if Philip acts as one in amity with us; if he does not keep possession of our dominions, contrary to his treaty; if he be not every where spiriting up enemies against us; all debates are at an end; we are undoubtedly obliged to live in peace, and I find it perfectly agreeable to you. But if the articles of our treaty, ratified by the most solemn oaths, remain upon record, open to public inspection; if it appears, that long before the departure of Diopithes and his colony, who are now accused of involving us in a war, Philip had unjustly seized many of our possessions (for which I appeal to your own decrees;) if, ever since that time, he has been constantly arming himself with all the powers of Greeks and barbarians, to destroy us; what do these men mean, who affirm we are either absolutely to declare war, or to observe the peace! You have no choice at all; you have but one just and necessary measure to pursue, which they industriously pass over. And what is this? To repel force by force. Unless they will affirm, that while Philip keeps from Attica and the Piræus, [3.] he does our state no injury,

---

[1.] Hovering about the Hellespont.] By the Hellespont we are to understand, not the strait itself that separates Europe from Asia, but the cities and countries all along the coast.

[2.] In the senate.] Into which Demosthenes

had been admitted, in the archonship of Themistocles, a little after the taking of Olynthus: and (if we may believe Æschines) not in the regular manner, but by intrigue and bribery.

[3.] The Piræus.] This is the first time the

makes no war against us. If it be thus they state the bounds of peace and justice, we must all acknowledge that their sentiments are inconsistent with the common rights of mankind, with the dignity and the safety of Athens.

Besides, they themselves contradict their own accusation of Diopithes. For, shall Philip be left at full liberty to pursue all his other designs, provided he keeps from Attica; and shall not Diopithes be permitted to assist the Thracians? and if he does, shall we accuse him of involving us in a war?—But this is their incessant cry, 'Our foreign troops commit outrageous devastations on the Hellespont: Diopithes, without regard to justice, seizes and plunders vessels! These things must not be suffered!' Be it so: I acquiesce! but while they are labouring to have our troops disbanded, by inveighing against that man whose care and industry support them (if they really speak from a regard to justice;) they should show us, that, if we yield to their remonstrances, Philip's army also will be disbanded: else, it is apparent that their whole aim is to reduce the state to those circumstances which have occasioned all the losses we have lately suffered. For be assured of this, that nothing hath given Philip such advantage over us, as his superior vigilance in improving all opportunities. For, as he is constantly surrounded by his troops, and his mind perpetually engaged in projecting his designs, he can, in a moment, strike the blow where he pleases. But we wait till some event alarms us: then we are in motion, then we prepare. To this alone I can impute it, that the conquests he hath lately made, he now enjoys in full security; while all your efforts are too late, all your vast expenses ineffectual: your attempts have served only to discover your enmity, and inclination to oppose him: and the consequences of your misconduct are still farther aggravated by the disgrace.

Know then, Athenians! that all our orators allege at present is but words, but idle pretences. Their whole designs, their whole endeavours, are to confine you within the city; that while we have no forces in the field, Philip may be at full liberty to act as he pleases. Consider the present posture of affairs. Philip is now stationed in Thrace, at the head of a large army; and (as we are here informed) sends for reinforcements from Macedon and Thessaly. Now, should he watch the blowing of the Etesian winds, march his forces to Byzantium, and invest it; in the first place, can you imagine that the Byzantines would persist in their present folly; or that they would not have recourse to you for assistance? I cannot think it. No: if there were a people in whom they less confided [1.] than in us, they would receive even these into their city, rather than give it up to him; unless prevented by the quickness of his attack. And should we be unable to sail thither, should there be no forces ready to support them, nothing can prevent their ruin.—But the extravagance and folly of these men exceed all bounds.—I grant it. Yet still they should be secured from danger; for this is the interest of our state. Besides, it is by no means clear that he will not march into the Chersonesus itself. On the contrary, if we may judge from the letter which he sent to you, he is determined to oppose us in that country. If then the forces stationed there be still kept up, we may defend our own dominions, and infest those of our enemy; if they be once dispersed and broken, what shall we do, if he attempt the Chersonesus?—Bring Diopithes to a trial.—And how will that serve us?—No: but we will despatch succours from hence. What if the winds prevent us?—But he will not turn his arms thither.—Who will be our surety for this? Consider, Athenians! is not the season of the year approaching, in which it is thought by some, that you are to withdraw your forces from the Hellespont, and abandon it to Philip? But suppose (for this too merits our attention,) that, at his return from Thrace, he should neither bend his force against the Chersonesus, nor Byzantium, but fall on Chalcis or Megara, as he lately did upon Oreum; [2.] which would be the wiser course, to oppose him here, and make Attica the seat of war, or to find him employment abroad? I think the latter.

Let these things sink deep into our minds; and let us not raise invidious clamours against

---

orator mentions this celebrated port of Athens. It was at first detached from the city, but afterward joined to it by two long walls, which the Greeks called the Legs of the Piræus; and from that time, by the advice of Themistocles, the Athenians made this their principal harbour. It would contain 400 ships of war; was well fortified, and furnished with a market, to which all the trading part of Greece resorted. Historians call it the triple port, for it really contained three: the first called Κάνθαρος, from a hero of that name: the second 'Αφροδίσιον, from two temples of Venus that were erected near it: the third Ζέα, because it was the mart for corn. *Tourreil.*

[1.] *If there were a people in whom they less confided, &c.*] In the third year of the 105th Olympiad, the Byzantines entered into a league with Chios, Cos, and Rhodes, against the Athenians, and withdrew themselves from their dominion. This is what Demosthenes calls their folly and extravagance. They had reason to think the Athenians would regard them as rebellious subjects, and treat them with the resentment of offended sovereigns; 'however,' says the orator, 'if they were reduced to the alternative of either submitting to Philip, or having recourse to you for protection, they would without hesitation choose the latter.' The event confirmed his prediction. Philip besieged Byzantium, the Byzantines had recourse to the Athenians, and Phocion, at the head of their army, obliged Philip to raise the siege. *Tourreil.*

[2.] *As he lately did upon Oreum.*] In the third Philippic, we shall find a particular account of the manner in which he reduced this city to his obedience.

those forces which Diopithes is endeavouring to keep up for the service of his country, or attempt to break them; let us rather prepare to reinforce them; grant their general the necessary supplies of money, and in every other instance favour his designs with a hearty zeal. Imagine this question proposed to Philip: 'Which would be most agreeable to you, that the forces commanded by Diopithes—(of whatever kind they be, for I shall not dispute on that head)—should continue in full strength and good esteem at Athens, and be reinforced by detachments from the city; or that the clamours and invectives of certain persons should prevail to have them broken and disbanded?' I think he would choose this latter. And are there men among us labouring for that which Philip would entreat the gods to grant him? and if so, is it still a question, whence our distresses have arisen?

Let me entreat you to examine the present state of Athens, with an unbiassed freedom; to consider how we are acting, and how our affairs are conducted. We are neither willing to raise contributions, nor do we dare to take the field, nor do we spare the public funds, nor do we grant supplies to Diopithes, nor do we approve of those subsidies he hath procured himself: but we malign him, we pry into his designs, and watch his motions. Thus we proceed, quite regardless of our interests; and while in words we extol those speakers who assert the dignity of their country, our actions favour their opposers. It is usual, when a speaker rises, to ask him, 'What are we to do?' Give me leave to propose the like question to you: 'What am I to say?' For if you neither raise contributions, nor take the field, nor

spare the public funds, nor grant subsidies to Diopithes, nor approve of those provisions he hath made himself, nor take the due care of our interests, I have nothing to say. If you grant such unbounded license to informers, as even to listen to their accusations of a man, for what they pretend he will do before it be yet done, what can one say?—

But it is necessary to explain to some of you the effect of this behaviour [1.] (I shall speak with an undaunted freedom, for in no other manner can I speak.)—It has been the constant custom of all the commanders who have sailed from this city, (if I advance a falsehood, let me feel the severest punishment,) to take money from the Chians, and from the Erythrians, and from any people that would give it; I mean, of the inhabitants of Asia. They who have but one or two ships take a talent; they who command a greater force raise a larger contribution. And the people who give this money, whether more or less, do not give it for nothing (they are not so mad;) no; it is the price they pay to secure their trading vessels from rapine and piracy, to provide them with the necessary convoys, and the like; however they may pretend friendship and affection, and dignify those payments with the name of free gifts. It is therefore evident, that as Diopithes is at the head of a considerable power, the same contributions will be granted to him. Else, how shall he pay his soldiers? how shall he maintain them, who receives nothing from you, and has nothing of his own? From the skies? No; but from what he can collect, and beg, and borrow. So that the whole scheme of his accusers is to warn all people to grant him nothing; as he is to suffer punishment for crimes

---

[1.] But it is necessary to explain to some of you the effect of this behaviour.] To the same purpose hath the sentence been translated by Wolfius and Tourreil. But this interpretation, which is acknowledged consonant to grammatical rules of construction, hath yet been stigmatized as a total perversion of the author's reasoning, and the sense of the context. Clamours had been raised against an Athenian general, who had exacted contributions from the islanders and Grecian settlements along the coast of Asia. Demosthenes appears as his advocate. He proceeds, as it is observed, to show, that it had ever been the custom of other commanders to raise the like contributions. Hence it is inferred, that the meaning of the phrase here quoted must be, that 'the general is warranted, by justice and custom, to act as he had done. The orator, indeed, doth proceed to give instances of this custom. But this conclusion I cannot admit: for whatever deference and respect the writers who have adopted it may justly claim, a greater deference and respect is due to the original, where we find a conclusion of a different nature, deduced in express terms. 'It hath been the constant custom,' saith Demosthenes, 'of all the commanders who have sailed from this city (if I advance a falsehood, let me feel the

severest punishment,) to take money from the Chians, and from the Erythrians, and from any people that would give it; I mean, of the inhabitants of Asia. They who have but one or two ships take a talent; they who command a greater force raise a larger contribution. And the people who give this money, whether more or less, do not give it for nothing (they are not so mad:) no; it is the price they pay to secure their trading vessels from rapine and piracy, to provide them with the necessary convoys, and the like; however they may pretend friendship and affection, and dignify those payments with the name of free gifts. It is therefore evident, that, as Diopithes is at the head of a considerable power, the same contributions will be granted to him. Else, how shall he pay his soldiers; how shall he maintain them, who receives nothing from you, and has nothing of his own? From the skies? No; but from what he can collect, and beg, and borrow.' Then follows the conclusion from the whole: Οὐδὲν ΟΥΝ ἄλλο ποιοῦσιν οἱ κατηγοροῦντες ἐν ὑμῖν η προλιγουσιν ἅπασι, &c. So that the whole scheme of his accusers (or the whole effect of their accusations) is to warn all people to grant him nothing, &c. This is the meaning (or this is the tendency) of their clamours.

yet to be committed, not for any he hath already committed, or in which he hath already assisted. This is the meaning of their clamours. 'He is going to form sieges! he leaves the Greeks exposed.' Have these men all this tenderness for the Grecian colonies of Asia? They then prefer the interest of foreigners to that of their own country. This must be the case, if they prevail to have another general sent to the Hellespont. If Diopithes commit outrages, if he be guilty of piracy, one single edict, [1.] Athenians! a single edict will put a stop to such proceedings. This is the voice of our laws; that such offenders should be impeached, [2.] and not opposed [3.] with such vast preparations of ships and money (this would be the height of madness:) it is against our enemies, whom the laws cannot touch,

that we ought, we must maintain our forces, send out our navies, and raise our contributions. But when citizens have offended, we can decree, we can impeach, we can recall. [4.] These are arms sufficient; these are the measures befitting men of prudence: they who would raise disorder and confusion in the state, may have recourse to such as these men propose.

But, dreadful as it is to have such men among us, yet the most dreadful circumstance of all is this. You assemble here, with minds so disposed, that if any one accuses Diopithes, or Chares, [5.] or Aristophon, [6.] or any citizen whatever, as the cause of our misfortunes, you instantly break forth into acclamations and applause. But if a man stands forth, and thus declares the truth, 'This is all trifling, Athe-

---

[1.] One single edict.] In the Greek Πινάκιον, which in this place may either signify the tablet which was fixed up in public, containing a citation of the accused party, and an account of the crimes of which he was accused; or that which was given to the judges who sat on his trial, to write their sentences upon. I have chosen the first of these senses.

[2.] That such offenders should be impeached.] The Greek words Εισαγγελλειν, and Εισαγγελια, which I have translated 'to impeach,' and 'impeachment,' are terms in the Athenian judicature; and relate to those particular kind of actions, which were not referred to any court of justice, but immediately brought before the senate of 500, or assembly of the people, and sometimes before the Archon: and in which both the accusation and defence were made by word of mouth, without any written articles.

[3.] And not opposed, &c.] The accusers of Diopithes raised loud clamours against his conduct. They insisted, that he had committed depredations on the Grecian colonies, and was meditating further hostilities against them, contrary to his commission and instructions. They declared, that a force should be despatched to defend them; which Demosthenes calls raising an army against Diopithes. 'It is against our enemies, saith he, 'whom our laws cannot reach that we are to raise our forces; when citizens have offended we can impeach them,' &c. But this interpretation hath been loaded with the heavy charge of absurdity. If the translator had a right to pronounce so peremptorily and so severely, he would declare, that, by the same rule, every ardent expression, every bold figure, every lively image, in short, every thing in eloquence, not literally and strictly consonant to metaphysical truth, might be pronounced equally absurd. The meaning of the passage here quoted, is said to be, we are not to protect the islanders by our armies, but to employ them against our enimies. But why were they to raise their armies against their enemies? Because their enemies were not punishable by their laws. Those, therefore, against whom they were not to raise their armies, must have been such as were punishable by the laws. This conclusion might, perhaps,

be deemed natural and necessary, even if the orator had not expressly pointed out both those against whom they were, and were not to raise their armies. 'Επι τους εχθρους, 'Against enemies.' And επι δ' ημας αυτους, but 'against yourselves,' i. e. our own citizens.

[4.] We can recall.] In the original, we have the Πάραλος, that is, the galley (called so from the hero Paralus, who with Theseus signalized himself against the Thebans.) The Athenians had two galleys, the Salaminian and Paralian, appointed for the most pressing occasions of the state. In allusion to this usage, Pericles was called the Salaminian galley, because he affected to appear in public only upon extraordinary emergencies. When Lysander had beaten the Athenian fleet at the Hellespont, the Paralian galley was despatched with the melancholy news to the people. And when Alcibiades was recalled from Sicily to defend himself against the charge of impiety, the Salaminian galley was ordered to bring him home. Both the one and the other were employed to recall such generals as were superseded. Tourreil.

[5.] Or Chares.] This apology (says Monsieur Tourreil) savours a little of faction and cabal: their ill success might with great justice have been charged upon Chares. Indeed what could have been expected from a general no less incapable than luxurious, who in all his military expeditions drew after him a train of musicians, whom he kept in pay at the expense of his troops? accordingly his enterprises were unsuccessful; and, to crown all his miscarriages, he lost the battle of Chaeronea. And yet this Chares was able to support himself to the last, by the credit of those orators who protected him.

[6.] Or Aristophon.] Another Athenian general. Aristotle (Rhet. l. ii. c. 23.) mentions a smart answer made to him by Iphicrates. Aristophon accused him of having betrayed the fleet which he commanded. Iphicrates, with that confidence which an established reputation inspires, asked him, Would you be guilty of such a piece of treachery? By no means, answered he. What! returned the other, can Iphicrates have committed what Aristophon would refuse to do?

nians! It is to Philip we owe our calamities: he hath plunged us in these difficulties; for had he observed his treaty, our state would be in perfect tranquillity:' this you cannot deny; but you hear it with the utmost grief, as if it were the account of some dreadful misfortune. The cause is this, (for when I am to urge the interest of my country, let me speak boldly.) Certain persons, who have been intrusted with public affairs, have for a long time past rendered you daring and terrible, in council; but in all affairs of war, wretched and contemptible. Hence it is that if a citizen, subject to your own power and jurisdiction, be pointed out as the author of your misfortunes, you hear the accusation with applause; but if they are charged upon a man who must first be conquered before he can be punished, then you are utterly disconcerted: that truth is too severe to be borne. Your ministers, Athenians! should take quite a contrary course. They should render you gentle and humane in council, where the rights of citizens and allies come before you: in military affairs, they should inspire you with fierceness and intrepidity; for here you are engaged with enemies, with armed troops. But now, by leading you gently on to their purposes by the most abject compliance with your humours, they have so formed and moulded you, that in your assemblies you are delicate, and attend but to flattery and entertainment; in your affairs, you find yourselves threatened with extremity of danger.

And now, in the name of Heaven, suppose that the states of Greece should thus demand [1.] an account of those opportunities which your indolence hath lost. 'Men of Athens! you are ever sending embassies to us; you assure us that Philip is projecting our ruin, and that of all the Greeks; you warn us to guard against this man's design. (And it is too true, we have done thus.) But, O most wretched of mankind! when this man had been ten months detained abroad; when sickness, and the severity of winter, and the armies of his enemies, rendered it impossible for him to return home; you neither restored the liberty of Euboea, nor recovered any of your own dominions. But while you sit at home in perfect ease and health, (if such a state may be called health,) Euboea is commanded by his two tyrants; [2.] the one, just opposite to Attica, to keep you perpetually in awe: the other to Scyathus. Yet you have not attempted to oppose even this. No; you have submitted; you have been insensible to your wrongs; you have fully declared, that if Philip were ten

times to die, it would not inspire you with the least degree of vigour. Why then these embassies, these accusations, all this unnecessary trouble, to us?'—If they should say this, what could we allege? what answer could we give? I know not!

We have those amongst us, who think à speaker fully confûted by asking, What then is to be done? To whom I answer, with the utmost truth and justness, Not what we are now doing.—But I shall be more explicit, if they will be as ready to follow, as to ask advice.

First then, Athenians! be firmly convinced of these truths: That Philip does commit hostilities against us, and has violated the peace, (and let us no longer accuse each other of his crimes;)—that he is the implacable enemy of this whole city, of the ground on which the city stands, of every inhabitant within these walls; even of those who imagine themselves highest in his favour. If they doubt this, let them think of Euthycrates and Lasthenes, the Olynthians. They who seemed the nearest to his heart, the moment they betrayed their country, were distinguished only by the superior cruelty of their death. But it is against our constitution that his arms are principally directed; nor, in all his schemes, in all his actions, hath he any thing so immediately in view, as to subvert it. And there is in some sort a necessity for this. He knows full well, that his conquests, however great and extensive, can never be secure, while you continue free; but that if once he meets with any accident, (and every man is subject to many,) all those whom he hath forced into his service will instantly revolt, and fly to you for protection. For you are not naturally disposed to grasp at empire yourselves; but to frustrate the ambitious attempts of others; to be ever ready to oppose usurpation and assert the liberty of mankind; this is your peculiar character. And therefore it is not without regret that he sees, in your freedom, a spy upon the incidents of his fortune. Nor is this his reasoning weak or trivial.

In the first place, therefore, we are to consider him as the enemy of our state, the implacable enemy of our free constitution. Nothing but the deepest sense of this can give you a true, vigorous, and active spirit. In the next place, be assured, that every thing he is now labouring, every thing he is concerting, he is concerting against our city; and that wherever any man opposes him, he opposes an attempt against these walls. For none of you can be weak enough to imagine that Philip's

---

[1.] Suppose that the state of Greece should thus demand, &c.] After the taking of Olynthus, when the Athenians were at last prevailed upon to declare war in form against Philip, they sent embassies to all the states of Greece, to represent the danger of his growing power, and to engage them to join against him. From hence the orator takes occasion to introduce this beautiful prosopopoeia, by which he throws

out the bitterest reproaches against his countrymen, so artfully, as not to give them offence, and yet at the same time sets the shamefulness of their misconduct in the strongest light. *Tourreil.*

[2.] By his two tyrants.] Philistides and Clitarchus; the one fixed at Eretria, opposite to Attica; the other at Oreum, over against Scyathus, an island subject to Athens.

desires are centred in those paltry villages of Thrace (for what name else can one give to Drongilus, and Cabyle, and Mastira, [1.] and all those places he is now reducing to his obedience?) that he endures the severity of toils and seasons, and braves the utmost dangers, for these; and has no designs upon the ports, and the arsenals, and the navies, and the silvermines, and all the other revenues of Athens; but that he will leave them for you to enjoy; while, for some wretched hoards of grain in the cells of Thrace, he takes up his winter quarters in the horrors of a dungeon? [2.] Impossible! No; these and all his expeditions are really intended to facilitate the conquest of Athens.

Let us then approve ourselves men of wisdom; and, fully persuaded of these truths, let us shake off our extravagant and dangerous supineness. Let us supply the necessary expenses; let us call upon our allies; let us take all possible measures for keeping up a regular army; so that, as he hath his force constantly prepared to injure and enslave the Greeks, yours too may be ever ready to protect and assist them. If you depend upon occasional detachments, you cannot ever expect the least degree of success: you must keep an army constantly on foot, provide for its maintenance, appoint public treasurers, and by all possible means secure your military funds: and while these officers account for all disbursements, let your generals be bound to answer for the conduct of the war. Let these be your measures, these your resolutions, and you will compel Philip to live in the real observance of an equitable peace, and to confine himself to his own kingdom, (which is most for our interest,) or we shall fight him on equal terms.

If any man thinks that the measures I propose will require expense, and be attended with much toil and trouble, he thinks justly. Yet, let him consider what consequences must attend the state, if these measures be neglected; and it will appear, that we shall really be gainers, by engaging heartily in this cause. Suppose some god should be our surety, (for no mortal ought to be relied on in an affair of such moment,) that if we continue quiet, and give up all our interests, he will not at last turn his arms against us; it would yet be shameful; it would (I call all the powers of heaven to witness!) be unworthy of you, unworthy the dignity of your country, and the glory of your ancestors, to abandon the rest of Greece to slavery, for the sake of private ease. I, for my part, would die, rather than propose so

mean a conduct: however, if there be any other person who will recommend it, be it so; neglect your defence; give up your interests! But if there be no such counsellor; if, on the contrary, we all foresee, that the farther this man is suffered to extend his conquests, the more formidable and powerful enemy we must find in him: why this reluctance? why do we delay? or when, my countrymen! will we perform our duty? Must some necessity compel us? What one may call the necessity of freemen, not only presses us now, but hath long since been felt: that of slaves, it is to be wished, may never approach us. And how do these differ? to a freeman, the disgrace of past misconduct is the most urgent necessity; to a slave, stripes and bodily pains. Far be this from us! It ought not to be mentioned!

I would now gladly lay before you the whole conduct of certain politicians; but I spare them. One thing only I shall observe: The moment that Philip is mentioned, there is still one ready to start up, and cry, 'What a happiness to live in peace! how grievous the maintenance of a great army! certain persons have designs upon our treasury!' Thus they delay your resolutions, and give him full liberty to act as he pleases! hence you gain ease and indulgence for the present (which I fear may, at some time, prove too dear a purchase;) and these men recommend themselves to your favour, and are well paid for their service. But in my opinion there is no need to persuade you to peace, who sit down already thoroughly persuaded. Let it be recommended to him who is committing hostilities; if he can be prevailed on, you are ready to concur. Nor should we think those expenses grievous which our security requires, but the consequences which must arise, if such expenses be denied. Then as to plundering our treasury, this must be prevented by intrusting it to proper guardians, not by neglecting our affairs. For my own part, Athenians! I am filled with indignation, when I find some persons expressing their impatience, as if our treasures were exposed to plunderers; and yet utterly unaffected at the progress of Philip, who is successively plundering every state of Greece; and this, that he may at last fall with all his fury upon you.

What then can be the reason, Athenians! that, notwithstanding all his manifest hostilities, all his acts of violence, all the places he hath taken from us, these men will not acknowledge that he hath acted unjustly, and that he is at war with us; but accuse those of embroiling you in a war, who call upon you to oppose

---

[1.] For what name else can one give to Drongilus, and Cabyle, and Mastira, &c.] Drongilus and Cabyle, however the orator affects to treat them with contempt, are yet mentioned in history. As to Mastira, it is entirely unknown: hence Harpocration suggested, that instead of Mastira we should read Bastira, a town of Thrace of that name having been mentioned in the history of Philip, written by Anaximenes, a work long time lost.

[2.] In the horrors of a dungeon.] In the original it is, in a Barathrum. There was a ditch or cavern in Athens of that name, into which criminals were precipitated. So that by this figure he not only represents the dreadful and deadly nature of the country, but at the same time sets Philip in the light of a wicked wretch, who merited the vilest and most ignominious fate. *Tourreil.*

him, and to check his progress? I shall tell you. That popular resentment which may arise from any disagreeable circumstances with which a war may be attended, (and it is necessary,/absolutely necessary, that a war should be attended with many such disagreeable circumstances,) they would cast upon your faithful counsellors, that you may pass sentence upon them, instead of opposing Philip; and they turn accusers, instead of meeting the punishment due to their present practices. This is the meaning of their clamours, that certain persons would involve you in a war: hence have they raised all these cavils and debates. I know full well, that before any Athenian had ever moved you to declare war against him, Philip had seized many of our dominions: and hath now sent assistance to the Cardians. If you are resolved to dissemble your sense of his hostilities, he would be the weakest of mankind if he attempted to contradict you. But suppose he marches directly against us, what shall we say in that case? He will still assure us, that he is not at war: such were his professions to the people of Oreum, when his forces were in the heart of their country; and to those of Pheræ, until the moment that he attacked their walls; and thus he at first amused the Olynthians, until he had marched his army into their territory. And will you still insist, even in such a case, that they who call upon us to defend our country are embroiling us in a war? Then slavery is inevitable. There is no other medium between an obstinate refusal to take arms, on your part, and a determined resolution to attack us, on the part of our enemy.

Nor is the danger which threatens us the same with that of other people. It is not the conquest of Athens which Philip aims at: no, it is our utter extirpation. He knows full well that slavery is a state you would not, or, if you were inclined, you could not submit to; for sovereignty is become habitual to you. Nor is he ignorant, that at any unfavourable juncture, you have more power to obstruct his enterprises, than the whole world besides.

Let us then be assured, that we are contending for the very being of our state; let this inspire us with abhorrence of those who have sold themselves to this man; and let them feel the severity of public justice: for it is not, it is not possible to conquer our foreign enemy, until we have punished those traitors who are serving him within our walls. Else, while we strike on these, as so many obstacles, our enemies must necessarily prove superior to us. —And whence is it that he dares treat you with insolence, (I cannot give his present conduct any other name,) that he utters menaces against you, while on others he confers acts of kindness? (to deceive them at least, if for no other purpose!) Thus, by heaping favours on the Thessalians, he hath reduced them to their present slavery. It is not possible to recount the various artifices by which he abused the wretched Olynthians, from his first insidious gift of Potidæa. But now he seduced the Thebans to his party, by making them masters of Bœotia, and easing them of a great and grievous war. And thus, by being gratified in some favourite point, these people are either involved in calamities known to the whole world, or wait with submission for the moment when such calamities are to fall upon them. I do not recount all that you yourselves have lost, Athenians! but in the very conclusion of the peace, how have you been deceived? how have you been despoiled? Was not Phocis, was not Thermopylæ, were not our Thracian dominions, Doriscum, Serrium, and even our ally Cersobleptes, [1.] all wrested from us? Is he not at this time in possession of Cardia? and does he not avow it? Whence is it, I say, that he treats you in so singular a manner? Because ours is the only state where there is allowed full liberty to plead the cause of an enemy; and the man who sells his country may harangue securely, at the very time that you are despoiled of your dominions. It was not safe to speak for Philip at Olynthus, until the people of Olynthus had been gained by the surrender of Potidæa. In Thessaly, it was not safe to speak for Philip, until the Thessalians had been gained by the expulsion of the tyrants, and the recovery of their rank of Amphictyons; nor could it have been safely attempted at Thebes, before he had restored Bœotia, and extirpated the Phocians. But at Athens, although he hath robbed us of Amphipolis, and the territory of Cardia: though he awes us with his fortifications in Eubœa; though he be now upon his march to Byzantium; [2.] yet his partisans may speak for Philip without any danger. Hence some of them, from the meanest poverty, have on a sudden risen to affluence; some from obscurity and disgrace, to eminence and honour: while you, on the contrary, from glory have sunk into meanness; from riches, to poverty: for the riches of a state I take to be its allies, its credit, its connexions; in all which you are poor. And by your neglect of these, by your utter insensibility to your wrongs, he is become fortunate and great, the terror of Greeks and Barbarians; and you abandoned and despised: splendid indeed is the abundance [3.] of your markets; but as to any

---

[1.] And even our ally Cersobleptes.] The late treaty of peace between Philip and the Athenians, was concluded without giving Cersobleptes (then in alliance with Athens) an opportunity of acceding to it: nor was any provision made by it for his security and protection. By this means Philip found himself at liberty to turn his arms against him; and a few years after drove him from his kingdom, and obliged him to become his tributary.

[2.] To Byzantium.] See the introduction to the following oration.

[3.] Splendid indeed is the abundance, &c.] They who opposed Philip's interest in the

real provision for your security, ridiculously deficient.

There are some orators, I find, who view your interests and their own in a quite different light. They would persuade you to continue quiet, whatever injuries are offered to you: they themselves cannot be quiet, though no one offers them the least injury. When one of these men rises, I am sure to hear, ' What ! will you not propose your decree ? will you not venture ? No ; you are timid, you want true spirit.'—I own, indeed, I am not, nor would I choose to be, a bold, an importunate, an audacious speaker. And yet, if I mistake not, I have more real courage than they who manage your affairs with this rash hardiness. For he who, neglecting the public interests, is engaged only in trials, in confiscations, in rewarding, in accusing, doth not act from any principle of courage ; but, as he never speaks but to gain your favour, never proposes measures that are attended with the least hazard : in this he has a pledge of his security, and therefore he is daring. But he who, for his country's good, oftentimes opposes your inclinations ; who gives the most salutary, though not always the most agreeable counsel ; who pursues those measures whose success depends more on fortune than on prudence, and is yet willing to be accountable for the event ; this is the man of courage, this is the true patriot ; not they who, by flattering your passions, have lost the most important interests of the state ; men whom I am so far from imitating, or deeming citizens of worth, that should this question be proposed to me, ' What services have you done your country ?' although I might recount the galleys I have fitted out, and the public entertainments I have exhibited, [1.] and the contributions I have paid, and the captives I have ransomed, [2.] and many like acts of benevolence, I would yet pass them all by, and only say, that my public conduct hath ever been directly opposite to theirs. I might, like them, have turned accuser, have distributed rewards and punishments : but this is a part I never assumed : my inclinations were averse ; nor could wealth or honours prompt me to it. No ; I confine myself to such counsels as have sunk my reputation ; but, if pursued, must raise the reputation of my country. Thus much I may be allowed to say, without exposing myself to envy.—I should not have thought myself a good citizen, had I proposed such measures as would have made me the first among my countrymen, but reduced you to the last of states : on the contrary, the faithful minister should raise the glory of his country ; and upon all occasions, advise the most salutary, not the easiest measures. To these nature itself inclines ; those are not to be promoted, but by the utmost efforts of a wise and faithful counsellor.

I have heard it objected, ' that indeed I ever speak with reason ; yet still this is no more than words ; that the state requires something more effectual, some vigorous actions.' Upon which I shall give my sentiments without the least reserve. The sole business of a speaker is, in my opinion, to propose the course you are to pursue. This were easy to be proved. You know, that when the great Timotheus moved you to defend the Eubœans, against the tyranny of Thebes, he addressed you thus : What, my countrymen ! when the Thebans are actually in the island, are you deliberating what is to be done ? what part to be taken ? Will you not cover the seas with your navies ? Why are you not at the Piræus ? why are you not embarked ?'—Thus Timotheus advised ; thus you acted ; and success ensued. But had he spoken with the same spirit, and had your indolence prevailed, and his advice been rejected, would the state have had the same success ? By no means. And so in the present case, vigour and execution is your part ; from your speakers you are only to expect wisdom and integrity.

I shall just give the summary of my opinion, and then descend. You should raise supplies, you should keep up your present forces, and reform whatever abuses may be found in them (not break them entirely upon the first complaint.) You should send ambassadors into

---

Athenian assembly, were ever urging the fallen condition of their country, and the dishonour of suffering another power to wrest that pre-eminence from her which had been enjoyed for ages. The speakers on the other side affected to despise the power of Philip, or insisted on the sincerity and uprightness of his intentions. But now, when the danger became too apparent, and his designs too flagrant to be dissembled, it appears that they had recourse to other arguments. They endeavoured to confine the views of the Athenians to what passed within their own walls ; displayed the advantages of their trade, the flourishing state of their commerce ; and perhaps recommended it as their true policy, to attend only to these, without making themselves a party in the quarrels of others, or loading the state with the expense of maintaining wars to support the power and interest of foreigners.

[1.] The public entertainments I have exhibited.] In the original it is, the offices of Choregus that I have discharged. Each of the ten tribes of Athens had their bands of musicians to perform in the feast of Bacchus, together with a poet, to compose the hymns and other pieces ; and these bands contended for a prize. The feasts were exhibited with great magnificence ; and in order to defray the charges, they appointed the richest citizen out of each tribe (or sometimes he offered himself) to exhibit them at his own cost. He was called the Choregus ; and if his band gained the prize, his name was inscribed, together with those of the tribe and the poet, upon the vase ; which was the reward of the conquerors. *Tourreil.*

[2.] The captives I have ransomed.] See the preface to the Oration on the Peace.

all parts, to reform, to remonstrate, to exert all their efforts in the service of their state. But above all things, let those corrupt ministers feel the severest punishment; let them, at all times, and in all places, be the objects of your abhorrence; that wise and faithful counsellors may appear to have consulted their own interest as well as that of others.—If you will act thus, if you will shake off this indolence, perhaps, even yet, perhaps, we may promise ourselves some good fortune. But if you only just exert yourselves in acclamations and applauses, and when any thing is to be done, sink again into your supineness, I do not see how all the wisdom in the world can save the state from ruin, when you deny your assistance.

THE TENTH ORATION AGAINST PHILIP:

Commonly called the Third.

PRONOUNCED IN THE SAME YEAR.

INTRODUCTION.

THE former oration had its effect. For, instead of punishing Diopithes, the Athenians supplied him with money, in order to put him in a condition of continuing his expeditions. In the mean time, Philip pursued his Thracian conquests, and made himself master of several places, which, though of little importance in themselves, yet opened him a way to the cities of the Propontis, and above all to Byzantium, which he had always intended to annex to his dominions. He had at first tried the way of negotiation, in order to gain the Byzantines into the number of his allies; but this proving ineffectual, he resolved to proceed in another manner. He had a party in the city, at whose head was the orator Python, that engaged to deliver him up one of the gates; but while he was on his march toward the city, the conspiracy was discovered, which immediately determined his master to take another route. His sudden counter-march, intended to conceal the crime of Python, really served to confirm it. He was brought to trial; but the credit and the presents of Philip prevailed to save him. The efforts of the Athenians to support their interests in Euboea, and the power which Philip had acquired there, and which every day increased, had entirely destroyed the tranquility of this island. The people of Oreum, divided by the Athenian and Macedonian factions, were on the point of breaking out into a civil war; when, under pretence of restoring their peace, Philip sent them a body of a thousand forces, under the command of Hipponicus; which soon determined the superiority to his side. Philistides, a tyrant, who had grown old in factions and public contests, was intrusted with the government of Oreum, which he administered with all possible severity and cruelty to those in the Athenian interest; while the other states of the island were also subjected to other Macedonian governors. Callias, the Chalcidian, whose inconstancy had made him espouse the interests of Athens, of Thebes, and Macedon, successively, now returned to his engagements with Athens. He sent deputies thither to desire assistance, and to prevail on the Athenians to make some vigorous attempt to regain their power in Euboea.

In the mean time, the king of Persia, alarmed by the accounts of Philip's growing power, made use of all the influence which his gold could gain at Athens, to engage the Athenians to act openly against an enemy equally suspected by them both. This circumstance, perhaps, disposed them to give the greater attention to the following oration.

PHILIPPIC THE THIRD.

Sosigenes Archon.—A. R. Philip.—19.—Olympiad. 109. An, 3.

THOUGH we have heard a great deal, Athenians! in almost every assembly, of those acts of violence which Philip hath been committing, ever since his treaty, not against ours only, but the other states of Greece: though all (I am confident) are ready to acknowledge, even they who fail in the performance, that we should every one of us exert our efforts, in council and in action, to oppose and to chastise his insolence: yet to such circumstances are you reduced by your supineness, that I fear (shocking as it is to say, yet) that, had we all agreed to propose, and you to embrace such measures, as would most effectually ruin our affairs, they could not have been more distressed than at present. And to this, perhaps a variety of causes have conspired: nor could we have been thus affected by one or two.—But, upon a strict and just inquiry, you will find it principally owing to those orators, who study rather to gain your favour, than to advance your interests. Some of whom (attentive only to the means of establishing their own reputation and power) never extend their thoughts beyond the present moment, and therefore think that your views are equally confined. Others, by their accusations and invectives against those at the head of affairs, labour only to make the state inflict severity upon itself; that, while we are thus engaged, Philip may have full power of speaking and of acting as he pleases. Such are now the usual methods of our statesmen, and hence all our errors and disorders.

Let me entreat you, my countrymen, that if I speak some truths with boldness, I may not be exposed to your resentment. Consider this; on other occasions, you account liberty of speech so general a privilege of all within your walls, that aliens and slaves [1.] are allowed to share it. So that many domestics may be found among you, speaking their thoughts with less reserve than citizens in some other states. But from your councils you have utterly banished it. And the consequence is this: in your assemblies, as you listen only to be pleased, you meet with flattery and indulgence: in the circumstances of public affairs, you find yourselves threatened with extremity of danger. If you have still the same dispositions, I must be silent: if you will attend to your true interests, without expecting to be flattered, I am ready to speak. For although our affairs are wretchedly situated, though our inactivity hath occasioned many losses, yet by proper vigour and resolution you may still repair them all. What I am now going to advance may possibly appear incredible; yet it is a certain truth. The greatest of all our past misfortunes is a circumstance the most favourable to our future expectations. And what is this? That the present difficulties are really owing to our utter disregard of every thing which in any degree affected our interests: for were we thus situated, in spite of every effort which our duty demanded, then we should regard our fortune as absolutely desperate. But now Philip hath conquered your supineness and inactivity: the state he hath not conquered. Nor have you been defeated; your force hath not even been exerted.

Were it generally acknowledged that Philip was at war with the state, and had really violated the peace, the only point to be considered would then be, how to oppose him with the greatest ease and safety. But since there are persons so strangely infatuated, that although he be still extending his conquests, although he hath possessed himself of a considerable part of our dominions, although all mankind have suffered by his injustice, they can yet hear it repeated in this assembly, that it is some of us who are embroiling the state

in war. This suggestion must first be guarded against; else there is reason to apprehend, that the man who moves you to oppose your adversary, may incur the censure of being the author of the war.

And, first of all, I lay down this as certain: if it were in our power to determine whether we should be at peace or war; if peace (that I may begin with this) were wholly dependent upon the option of the state, there is no doubt but we should embrace it. And I expect, that he who asserts it is, will, without attempting to prevaricate, draw up his decree in form, and propose it to your acceptance. But if the other party had drawn the sword, and gathered his armies round him; if he amuse us with the name of peace, while he really proceeds to all kinds of hostilities; what remains but to oppose him? To make professions of peace, indeed, like him;—if this be agreeable to you, I acquiesce. But if any man takes that for peace, which is enabling him, after all his other conquests, to lead his forces hither, his mind must be disordered: at least, it is our conduct only toward him, not his toward us, that must be called a peace. But this it is for which all Philip's treasures are expended; that he should carry on the war against you, but that you should make no war on him.—Should we continue thus inactive, till he declares himself our enemy, we should be the weakest of mortals. This he would not do, although he were in the heart of Attica, even at the Piræus, if we may judge from his behaviour to others. For it was not till he came within a few miles [2.] of Olynthus that he declared, that 'either the Olynthians must quit their city, or he his kingdom.' Had he been accused of this at any time before, he would have resented it, and ambassadors must have been despatched to justify their master. In like manner, while he was moving toward the Phocians, he still affected to regard them as allies and friends: nay, there were actually ambassadors from Phocis, who attended him in his march; and among us were many who insisted that this march portended no good to Thebes. Not long since, when he went into Thessaly with all the appearance of amity, he possessed himself of Pheræ. And it is but now he told the wretched people of Oreum that he had, in all affection, sent some forces to inspect their affairs: for that he heard they laboured under disorders and seditions; and that true friends and allies should not be at

---

[1.] Aliens and slaves.] The Athenians piqued themselves upon being the most independent and most humane of all people. With them a stranger had liberty of speaking as he pleased, provided he let nothing escape him against the government. So far were they from admitting him into their public deliberations, that a citizen was not permitted to touch on state affairs in the presence of an alien. Their slaves enjoyed a proportionable degree of indulgence. The Saturnalia, when they were allowed to assume the character of

masters, was originally an Athenian institution, and adopted at Rome by Numa. A Sparta and Thessaly, on the contrary, slaves were treated with such severity, as obliged them frequently to revolt. The humanity Athens had its reward; for their slaves d them considerable service on several occ sions; at Marathon, in the war of Egina, an at Arginusæ. *Tourreil.*

[1.] A few miles, &c.] In the original, 'for stadia,' about five miles,

sent upon such occasions. And can you imagine, that he who chose to make use of artifice rather than open force, against enemies by no means able to distress him, who at most could but have defended themselves against him; that he will openly proclaim his hostile designs against you; and this when you yourselves obstinately shut your eyes against them? Impossible! He would be the absurdest of mankind, if, while his outrages pass unnoticed, while you are wholly engaged in accusing some among yourselves, and endeavouring to bring them to a trial, he should put an end to your private contests, warn you to direct all your zeal against him, and so deprive his pensioners of their most specious pretence for suspending your resolutions, that of his not being at war with the state. Heavens! is there any man of a right mind who would judge of peace or war by words, and not by actions? Surely, no man. To examine then the actions of Philip.—When the peace was just concluded, before ever Diopithes had received his commission, or those in the Chersonesus had been sent out, he possessed himself of Serrium and Doriscum, and obliged the forces our general had stationed in the citadel of Serrium and the Sacred Mount, to evacuate these places. From these proceedings, what are we to judge of him? The peace he had ratified by the most solemn oaths.—And let it not be asked, [1.] of what moment is all this? or how is the state affected by it? Whether these things be of no moment, or whether we are affected by them or no, is a question of another nature. Let the instance of violation be great or small, the sacred obligation of faith and justice is, in all instances, the same.

But farther: when he sends his forces into the Chersonesus, which the King, which every state of Greece acknowledged to be ours; when he confessedly assists our enemies, and braves us with such letters, what are his intentions? for they say, he is not at war with us. For my own part, so far am I from acknowledging such conduct to be consistent with his treaty, that I declare, that by his attack of the Megareans, by his attempts upon the liberty of Euboea, by his late incursion into Thrace, by his practices in Peloponnesus, and by his constant recourse to the power of arms in all his transactions, he has violated the treaty, and is at war with you; unless you will affirm, that he who prepares to invest a city is still at peace until the walls be actually assaulted. You cannot, surely, affirm it! He whose designs, whose whole conduct, tends to reduce me to subjection, that man is at war with me, though not a blow hath yet been given, not one weapon drawn. And if any accident should happen, to what dangers must you be exposed! The Hellespont will be no longer yours; your enemy will become master of Megara and Euboea: the Peleponnesians will he gained over to his interest. And shall I say, that the man who is thus raising his engines, and preparing to storm the city, that he is at peace with you? No: from that day in which Phocis fell beneath his arms, I date his hostilities against you. If you will instantly oppose him, I pronounce you wise: if you delay, it will not be in your power when you are inclined. And so far, Athenians! do I differ from some other speakers, that I think it now no time to debate about the Chersonesus or Byzantium; but that we should immediately send reinforcements, and guard these places from all accidents, supply the generals stationed there with every thing they stand in need of, and extend our care to all the Greeks, now in the greatest and most imminent danger. Let me entreat your attention, while I explain the reasons which induce me to be apprehensive of this danger; that if they are just, you may adopt them, and be provident of your own interests at least, if those of others do not affect you; or if they appear frivolous and impertinent, you may now, and ever hereafter, neglect me as a man of an unsound mind.

That Philip, from a mean and inconsiderable origin, hath advanced to greatness; that suspicion and faction divide all the Greeks; that it is more to be admired that he should become so powerful from what he was, than that now, after such accessions of strength, he should accomplish all his ambitious schemes; these, and other like points which might be dwelt upon, I choose to pass over. But there is one concession, which, by the influence of your example, all men have made to him, which hath heretofore been the cause of all the Grecian wars. And what is this? an absolute power to act as he pleases, thus to harass and plunder every state of Greece successively, to invade and to enslave their cities. You held the sovereignty of Greece seventy-three years: [2.] the Lacedemonians commanded for the space of twenty-nine years: [3.] and in those latter times, after the battle of Leuctra, the Thebans were in some degree of eminence. Yet neither to you, nor to the Thebans, nor to the Lacedemonians, did the Greeks ever grant this uncontrolled power: far from it. On the contrary, when you, or rather the Athenians of that age, seemed to treat some persons not with due moderation, it was universally resolved to take up arms; even they who had no private complaints es-

---

[1.] Let it not be asked, &c.] The partisans of Philip affected to speak with contempt of these places. To deny the right of Athens to them was dangerous and unpopular; they therefore endeavoured to represent them as beneath the public regard.

[2.] Seventy-three years.] See a note on Olynth. II. p. 20.

[3.] Twenty-nine years.] That is, from the destruction of Athens by Lysander, in the last year of the 93d Olympiad, to the first war in which the Athenians, when re-established by Conon, engaged against Sparta, to free themselves and the other Greeks from the Spartan yoke, in the last year of the 100th Olympiad. *Tourreil.*

poused the cause of the injured. And when the Lacedemonians succeeded to your power, the moment that they attempted to enlarge their sway, and to make such changes in affairs as betrayed their ambitious designs, they were opposed by all, even by those who were not immediately affected by their conduct. But why do I speak of others? we ourselves, and the Lacedemonians, though from the first we could allege no injuries against each other, yet, to redress the injured, thought ourselves bound to draw the sword. And all the faults of the Lacedemonians in their thirty years, and of our ancestors in their seventy years, do not amount to the outrages which Philip hath committed against the Greeks, within less than thirteen years of power: [1.] or, rather, do not all make up the smallest part of them. This I shall easily prove in a few words.

Olynthus, and Methone, and Apollonia, and the two-and-thirty cities of Thrace, I pass all over; every one of which felt such severe effects of his cruelty, that an observer could not easily determine whether any of them had ever been inhabited or no. The destruction of the Phocians, a people so considerable, shall also pass unnoticed. But think on the condition of the Thessalians. Hath he not subverted their states and cities?—hath he not established his tetrarchs over them: that not only single towns, but whole countries, [2.] might pay him vassalage?—are not the states of Euboea in the hands of tyrants, and this an island bordering on Thebes and Athens?—are not these the express words of his letters, 'they who are willing to obey me may expect peace from me'? And he not only writes, but confirms his menaces by actions. He marches directly to the Hellespont; but just before he attacked Ambracia; Elis, [3.] one of the chief cities of Peloponnesus, is in his possession; not long since, he entertained designs against Megara. All Greece, all the barbarian world, is too narrow for this man's ambition. And though we Greeks see and hear all this, we send no embassies to each other, we express no resentment: but into such wretchedness are we sunk, (blocked up within our several

cities,) that even to this day we have not been able to perform the least part of that, which our interest or our duty demanded; to engage in any associations, or to form any confederacies; but look with unconcern upon this man's growing power, each fondly imagining, (as far as I can judge,) that the time in which ano ther is destroyed is gained to him, without ever consulting or acting for the cause of Greece; although no man can be ignorant, that, like the regular periodic return of a fever, or other disorder, he is coming upon those who think themselves most remote from danger.

You are also sensible, that whatever injuries the Greeks suffered by the Lacedemonians, or by us, they suffered by the true sons of Greece. And one may consider it in this light. Suppose a lawful heir, born to an affluence of fortune, should, in some instances, be guilty of misconduct; he indeed lies open to the justest censure and reproach; yet it cannot be said, that he hath lavished a fortune to which he had no claim, no right of inheritance. But should a slave, should a pretended son, waste those possessions which really belonged to others, how much more heinous would it be thought! how much more worthy of resentment! And shall not Philip and his actions raise the like indignation? he, who is not only no Greek, noway allied to Greece, but sprung from a part of the barbarian world unworthy to be named; a vile Macedonian! where formerly we could not find a slave fit to purchase! And hath his insolence known any bounds? Besides the destruction of cities, doth he not appoint the Pithian games, [4.] the common entertainment of Greece; and, if absent himself, send his slaves to preside? Is he not master of Thermopylæ? Are not the passes into Greece possessed by his guards and mercenaries? Hath he not assumed the honours of the temple, [5.] in opposition to our claim, to that of the Thessalians, that of the Doreans, and of the other Amphictyons; honours, to which even the Greeks do not pretend? Doth he not prescribe to the Thessalians, how they shall be governed? Doth he not send out his forces, some to Pothnus, to expel the Eretrian

[1.] Thirteen years of power.] Philip had now reigned nineteen years. But being at first engaged in wars with his neighbours, he did not begin to make any considerable figure in Greece until the eighth year of his reign, when, after the taking of Methone, he expelled the tyrants of Thessaly, and cut off the Phocian army commanded by Onomarchus. From this period, Demosthenes begins his computation. *Tourreil.*

[2.] Whole countries, &c.] The word in the original signifies, a number of different people dependent on one principal state or city.

[3.] Elis, &c.] He made himself master of this place by treaty, not by force of arms. Elis entered into the league of the Amphictyons, by which Philip was acknowledged as their chief: and maintained its freedom till after the death of Alexander. *Tourreil.*

[4.] The Pithian games, &c.] To this honour he was admitted by being made an Amphictyon, and declared head of the sacred league. By 'his slaves,' we are to understand no more than his subjects; for those republicans affected to speak thus of the subjects of every king or tyrant. *Tourreil* and *Olivet.*

[5.] The honors of the temple, &c.] Προμαντείαν, the right of precedency in consulting the oracle of Delphos. This the Phocians had enjoyed, as being in possession of the temple; and Philip was invested with it, as well as their other privileges. It was thought of considerable consequence to the Greeks, as appears from the first article of a peace made between the Athenians and the allies of Lacedemon. See Thucyd. B. 5. *Tourreil.*

colony: some to Oreum, to make Philistides tyrant? And yet the Greeks see all this without the least impatience. Just as at the fall of hail; every one prays it may not alight on his ground, but no one attempts to fend himself against it: so they not only suffer the general wrongs of Greece to pass unpunished, but carry their insensibility to the utmost, and are not roused even by their private wrongs. Hath he not attacked Ambracia and Leucas, cities of the Corinthians? Hath he not wrested Naupactus from the Achæans, [1.] and engaged by oath to deliver it to the Ætolians? Hath he not robbed the Thebans of Echinus? [2.] Is he not on his march against the Byzantines? [3.] And are they not our allies? I shall only add, that Cardia, the chief city of the Chersonesus, is in his possession. Yet these things do not affect us: we are all languid and irresolute: we watch the motions of those about us, and regard each other with suspicious eyes; and this, when we are all so manifestly injured. And if he behaves with such insolence toward the general body, to what extravagances, think ye, will he proceed when master of each particular state?

And now, what is the cause of all this? (for there must be some cause, some good reason to be assigned, why the Greeks were once so jealous of their liberty, and are now ready to submit to slavery.) It is this, Athenians! Formerly, men's minds were animated with that which they now feel no longer, which conquered all the opulence of Persia, maintained the freedom of Greece, and triumphed over the powers of sea and land: but now that it is lost, universal ruin and confusion overspread the face of Greece. What is this? Nothing subtle or mysterious: nothing more than a unanimous abhorrence of all those who accepted bribes from princes, prompted by the ambition of subduing, or the bare intent of corrupting, Greece. To be guilty of such practices was accounted a crime of the blackest kind; a crime which called for all the severity of public justice: no petitioning for mercy, no pardon was allowed. So that neither orator nor general could sell those favourable conjunctures, with which fortune oftentimes assists the supine against the vigilant, and renders men, utterly regardless of their interests, superior to those who exert their utmost efforts: nor were mutual confidence among ourselves, distrust of tyrants and barbarians, and such like noble principles, subject to the power of gold. But now are all these exposed to sale, as in a public mart; and, in exchange, such things have been introduced, as have affected the safety, the very vitals, of Greece. What are these? Envy, when a man hath received a bribe; laughter, if he confess it; pardon, if he be convicted; resentment at his being accused; and all the other appendages of corruption. For as to naval power, troops, revenues, and all kinds of preparations, every thing that is esteemed the strength of a state, we are now much better, and more amply provided, than formerly: but they have lost all their force, all their efficacy, all their value, by means of these traffickers.

That such is our present state, you yourselves are witnesses, and need not any testimony from me. That our state, in former times, was quite opposite to this, I shall now convince you, not by any arguments of mine, but by a decree of your ancestors, which they inscribed upon a brazen column erected in the citadel; not with a view to their own advantage, (they needed no such memorials to inspire them with just sentiments;) but that it might descend to you, as an example of the great attention due to such affairs. Hear then the inscription: 'Let Arthmius [4.] of Zelia, the son of Pytho-

---

[1.] Wrested Naupactus from the Achæans, &c.] Naupactus was not a city of the Achæans, but of the Locri Ozolæ. Possibly Demosthenes speaks with the liberty of an orator, and founds his assertion on some alliance which Naupactus might have had with the Achæans against the Ætolians, its inveterate enemies. This city, thus delivered up, remained ever after under the jurisdiction of Ætolia, and is mentioned by Livy and Polybius as the principal city of that country. *Tourreil.*

[2.] Echinus.] There were two places of this name: the one in Acarnania; the other, which is here spoken of, founded by the Thebans on the Maliac Gulf. *Tourreil.*

[3.] Against the Byzantines?] He had threatened them already, but had not as yet executed his threats: for we learn from history, that Philip, having for a considerable time besieged Perinthus, raised the siege, in order to march to that of Byzantium. If the siege of Perinthus had preceded this oration, Demosthenes could not have forgotten so memorable an expedition, in recounting the enterprises of Philip. Probably this prince made a feint of marching to Byzantium, in order to conceal his designs against Perinthus. *Tourreil.*

In the introduction to this oration, the reader has another account of Philip's first march against Byzantium.

[4.] Let Arthmius, &c.] This, in a few words, was the occasion of publishing this terrible decree against Arthmius, of which Themistocles was the author. Egypt had thrown off the yoke of Artaxerxes Longimanus. A formidable army marched to reduce the rebels; but failed of success, as Athens had provided for their defence. The resentment of Artaxerxes then turned against the Athenians. He sent Megabyzus, and other secret agents, into Peloponnesus, to raise up enemies against them by the force of bribery: and to blow up the flame of resentment and jealousy in Sparta, which was ever ready to break out. But the attempt was ineffectual. Arthmius probably was one of the king of Persia's agents in this affair; and Diodorus, who does not name him, includes him however in the general appellation of 'the emissaries of Artaxerxes.' *Tourreil.*

max, be accounted infamous, and an enemy to the Athenians and their allies, both he and all his race.' Then comes the reason of his sentence : 'Because he brought gold from Media into Peloponnesus.'—Not to Athens. This is the decree. And now, in the name of all the gods, reflect on this! think what wisdom, what dignity, appeared in this action of our ancestors! one Arthmius of Zelia, a slave of the King's, (for Zelia is a city of Asia,) in obedience to his master, brings gold, not into Athens, but Peloponnesus. This man they declare an enemy to them and their confederates, and that he and his posterity shall be infamous. Nor was this merely a mark of ignominy ; for how did it concern this Zelite whether he was to be received into the community of Athens or no? The sentence imported something more : for, in the laws relating to capital cases, it is enacted, that 'when the legal punishment of a man's crime cannot be inflicted, he may be put to death.' And it was accounted meritorious to kill him. 'Let not the infamous man,' saith the law, 'be permitted to live.' Intimating, that he is free from guilt who executes this sentence.

Our fathers, therefore, thought themselves bound to extend their care to all Greece : else they must have looked with unconcern at the introduction of bribery into Peloponnesus. But we find they proceeded to such severity against all they could detect in it, as to raise monuments of their crimes. Hence it was (and no wonder) that the Greeks were a terror to the Barbarians, not the Barbarians to the Greeks. But now it

is not so : for you do not show the same spirit, upon such or upon any other occasions. How then do you behave? you need not be informed. Why should the whole censure fall on you? the conduct of the rest of Greece is no less blameable. It is my opinion, therefore, that the present state of things demands the utmost care, and most salutary counsel. What counsel? Shall I propose it? and will ye not be offended?—Read this memorial.

[*Here the secretary reads. And the speaker resumes his discourse.*]

And here I must take notice of one weak argument made use of, to inspire us with confidence : That Philip is not yet so powerful as the Lacedemonians once were, who commanded by sea and land, were strengthened by the alliance of the King, [1.] were absolute and uncontrolled; and yet we made a brave stand against them; nor was all their force able to crush our state. In answer to this, I shall observe, that, amidst all the alterations and improvements which have happened in affairs of every kind, nothing hath been more improved than the art of war : for, in the first place, I am informed, that at that time the Lacedemonians, and all the other Greeks, used to keep the field four or five months, just the convenient season ; and having so long continued their invasion, and infested the territories of their enemy with their heavy-armed and domestic forces, they retired into their own country. Then, such was the simplicity, I should say the national spirit [2.] of that age, that the power of gold was never called to their assistance : but

---

[1.] Were strengthened by the alliance of the King.] After the expedition into Sicily, an expedition as unfortunate as it was imprudent, the Athenians might still have supported themselves, if the king of Persia had not concurred to precipitate their ruin. Tissaphernes, the satrap of Darius Nothus, conducted the first alliance between his master and the Lacedemonians. This alliance had at that time no very great effect. But when Cyrus the younger was sent, by order of his father, to command in Asia Minor, Lysander gained the affection of this young prince, who soon made him able to give law to Athens. It is this period which Demosthenes points out. *Tourreil.*

[2.] I should say the national spirit, &c.] Circumstances peculiar to any people, singular customs, particular relations, and the like, give rise to words and phrases, incapable of being precisely rendered into any other language. And such I take to be the words πολιτικῶς. Every particular state of Greece was a member of a larger political body, that of the nation, in which all the several communities were united by national laws, national customs, and a national religion. This I have explained at large, on another occasion. (See Prelim. Dissert. to the Life of Philip.) The word πολιτικῶς, therefore, I understand as expressive of that duty which each state owed to the Helenic Body, which prescribed bounds and laws to their wars, and forbade their passions, contests, and animosities against each

other, to break out into any excesses which might affect the welfare of the nation. They were to fight, not as inveterate foes, but competitors for power and honour. To recur to bribery in order to defeat their antagonists, was to be guilty of corrupting the morals, of what, in an extensive sense, may be called their country. In like manner, the word 'civilis,' in Latin, is used in a sense somewhat analogous to this, as denoting the regard which every citizen should pay to the rights of others, in opposition to despotism, pride, imperiousness, and all those passions which are enemies to liberty and the general good. Thus we find in Tacitus, 'Juveni civile ingenium, mira comitas. Ann. 1. Silentium ejus non civile, ut crediderat, sed in superbiam accipiebatur.' Ann. 6. And of Tiberius, the historian says, 'Liberatus metu, civilem se admodum inter initia, ac paulo minus quam privatum egit.' I have observed, in a note on the exordium of the Second Philippic, that a regard to the interest of Greece was generally the most extensive affection in the minds of its inhabitants. And that the extensive social affections were denoted by the Greek word πολιτικὸν, we learn from Cicero. Let the following quotation, from the fifth book of his treatise de Finibus, suffice on this occasion : 'Cum sic hominis natura generata sit, ut habeat quiddam innatum quasi civile et populare quod Græc Πολιτικὸν vocant, quicquid aget quæque vir tus, id a communitate, et ea quam exposu

all their wars were fair and open. Now, on the contrary, we see most defeats owing to treachery; no formal engagements, nothing left to the decision of arms. For you find the rapid progress of Philip is not owing to the force of regular troops, but to armies composed of light horse and foreign archers. With these he pours down upon some people, already engaged by civil discord and commotions: and when none will venture out in defence of their state, on account of their private suspicions, he brings up his engines, and attacks their walls. Not to mention his absolute indifference to heat and cold, and that there is no peculiar season which he gives to pleasure. Let these things sink deep into all our minds: let us not suffer his arms to approach these territories: let us not proudly [1.] depend on our strength, by forming our judgments from the old Lacedemonian war: but let us attend, with all possible precaution, to our interests and our armaments: and let this be our point in view; to confine him to his own kingdom; not to engage him upon equal terms in the field. For, if you be satisfied with committing hostilities, their nature hath given you many advantages [2.] (let us but do our part.) The situation of his kingdom, for instance, exposes it to all the fury of an enemy: not to speak of many other circumstances. But if we once come to a regular engagement, there his experience must give him the superiority.

But these are not the only points that require your attention: nor are you to oppose him only by the arts of war. It is also necessary that reason and penetration should inspire you with an abhorrence of those who plead his cause before you: ever bearing in mind the absolute impossibility of conquering our foreign enemy, until we have punished those who are serving him within our walls. But this, I call the powers of heaven to witness, ye cannot, ye will not do! No: such is your infatuation, or madness, or—I know not what to call it, (for I am oftentimes tempted to believe, that some power, more than human, is driving us to ruin,) that through malice, or envy, or a spirit of ridicule, or some like motive, you command hirelings to speak, (some of whom dare not deny that they are hirelings,) and make their calumnies serve your mirth. Yet, shocking as this is, there is something still more shocking: these men are allowed to direct the public affairs with greater security than your faithful counsellors.—And now observe the dreadful consequences of listening to such wretches.—I shall mention facts well known to you all.

In Olynthus, the administration of affairs was divided between two parties. The one, in the interest of Philip, entirely devoted to him; the other, inspired by true patriotism, directed all their efforts to preserve the freedom of their country. To which of those are we to charge the ruin of the state? or who betrayed the troops, and by that treachery destroyed Olynthus?—The creatures of Philip. Yet while their city stood, these men pursued the advocates for liberty with such malicious accusations and invectives, that an assembly of the people was persuaded even to banish Apollonides.

But this is not the only instance. The same custom hath produced the same calamities in other places. In Eretria, at the departure of Plutarchus and the foreign troops, when the people had possession of the city and of Porthmus, some were inclined to seek our protection, some to submit to Philip. But being influenced by this latter party, on most, or, rather, all occasions, the poor unfortunate Eretrians were at length persuaded to banish their faithful counsellors. And the consequence was this: Philip, their confederate and friend, detached a thousand mercenaries under the command of Hipponicus, raised the fortifications of Porthmus, set three tyrants over them, Hipparchus, Automedon, and Clitarchus; and after that, when they discovered some inclination to shake off the yoke, drove them twice out of their territory; once by the forces commanded by Eurylochus: and again, by those under Parmenio.

To give but one instance more. In Oreum, Philistides was the agent of Philip; as were Menippus and Socrates, and Thoas, and Agapæus, the present masters of that city. And this was universally known. But there was one Euphræus, a man for some time resident at Athens, who stood up against captivity and slavery. Much might be said of the injurious and contemptuous treatment which he received from the people of Oreum, upon other occasions. But the year before the taking of the city, as he saw through the traitorous designs of Philistides and his accomplices, he brought a formal impeachment against them. Immediately, considerable numbers form themselves into a faction, (directed and supported by Philip,) and hurry away Euphræus to prison, as a disturber of the public peace. The people of Oreum were witnesses of this; but, instead of defending him, and bringing his enemies to condign punishment, showed no resentment toward them; but approved, and triumphed in his sufferings. And now the faction, possessed of all the power they wished for, laid their schemes for the ruin of the city, and were carrying them into execution. Among the people, if any man perceived

---

charitate, atque societate humana, non abhorrebit.' The authority of a writer, who devoted so much of his attention to the moral and political learning of the Greeks, and took so much pains to explain it to his countrymen, may surely be deemed decisive.

[1.] Let us not proudly, &c.] In the original ἐκτραχηλισθῆναι, which, besides the signification

which Wolfius assigns it, is frequently rendered ' insolescere, superbire.'

[2.] Many advantages.] Although the Athenians had lost Amphipolis, Pydna, and Potidæa, they were still in possession of Thassus, Lemnos, and the adjacent islands, from whence they might readily have attempted a descent on Macedon. *Tourreil.*

8   †

this, he was silent; struck with the remembrance of Euphræus and his sufferings. And to such dejection were they reduced, that no one dared to express the least apprehension of the approaching danger, until the enemy drew up before their walls, and prepared for an assault. Then some defended, others betrayed, their state. When the city had thus been shamefully and basely lost, the faction began to exercise the most tyrannic power, having, either by banishment or death, removed all those who had deserted their own cause, and that of Euphræus; and were still ready for any noble enterprise. Euphræus himself put an end to his own life: and thus gave proof, that, in his opposition to Philip, he had been actuated by a just and pure regard to the interest of his country.

And now what could be the reason (you may possibly ask with surprise) that the people of Olynthus, and those of Eretria, and those of Oreum, all attended with greater pleasure to the advocates of Philip than to their own friends? The same reason which prevails here. Because they, who are engaged on the part of truth and justice, can never, even if they were inclined, advance any thing to recommend themselves to favour; their whole concern is for the welfare of the state. The others need but to sooth and flatter, in order to second the designs of Philip. The one press for supplies; the others insist that they are not wanted: the one call their countrymen to battle, and alarm them with apprehensions of danger; the others are ever recommending peace, until the toils come too near to be escaped. And thus, on all occasions, one set of men speak but to insinuate themselves into the affections of their fellow-citizens; the other to preserve them from ruin: till, at last, the interests of the state are given up; not corruptly or ignorantly, but from a desperate purpose of yielding to the fate of a constitution thought to be irrecoverably lost. And, by the powers of heaven! I dread, that this may prove your case; when you find that reflection cannot serve you! And when I turn my eyes to the men who have reduced you to this, it is not terror [1.] that I feel; it is the utmost detestation. For, whether they act through design or ignorance, the distress to which they are reducing us is manifest. But far be this distress from us, Athenians! It were better to die ten thousand deaths, than to be guilty of a servile complaisance to Philip, and to abandon any of your faithful counsellors! The people of Oreum have now met a noble return for their confidence in Philip's creatures, and their violence toward Euphræus. The Eretrians are nobly rewarded for driving out our ambassador and committing their affairs to Clitarchu Captivity, and stripes, and racks, are their r ward. Great was his indulgence to the Oly thians, for choosing Lasthenes their gener and banishing Apollonides. It were folly ar baseness to be amused with such false hop as theirs, when neither our counsels direct u nor our inclinations prompt us, to the pursu of our true interests; and to suffer those wl speak for our enemies to persuade us that tl state is too powerful to be affected by any a cident whatever. It is shameful to cry ot when some event hath surprised us, 'He vens! who could have expected this? W should have acted thus and thus; and avoid these and these errors.' There are mai things the Olynthians can now mention, whic if foreseen in time, would have prevented th destruction. The people of Oreum can me tion many: those of Phocis many: every sta that hath been destroyed can mention mai such things. But what doth it avail them nov While the vessel is safe, whether it be gre or small, the mariner, the pilot, every pers should exert himself in his particular static and preserve it from being wrecked, either villany or unskilfulness. But when the s hath once broken in, all care is vain. A therefore, Athenians! while we are yet sa possessed of a powerful city, favoured wi many resources, our reputation illustrious What are we to do? (perhaps some have with impatience to ask.)—I shall now give r opinion, and propose it in form; that, if a proved, your voices may confirm it.

Having, in the first place, provided for yc defence, fitted out your navy, raised your st plies, and arrayed your forces, (for althou all other people should submit to slavery, y should still contend for freedom;) having ma such a provision, (I say,) and this in the sic of Greece, then we are to call others to th duty; and, for this purpose, to send ambas dors into all parts, to Peloponnesus, to Rhod to Chios, and even to the KING, (for he is no means unconcerned in opposing the rapid of this man's progress.) If ye prevail, ye v have sharers in the dangers and expense wh may arise; at least you may gain some respi and as we are engaged against a single per and not the united powers of a commonweal this may be of advantage; as were those e bassies of last year into Peloponnesus, those remonstrances which were made in se ral places by me, and Polydatus, that true triot, and Hegesippus, and Clitomachus, s Lycurgus, and the other ministers; wh checked his progress, prevented his attack

***

[1.] It is not terror, &c.) The word in the original signifies the most abject fear and dismay; and the whole passage seems to have a particular reference or allusion. Possibly some of Philip's partisans might have accused Demosthenes of being thus affected at their sight; while they magnified their own integrity and resolution, their true discernment, and patric zeal for the interest of their country: possibly might have called out for severe p ishment on the man who dared to utter most bitter invectives against a powerful pri in alliance with Athens.

Ambracia, and secured Peloponnesus from an invasion.

I do not mean that we should endeavour to raise that spirit abroad, which we ourselves are unwilling to assume. It would be absurd to neglect our own interests, and yet pretend a regard to the common cause; or, while we are insensible to present dangers, to think of alarming others with apprehensions of futurity. No: let us provide the forces in the Chersonesus with money, and every thing else that they desire. Let us begin with vigour on our part: then call upon the other Greeks; convene, instruct, exhort them. Thus it becomes a state of such dignity as ours. If you think the protection of Greece may be intrusted to the Chalcidians and Megareans, and so desert its cause, you do not think justly. It will be well if they can protect themselves. No: this is your province; this is that prerogative transmitted from your ancestors, the reward of all their many, and glorious, and great dangers. If every man sits down in ease and indulgence, and studies only to avoid trouble, he will certainly find no one to supply his place; and I am also apprehensive, that we may be forced into all that trouble to which we are so averse. Were there persons to act in our stead, our inactivity would have long since discovered them: but there are really none.

You have now heard my sentiments. You have heard the measures I propose, and by which I apprehend our affairs may be yet retrieved. If any man can offer some more salutary course, let him arise, and declare his opinion. And whatever be your resolution, the gods grant that we may feel its good effects.

THE ELEVENTH ORATION AGAINST PHILIP:

Commonly called the Fourth.

PRONOUNCED IN THE ARCHONSHIP OF NICOMACHUS, THE YEAR AFTER THE FORMER ORATION.

INTRODUCTION.

Soon after the preceding oration, the Athenian succours arrived at Euboea. Demosthenes had proposed the decree for them; and the command was given to Phocion, whom the Athenians gladly employed on all extraordinary emergencies, and who was always ready to serve them, at the same time that he highly condemned their conduct.

Demosthenes attended Phocion, not in a military character, but to endeavour to gain over the people of Euboea to the Athenian interest; in which he had some success: while the general, on his part, acted with so much conduct and resolution, that the Macedonians were forced to abandon the island; and the Euboeans entered into a treaty of alliance with Athens.

In the mean time Philip marched along the Hellespont, to support his fleet then in view, and to prevent Diopithes from cutting off his provisions. When he had crossed the Isthmus of the Chersonesus, he returned, and by a forced march arrived with the choice of his army at Cardia; where he surprised Diopithes, and defeated him in an action in which that general fell. This he affected to consider not as an open breach of his treaty, but only as the consequence of the protection he had granted to the Cardians, and an act of particular revenge he had determined to take on Diopithes.

Philip then joined his army, and encamped before Perinthus, a place considerable by its commerce and situation, ever firm to the Athenians, and consequently dreadful and dangerous to Philip. The Perinthians defended themselves with a courage almost incredible, and which, it appeared, could not be abated by danger or fatigue. Philip, on his part, pressed them by all the methods of assault; and after many vigorous efforts on each side, when the city was just on the point of being taken by assault, or of being obliged to surrender at discretion, fortune provided for it an unexpected succour.

The fame of Philip's arms having alarmed the court of Persia, Ochus sent his letters mandatory to the governors of the maritime provinces, directing them to supply Perinthus with all things in their power; in consequence of which they filled it with troops and provisions. While the Byzantines, justly conceiving their own turn would be next, sent into the city the flower of their youth, with all other necessaries for an obstinate defence.

The Perinthians, thus reinforced, resumed their former ardour. And as all they suffered was on account of Athens, they despatched ambassadors thither, to demand the speedy and effectual assistance of that state. On this occasion Demosthenes pronounced the following oration.

PHILIPPIC THE FOURTH. [1.]

Nicomachus, Archon.—A. R. Philip. 20.—Olympiad. 109. An. 4.

As I am persuaded, Athenians! that you are now convened about affairs of greatest moment, such as affect the very being of the state, I shall endeavour to speak to them in the manner most agreeable to your interests.

There are faults of no late origin, and gradually increased to no inconsiderable number, which have conspired to involve us in the present difficulties. But, of all these, what at this time most distresses us is this; that your minds are quite alienated from public affairs; that your attention is engaged just while you are assembled, and some new event related; then each man departs, and, far from being influenced by what he hath heard, he does not even remember it.

The insolence and outrage with which Philip treats all mankind, are really as great as you hear them represented. That it is not possible to set bounds to these, by the force of speeches and debates, no one can be ignorant; for if other arguments cannot convince, let this be weighed: whenever we have had occasion to plead in defence of our rights, we have never failed of success, we have never incurred the censure of injustice: but all places and all persons must acknowledge that our arguments are irresistible. Is he then distressed by this? and are our affairs advanced? By no means! For as he proceeds to take up arms, leads out his troops, and is ready to hazard his whole empire in pursuit of his designs, while we sit here, pleading, or attending to those who plead the justness of our cause, the consequence (and I think the natural consequence) is this; actions prove superior to words; and men's regards are engaged, not by those arguments which we have advanced, or may now advance, how just soever, but by the measures we pursue; and these are by no means fitted to protect any of the injured states: to say more of them is unnecessary.

As, then, all Greece is now divided into two parties; the one composed of those who desire neither to exercise, nor to be subject to arbitrary power, but to enjoy the benefits of liberty, laws, and independence; the other, those who, while they aim at an absolute command of their fellow-citizens, are themselv the vassals of another person, by whose mea they hope to obtain their purposes: his par sans, the affecters of tyranny and despotis are superior every where. So that of all t popular constitutions, I know not whether o be left firmly established, except our ow And they who in the several states have be raised by him to the administration of affai have their superiority secured by all the mea which can advance a cause. The first a principal is this: When they would bri those who are capable of selling their integri they have a person ever ready to supply the In the next place, (and it is of no less n ment,) at whatever season they desire it, th are forces at hand to overwhelm their op sers: while we, Athenians! are not only ficient in these particulars, but unable even awaken from our indolence; like men reduc by some potion [2.] to a lethargic state. consequence of this, (for I hold it necessa to speak the truth,) we are fallen into su contempt and infamy, that, of the people i mediately threatened with danger, some c tend with us for the honour of commandin some about the place of conference; [3.] wl others determine rather to trust to their o strength than to accept of your assistance.

And why am I thus particular in recount these things? I call the gods to witness, t I would not willingly incur your displeasu but I would have you know, and see, that public as well as in private affairs, contin indolence and supineness, though not im diately felt in every single instance, of on sion, yet, in the end, must affect the gen welfare. You see this in the instances Serrium and Doriscum. When the peace made, we began with neglecting these pla (Perhaps some of you have never heard them.) And these places, thus abandoned despised, lost you Thrace and your ally C sobleptes. Again, when he saw that this not rouse you, and that you sent no assistar he razed Porthmus; and to keep us in conti al awe, erected a tyranny in Euboea, against Attica. This was disregarded: and attempt upon Megara was well nigh success

---

[1.] We shall find in this oration many things which occur in those that are precedent; and as it is on the same subject, already exhausted by so many orations, it was in some sort necessary for the orator to make use of repetitions. And it should seem, that in such a case repetition is by no means a fault, particularly as we may consider this as a recapitulation of all the others; and may in effect call it the peroration of the Philippics. In which the orator resumes the arguments he had already made use of; but, in resuming them, gives them new force, as well by the manner in which they are disposed, as by the many additions with which they are heightened. *Tourreil.*

[2.] Like men reduced by some potion, &c.] In the original, 'like men who have drun mandragora;' an herb ranked by natura among those of a soporiferous kind. It se to have been a proverbial phrase, to sig indolent and negligent persons. *Tourrei*

[3.] For the honour of commanding, s about the place of conference.] In all the c federate wars of the Greeks, that state wl was acknowledged the most powerful had honour of giving a commander-in-chief, of appointing the place of general congres concerting the operations. In the Per war we find the Lacedemonians and Athen sometimes contending for these points; wl in effect was a dispute which of these st was most respectable.

Still ye were insensible, expressed no impatience, no inclination to oppose him. He purchased Antronæ; and soon after got possession of Oreum. I pass over many things; Pheræ, the march to Ambracia, the massacre of Elis, [1.] and thousands of the like actions: for it is not my design to give a detail of Philip's acts of outrage and injustice; but to convince you, that the property and liberty of mankind will never be secure from him, until he meets with some effectual opposition.

There are persons who, before they hear affairs debated, stop us with this question, 'What is to be done?' not that they may do it, when informed, (for then they would be the best citizens,) but to prevent the trouble of attending. It is my part, however, to declare what we are now to do.

First, then, Athenians! be firmly persuaded of this: that Philip is committing hostilities against us, and has really violated the peace: that he has the most implacable enmity to this whole city; to the ground on which this city stands; to the very gods of this city: (may their vengeance fall upon him!) but against our constitution is his force principally directed; the destruction of this is, of all other things, the most immediate object of his secret schemes and machinations. And there is, in some sort, a necessity that it should be so. Consider; he aims at universal power; and you he regards as the only persons to dispute his pretensions. He hath long injured you; and of this he himself is fully conscious; for the surest barriers of his other dominions are those places which he hath taken from us: so that if he should give up Amphipolis and Potidæa, he would not think himself secure in Macedon. He is then sensible, both that he entertains designs against you, and that you perceive them; and as he thinks highly of your wisdom, he judges that you hold him in the abhorrence he deserves. To these things (and these of such importance) add, that he is perfectly convinced that although he were master of all other places, yet it is impossible for him to be secure, while your popular government subsists: but that if any accident should happen to him, (and every man is subject to many,) all those who now submit to force would seize the opportunity, and fly to you for protection: for you are not naturally disposed to grasp at power, or to usurp dominion; but to prevent usurpation, to wrest their unjust acquisitions from the hands of others, to curb the violence of ambition, and to preserve the liberty of mankind, is your peculiar excellence. And therefore it is with regret he sees, in that freedom you enjoy, a spy upon the incidents of his fortune: nor is this his reasoning weak or trivial. First, then, he is on this account to be regarded as the implacable enemy of our free and popular constitution. In the next place, we should be fully persuaded that all those things which now employ him, all that he is now projecting, he is projecting against this city. There can be none among you weak enough to imagine, that the desires of Philip are centred in those paltry villages [2.] of Thrace; (for what name else can we give to Drongilus, and Cabyle, and Mastira, and all those places now said to be in his possession?) that he endures the severity of toils and seasons, and exposes himself to the utmost dangers for these; and has no designs upon the ports, and the arsenals, and the navies, and the silver-mines, and other revenues, and the situation, and the glory of Athens, (which never may the conquest of this city give to him or any other!) but will suffer us to enjoy these: while, for those trifling hoards of grain he finds in the cells of Thrace, he takes up his winter-quarters in all the horrors of a dungeon. It cannot be! Even in his march thither he had these in view; these are the chief objects of all his enterprises.

Thus must we all think of him. And let us not oblige that man, who hath ever been our most faithful counsellor, to propose the war in form: that would be to seek a pretence to avoid it, not to pursue the interest of our country. To yourselves I appeal: if after the first, or the second, or the third of Philip's infractions of his treaty, (for there was a long succession of them,) any man had moved you to declare hostilities against him, and he had given the same assistance to the Cardians, as now, when no such motion came from any Athenian, would not that man have been torn to pieces? would you not have cried out, with one voice, that it was this which made him ally to the Cardians? Do not then seek for some person whom you may hate for Philip's faults, whom you may expose to the fury of his hirelings. When your decree for war hath once passed, let there be no dispute, whether it ought or ought not to have been undertaken. Observe his manner in attacking you: imitate it in your opposition: supply those who are

---

[1.] Pheræ, the march to Ambracia, the massacre of Elis.] An orator does not always pique himself on an exact adherence to history; but sometimes disguises facts, or aggravates them, when it serves his purpose. One would imagine that Philip had committed some terrible outrages at Pheræ; and yet he only restored the liberty of that city, by expelling its tyrants. And as to the massacre of Elis, it is not to be imputed immediately to Philip. He had, indeed, as chief of the allies in the sacred war, and head of the Amphictyons, suggested the resolution of proscribing the Pho-

cians, and all the favourers of their impiety. Some of these, who had fled into Crete with their general Phalecus, joined with a body of men who had been banished from Elis, made an inroad into Peloponnesus, and attempted an attack upon their countrymen; who, with the assistance of the Arcadians, obliged the rebellious army to surrender at discretion; and, in obedience to the decree of the Amphictyons, put it to the sword. *Tourreil*.

[2.] Those paltry villages, &c.] See the notes of the oration on the state of the Chersonesus, p. 48.

now opposing him, with money, and whatever else they want: raise your supplies; prepare your forces, galleys, horse, transports, and all other necessaries of a war. At present your conduct must expose you to derision. Nay, I call the powers to witness, that you are acting as if Philip's wishes were to direct you. Opportunities escape you; your treasures are wasted; you shift the weight of public business upon others; break into passion; criminate each other.—I shall now show whence these disorders have proceeded, and point out the remedy.

You have never, Athenians! made the necessary dispositions in your affairs, or armed yourselves in time, but have been ever led by events. Then, when it proves too late to act, you lay down your arms. If another incident alarms you, your preparations are resumed, and all is tumult and confusion. But this is not the way. It is impossible ever to secure the least success by occasional detachments. No; you must raise a regular army, provide for its subsistence, appoint state treasurers, and guard the public money with the strictest attention: oblige those treasurers to answer for the sums expended, and your general for his conduct in the field: and let this general have no pretence [1.] to sail to any other place, or engage in any other enterprise than those prescribed. Let these be your measures, these your resolutions; and you will compel Philip to live in the real observance of an equitable peace, and to confine himself to his own territory, or you will engage him upon equal terms. And perhaps, Athenians! perhaps, as you now ask, 'What is Philip doing? whither is he marching?' so there may come a time when he will be solicitous to know whither our forces have directed their march, or where they are to appear.

If it be objected, that these measures will be attended with great expense, and many toils and perplexities, I confess it. (It is necessary, absolutely necessary, that a war should be attended with many disagreeable circumstances.) But let us consider what consequences must attend the state, if we refuse to take this course; and it will appear that we shall really be gainers by a seasonable performance of our duty. Suppose some god should be our surety, (for no mortal can be depended on in an affair of such moment,) that, although you are quite inactive and insensible, yet he will not at last lead his armies hither; still it would be ignominious, it would (I call every power of Heaven to witness!) be beneath you, beneath the dignity of your state, beneath the glory of your ancestors, to abandon all the rest of Greece to slavery, for the sake of private ease. I, for

my part, would rather die, than propose such a conduct: if, however, there be any other person to recommend it to you, be it so; make no opposition; abandon all affairs: but if there be no one of this opinion; if, on the contrary, we all foresee, that the farther this man is suffered to extend his conquests, the more dangerous and powerful enemy we must find in him; why is our duty evaded? why do we delay? or when will we be disposed to exert ourselves, Athenians? Must some necessity press us? What one may call the necessity of freemen not only presseth us now, but hath long since been felt; that of slaves, it is to be wished may never approach us. How do these differ? To freemen the most urgent necessity is dishonour; a greater cannot, I think, be assigned: to slaves, stripes and tortures. Far be this from us! It ought not to be mentioned!

And now, the neglect of those things, to which your lives and fortunes should be devoted, it must be confessed is by no means justifiable: far from it! some pretence, however, may be alleged in its excuse. But to refuse even to listen to those things which demand your utmost attention, which are of the greatest moment to be fully considered, this deserves the most severe censure. And yet you never attend, but upon occasions like this, when the danger is actually present; nor in time of disengagement, do you ever think of consulting: but while he is preparing to distress you, instead of making like preparations, and providing for your defence, you are sunk in inactivity: and if any one attempts to rouse you, he feels your resentment. But when advice is received that some place is lost, or invested, then you attend, then you prepare. The proper season for attending and consulting, was then, when you refused: now when you are prevailed upon to hear, you should be acting, and applying your preparations. And by this supineness is your conduct distinguished from that of all other nations: they usually deliberate before events: your consultations follow them.——There is but one course left, which should long since have been pursued: but still may be of service.—This I shall lay before you.

There is nothing which the state is more concerned to procure on this occasion than money. And some very favourable opportunities present themselves, which, if wisely improved, may possibly supply our demands. In the first place, they whom the king regards [2.] as his faithful and strenuous adherents are the implacable enemies of Philip, and actually in arms against him. Then the man who was [3.] Philip's assistant and counsellor in all his

---

[1.] Have no pretence, &c.] See note on Phil. 1. p. 16.

[2.] They whom the king regards, &c.] He probably means the Thebans, who had given Ochus powerful assistance in the siege of Pelusium; and who were now much provoked at Philip, on account of Echinus, which he had taken from them. *Tourreil.*

[3.] Man who was, &c.] As Philip seems to have already projected an expedition into Asia, he received with open arms all the malcontents of Persia, and held secret intelligence with the rebel satraps. Hermias, the tyrant of Artans, a city of Mysia, was of this number; and had been in confidence with Philip. Mentor, the Rhodian, general of the Persian army,

designs against the king, hath been lately seized, so that the king will be informed of his practices, not by our accusations, to which he might suppose our private interest prompted us, but by the very agent and conductor of them. This will give weight to your assertions; and there will be nothing left for your ministers to urge, but what the king will gladly attend to: that we should unite to chastise the man who hath injured us equally: that Philip will be much more formidable to the king, if his first attack be made on us: for that, if he should be permitted to gain any advantage here, he will then march against him free from all apprehensions. For all these reasons, I think you should send ambassadors to treat with the king: and lay aside those idle prejudices, which have so often been injurious to your interests; 'that he is a barbarian, our common enemy, and the like.' For my own part, when I find a man apprehending danger from a prince, whose residence is in Susa and Ecbatana, and pronouncing him the enemy of our state, who formerly re-established its power, [1.] and but now made us [2.] such considerable offers, (if you rejected them, that was no fault of his,) and yet speaking in another strain of one who is at our gates, who is ex-

tending his conquests in the very heart of Greece, the plunderer of the Greeks, I am astonished: and regard that man, whoever he is, as dangerous, who doth not see danger in Philip.

There is another affair, wherein the public hath been injured, which hath been attacked most unjustly and indecently; which is the constant pretence of those who refuse to perform their duty to the state; to which you will find the blame of every omission, which every man is guilty of, constantly transferred. I cannot speak of it without great apprehensions. Yet I will speak: for I think I can serve my country, by advancing some things both in behalf of the poor [3,] against the rich, and of the rich against the necessitous; if we first banish those invectives, unjustly thrown out against the theatrical funds; and those fears that such an appointment cannot subsist without some dismal consequences; an appointment which, above all others, may be most conducive to our interests, and give the greatest strength to the whole community.

Attend then, while I first plead for those who are thought necessitous. There was a time, not long since, when the state could not raise more than one hundred and thirty talents; [4.]

---

drew him to an interview by feigned promises, where he seized him, and sent him in chains to Ochus. Instead of *ανάρπαστος*, some copies have *ανάστατος*, brought back: in which case it must be understood of Memnon or Artabazus, two rebellious satraps, who had taken refuge in Philip's court, but, by the mediation of Mentor, were reconciled to the king of Persia. *Ulpian. Tourreil.*

[1.] Who formerly re-established its power.] That is, when Conon, by the assistance Artaxerxes Mnemon, beat the Lacedemonian fleet at Cnidos, and restored the liberty and splendour of his country.

[2.] And but now made us, &c.] Artaxerxes Ochus, in order to reduce Egypt, which had revolted from him, solicited succours from the principal cities of Greece. Argos and Thebes consented; but from Athens and Lacedemon he could obtain only vain professions of friendship. He had, without doubt, offered large advantages to such people as would concur with him. Demosthenes here insinuates an accusation of the imprudence of Athens, in rejecting these offers. *Tourreil.*

[3.] Some things both in behalf of the poor, &c.] The theatrical distributions afforded a perpetual occasion of public contests between the several orders of the state. The poor were ever dissatisfied that the rich citizens shared the largesses, which they considered as their own peculiar right; and the rich beheld with impatience the dissipation of the public funds, which threw the whole weight of the supplies on them. But there was still a greater cause of complaint. The revenues of the state were always sufficient to defray the immense expenses of feasts and entertainments. And, in this case, some factious leader, who was willing to gain popularity, would pro-

pose to tax the rich; or, perhaps, by some infamous calumnies, would raise a prosecution, which would bring in a large pecuniary one. The rich, it may be imagined, were alarmed at such proceedings: they inveighed loudly against the authors of them, and sometimes ventured to accuse them in form, and bring them to trial. When their baseness and evil designs were publicly exposed, the people were ashamed to avow their intentions of supporting such flagrant injustice. Their clamours were loud against the person accused. But as in all judicial processes they gave their vote by ballot, they then had an opportunity of saving their friend.

All that the orator here says in defence of the theatrical appointments, is expressed with a caution and reserve quite opposite to his usual openness and freedom; and which plainly betray a consciousness of his being inconsistent with his former sentiments. How far he may be excused by the supposed necessity of yielding to the violent prepossessions of the people, and giving up a favourite point, I cannot pretend to determine. But it certainly is not very honourable to Demosthenes, to suppose, (with Ulpian,) that his former opposition was merely personal; and that the death of Eubulus now put an end to it.

[4.] The state could not raise more than one hundred and thirty talents.] We must understand this of those revenues raised out of Attica only: for the contributions of the allies, according to the taxation of Aristides, amounted to four hundred and sixty talents annually, and Pericles raised them yet higher. In order to know the real value of their revenues, we should consider the prices of things. In the time of Solon, an ox was sold at Athens for five drachmæ, as we learn from Plutarch, and yet none of those who were to command or to contribute to the equipment of a galley, ever had recourse to the pretence of poverty to be exempted from their duty; but vessels were sent out, money was supplied, and none of our affairs neglected. After this (thanks to fortune!) our revenues were considerably improved; and instead of one hundred, rose to four hundred talents; and this without any loss to the wealthy citizens, but rather with advantage: for they share the public affluence, and justly share it. Why then do we reproach each other? why have we recourse to such pretences, to be exempted from our duty? unless we envy the poor that supply with which fortune hath favoured them. I do not, and I think no one should blame them: for in private families I do not find the young so devoid of respect to years, or indeed any one so unreasonable and absurd, as to refuse to do his duty, unless all others do quite as much: such perverseness would render a man obnoxious to the laws against undutiful children; for to nothing are we more inviolably bound, than to a just and cheerful discharge of that debt, in which both nature and the laws engage us to our parents. And as we, each of us, have our particular parents, so all our citizens are to be esteemed the common parents of the state; and therefore, instead of depriving them of what the state bestows, we ought, if there were not this provision, to find out some other means of supplying their necessities. If the rich proceed upon these principles, they will act agreeably, not to justice only, but to good policy, for to rob some men of their necessary subsistence, is to raise a number of enemies to the commonwealth.

To men of lower fortunes I give this advice; that they should remove those grievances of which the wealthier members complain so loudly and so justly, (for I now proceed in the manner I proposed, and shall not scruple to offer such truths as may be favourable to the rich.) Look out, not through Athens only, but every other state, and, in my opinion, you will not find a man of so cruel, so inhuman a disposition, as to complain, when he sees poor men, men who even want the necessaries of life, receiving those appointments. Where then lies the difficulty? whence this animosity? When they behold certain [1.] persons charg-

ing private fortunes with those demands which were usually answered by the public; when they behold the proposer of this immediately rising in your esteem, and (as far as your protection can make him) immortal; when they find your private votes entirely different from your public clamours: then it is that their indignation is raised: for justice requires, Athenians! that the advantages of society should be shared by all its members. The rich should have their lives and fortunes well secured; that so, when any danger threatens their country, their opulence may be applied to its defence. Other citizens should regard the public treasure as it really is, the property of all, and be content with their just portion; but should esteem all private fortunes as the inviolable right of their possessors. Thus a small state rises to greatness, a great one preserves its power.

But it may be said, that possibly these are the duties of our several citizens: yet that they may be performed agreeably to the laws, some regulations must first be made.—The causes of our present disorders are many in number, and of long continuance. Grant me your attention, and I shall trace them to their origin.

You have departed, Athenians! from that plan of government which your ancestors laid down. You are persuaded by your leaders, that to be the first among the Greeks, to keep up your forces ready to redress the injured, is an unnecessary and vain expense. You are taught to think, that to lie down in indolence, to be free from public cares, to abandon all your interests one by one, a prey to the vigilance and craft of others, is to be perfectly secure, and surprisingly happy. By these means, the station which you should have maintained is now seized by another, and he is become the successful, the mighty potentate. And what else could have been expected? for as the Lacedemonians were unfortunate, the Thebans engaged in the Phocian war, and we quite insensible; he had no competitor for a prize so noble, so great, so illustrious, which for a long time engaged the most considerable states of Greece in the severest contests, Thus is he become formidable, strengthened by alliances, and attended by his armies; while all the Greeks are involved in so many

---

in the life of Solon. A hog in the time of Aristophanes was worth three drachmæ, as appears from one of his comedies, called 'the Peace.' *Olivet.*

A drachma, according to Arbuthnot, was equal to 7 3-4d. of our money. A hundred drachmæ made a mina, or 3l. 4s. 7d. We may also, from the same author, add to the foregoing note these particulars. In the time of Solon, corn was reckoned at a drachma the medimnus, or 4s. 6d. per quarter. In the time of Demosthenes it was much higher, at five drachmæ the medimnus, which makes it 1l. 2s. 7 3-4d. per quarter. In Solon's time the price of a sheep was 7 3-4d. A soldier's

daily pay was a drachma. The yearly salary of a common schoolmaster at Athens was a mina. In the early times of the republic, five hundred drachmæ were thought a competent fortune for a gentlewoman, 16l. 2s. 11d. To Aristides's two daughters, the Athenians gave three thousand drachmæ, 96l. 17s. 2d. The arts and sciences were rated very high: and though the price of a seat in the theatre was no more than two oboli, or 2 1-4d., yet the performers were rewarded magnificently. When Amœbæus sang in the theatre of Athens, his pay *per diem* was a talent.

[1.] When they behold certain, &c.] See note on the preceding page.

and so great difficulties, that it is hard to say where they may find resources. But of all the dangers of the several states, none are so dreadful as those which threaten ours : not only because Philip's designs aim principally at us, but because we, of all others, have been most regardless of our interests.

If, then, from the variety [1.] of merchandizes and plenty of provisions, you flatter yourselves that the state is not in danger, you judge unworthily and falsely. Hence we might determine whether our markets were well or ill supplied : but the strength of that state, which is regarded by all who aim at the sovereignty of Greece as the sole obstacle to their designs, the well known guardian of liberty, is not surely to be judged of by its vendibles. No : we should inquire whether it be secure of the affections of its allies ; whether it be powerful in arms. These are the points to be considered : and in these, instead of being well provided, you are totally deficient. To be assured of this, you need but attend to the following consideration. At what time have the affairs of Greece been in the greatest confusion ? I believe it will not be affirmed, that they have ever been in greater than at present. For in former times Greece was always divided into two parties; that of the Lacedemonians, and ours. All the several states adhered to one or the other of these. The King, while he had no alliances here, was equally suspected by all. By espousing the cause of the vanquished, [2.] he gained some credit, until he restored them to the same degree of power with their adversaries; after that, he became no less hated [3.] by those whom he had saved, than by those whom he had constantly opposed. But now, in the first place, the king lives in amity with all the Greeks, (indeed, without some immediate reformation in our conduct, we must be excepted.) In the next place there are several cities which affect the characters of guardians and

protectors. They are all possessed with a strong passion for pre-eminence ; and some of them (to their shame !) desert, and envy, and distrust each other. In a word, the Argians, Thebans, Corinthians, Lacedemonians, Arcadians, and Athenians, have all erected themselves into so many distinct sovereignties. But among all these parties, all these governing states, into which Greece is broken, there is not one (if I may speak freely) to whose councils [4.] fewer Grecian affairs are submitted, than to ours : and no wonder ; when neither love, nor confidence, nor fear, can induce any people to apply to you. It is not one single cause that hath effected this, (in that case, the remedy were easy;) but many faults, of various natures and of long continuance. Without entering into a particular detail, I shall mention one in which they all centre :—but I must first entreat you not to be offended, if I speak some bold truths without reserve.

Every opportunity which might have been improved to your advantage hath been sold. The ease and supineness in which you are indulged have disarmed your resentment against the traitors ; and thus others are suffered to possess your honours.—But, at present, I shall take notice only of what relates to Philip. If he be mentioned, immediately there is one ready to start up, and cry, ' We should not act inconsiderately ; we should not involve ourselves in a war.' And then he is sure not to forget the great happiness of living in peace, the misfortune of being loaded with the maintenance of a large army, the evil designs of some persons against our treasures; with others of the like momentous truths.

But these exhortations to peace should not be addressed to you : your conduct is but too pacific : let them rather be addressed to him who is in arms. If he can be prevailed on, there will be no difficulty on your part. Then it cannot be thought a misfortune to provide

---

[1.] If then from the variety, &c.] See note on the oration on the State of the Chersonesus, p. 49.

[2.] By espousing the cause of the vanquished, &c.] Lacedemon first entered into an alliance with Darius Nothus, by the mediation of Tissaphernes; which enabled Lysander to conquer Athens. Conon obtained from Artaxerxes Mnemon the succours necessary to revenge his country, and to re-establish it. And it was with reason that the kings of Persia attended to the preservation of the due balance between the Grecian States, lest the prevailing power might turn its thoughts to Asia, and attempt an invasion there. *Tourreil.*

[3.] He became no less hated, &c.] Lacedemon had no sooner subjected the Athenians, by the help of Darius, but she ravaged the Persian provinces in Asia Minor, and joined with the rebellious satraps. And as soon as the Athenians were delivered by Artaxerxes from the Spartan yoke, they espoused the quarrel

of Evagoras, who had revolted from Artaxerxes, and usurped a great part of the kingdom of Cyprus. Benefits could not bind these states. Interest alone formed their engagements, and interest dissolved them. The picture here exhibited of the conduct of the Greeks toward the kings of Persia, is by no means flattering, in point of morals. But it is not in ancient times only that we find morals must be silent, when politics speaks. *Tourreil.*

[4.] To whose councils, &c.] The ruling states of Greece accounted it their greatest glory to see and hear a number of ambassadors in their assemblies, soliciting their protection and alliance. The conquests which Philip made in Thrace had put an end to many applications of this sort, which had formerly been addressed to the Athenians. And their indolence made people decline any engagements with them. Foreigners were persuaded, that they who were insensible to their own interests, were not likely to grant the due attention to those of others.

9

for our security at the expense of some part of our possessions; the consequences that must arise, if this provision be neglected, rather deserve that name. And as to the plundering of your treasury, this must be prevented, by finding some effectual means to guard it: not by neglecting your interests. Nor can I but express the utmost indignation, when I find some of you complaining that your treasures are plundered, though it be in your power to secure them, and to punish the guilty; and yet looking on with indifference, while Philip is plundering every part of Greece successively: and this, that he may at last destroy you.

And what can be the reason, Athenians! that when Philip is guilty of such manifest violations of justice, when he is actually seizing our cities, yet none of these men will acknowledge that he acts unjustly, or commits hostilities; but assert, that they who rouse you from your insensibility, and urge you to oppose these outrages, are involving you in war? This is the reason: that whatever accidents may happen in the course of the war, (and there is a necessity, a melancholy necessity, that war should be attended with many accidents,)"they may lay the whole blame upon your best and most faithful counsellors. They know, that if with a steady and unanimous resolution you oppose the insolent invader, he must be conquered and they deprived of a master, whose pay was ever ready. But if the first unhappy accident calls you off to private trials and prosecutions, they need but appear as accusers, and two great points are secured; your favour, and Philip's gold; while you discharge the vengeance due to their perfidy against your faithful speakers. These are their hopes; these the grounds of their complaints, that certain persons are involving you in war. For my own part, this I know perfectly, that although it hath never been proposed by any Athenian to declare war, yet Philip hath seized many of our territories, and but just now sent succours to the Cardians. But if we will persuade ourselves that he is not committing hostilities, he would be the most senseless of mortals, should he attempt to undeceive us: for when they who have received the injury deny it, must the offender prove his guilt? But when he marches directly hither, what shall we then say? He will still deny that he is at war with us, (as he did to the people of Oreum, until his forces were in the heart of their dominions; as he did to those of Pheræ, until he was upon the point of storming their walls; as he did to the Olynthians, until he appeared in their territories at the head of an army.) Shall we then say, that they who urge us to defend our country are involving us in war? if so, we must be slaves. There is no medium! Nor is your danger the same with that of other states. Philip's design is not to enslave, but to extirpate, Athens. He knows, that a state like yours, accustomed to command, will not, or, if it were inclined, cannot, submit to slavery; he knows, that if you have an opportunity, you can give him more disturbance than any other people:

and therefore if ever he conquers us, we may be sure of finding no degree of mercy.

Since, then, you are engaged in defence of all that is dear to you, apply to the great work with an attention equal to the importance of it: let the wretches who have openly sold themselves to this man, be the objects of your abhorrence; let them meet with the utmost severity of public justice. For you will not, you cannot conquer your foreign enemies, until you have punished those that lurk within your walls. No; they will ever prove so many obstacles to impede our progress, and to give our enemies the superiority.

And what can be the reason that he treats you with insolence, (for I cannot call his present conduct by another name;) that he utters menaces against you, while he at least condescends to dissemble with other people, and to gain their confidence by good offices? Thus, by heaping favours upon the Thessalians, he led them insensibly into their present slavery. It is not possible to enumerate all the various artifices he practised against the wretched Olynthians, (such, among others, was the putting them in possession of Potidæa.) In his late transactions with the Thebans, he enticed them to his party, by yielding Bœotia to them, and by freeing them from a tedious and distressing war. And thus, after receiving their several insidious favours, some of these people have suffered calamities but too well known to all; others must submit to whatever may befall them. What you yourselves have formerly lost, I shall not mention; but in the very treaty of peace, in how many instances have we been deceived? how have we been despoiled? Did we not give up Phocis and the Straits? Did we not lose our Thracian dominions, Doriscum, Serrium, and even our ally Cersobleptes? Is he not in possession of Cardia? and doth he not now avow his usurpation? Whence is it, then, that his behaviour toward you is so different from that toward others? Because, of all the Grecian states, ours is the only one in which harangues in favour of enemies are pronounced with impunity; and the venal wretch may utter his falsehoods with security, even while you are losing your dominions. It was not safe to speak for Philip at Olynthus, until the people had been gained by Potidæa. In Thessaly, it was not safe to speak for Philip, until that people had been gained by the expulsion of their tyrants, and by being reinstated in the council of Amphictyons. Nor could it have been safely attempted at Thebes, until he had given them up Bœotia, and exterminated the Phocians. But at Athens, without the least danger, may Philip be defended, although he hath deprived us of Amphipolis and the territory of Cardia; although he threatens our city by his fortifications in Eubœa; although he is now marching to Byzantium. Hence some of his advocates have risen from penury to affluence, from obscurity and contempt to honour and eminence; while, on the other hand, you have sunk from glory to disgrace, from wealth to poverty; for the riches of a state I take to be the number, fidelity, and affection of its allies; in all which you are notoriously deficient. And by your total insensibility, while your affairs are thus falling into ruin, he is become successful, great, and formidable to all the Greeks, to all the barbarians; and you, deserted and inconsiderable; sumptuous indeed in your markets, but in every thing relating to military power, ridiculous.

There are some orators, I find, who view your interests and their own in a quite different light. To you they urge the necessity of continuing quiet, whatever injuries you are exposed to; they themselves find this impossible, though no one offers them the least injury. To you I speak, Aristodemus! [1.] Suppose a person should, without severity, ask you this question: 'How is it, that you, who are sensible (for it is a well-known truth) that the life of private men is serene and easy, and free from danger; that of statesmen, invidious and insecure, subject to daily contests and disquiets; should yet prefer the life encompassed with dangers, to that of peace and disengagement?' What could you say? Suppose we admit the truth of the very best answer you could make, 'that you were prompted by a desire of honour and renown:' is it possible, that you, who engaged in such painful undertakings, who despised all toils and dangers, for the sake of these, should advise the state to give them up for ease and indulgence? You cannot surely say, that it was incumbent upon you to maintain a degree of eminence in the city; and that the city was not concerned to maintain her eminence in Greece! Nor do I see how the public safety requires that we should confine ourselves to our own concerns, and yet, that an officious intrusion into those of others should be necessary for your safety. On the contrary, you are involving yourself in the greatest dangers, by being unnecessarily assiduous; and the city by being quite inactive. 'But then you

have an illustrious 'reputation, derived from your family, which it would be shameful not to support; while on the contrary, nothing has been transmitted from our fathers, but obscurity and meanness.' This is equally false. Your father was like you, and therefore base and infamous. To the honour of our ancestors, let all Greece bear witness; twice rescued, [2.] by their valour, from the greatest dangers.

There are persons, then, who do not act with the same firmness and integrity, in the conduct of their own affairs and those of the state. Is not this the case, when some of them, after escaping from prison, have raised themselves so high, as to forget their former condition; and yet have reduced a state, whose pre-eminence in Greece was but now universally acknowledged, to the lowest degree of infamy and meanness?—I could say more on these and other points, but I forbear: for it is not want of good counsel that now distresses, or ever hath distressed you. But when your true interests have been laid before you, and that you have been unanimous in your approbation, you can, with equal patience, attend to those who endeavour to discredit, to overthrow all that hath been advanced. Not that you are ignorant of their characters, (for you can, at first glance, distinguish the hireling and agent of Philip from the true patriot;) but that, by impeaching your faithful friends, and by turning the whole affair into ridicule and invective, you may find a pretence for a general neglect of your duty.

You have now heard truths of the highest moment, urged with all freedom, simplicity, and zeal. You have heard a speech not filled with flattery, danger, and deceit; calculated to bring gold to the speaker, and to reduce the state into the power of its enemies. It remains, therefore, that the whole tenor of your conduct be reformed! if not, that utter desolation, which will be found in your affairs, must be imputed wholly to yourselves.

[1.] To you I speak, Aristodemus!] He was by profession a player; and was one of the ten ambassadors which the Athenians had sent to the court of Macedon, to treat about the peace. At his return Demosthenes proposed a decree for crowning this very man for his good services, whom he here inveighs against with so much bitterness.

[2.] Twice rescued, &c.] First, at Marathon, and afterward at Salamis. Isocrates mentions a third time, when they delivered Greece from the Spartan yoke. Demosthenes (frequently speaks of this in the highest terms, but) here rather chooses to lessen the glory of his country than to recall an event which reflected on the Lacedemonians, now in alliance with Athens. *Tourreil.*

THE TWELFTH ORATION AGAINST PHILIP:

Commonly called the Oration on the Letter.

PRONOUNCED IN THE ARCHONSHIP OF THEOPHRASTUS, THE YEAR AFTER THE
FOREGOING ORATION.

TO WHICH IS PREFIXED PHILIP'S LETTER TO THE ATHENIANS.

INTRODUCTION.

THE former oration inspired the Athenians with the resolution to send succours to all the cities that were threatened by Philip's arms; and their first step was to despatch to the Hellespont a convoy with provisions; which weighed anchor in view of Selymbria, a city of the Propontis, then besieged by the Macedonians, and was there seized by Amyntas, Philip's admiral. The ships were demanded by the Athenians, and returned by Philip, but with declarations sufficiently alarming.

The obstinate valour of the Perinthians had forced Philip to turn the siege into a blockade. He marched off with a considerable body of his army, to attack other places; and made an incursion into the territories of Byzantium. The Byzantines shut themselves up within their city, and despatched one of their citizens to Athens, to desire the assistance of that state; who, with some difficulty prevailed to have a fleet of forty ships sent out, under the command of Chares.

As this general had not the same reputation in other places as at Athens, the cities by which he was to pass refused to receive him: so that he was obliged to wander for some time along the coasts, extorting contributions from the Athenian allies; despised by the enemy, and suspected by the whole world. He appeared at last before Byzantium; where he met with the same mortifying treatment as in other places, and was refused admission: and shortly after was defeated by Amyntas in a naval engagement, in which a considerable part of his fleet was either sunk or taken.

Philip had for some time perceived, that, sooner or later, he must inevitably come to a rupture with the Athenians. His partisans were no longer able to lull them into security. Their oppositions to his designs, however imperfect and ineffectual, were yet sufficient to alarm him. He therefore determined to endeavour to abate that spirit which now began to break through their inveterate indolence; and for this purpose sent them a letter, in which, with the utmost art, he laid open the causes of complaint he had against them, and threatened them with reprisals. This letter was not received at Athens till after the news of Chares's defeat.

Philip had now laid siege to Byzantium; and exerted all his efforts to make himself master of that city. On the other hand the Athenians were disheartened by the ill success of their commander, and began to repent of having sent any succours; when Phocion, who always assumed the liberty of speaking his sentiments freely, assured them that, for once, they themselves had not been in fault; but that their general only was to blame. He was immediately desired to take on himself the charge of relieving Byzantium; and set sail with a numerous body of forces. He was received with the greatest demonstrations of joy; and his whole conduct expressed the utmost wisdom and moderation. Nor was his valour less conspicuous: he sustained many assaults with an intrepidity worthy of the early ages of the commonwealth; and at last obliged Philip to raise the siege.

Phocion then departed amidst the general acclamations of the people whom he had saved. He proceeded to the relief of the colonies of the Chersonesus, who were ever exposed to the attacks of the Cardians. In his way he took some vessels laden with arms and provisions for the enemy: and obliged the Macedonians, who had attempted Sestos, to abandon their enterprise, and shut themselves up in Cardia.

And thus, after various expeditions highly honourable to himself and to his country, Phocion returned home, where he found the Athenians engaged in a debate on Philip's letter; on which occasion Demosthenes pronounced his last oration against Philip. To have answered the letter particularly, would have been very difficult: for though Athens had the better cause, yet many irregularities had really been committed; which Philip knew how to display in their full force. The orator therefore makes use of his art to extricate himself from the difficulty; avoids all former discussions of facts; and applies himself at once to raise the lively passions: affects to consider this letter as an open declaration of war; inflames the imaginations of his hearers with the idea; and speaks only of the means to support their arms against so powerful an enemy.

PHILIP'S LETTER [1.] TO THE ATHENIANS.

Theophrastus, Archon.—A. R. Philip. 21—Olympiad. 110. An. 1.

Philip, to the Senate and People of Athens, greeting:

As the embassies I have frequently sent, to enforce those oaths and declarations by which we stand engaged, have produced no alteration in your conduct, I thought it necessary thus to lay before you the several particulars in which I think myself aggrieved. Be not surprised at the length of this letter; for as I have many causes of complaint, it is necessary to explain them all distinctly.

First then, when Nicias the herald [2.] was forcibly taken out of my own territory; instead of punishing the author of this outrage, as justice required, you added to his wrongs, by keeping him ten months in prison: and the letters intrusted to him, by us, [3.] you read publicly in your assembly. Again; when the ports of Thassus were open [4.] to the Byzantine galleys, nay, to any pirates that pleased, you looked on with indifference; although our treaties expressly say, that such proceedings shall be considered as an actual declaration of war. About the same time it was that Diopithes made a descent upon my dominions, carried off in chains the inhabitants of Crobyle and Tiristasis, [5.] ravaged all the adjacent parts of Thrace, and at length proceeded to such a pitch of lawless violence, as to seize Amphilochus, [6.] who went, in quality of an ambassador, to treat about the ransom of prisoners: whom, after he had reduced him to the greatest difficulties, be compelled to purchase his freedom at the rate of nine talents. And this he did with the approbation of his state. Yet the violation of the sacred character of heralds and ambassadors is accounted, by all people, the height of impiety: nor have any expressed a deeper sense of this, than you yourselves: for when the Megareans had put Anthemocritus to death, [7.] the people proceeded so far as to exclude them from the mysteries; and erected [8.] a statue before the gates, as a monument of their

---

[1.] This letter is a masterpiece in the original. It has a majestic and a persuasive vivacity; a force and justness of reasoning sustained through the whole; a clear exposition of facts, and each followed by its natural consequence; a delicate irony: in short a noble and concise style, made for kings who speak well, or have taste and discernment at least to make choice of those who can make them speak well. If Philip was himself the author of this letter, as it is but just to believe, since we have no proof to the contrary, we may reasonably pronounce of him, as was said of Cæsar, ' that he wrote with that spirit with which he fought. Eodem animo dixit, quo bellavit. Quint. Inst. l. 10. c. 17.' *Tourreil.*

[2.] When Nicias the herald, &c.] Probably he had been seized upon his journey from Thrace to Macedon, by Diopithes, at the time of his invading Philip's Thracian dominions, as mentioned in the preface to the oration on the State of the Chersonesus. *Tourreil.*

[3.] And the letters intrusted to him, by us, &c.] The Athenians hoped, by opening this packet, to get some light into Philip's secret schemes and practices against them. There were found in it some letters directed to Olympias, Philip's queen, which they treated with a most scrupulous respect, and took care she should receive them in the same condition in which they had been intercepted. *Tourreil.*

[4.] When the ports of Thassus were open, &c.] The Athenians had engaged, by an article of their treaty, that the Thassians, who were their subjects, should not receive any ships that committed piracies on the subjects or allies of Philip. Thisarticle had not been strictly observed; perhaps on account of Philip's own infidelity. *Tourreil.*

[5.] Crobyle and Tiristasis.] The first of these places is quite unknown. Tiristasis is placed by Pliny in the Thracian Chersonesus.

[6.] As to seize Amphilochus.] It is impossible to save the honour of Diopithes, but by denying the fact; at least in the manner that Philip represents it. *Tourreil.*

[7.] For when the Megareans had put Anthemocritus to death, &c.] Philip, here, beats the Athenians with their own weapons, and cites, very much to the purpose, the example of a memorable vengeance, which they had taken about an age before, upon the Megareans. They had accused this people of favouring a revolt of their slaves, and of profaning a tract of consecrated land; and upon this account excluded them from all advantages of commerce in the ports and markets of Athens. Thucydides stops here; but Pausanias adds, that Anthemocritus went from Athens in quality of a herald, to summon the Megareans to desist from their sacrilege, and that for answer they put him to death. The interest of the gods served the Athenians, for a pretence; but the famous Aspasia, whom Pericles was so violently in love with, was the true cause of their rupture with Megara. Some young Athenians, heated by wine, had taken away from Megara a remarkable courtezan, called Simætha; and the Megareans, by way of reprisal, seized two Athenian ladies of the same character, that were in Aspasia's train. Pericles espoused his favourite's quarrel; and, with the power which he then possessed, easily persuaded the people to whatever he pleased. They thundered out a decree against the Megareans, forbidding all commerce with them upon pain of death: they drew up a new from of an oath, by which every general obliged himself to invade the territories of Megara twice every year. This decree kindled the first spark of contention, which at length flamed out in the Peloponnesian war. It was the work of three courtezans. The most illustrious events have sometimes as shameful an origin. *Tourreil.*

[4.] To exclude them from the mysteries;

crime. And is not this shocking; to be avowedly guilty of the very same crimes, for which your resentment fell so severely upon others, when you yourselves were aggrieved? In the next place, Callias, your general, hath made himself master of all the towns upon the bay of Pagasæ; though comprehended in the treaty made with you, and united in alliance to me. Not a vessel could steer its course toward Macedon, but the passengers were all treated by him as enemies, and sold: and this his conduct hath been applauded by the resolutions of your council. So that I do not see how you can proceed farther, if you actually declare war against me. For when we were at open hostilities, you did but send out your corsairs, make prize of those who were sailing to my kingdom, assist my enemies, and infest my territories. Yet now, when we are professedly at peace, so far have your injustice and rancour hurried you, that you have sent ambassadors to the Persian [1.] to persuade him to attack me; which must appear highly surprising; for before that prince had subdued Egypt and Phœnicia, it was resolved, [2.] that, if he attempted any new enterprises, you would invite me, as well as all the other Greeks, to an association against him. But now, with such malice am I pursued, that you are, on the contrary, confederating with him against me. In former times, I am told, your ancestors objected it as an heinous crime to the family [3.] of Pisistratus, that they had led the Persian against the Greeks: and yet you are not ashamed to commit the very same action, for which you were continually inveighing against those tyrants.

But your injustice hath not stopped here. Your decrees command me to permit Teres and Cersobleptes to reign [4.] unmolested in Thrace, as being citizens of Athens—I do not know that they were included in our treaty, that their names are to be found in the records of our engagements, or that they are Athenians. But this I know, that Teres served in my army against you; and that when Cersobleptes proposed to my ambassadors to take the necessary oaths, in order to be particularly included in the treaty, your generals prevented him, by declaring him an enemy to the Athenians. And how is this equitable or just? when it serves your purposes, to proclaim him the enemy of your state; when I am to be calumniated, to give him the title of your citizen; when Sitalces was slain, [5.] to whom you granted the privileges of your city, instantly to enter into an alliance with his

---

and erected, &c.] All the Greeks had, ordinarily, a right to be initiated into what were called the lesser mysteries which the Athenians celebrated at Eleusis, in honour of Ceres and Proserpine. But upon the death of Anthemocritus, the Megareans were excluded; and a statue or tomb erected in honour of this herald, on the road leading from Athens to Eleusis, near the gate called Dipylon. According to Aristophanes, (in Acharn. Act 2. Sc. 5.) the Megareans denied this murder, and threw the whole blame of it upon Aspasia and Pericles. *Tourreil.*

[1.] You have sent ambassadors to the Persian, &c.] Diodorus informs us, that about this time the satraps of the lesser Asia had obliged Philip to raise the siege of Perinthus. The historian does not say that the Athenians invited them; but Philip complains of it here; and Pausanias observes, that in this expedition the Persian forces were commanded by Apollodorus, an Athenian general. We may observe, with what disrespect Philip (whose ancestors, in their greatest prosperity, never aspired higher than to the alliance of some satrap) here speaks of the Great King—' The Persian!' *Tourreil.*

[2.] Before that prince had subdued Egypt and Phœnicia, it was resolved, &c.] Artaxerxes Ochus, who governed Persia at that time, before his reduction of these revolted provinces, had marched into the lesser Asia, against Artadazus, a rebellious satrap. The approach of the Persians alarmed the Greeks: and Athens conceived a design of attacking them in their own country. This gave occasion to the oration of Demosthenes, entitled, Περὶ τῶν Συμμοριῶν. Philip pretends that they had resolved to admit him into the confederacy which

was then forming in favour of the Greeks, with whom he affects to rank, and by his expressions removes every idea of foreigner and barbarian, which are the representations that the orator frequently makes of him. *Tourreil.*

[3.] Your ancestors objected it as an heinous crime to the family, &c.] The comparison which Philip makes here, between the sons of Pisistratus and the orators who advised an alliance with Persia, is founded upon a history too well known to be enlarged upon. It is undoubtedly by no means just: for, in different conjunctures, the good citizen may employ the same forces to save his country, that the wicked one had formerly employed to destroy it. However, the turn he gives it was the fittest in the world to affect the people, who thought it their greatest honour to express an inveterate hatred to the Persians. *Tourreil.*

[4.] To permit Teres and Cersobleptes to reign, &c.] History speaks only of Cersobleptes. They had suffered him to be overthrown by Philip: and, when they found how nearly they themselves were affected by his fall, employed those decrees to endeavour to restore him. *Tourreil.*

[5.] When Sitalces was slain, &c.] This Sitalces was the grandfather of Cersobleptes. In the beginning of the Peloponnesian war, he rendered the Athenians such important services, that they, by way of acknowledgment, admitted his son Sadocus into the number of their citizens. In the eighth year of this war, Sitalces was killed in a battle against the Triballi. His nephew Seuthes seized the kingdom, in prejudice of his children, and hence became suspected of being the cause of his death. Philip argues, from this suspicion, as if it were an undoubted truth. *Tourreil.*

murderer; yet to engage in a war with me on account of Cersobleptes? and this, when you are sensible that not one of these your adopted citizens have ever showed the least regard to your laws or determinations.—But to bring this affair to a short issue. You granted the rights of your community [1.] to Evagoras of Cyprus, [2.] to Dionysius the Syracusan, and to their descendants. Prevail therefore upon the men who have dispossessed each of these, to restore them to their dominions, and you shall recover from me all those territories of Thrace [3.] which Teres and Cersobleptes commanded. But if you have nothing to urge against those who expelled them, and yet are incessantly tormenting me, am not I justly warranted to oppose you?—I might urge many other arguments upon this head, but I choose to pass them over.

The Cardians, [4.] I freely declare, I am determined to support, as my engagements to them are prior to our treaty; and as you refused to submit your differences with them to an arbitration, though frequently urged by me: nor have they been wanting in the like solicitations. Should not I, therefore, be the basest of mankind, to abandon my allies, and to show greater regard for you, my inveterate opposers, than for my constant and assured adherents?

Formerly, (for I cannot pass this in silence,) you contented yourselves with remonstrating upon the points above mentioned. But lately, upon the bare complaint of the Peparethians, that they had been severely treated by me, you proceeded to such outrage, as to send orders to your general to revenge their quarrel. Yet the punishment which I inflicted was no way equal to the heinousness of their crime: as they had, in time of peace, seized

Halonesus; nor could be prevailed upon, by all my solicitations, to give up either the island or the garrison. · The injuries I received from the Peparethians were never thought of, but their punishment commanded all your attention, as it afforded a pretence for accusing me, although I did not take the island either from them, or from you, but from the pirate Sostratus. If, then, you confess that you delivered it to Sostratus, you confess yourselves guilty of sending out pirates: if he seized it without your consent, how have I injured you by taking possession of it, and by rendering it a secure harbour? Nay, so great was my regard to your state, that I offered to bestow on you this island: but this was not agreeable to your orators: they [5.] would not have it accepted, but resumed. So that if I complied with their directions, I proclaimed myself a usurper: if I still kept possession of the place, I became suspected to the people. I saw through these artifices, and therefore proposed to bring our differences to a judicial determination: and if sentence was given for me, to present you with the place: if in your favour, to restore it to the people. This I frequently desired: you would not have it: the Peparethians seized the island. What then was I to do? Should I not punish the violators of oaths? Was I tamely to bear such an audacious insult? If the island was the property of the Peparethians, what right have the Athenians to demand it? If it be yours, why do you not resent their usurpation?

So far, in short, have our animosities been carried, that, when I had occasion to despatch some vessels to the Hellespont, I was obliged to send a body of forces through the Chersonesus, to defend them against your colonies, who are authorized to attack me by a decree

---

[1.] You granted the rights of your community, &c.] What idea must we form of the splendour of that city, where even kings solicited for the rank of private citizens! The other states of Greece affected the same kind of grandeur. At a time when ambassadors from Corinth were congratulating Alexander on his victories, they made him an offer of the freedom of their city, as the greatest mark of honour possible. Alexander, now in the full splendour of his fortune, disdained to return them any answer but a contemptuous smile. This stung the ambassadors to the quick, and one of them was bold enough to say, 'Know, Sir, that the great Hercules and you are the only persons whom Corinth has ever deigned to distinguish in this manner.' This softened the prince: he received them with all possible marks of respect, and accepted of a title which had been so dignified. *Tourreil.*

[2.] To Evagoras of Cyprus.] The Athenians erected a statue to Evagoras, the elder of that name, and declared him a citizen of Athens, for having assisted Conon in restoring their liberty. He caused Salamis to revolt from the Persian, and subdued most part of the island of Cyprus; but was afterward reduced, and

fell by the hands of Nicocles. His son, Evagoras the younger, however, asserted his claim to the kingdom of Cyprus, and was supported by the Athenians against Protagoras, the successor of Nicocles. But his attempts were not successful. Protagoras supplanted him at the court of Persia, where he had been in full favour. He was cited to answer to some heads of an accusation; and, upon his justifying himself, he obtained a government in Asia, well worth his little kingdom. But his bad conduct soon obliged him to abdicate, and fly into Cyprus; where he perished wretchedly. *Tourreil.*

[3.] All those territories of Thrace.] In the original, τὴν Θρᾴκην, ὅσην, &c. By the ironical pomp of this expression, he sets their dominions (which were really inconsiderable) in the most contemptuous light. *Tourreil.*

[4.] The Cardians, &c.] See the Preface to the oration on the State of the Chersonesus.

[5.] But this was not agreeable to your orators: they, &c.] Demosthenes, in particular, opposed their receiving a restitution under the name of a present.

of Polycrates, [1.] confirmed by the resolutions of your council. Nay, your general has actually invited the Byzantines to join him; and he has every where publicly declared, that he has your instructions to commence hostilities at the first favourable opportunity. All this could not prevail upon me to make any attempt upon your city, or your navy, or your territories, although I might have had success in most, or even all of them. I chose rather to continue my solicitations to have our complaints submitted to proper umpires. And which, think ye, is the fittest decision, that of reason or of the sword? Who are to be judges in your cause, yourselves or others? What can be more inconsistent, than that the people of Athens, who compelled the Thassians and Maronites [2.] to bring their pretensions to the city of Stryma to a judicial decision, should yet refuse to have their own disputes with me determined in the same manner? particularly as you are sensible that, if the decree be against you, still you lose nothing; if in your favour, it puts you in possession of my conquests.

But what appears to me most unaccountable is this: when I sent you ambassadors, chosen from all the confederated powers, on purpose to be witness of our transactions; when I discovered the sincerest intentions of entering into reasonable and just engagements with you, in relation to the affairs of Greece; you even refused to hear these ambassadors on that head. It was then in your power to remove all their apprehensions, who suspected any danger from my designs, or to have openly convicted me of consummate baseness. This was the interest of the people; but the orators could not find their account in it; for they are a set of men, to whom (if I may believe those that are acquainted with your polity) peace is war, and war is peace; [3.] as they are always sure to make a property of the generals, either by aiding their designs, or by malicious prosecutions. Then they need but throw out some scandalous invectives against persons of worth and eminence, citizens or foreigners, and they at once acquire the character of patriots, among the many. I could have easily silenced their clamours against me, by a little gold; and even have converted them into praises: but I should blush to purchase your friendship from such wretches. To such insolence have they proceeded upon other occasions, that they even dared to dispute my title to Amphipolis; which is founded, I presume, upon reasons beyond their power to invalidate: for if it is to belong to those who first conquered it, what can be juster than our claim? Alexander our ancestor, was the original sovereign: [4.] as appears from the golden statue [5.] which he erected at Delphos, from the first fruits of the Persian spoils taken there. But if this admits of contest, and it is to continue the property of those who were last in possession, it is mine by this title too, (for I took it from the Lacedemonian inhabitants, who had dispossessed you:) [3.] and all cities are held either by hereditary right or by the right of conquest.

[1.] By a decree of Polycrates.] This orator had great credit at Athens, and on many occasions favoured the designs of Philip. Possibly he acted otherwise upon this occasion, the better to conceal his attachment, or that he might afterward sell his integrity at a dearer rate. *Tourreil*.

[2.] Who compelled the Thassians and Maronites, &c.] The first of these people inhabited an island in the Egean sea: the other, a maritime place in Thrace. The Thassians had founded Stryma, according to Herodotus; but as it was in the neighbourhood of Maronea, probably the Maronites had, in quality of protectors, or benefactors, acquired some pretensions to it. *Tourreil*.

[3.] Peace is war, and war is peace, &c.] Aristotle, in his Rhetor. l. 3, c. 10, quotes this (nearly) as an example of an agreeable antithesis: which, joined to the force, and, what is more, to the order of the arguments contained in this letter, inclines me to think that Aristotle was his secretary on this occasion. But my conjecture, whether well or ill founded, does not detract from Philip, in point of genius and spirit. The true talent of a king is to know how to apply the talents of others to the best advantage. And we do not want other proofs of Philip's abilities in writing: witness his letter to Aristotle on the birth of Alexander. *Tourreil*.

[1.] Alexander, our ancestor, was the original sovereign.] Philip asserts boldly, without giving himself much trouble even to preserve probability: for in the time of Alexander, the contemporary of Xerxes, there was no city, no fortified post, in the place Amphipolis was afterward raised; nor was it till thirty years after the defeat of the Persians that Agnon founded it. *Tourreil*.

[5.] As appears from the golden statue, &c.] Herodotus speaks of this statue, and places it near the colossal statue which the Greeks raised, according to custom, out of the Persian spoils. The proximity of these statues serves Philip as a foundation for giving his ancestors an honour which really belonged to the Greeks. Solinus mentions, that Alexander, a very rich prince, made an offering of a golden statue of Apollo in the temple of Delphos, and another of Jupiter in the temple of Elis; but not that the Persian spoils were any part of these offerings.—This Alexander, surnamed Φιλέλλην, 'friend of Greeks,' had the reputation of an able politician, but not of a good soldier, or great commander. He served the Persians a long time, rather by force than inclination; and, before the battle of Salamis, declared, of a sudden, for the Greeks. *Tourreil*.

[6.] I took it from the Lacedemonian inhabitants, who had dispossessed you, &c.] Brasidas, the Lacedemonian general, took Amphipolis from the republic of Athens: and by the assistance of Sparta, it afterward

And yet you, who neither were the original possessors, nor are now in possession, presume to lay claim to this city, under pretence of having held it for some short time; and this, when you have yourselves given the strongest testimony in my favour: for I frequently wrote to you upon this head; and you as often acknowledged me the rightful sovereign: and by the articles of our late treaty, the possession of Amphipolis, and your alliance, were both secured to me. What title therefore can be better established? It descended to us from our ancestors; it is ours by conquest; and, lastly, you yourselves have acknowledged the justice of our pretensions; you who are wont to assert your claim, even when it is not supported by right.

I have now laid before you the grounds of my complaints. Since you have been the first aggressors; since my gentleness and fear of offending have only served to increase your injustice, and to animate you in your attempts to distress me: I must now take up arms; and I call the gods to witness to the justice of my cause, and the necessity of procuring for myself that redress which you deny me.

THE ORATION ON THE LETTER. [1.]

Theophrastus, Archon.—A. R. Philip. 21. *—Olympiad.* 110. *An.* 1.

Now, Athenians! it is fully evident to you all, that Philip made no real peace with us, but only deferred hostilities. When he surrendered Halus to the Pharsalians, [2.] when

he completed the ruin of Phocis, when he overturned all Thrace, [3.] then did he really attack the state under the concealment of false allegations and unjust pretensions; but now he hath made a formal declaration of war, by this his letter. That we are not to look with horror upon his power; that, on the other hand, we are not to be remiss in our opposition, but to engage our persons, our treasures, and our navies; in one word, our whole strength, freely, in the common cause; these are the points I would establish.

First then, Athenians! the gods we may justly regard as our strongest allies and assistants; since in this unjust violation of his treaty, he hath trampled upon religion, and despised the most solemn oaths. In the next place, those secret practices to which his greatness hath hitherto been owing, all his arts of deceiving, all his magnificent promises, are now quite exhausted. The Perinthians, and the Byzantines, and their confederates, [4.] have at length discovered, that he intends to treat them as he formerly treated the Olynthians. The Thessalians are no longer ignorant that he affects to be the master, and not the leader, of his allies. The Thebans begin to see danger in his stationing a garrison at Nicæa, [5.] his assuming the rank of an Amphictyon, his bringing into Macedon the embassies from Peloponnesus, [6.] and his preventing them in seizing the advantage of an alliance with the people of that country. So that, of those who have hitherto been his friends, some are now irreconcileably at war with him; others no longer serve him with zeal and sincerity; and all have their suspicions and complaints. Add to this, (and it is

---

maintained its independence, until it fell into the power of Philip. *Tourreil.*

[1.] It must be confessed, that this oration consists almost wholly of repetitions. This great man seems to have thought himself superior to all vain criticism; and, only concerned for the safety of Athens, was in no pain about his private glory. He speaks as an orator whose end is to persuade and convince; not as a declaimer, who seeks only to give pleasure and excite admiration. He therefore resumes those topics he had already made use of, and gives them new force, by the close and lively manner in which he delivers them.

[2.] When he surrendered Halus to the Pharsalians, &c.] Halus was a town of Thessaly, upon the river Amphrysus. Parmenio besieged and took it; after which Philip put the people of Pharsalia in possession of it. *Tourreil.*

[3.] When he overturned all Thrace, &c.] This is the language of an orator, who, to represent Philip's outrages with the greater aggravation, takes the liberty of speaking of a part of that country as of the whole. Philip had indeed made himself master of the territories of Teres and Cersobleptes, both kings in Thrace, and allies of the Athenians. But Pausanias observes, that, before the Ro-

mans, no one had ever made an entire conquest of Thrace. *Tourreil.*

[4.] And their confederates.] The inhabitants of Chios, Rhodes, and some other places, joined to defeat Philip's designs upon Perinthus and Byzantium. *Tourreil.*

[5.] At Nicæa.] This town was situated near Thermopylæ, and was counted among the principal towns of the Locrians, (Epicnemidii,) the neighbours and allies of the Bœotians and Thebans. Philip made himself master of it at the time that he seized Thermopylæ, under pretence of putting an end to the sacred war. *Tourreil.*

[6.] His bringing into Macedon the embassies from Peloponnesus, &c.] Probably this was at the time when he interested himself in the disputes between Sparta and the Argians and Messenians, as mentioned in the preface to the Second Philippic Oration.—Strabo mentions an application of the Argians and Messenians to Philip, to regulate a contest between them and Lacedemon, about their boundaries. And Pausanias declaims against the pride of Gallus, a Roman senator, who thought it derogated from his dignity to decide the differences of Lacedemon and Argos; and disdained to muddle with a mediation, which Philip had formerly not only accepted, but courted. *Tourreil.*

10   †

of no small moment,) that the satraps of Asia have just now forced him to raise the siege of Perinthus, by throwing in a body of hired troops : and as this must make him their enemy, [1.] and as they are immediately exposed to danger, should he become master of Byzantium, they will not only readily unite their force with ours, but prevail upon the king of Persia to assist us with his treasure ; who, in this particular, far exceeds all other potentates ; and whose influence in Greece is so great, that formerly when we were engaged in a war with Lacedemon, he never failed to give the superiority to [2.] that party which he espoused : and now, when he unites with us, he will with ease subdue the power of Philip.

I shall not mention, as a balance to these so considerable advantages, that he hath taken the opportunity of the peace to make himself master of many of our territories, our ports, and other like conveniences. For it is observable, that where affection joins, and one common interest animates the confederating powers, there the alliance is never to be shaken ; but where subtle fraud, and passions insatiable, and perfidy and violence have formed it, (and these are the means which he hath used,) the least pretence, the slightest accident, gives it the fatal shock, and in an instant it is utterly dissolved. And from repeated observations I am convinced, Athenians! that Philip not only wants the confidence and affection of his allies, but even in his own kingdom he is by no means happy in that well-established regularity, and those intimate attachments, which might be expected. The power of Macedon, indeed, as an ally, may have some effect ; but if left to itself, is insufficient ; and when compared with his pompous enterprises, quite contemptible. And then his wars, his expeditions, all those exploits which have given him this splendour, are the very means of rendering it yet weaker : for you are not to imagine, Athenians ! that Philip and his subjects have the same desires. He is possessed with the love of glory ; they wish only for security. The object of his passion must be attended with danger ; and they but ill endure a banishment from their children, parents, wives ; a life worn out with toils, and exposed to continual perils in his cause.

Hence we may learn how his subjects in general are affected to their prince. But then his guards and officers of his foreign troops ; these, you will find, have some military reputation : yet they live in greater terrors than the obscure and mean. These are exposed only to their avowed enemies ; the others have more to fear from calumny and flattery, than in the field. The one, when engaged in battle, but share the common danger : the others, besides their part, and this not the least of that danger, have also their private apprehensions from the temper of their prince. Among the many, when one hath transgressed, his punishment is proportioned to his crime : the others, when they have most eminently distinguished themselves, are then, in open defiance of all decency, treated with the greatest insolence and disdain.

That these are incontestable truths, no reasonable man can doubt : for they who have lived with him assure us, that his ambition is so insatiable, that he will have the glory of every exploit ascribed wholly to himself ; and is much more incensed against such commanders as have performed any thing worthy of honour, than against those whose misconduct hath ruined his enterprises. But if this be the case, how is it that they have persevered so long in their attachment to his cause ? It is for this reason, Athenians ! because success throws a shade on all his odious qualities, (for nothing veils men's faults from observation so effectually as success :) but let any accident happen, and they will be perfectly discovered. Just as in our bodies ; while we are in health, our inward defects lie concealed ; but when we are attacked by a disorder, then they are all sensible, in the vessels, in the joints, or wherever we are affected : so in kingdoms and governments of every kind, while their arms are victorious, their disorders escape the common observation ; but a reverse of fortune, (and this he must experience, as he has taken up a burden much beyond his strength,) never fails to lay them open to every eye.

If there be a man among you, Athenians ! who regards Philip as a powerful and formidable enemy, on account of his good fortune, such cautious foresight bespeaks a truly prudent mind. Fortune indeed does greatly influence, or rather has the entire direction of all human affairs : but there are many rea-

---

[1.] As this must make him their enemy.] This proved an exact prediction of what happened some time after. Alexander, in his letter to Darius, alleges, as one of the principal subjects of their rupture, the powerful succours which Perinthus received from the Persian satraps. Arrian, l. 1. *Tourreil.*

[2.] He never failed to give the superiority to, &c.] History represents the king of Persia as the supreme arbiter of the fate of Athens and Lacedemon, during the whole time of their quarrels. Darius Nothus joined with the Lacedemonians ; and Lysander, their general, de-

stroyed Athens. Artaxerxes Mnemon protected Conon, the Athenian general ; and immediately Athens resumed her former splendour. Lacedemon afterward joined in alliance with the Great King ; and this intimidated the Athenians, and obliged them to seek for peace. Artaxerxes dictated the articles of it, threatening to declare against those who should refuse to subscribe to them. Athens instantly obeyed. Thus it was that a foreign power lorded it over the Greeks, and by means of their divisions had the absolute command of their fate. *Tourreil.*

sons to expect much more from the fortune of Athens, than that of Philip. We can boast of an authority in Greece, derived from our ancestors, not only before his days, but before any one prince of Macedon. They all were tributaries of Athens: Athens never paid that mark of subjection to any people. In the next place, the more inviolably we have adhered to piety and justice, the greater may be our confidence in the favour of the gods. But if this be the case, how is it that, in the late war, his arms had such superior fortune? This is the cause, (for I will speak with undaunted freedom:) he takes the field himself, endures its toils, and shares its dangers: no favourable incident escapes him, no season of the year retards him. While we (for the truth must not be concealed) are confined within our walls, in perfect inactivity, delaying, and voting, and wandering through the public places, in search of news. Can any thing better deserve the name of 'new,' than that one sprung from Macedon should insult Athens, and dare to send such letters as you have just heard recited? That he should have his armies and his orators in pay? (Yes, I call Heaven to witness, there are those among us, who do not blush to live for Philip, who have not sense to perceive that they are selling all the interests of the state, all their own real interests, for a trifling pittance!)— While we never once think of preparing to oppose him; are quite averse to hiring troops, and want resolution to take up arms ourselves. No wonder, therefore, that he had some advantage over us in the late war: on the contrary, it is really surprising that we, who are quite regardless of all that concerns our cause, should expect to conquer him, who leaves no means omitted that may assure his success.

Let things be duly weighed, Athenians! and deeply impressed upon your minds. Consider, that it is not at your option, whether to profess peace or no; for he hath now made a declaration of war, and hostilities are commenced. Spare no expenses, public or private: let a general ardour appear for taking arms: appoint abler commanders than you have hitherto chosen: for it must not be imagined, that the men who from a state of prosperity have reduced us to these difficulties, will again extricate us, and restore us to our former splendour: nor is it to be expected, that, if you continue thus supine, your cause will find other assertors. Think, how infamous it is, that you, whose ancestors were exposed to such incessant toils, and so great dangers, in the war with Lacedemon, should refuse to engage with resolution in defence of that rightful power which they transmitted to us! how shameful, that this Macedonian should have a soul so daring, that, to enlarge his empire, his whole body is covered with wounds; and that the Athenians, they whose hereditary character it is to yield to none, but to give law to all their adversaries, are now supine and enervated, insensible to the glory of their fathers, and regardless of the interests of their country!

That I may not detain you, my sentence is this: that we should instantly prepare for war, and call upon the other states of Greece to join in the common cause; not by words but by actions; for words, if not attended with actions, are of no force. Our professions particularly have always had the less weight, as we are confessedly superior to the rest of Greece, in prompt address and excellence of speaking.

CONCLUSION.

HAVING thus far traced the progress of Philip's attempts on Greece, it may be no improper conclusion to continue the account down to his final triumph over the liberty of that country.

We have seen the Athenians, at last, exerting themselves in a matter worthy of that renowned people. And Philip, now returning from his Scythian expedition, in which he had engaged, when foiled in his attempts on Perinthus and Byzantium, found himself considerably distressed and harassed by the hostilities of Athens. To extricate himself from these difficulties, he formed a bold and subtle project of entering Greece: and so laid his scheme, as to make the Athenians themselves the instruments of his designs.

By his intrigues he procured Æschines to be sent as their deputy to the council of Amphictyons. This was in reality of the highest consequence: for no sooner had the deputy taken his seat, but a question was moved, Whether the Locrians of Amphissa had not been guilty of sacrilege, in ploughing the fields of Cirrha, contiguous to the temple of Delphos? Sentiments were divided. Æschines proposed a view: this was decreed: and when the Amphictyons came to take it, the Locrians, jealous of their property, and no doubt inflamed by those who were in the secret of the whole design, fell on those venerable persons, and obliged them to consult their safety by flight. Such an outrage was judged to demand the severest punishment; and it was decreed that all Greece should join in inflicting it. But when the army came to a place of rendezvous, their appearance gave no great prospect of success. His agents and partisans then arose, and by their artful representations, prevailed upon the Amphictyons to declare Philip general of the Grecian forces, and to invite him to execute their decrees. As the event was expected, his army was ready. He marched into Greece: but instead of attacking the Locrians, he immediately seized Elatæa, a city of Phocis, of the utmost moment, as it awed Bœotia, and opened him a passage into Attica.

This step struck Greece with astonishment. Athens particularly received the news with inexpressible confusion. The people ran dismayed to an assembly, and called on their usual counsellors to give their opinion in this critical juncture. Demosthenes arose; and his eloquence was exerted to animate their drooping courage: by his advice ambassadors were sent through Greece, and particularly to Thebes, to engage the states to rise at once to oppose the Macedonian torrent before it bore down all. Demosthenes himself headed the embassy to the Thebans. He found a powerful antagonist in Python, Philip's agent: yet, in spite of his remonstrances, he so fired that people, that they at once forgot all the favours Philip had conferred on them, and joined against him with the most cordial zeal. The confederates met at Eleusis. The Pythian priestess uttered the most terrible predictions, and threatened them with the severest fate; but Demosthenes took care to prevent the effect of this, by treating her oracles with contempt, which, he declared, were dictated by Philip, and calculated to serve his interests.

This prince now saw all his arts defeated; and therefore resolved upon an engagement as his last resource. He advanced to Chero-næa, in the neighbourhood of which city the confederates were encamped, under the command of Chares and Lysicles, two Athenian generals, by no means worthy of commanding so illustrious an army. The next day, by sunrise, both armies were in the field. Alexander, then but nineteen years old, surrounded by a number of experienced officers, commanded the left wing of the Macedonians. He began the onset: and was bravely opposed by the Sacred Band of the Thebans. On the right Philip himself commanded, where the Athenians made their attack with such vigour as obliged his soldiers to give ground. The advantage was pursued with the most imprudent and intemperate heat. But while the Athenians were rushing on without any order, Philip bore down upon them with his phalanx, and obtained an easy, though a bloody victory. At the same time, and with a like effusion of blood, Alexander triumphed over the Thebans.

Thus were the confederates totally overthrown, and the liberty of Greece lost for ever.

THE

ORATIONS OF DEMOSTHENES.

On Occasions of Public Deliberation.

TO WHICH IS ADDED,

THE ORATION OF DINARCHUS AGAINST DEMOSTHENES.

PREFACE.

THE public Orations of Demosthenes here presented to the reader, are not indeed of the same interesting nature with those of the former part of this volume, but such as have been always deemed well worthy the regards of the learned. And if we may ever hope to gain an attention to the remains of this eloquent statesman, we must look for it in Britain, where a love of liberty possesses its inhabitants, and a freedom of debate (the natural consequence of a freedom of constitution) is held sacred and inviolable : where opposite opinions, accidental abuses and corruptions, various plans of policy, contentions for power, and many other causes, conspire to animate its counsellors, and call forth their abilities ; where a profusion of glittering ornament, gay flights of fancy, and figurative eloquence, do by no means form the character of national eloquence : but simplicity and severity of reasoning, force, and energy, eminently distinguish the speakers of every kind, from those of the neighbouring nations, and where, above all, a warm benevolence of heart, confessedly the glory of its citizens, may, at some times, engage their attention to the interests and concerns of a people, who experienced the vicissitudes of integrity and corruption, happiness and misfortune ; who were disgraced or renowned, just as their councils were weak or well directed.

The history of the wars, negotiations, government, and policy, of the conquests and defeats, of the progress and declension, of all ancient states, is universally allowed to be a study highly delightful and interesting to the ingenious mind. The harangues and counsels of their statesmen are no inconsiderable part of this history. Nor can it be deemed a useful or unaffecting occupation to inquire, what were the arguments used in a free assembly, on any occasions where the public interests were concerned ; what were the topics urged to awaken the indolence, or to check the violence of the people ; to elevate their hopes, or to alarm their apprehensions ; to correct their prejudices, and to reform their abuses : what schemes of policy were proposed, what measures suggested ; what artifices were used, what arguments urged by contending parties, to establish their power and interest : what motives were proposed to engage the community in war, or to inspire the people with pacific dispositions : to prompt them to form, or to dissolve alliances ; to extend their views to the interests and concerns of foreigners, or to confine their regards to their own security. These, I say, and such like, are by no means unworthy of attention : and these we find in a translation of an ancient orator, executed with any tolerable care and fidelity, however it may be discovered, by the learned reader, inferior to the illustrious original, in dignity of expression, and excellence of style and composition.

Or if we consider the remains of an ancient orator in a critical view, merely as the productions of art and genius, it can be no unworthy curiosity to endeavour at gaining a just, though faint idea of that excellence which, we are told, had such wonderful effects. The appearance of a great public speaker, and the power of his eloquence, are so feelingly described by Cicero, that we may be certain the piece was copied for himself, and from what he accounted his greatest glory. [1.] ' Give me the orator,' saith he, ' who can produce the following effects. When it is once known that he is to speak, let there be the utmost impatience to secure places in the court, which must be instantly crowded ; let all be hurry and eagerness ; the clerks and officers must fly up and down with an obliging

---

[1.] Volo hoc oratori contingat, ut cum auditum sit eum esse dicturum, locus in subselliis occupetur, compleatur tribunal; gratiosi scribæ sint in dando et cedendo loco, corona multiplex, judex erectus; cum surgit is qui dicturus sit, significetur a corona silentium; deinde crebræ assentationes, multæ admirationes; risus, cum velit; cum velit, fletus; ut qui hæc procul videat, etiamsi, quid agatur nesciat, placere tamen, et in scena esse Roscium intelligat. Hæc cui contingat, eum scito Attice dicere : ut de Pericle audivimus, ut de Hyperide, ut de Æschine; de ipso quidem Demosthene maxime. *Cic.* in *Brut.*

solicitude, to provide seats and accommodations for the assembly. The auditors must press forward in a crowded circle. Let the judge be roused to the utmost attention. When the speaker rises, the audience must command silence, all must be hushed, till some marks of approbation are extorted, and expressions of wonder break out at frequent intervals. If he would inspire them with mirth, the smile must be universal; if with sorrow, their tears must instantly flow. So that a person at a distance, though he does not know directly what piece is acting, must yet be witness of the powerful impression, and assured that some great favourite actor is on the stage. He that has such power, we may pronounce the truly complete speaker. As we have heard of Pericles, as of Hyperides, as of Æschines; but chiefly of Demosthenes himself.[1]

And if Demosthenes appeared with so great splendour in his judicial pleadings, his speeches in public deliberations seem to have been attended with circumstances still more honourable, and with proofs of his abilities still more forcible. He generally acted in scenes of turbulence and public confusion. The speakers of the opposite party had first laboured to prepossess the people against the sentiments he was to deliver: to this their own corrupted inclinations conspired, and vengeance was denounced against all that should dare to control them. In the midst of clamour and commotion the orator arises: his adversaries dread him, and endeavour to drown his remonstrances in tumult. By degrees he gains a patient audience. Opposition is checked, dismayed, and silenced. His countrymen hang on him as on some oracle, that denounces destruction on their vices and misconduct, and points out the only way to security. They feel their own weakness and unworthiness, they acknowledge the justice of his severity: they resign themselves to his direction, and rush enthusiastically forward to the dangerous field of glory which he points out to them. Such were generally the immediate impressions, though not always permanent and effectual.

At other times he appeared when a universal terror and dismay had seized the assembly; when the enemy seemed to be at their gates; when destruction appeared inevitable, and despair had buried the faculties of those speakers in a mournful silence, who in times of less danger were ever forward to take the lead. Then did their country (as Demosthenes himself describes the solemn scene) call on her sons, to aid and support her by their counsels in this affecting hour of distress. But in a case of extreme difficulty, who can dare to propose any measures whose event must be precarious, where ill success may be imputed to the first adviser, and be severely avenged as his crime? Neither the dangerous situation of affairs, nor the well-known injustice and capriciousness of his countrymen, could deter Demosthenes. He is known on such occasions to have arisen in the assembly, and, by his appearance only, to have inspired his countrymen with some confused expectation of relief. He has awakened them from their despair, and gradually calmed their apprehensions; he has dispelled the mist of terror, and diffused bright hopes and cheerful expectations through the assembly. Confidence and resolution, magnanimity and courage, indignation and martial rage, vigorous efforts and generous contempt of danger, have fully confessed the irresistible force and energy of the speaker.

Such effects were a full reward for the patient assiduity with which Demosthenes laboured to qualify himself for a public speaker and leader; not by weighing words, culling rhetorical flowers, and arranging periods; but by collecting a large treasure of political knowledge, with which his most early performances appear to be enriched; by learning and habituating himself to strict and solid reasoning, by studying the human heart, and the means of affecting it; by acquiring, from constant practice, a promptness which no difficulties could embarrass, an acuteness which no opposition, however subtle and unexpected, could disconcert; and a copiousness inexhaustible; prepared for all emergencies; ever flowing, and ever abundantly supplied from its rich and bountiful source.

'Eloquence,' saith an admired writer, [1.] 'must flow like a stream that is fed by an abundant spring, and not spout forth a little frothy stream, on some gaudy day, and remain dry for the rest of the year.' Such was the eloquence of all those illustrious ancients that history hath celebrated; and such, in every free state, must be the eloquence which can really bring advantage to the public, or honour to the possessor. The voice may be tuned to the most musical perfection: the action may be modelled to the utmost grace and propriety; expressions may be chosen, of energy, delicacy, and majesty; the period may be taught to flow with all the ease and eloquence of harmonious modulation: yet these are but inferior parts of genuine eloquence; by no means the first and principal, much less the sole objects of regard. The weapon of the orator should be bright and glittering indeed; but this should arise from the keenness of its edge: it should be managed with grace; but with such a grace as is an indication of consummate skill and strength.

We are told of a Grecian general, who, when he travelled, and viewed the country round him, revolved in his mind how an army might be there drawn up to the greatest advantage; how he could best defend himself, if attacked from such a quarter; how advance with greatest security; how retreat with least danger. Something similar to this should be the practice and study of a public speaker. And thus was Demosthenes, for the most part, employed, in his days of retirement and severe application. It is indeed insinuated by his enemy, [2.] that he was more solicitous about rounding a period,

---

[1.] Lord Bolingbroke, Spirit of Patriotism.

[2.] Æschines in Ctesiph.

than preserving his country. But this is an object fitted rather to the minute regards of such a speaker as the noble author, quoted above, describes with so just a contempt; whose whole abilities consist in providing a slender fund for some particular occasion, when perhaps, a weak or wicked cause is to be graced and ornamented; who lays on his thin covering, with the utmost care and most scrupulous nicety: which dazzles for a moment, till the first blast of true forcible eloquence puffs away the flimsy produce of his labours, and leaves all beneath in its native condition of deformity and shame.

But to return from this digression. Ancient eloquence in general, and that of Demosthenes in particular, we are told, had wonderful effects. The impression was strong and violent; the consequences, sometimes, of the utmost moment. But by reading the orator in a modern language, how fully and justly soever it might be possible to express the genius and general spirit of the original, or by consulting the original itself, we are always affected with the like impressions; or, can we always trace the artifice, or feel the force, which produced effects so magnificently described? By no means! And this is partly to be imputed to the fault of the reader, partly to a difference of circumstances:

He who applies himself to the study of Demosthenes, after a long intercourse with writers of a different character; who hath been accustomed to pointed periods, phrases of affected delicacy, fanciful allusions, figures and images calculated to dazzle and delight the eye, rather then illuminate, and cast the full glory of evidence round simple truth; he, I say, must throw by the author in disgust, or labour through him in a cold and lifeless progress, which must serve but to fatigue and disappoint him. He whose taste is ever so justly formed to relish simplicity and true manly grace, must yet read the orator to great disadvantage, if entirely a stranger to the spirit of free uncontrolled debate. Liberty (if we may so speak) hath its own ideas and its own language, whose force cannot always be felt, or even its meaning rightly and throughly conceived by strangers.

Tourreil, the French interpreter of Demosthenes, and Lucchesini, the Italian commentator, seem to have been instances of what is here advanced. The first appears to have had no just taste for the simplicity of modest Attic elegance. He dressed out his author in all that finery, to which he annexed the notions of grace and beauty: and presented him to his countrymen turgid and inflated, encumbered and disgraced by adventitious ornaments. The latter lived and wrote in a country where the voice of liberty is but seldom and faintly heard; where political transactions are of a confined nature, and not generally discussed in bold and spirited debate: where parties are seldom formed, public dissensions seldom raised; no grand interests boldly asserted: no political measures freely

censured. And the effect seems to have been this: the commentator appears shocked at the free, lively, and animated exertions of Demosthenes; he endeavours to reduce him within more sober bounds: and is sometimes, perhaps misled by trying his expressions by the rules of cold precision. Passages might be produced to warrant these observations; but I shall content myself with just hinting at one, of which notice has been taken in this volume, [1.] and which seems to prove what may be deemed the boldest assertion, that Demosthenes cannot be, always, even understood, but in a country of liberty. 'I am sensible,' saith the orator, 'that the Persian is the common enemy of the Greeks.' To the Italian, this assertion was strange and unaccountable, at a time when the two nations were at peace, and when treaties actually subsisted between them. History was ransacked and tortured for some plausible pretence or grounds for this extraordinary declaration. But in Britain such pains were needless: there, no idea is more familiar than that of a natural and hereditary enemy.

The reader's taste, however, may be strictly just: he may be well acquainted with the sentiments and language of liberty; he may be duly instructed in the history of an ancient people; he may suffer their affairs and interests to make a lively and forcible impression on his mind: yet still, though well prepared for the perusal of an orator, he cannot always perceive his whole force and artifice; as at this distance of time, facts may appear trivial, and arguments inconclusive, which fired every imagination, and silenced all opposition, in the assembly to which they were originally addressed. We know, in general, the genius, character, and temper of a people, whom the orator may have endeavoured to effect: we can, therefore, in general, conceive and must acknowledge his force and delicacy, the propriety and energy of his representations: they must please and surprise us, and sometimes affect and warm us; and such impressions sufficiently reward our attention. But, in particular passages, the traces of excellence must be faint, or, perhaps, totally effaced: where the art and force of the speaker consist in a judicious attention to particular circumstances of times, occasions, conjunctures of affairs, and dispositions of the auditors. A modern reader is struck with some particular argument or topic; he is, perhaps, disappointed to find, that it is not extended and enlarged on. But it is possible, nay very likely, that the disposition of those who heard it, required but a single hint, and that a minute detail would have tired and offended. We read that such a particular stroke of eloquence had wonderful effects; that such a passage raised a general acclamation, affected, transported, or terrified; we examine this passage by the general rules of criticism, and we pronounce it inadequate to the wonderful effects ascribed to it. But here we seem to

[.1] See Oration on the Classes.

confine our regards to our own sentiments, our own passions, and our own situations: we argue from our own feelings to those of other persons, in circumstances totally different. Cicero, by introducing the mention of the battle of Pharsalia, and the danger which Cæsar there encountered, (in a manner artful and lively indeed, but such as by no means indicates a surprising or singular elevation of genius,) is said to have made this hero turn pale and tremble. And why should we doubt of the reality of these effects? We can read of this battle of Pharsalia without emotion; but it was a more important object to a Roman; still more affecting to the soldier who fought in that famous field: but to the general who there gained the victory, and by this victory rescued himself from destruction, and obtained the sovereignty of the world, what object can be conceived more capable of alarming his passions, and filling his mind with the most turbulent emotions?

But it may be said, that however true the general position, yet the instance brought to illustrate it, is but unhappily chosen: for that, in this case, Cæsar's emotion was but pretended. [1.] He was himself an accomplished orator, and knew all the windings of the art—he courted Cicero's friendship, he saw where his vanity and his weakness lay; with perfect address, therefore, he played back the orator's art upon himself; his concern was feigned.—With deference to the author here quoted, I must declare that I cannot think this suggestion well warranted; no more than I can suppose that Octavia, the sister of Augustus, meant to pay a compliment to the poet, and but pretended concern, when she appeared to faint at the recital of the famous passage in the sixth Eneid:

'Heu miserande puer! Si qua fata aspera rumpas,
Tu Marcellus, Eris.'

If Cæsar was too well acquainted with the arts of eloquence, and of consequence, too well armed against them, to receive any real impression from the efforts of Cicero; this orator, who was equally well acquainted with those arts, the proper occasions of exerting them, and the effects to be expected from them, could not well be deceived by any unnatural semblance of emotion. I say unnatural semblance; because it is supposed, that such emotion, in such a case, is contrary to reason and the nature of things: and therefore Cicero, amidst all his vanity,

must have seen and despised the injudicious artifice.

The truth seems to be, that, in minds the most enlightened, the passions frequently retain a considerable degree of strength; and when kindled by some touch of the orator's address, the combustion is too sudden, as well as too violent, to be effectually suppressed by reason. At least the ancients seem persuaded of this; for whatever may be said of eloquence being made for the multitude and the forum, [2.] yet when they addressed themselves, not to the populace, but to select and refined judges, they were by no means (as Quintilian expresses it) quadam eloquentiæ frugalitate contenti, ac manum semper intra pallium continentes. On the contrary, some of the noblest and boldest efforts of art were exerted, some of the sublimest flights of genius indulged, on such occasions. To be convinced of this, we need but turn to any of the judicial pleadings of Cicero. Take the beautiful passage, in an oration against Verres, quoted by Mr. Hume, in his elegant Essay on Eloquence; or read the following passage in the oration for Milo, [3.] 'On you, ye Albanian mounts and groves, on you I call. Bear witness for me, ye ruined altars of Alba (equal in sanctity to the Roman shrines,) destroyed, and buried under the profane edifices raised by his outrageous sacrilege. Your influence, your power it was which then prevailed. Your divinity, then, triumphed, and completed its vengeance on all his profanations. And thou, O holy Jove, didst then at length look down from thy mount: then didst thou execute thy justice on the wretch, whose wickedness and abandoned impurity had so often polluted thy lakes, thy groves, thy boundaries. To thee, to thee, and in thy presence, did he pay the late, but justly merited punishment.'—That the circumstances of the trial contributed to animate the orator's style, is certain, as he himself informs us. [4.] Yet, amidst all this enthusiasm, the consummate master must have had a due regard to propriety. He could not have forgotten that he addressed himself immediately to a few selected judges; and if such elevated strains of eloquence sometimes failed of success in select assemblies, and before judges of penetration and refinement, the same may be observed of sober, solid, and just argument. Modern times are acquainted with refined assemblies in which affairs of highest moment are commonly discussed: and if the spirited and impassioned orator

---

[1.] See Brown's Essay on Ridicule.
[2.] Cicero in Brut.
[3.] Vos enim jam Albani tumuli atque luci, vos inquam imploro a'que obtestor, vosque Albanorum obrutæ aræ, sacrorum populi Romani sociæ et æquales, quas ille præceps amentia, cæcis prostratisque sanctissimis lucis, substructionum insania molibus oppresserat; vestræ tum aræ, vestiæ religiones vigue-

runt, vestra vis valuit, quam ille omni scelere polluerat; tuque ex tuo edito monte Latiari, sancte Jupiter, cujus ille lacus, nemora, finesque sæpe omni nefario stupro, et scelere maculara, aliquando ad eum puniendum oculos aperuisti; vobis illæ, vobis, vestro in conspectu sero sed justæ tamen, et debitæ pœnæ solutæ sunt.
[4.] In Brut.

doth not, on all occasions, obtain a majority in such assemblies, they do not always impute it to the superior strength of reason, that fortifies his hearers against the assaults of eloquence.

In poetry the impression made upon the hearer is so far from being lessened or defeated by his refinement and understanding, that it is really heightened and increased in proportion to the accuracy of his judgment and the delicacy of his sentiments. And although the man of sense, who, in this case, resigns himself up to the pleasing delusion, guards and arms himself against all artifice in that of eloquence, it might not be difficult to show how this vigilance is sometimes defeated and eluded. But the points which I am at present concerned to establish, are no more than these : That the wonderful effects ascribed to ancient eloquence are not mistaken or exaggerated : That its force was really extraordinary, and its impressions, in proportion, violent ; but that the reader who applies himself to study the remains of an ancient orator, and of Demosthenes in particular, may sometimes be disappointed in his sanguine expectations of delight, if he hath been long accustomed to compositions of less intrinsic worth, though of more glittering ornament ; if he is in general unused to the energy of a free debate ; if he is unacquainted with the history and character of the people to whom the orator addressed himself ; or if he precipitately judges of the real force and efficacy of his eloquence from his own sentiments and feelings, without making the necessary allowance for a difference of times, circumstances, passions, and dispositions.

He who will not acknowledge that some particular traces of that exquisite skill which our orator possessed, are now become faint and obscure, pays him a veneration rather too implicit. And he who does not still perceive, and feel, his rapid harmony exactly adjusted to the sense ; his vehement reasoning without any appearance of art ; his disdain, anger, boldness, freedom, involved in a continued stream of argument, [1.] may justly suspect his own deficiency in point of taste : nor is it any indication of a superior strength of reason, if he does not sometimes accompany the orator in these impetuous passions and exalted sentiments which animate his compositions.

It is a common observation, how much an orator is assisted by the charms of action or pronunciation, which Demosthenes is said to have regarded as the chief part, or rather the whole, of his art ; and, how much the loss of these must diminish his lustre. Yet there are other advantages which such a speaker derives from subjecting his works to a private review, to a strict, dispassionate, and reiterated study. The justness of his reasoning, the soundness of his policy, the worth and elevation of his sentiments, (and

these are the really valuable parts of an orator, are thus brought to a new and severe trial : and if, on such a trial, these excellencies preserve their weight and lustre, this is an additional proof that they are real and intrinsic. What Longinus observes of the sublime, is equally applicable to all the excellencies of an orator ; that, if they are really genuine, we must form the higher ideas of them, the more frequently and attentively they are considered ; and that the true and indisputable proof of a writer's value arises from the consenting approbation of all ages, professions, and inclinations. This last and final sanction our author's merit hath received from private examination, though, at this time, but a part of his merit can thus appear. And hence, again, we may form a judgment of the force and influence of his living eloquence. If he still commands our approbation, and even warms our hearts, how must the Rhodians have been affected when Æschines read his celebrated performance to that people ! And if they were strongly affected, how must the speaker himself have shaken and transported the souls of his hearers, in the Athenian assembly !

. It may be said, that the excellence of this author in the original, is a point too plain to require proof or illustration ; that it is universally acknowledged, and has been the subject of repeated praise ; but that this consummate excellence of the original necessarily inspires a prejudice against all attempts to copy it in another language ; that such attempts are presumptuous ; the learned despise them, others are deceived by them, and made to think with less honour of the great author, than his own genuine undisguised merit must ever obtain.

I could wish that this objection could be easily eluded, and that I could persuade myself that the present work did not enforce and confirm it. However, something I presume to say, in apology for such attempts, and for the manner in which they are executed.

It hath been already observed, that the sentiments and arguments of an ancient orator may be conveyed to the reader in a translation executed with tolerable care and fidelity. To this we may add the manner and order in which he arranges his thoughts ; no inconsiderable part of his address and artifice. And surely the attention of the reader unskilled in ancient languages, is rather liberally rewarded by these advantages ; although the learned may despise the inglorious toil of the translator, whose composition disgraces his noble original. Yet, even in this point, should our attempts be judged with some degree of candour and indulgence. An ancient language, even were it not superior to our own, must ever be read with favourable prejudice. Antiquity renders it respectable and venerable, its sounds and phrases are not debased by common and familiar use, but preserve their dignity in a stately and solemn retirement.

[1.] See Hume's Essay on Eloquence.

11 †

Longinus speaks of some vulgar phrases to be found in Demosthenes; but all such now lie concealed: and, unless the image conveyed be low, nothing can appear in the language humbled or debased; all flows on in one equal course of decency, grandeur, and dignity. But this is not the case in our own language. Familiarity tempts us to regard it with less reverence. "Its phrases and expressions are in constant use; and what we hear and pronounce every day, cannot easily endure a comparison with a language to whose very name we have been long taught to annex the ideas of grandeur and excellence. If in our composition we adhere scrupulously to the simple and natural form, the pomp and dignity of the original may seem to be lost and degraded. In order to avoid this extreme, we sometimes recur to a grave and laboured style, transpositions unnatural, and periods distorted; an unpardonably awkward substitute to ease and graceful majesty. And scarcely can we steer our course so happily, but that we must be in danger of touching, or appearing to touch, on one or other of these dangerous extremes.

But our difficulties appear stronger, and our claim to indulgence more just, when the real excellence of the ancient languages is considered. The Greek, in particular, is superior even to that of the Romans in point of sweetness, delicacy, and copiousness. This is the judgment of the great Roman critic. [1.] And with him an English translator still may say, [2.] 'He that expects from us the grace and delicacy of the Attic style, must give us the same sweetness, and an equal copiousness of language.' To acknowledge this inferiority in our own language, is not to derogate from its real merit. It is a weapon keen and forcible, if carefully preserved, and wielded with due skill. But he who should attempt to follow the great writers of antiquity in every maze and winding, through which their advantages enabled them, and their circumstances obliged them, to direct their course; he who should labour through all the straits of a minute and scrupulous imitation, to express their words, and dispose of their periods, exactly in the same form and order, must be equally inattentive to the genius of the language from which he copies, and to that of his own: equally inattentive to the excellences of this, and to its comparative defects. At least this is a state of subjection to which the present translator thought it by no means necessary to stoop, and if in this he should be judged to have taken too great a liberty, he flies for shelter to the authority of Quintilian, [3.] who compares the copy formed from the outward

traces and aspect of the original, to those airy phantoms which were supposed by Epicurus to issue from all bodies. If it may be thought a violation of the Attic simplicity, that he hath sometimes ventured on an epithet, a metaphor, or some other figurative form of speech, to express what is natural and unadorned in the original, let it be remembered, that in this he confines himself within much stricter bounds than the same great critic prescribes to those who translated from the Greek into Latin. In such works he tells us, 'Figuras—quibus maxime ornatur oratio, multas ac varias excogitandi etiam necessitas quædam est: quia plerumque a Græcis Romana dissentiunt. lib. x. cap. 5.' And in imitations of every kind in a language inferior to that of the original, in order to supply the defect, his rule is this: 'Oratio translationum nitore illuminanda,' lib. xii. cap. 10.

To exhibit Demosthenes such as he would have appeared in an English assembly similar to that of Athens, should certainly be the scope of his translator. Though he may be unfortunate in his aim, a voluntary deviation would be unpardonable. And an English Demosthenes would undoubtedly attend to the genius of his language. To express his dignity and majesty, he would not assume a constrained, uncouth, and perplexed air. He would have confined himself within the modest bounds of Atticism, but of English Atticism, (if the expression may be allowed.) He would have adopted a greater share of ornament, because a greater share of ornament would not be inconsistent with neatness, decent elegance, and manly dignity.

If it be still observed, that our language has been corrupted, and the cause of learning disgraced by translation, it might be easy to show in what cases this has been, and must be, the consequence: and that an attempt to copy the excellences of ancient writers of renown, does not necessarily fall under this censure. Or if the meanness and insignificance of the employment should be urged, a translator might observe, in the fulness of his vanity, that the great Roman orator himself thought it not beneath his dignity to publish his translations from Plato, Xenophon, and Demosthenes. But as to the utility of this employment, it need not be pointed out or defended, to the learned. As to its dignity, the translator is not at all solicitous to maintain it. He is ready to acknowledge, that the pittance of reputation to be acquired in this way is but trifling and insignificant, if he is so fortunate as to meet with that candour and indulgence which have hitherto favoured his attempts.

[1.] Quintil. Inst. Orat. lib. xii. cap. 10.
[2.] Quare qui a Latinis exigit illam gratiam sermonis Attici, det mihi in loquendo eandem jucunditatem, et parem copiam.
[3.] Nec—sufficiat imaginem virtutis effingere, et solam ut sic dicerem cutem vel potius

illas Epicuri figuras quas e summis corporibus dicit effluere. Hoc autem illis accidit qui non introspectis penitus virtutibus, ad primum se velut aspectium orationis aptarunt, et cum iis felicissime cessit imitatio verbis atque numeris sunt non multum differentes. lib. x. cap. 2.

THE ORATION ON THE CLASSES:

PRONOUNCED IN THE ARCHONSHIP OF DIOTIMUS, THE THIRD YEAR OF THE HUNDRED AND SIXTH OLYMPIAD.

INTRODUCTION.

THE title of this oration is taken from one particular part of it, in which the speaker enlarges on the method of dividing the citizens into Σνμμορίαι, or Classes, in order to raise the supplies, and to answer the exigencies of the state. The design of it was, to allay an extravagant ferment which had been raised at Athens, and to recommend caution and circumspection at a time when danger was apprehended. Artaxerxes Ochus, king of Persia, had been for some time employed in making preparations for war. These were represented to the Athenians as the effect of a design formed against Greece, and against their states in particular. They were conscious of having given this prince sufficient umbrage, by the assistance which their general, Chares, had afforded to some of his rebellious subjects: they were entirely possessed by the notions of their own importance, and therefore readily listened to their suggestions, who endeavoured to persuade them that some important blow was meditated against their dominions. An assembly of the people was convened: and the general temper both of the speakers and the auditors are distinctly marked out in several passages of the oration. The bare mention of a war with Persia, at once recalled to their minds the glorious days of their ancestors, and the great actions of Athens and her generals against the barbarians. These were now displayed with all the address and force of eloquence, and the people urged to imitate the bright example of antiquity; to rise up in arms against the Persian, and to send their ambassadors through Greece, to summon all the states to unite with Athens against the common enemy. To flatter the national vanity of their countrymen, was an expedient which many speakers had found effectual for establishing their power and credit in the assembly. And possibly some might have spoken, with a corrupt design of diverting the attention of their countrymen from those contests and dangers in which they were more immediately concerned. But however this may be, the impropriety of those bold and precipitate measures which they recommended, is urged with the utmost force in the following oration; in which we shall find the speaker moderating the unseasonable zeal of his countrymen, without absolutely shocking their prejudices. Demosthenes is most generally known as an orator, by the fire and energy with which he rouses his countrymen to arms. But the delicacy of address and artifice, which he displays in this and many of the following orations, is a part of his character no less worthy of attention. A youth of twenty-eight years, thoroughly acquainted with the constitution, interests, and connexions of his country, rising for the first time in a debate on public affairs, opposing himself with boldness and resolution, and at the same time with the utmost art and insinuation, to the general bent of the assembly; calming the turbulence of his countrymen, and presenting their true interests to their view, in the strongest and most striking colours; is an object truly pleasing and affecting.

THE

ORATION ON THE CLASSES. [1.]

Diotimo, Archon.—Olympiad. 106. *An.* 3.

THE men who thus dwell upon the praises of your ancestors, seem to me, ye men of Athens! to have chosen a subject fitted rather

---

[1.] That this oration was pronounced in the third year of the hundred and sixth Olympiad, we are assured by Dionysius, (in Epist. ad Ammæum,) and that Demosthenes was at this time in his twenty-eighth year. Plutarch, indeed, (if he be the author of the 'Lives of the Ten Orators,') places his nativity in the fourth year of the ninety-eighth Olympiad. But, not to mention the inaccuracies in this tract, the orator himself declares, in his oration against Midias, that he was then in his thirty-second year. This oration was spoken in the archonship of Callimachus, that is (according to Diodorus) in the fourth year of the hundred and seventh Olympiad. And therefore, by calculating from hence, the reader will find the authority of Dionysius, as to the time of our orator's birth, clearly and fully confirmed.

How then came it to pass, that he was allowed to speak on public affairs before the age of thirty years? for in the Attic laws respecting public speakers, it is expressly enacted, Μη εισελθείν τινα ειπείν μηπω τριακοντα ετη γεγονοτα. 'Let no man enter the assembly to speak, who hath not yet attained to the age of thirty.' The solution of this difficulty by Lucchesini seems solid and satisfactory. I know, saith he, there are some who assert, that this, as well as some other laws of Athens, fell into disuse; but such a method of solving the difficulties of antiquity, without any manner of proof or authority, is unsafe and fallacious. Besides, the assertion is contradicted by Æschines, who, in his oration against Timarchus, declares, That not only this, but other severer laws, relative to public speakers, were in full

to gratify the assembly, than to do the due honour to those on whom they lavish their applause. As they attempt to speak of actions which no words can worthily describe, the illustrious subject adorns their speech, and gives them the praise of eloquence; while their hearers are made to think of the virtues of those heroes with much less elevation than these virtues of themselves inspire. To me, time itself seems to be the noblest witness to their glory. A series of so many years hath now passed over, and still no men have yet appeared, whose actions could surpass those patterns of perfection. It shall be my part therefore, solely to endeavour to point out the means which may enable you most effectually to prepare for war. For, in fact, were all our

speakers to proceed in a pompous display of their abilities, such parade and ostentation could not possibly prove of the least advantage to the public: but if any man whatever will appear, and can explain to your full satisfaction what kind of armament, how great, and how support, may serve the present exigencies of the state, then all these alarms must instantly be dispelled. This I shall endeavour to the utmost of my abilities, having first briefly declared my opinion of our situation with respect to the King.

I do regard the King as the common enemy of all the Greeks. [1.] But I cannot, for that reason, advise, that we should be the only people to undertake a war against him: for I do not find the Greeks [2.] themselves united

---

force. In my opinion, the difficulty should rather be explained in this manner: Among the other magistrates who were chosen every year at Athens, there were ten orators appointed by lot, whose business it was to deliver their opinions in the assemblies on all affairs that concerned the state; and for which they received the gratuity of a drachma [seven pence three farthings] from the treasury. To these only must that law of Athens, which determines the age of orators, be construed to extend. As it was their duty to deliver their opinions in the senate, they ought of course to be of the senatorial age: but no person could be admitted to the senate, who had not completed his thirtieth year. But as for the law of Solon, it excludes no citizen whatsoever from the liberty of speaking, who might attend the assembly; nor had the seniors any other privilege than that of speaking first. The law runs thus : ' Let the senior first propose such measures as he thinks most expedient for the republic, and after him such other citizens as choose it, according to the order of their age.' Æschines cites it in the same words against Ctesiphon. No mention is here made of thirty years. Such of the citizens as were in their twentieth year might attend the assembly, and had their names enrolled. That they had a share in the administration, and might speak in public at this age, is confirmed by Lucian, in his Jupiter Tragœdus, where Momus thus addresses Apollo: ' You are now become a legal speaker, having long since left the class of young men, and enrolled your name in the books of the Duodecemviri.' Now, that the citizens were considered as having arrived at the age of manhood in their eighteenth year, we learn from Demosthenes in his oration against Aphobus. For his father died when he was but seven years old, and he remained for ten years under the care of his guardian; at which time, being released from his hands, he pleaded his own cause against him. Now his father had given directions that he should be under a guardian till he had arrived at the age of manhood: and this he did, as soon as he had reached his eighteenth year; all which is collected from his own words. These circumstances considered, it is very easy to suppose

that Demosthenes spoke in public, as he really did, in his eight-and-twentieth year. Nor does any manner of difficulty arise from what he says himself in his oration for the Crown : ' When the Phocian war was raised, &c., for I had then no hand in the administration :' that war being begun in the second year of the hundred and sixth Olympiad, under the archonship of Callistratus, at a time when our orator was only in the twenty-seventh year of his age.

[1.] The commentators who endeavour to account for this assertion, by considering the present state of Greece, or any late transactions with Persia, seem to examine the orator too rigidly, and with too much coldness and abstraction. It is by no means the result of any recent events. It had been the language of Greece for ages; the language of poets, historians, and orators. Even in those times of corruption, the popular leaders seldom ventured to use any other, particularly in an assembly where national vanity was so predominant as in that of Athens. Whatever treaties had been made with the king of Persia, however peace might have now subsisted between him and the Greeks, still he was their natural enemy.

[2.] The sacred war now raged in Greece. The Phocians, Lacedemonians, and Athenians, were engaged on one side; the Bœotians, Thessalians, Locrians, and some other inferior states, on the other : each party was harassed and exhausted by the war. The Phocians had reason to complain of the Athenians, who proved a useless and inactive ally. Whatever connexions had lately subsisted between Athens and Sparta, this latter state still hated its ancient rival, and was impatient to recover its former splendour and power. A prospect of assistance from Persia must have at once determined the Lacedemonians to detach themselves from the confederacy, and to act against the Athenians; particularly if any plausible pretence could be alleged for uniting with the Persian. The Phocians, who were not always influenced by the most religious engagements, might fairly be suspected of making no scruple to accept effectual assistance from the Great King, and at once renouncing their alliance to each other in sincere affection : nay, some among them seem to have more confidence in him than in certain of their own body. In such circumstances, I account it of the utmost moment that we should be strictly attentive to the origin of this war, that it may be free from every imputation of injustice. Let our armament be carried on with vigour; but let us carefully adhere to the principles of equity. For in my opinion, Athenians! the states of Greece (if it be once evident and incontestable that the king makes attempts against them) will instantly unite, and express the most ardent gratitude to those who arose before them, who, with them, still stand faithfully and bravely to repel these attempts. But while this is yet uncertain, should you begin hostilities, I fear we may be obliged to fight against an enemy reinforced by those very men for whose interests we were so forward to express our zeal. Yes! he will suspend his designs, (if he hath really designs against the Greeks;) his gold will be dispersed liberally amongst them; his promises of friendship will be lavished upon them: while they, distressed in their private wars, and attentive only to support them, will disregard the general welfare of the nation.

Into such confusion, into such weak measures, let us not precipitate the state. With respect to the king, you cannot pursue the same counsels with some others of the Greeks. Of these, many might, without the charge of inconsistency, neglect the rest of Greece, while engaged in the pursuit of private interest. But of you it would be unworthy, even though directly injured, to inflict so severe a punishment on the guilty, as to abandon them to the power of the barbarian.

Thus are we circumstanced: and let us then be careful that we do not engage in this war upon unequal terms; that he whom we suppose to entertain designs against the Greeks, may not recommend himself to their confidence, so as to be deemed their friend. And how shall these things be effected? By giving public proof that the forces of this state are well appointed, and complete for action;

but that in this our procedure we are determined to adhere inviolably to justice.

Let the bold and hazardous, who are vehement in urging you to war, attend to this. It is not difficult when an assembly is convened, to acquire the reputation of courage: no; nor, when dangers are actually impending, to speak with an impassioned boldness. But it is truly difficult, and it is our duty, in the time of danger, to support the character of superior bravery; in our councils, to display the same superiority of wisdom.

I, on my part, ye men of Athens! think that a war with the king may prove dangerous; in a battle, the consequence of such a war, I see no danger. And why? Because wars of every kind require many advantages, of naval force, of money, and of places. Here he is superior to the state. In a battle, nothing is so necessary to ensure success as valiant troops; and of these, we and our confederates can boast the greater number. For this reason, I earnestly recommend to you, by no means to be the first to enter on a war: but for an engagement, I think you should be effectually prepared. Were there one method of preparing to oppose barbarians, and another for engaging with Greeks, then we might expect, with reason, that any hostile intentions against the Persian must be at once discovered. But as in every armament the manner is the same, the general provisions equally the same, whether our enemies are to be attacked, or our allies to be protected, and our rights defended; why, when we have avowed enemies, [1.] should we seek for others? Shall we not prepare against the one, and be ready to oppose the other, should he attempt to injure us?——Call now upon the Greeks to unite with you.—But suppose ye should not readily concur with them in all their measures, (as some are by no means favourably inclined to this state,) can it be imagined that they will obey your summons?——'Certainly: for we shall convince them that the king forms designs against their interests, which they do not foresee.'—Ye powers! is it possible, that you can be thus persuaded? Yes;

---

with the Athenians. The Italian commentator supposes, that the orator expresses his apprehensions only of the Lacedemonians, and that they are particularly pointed out, as the men who have more confidence in the Persian than in their own brethren; and who would sacrifice every consideration to the support of their wars with the Greeks. The Phocians, he observes, could not possibly unite with the Persians, on account of the former injuries they had received from them, as well as of their invariable union with Athens. But a view of the politics of Greece, and indeed of the politics of all ages and nations, may convince us, that too much stress is not to be laid on such an argument. Nor was there less to fear from the confederates on the other side. They fought with an inveterate and implacable rancour; and all their efforts were scarcely sufficient to support the quarrel. Their strength was continually wasting, and their treasures were quite exhausted; the most favourable occasion for the Great King to gain them to his purposes. The speaker indeed declares, in another part of this oration, that the Thebans would not concur with the Persian in any design confessedly formed against the nation of Greece. Yet still they might, in their present circumstances, and in a cause which they affected to consider as the cause of the nation, accept of his assistance. They actually did accept of it in the course of this war.

[1.] The Bœotians, Thessalians, &c. were the avowed enemies of Athens, in consequence of the attachment of this state to Phocis; and the king of Macedon, by his invasions of their settlements in Thrace, and other acts of hostility.

I know you are. But whatever apprehensions you may raise, they must influence these Greeks less forcibly than their disputes with you and with each other; and therefore the remonstrances of your ambassadors will but appear like the tales of idle wanderers. [1.] If on the other hand ye pursue the measures now proposed, there is not a single state of Greece that will hesitate a moment to come in, and to solicit your alliance, when they see our thousand horse, [2.] our infantry as numerous as could be wished, our three hundred ships; an armament which they must regard as their surest refuge and defence. Should you apply for their assistance, you must appear as suppliants: should they refuse it, you incur the shame of a repulse. But if, while your forces are completed, you suspend your operations, the protection you then grant to them must appear as the consequence of their request: and, be assured, they will all fly to you for this protection.

With these and the like reflections deeply impressed upon my mind, I have not laboured to prepare a bold, vain, tedious harangue. No, my fellow-citizens! our preparations have been the sole object of my thoughts, and the manner of conducting them with effect and expedition. Grant me your attention; and if my sentiments be approved, confirm them by your voices. *It is then the first and most important part of preparation, to possess your minds with due resolution; so that every citizen, when called to action, may exert himself with alacrity and zeal. You know that in every instance, where, having first resolved on your designs in concert, every single member deemed it incumbent on him to labour vigorously in the execution, you have never once proved unsuccessful. But whenever we have first decreed, and then each man hath turned his eyes on others, fondly imagining that he himself need not act, that his neighbour would do all; our designs have never once been executed.

With these sentiments, and these vigorous resolutions, I recommend that you should proceed to the appointment of your twelve hundred; and raise them to two thousand, by a farther addition of eight hundred. Thus, when all necessary deductions are made, of those who by their condition [3.] are excused from contributing, or by any circumstances are unable to contribute, still the original number of twelve hundred will remain complete. These I would have formed into twenty classes, each consisting of sixty citizens, agreeably to the

---

[1.] In the original οὐδὶν οὖν ἀλλ' ἢ ΡΑΨΩΙ-ΔΗΣΟΥΣΙΝ οἱ πρίσβεις περιϊόντες. It was urged by the speakers on the other side, that ambassadors should be sent through Greece, to represent the dangerous designs of the Persian, and to exhort the several states to suspend their private animosities, and to unite with the Athenians against the common enemy. The orator, who is endeavouring to represent the useless and inoffectual nature of such a measure, compares these ambassadors to the ancient rhapsodists, or bards, whose lives were spent in travelling, and amusing their entertainers with songs and poems. And this similitude seems to arise not only from their repeating the same declarations, but from the circumstance of going from city to city, and exciting curiosity by their speeches, without any other effect.

[2.] At first sight it may appear extraordinary that the orator should speak in high terms of such a body as one thousand horse. But we must consider that Attica was a mountainous country, and therefore unfit for breeding horses. In the infancy of the state, when Athens was governed by kings, their cavalry amounted to no more than ninety-six, each ναυκράρια, or twelfth part of a tribe, furnishing two. But the number of such divisions was then but forty-eight, as the tribes were originally but four. This small body was at first an object of derision to the Persians, at Marathon; but afterward proved formidable and dangerous. After the defeat of the Persians, the city began to increase in power, and was enabled to raise a body of three hundred horse; which, in the time of the Peloponnesian war, was augmented to twelve hundred, (as we learn from Thucyd. B. II. and Æschines Παραπ.) This was the greatest body of cavalry the Athenians ever possessed, which seems, by the distresses of the state, to have been reduced to a thousand in the time of Demosthenes, as he mentions no greater number, though it was his business rather to magnify their force in this passage, than to extenuate it. The Equestrian Order was a rank of dignity at Athens, as among the Romans. But in later times the citizens were allowed to keep this rank, and to substitute others to serve in their stead. Lucchesini.

[3.] Those who by their condition, &c.] These are particularly specified in the original, ἐπικλήρων, 'maiden heiresses;' ὀρφανῶν, 'orphans of the other sex;' κληρουχικῶν, 'men appointed to form a colony;' and κοινωνικων, 'men incorporated into certain societies, which were exempted from contributing.' From whence it seems evident, that the duty and honour of composing the twelve hundred, who were to supply the exigencies of the state, must have been annexed to certain families; and continued to them, when time and various circumstances might have produced alterations of fortune in many. The inconveniences which arose from hence were partly removed by the ἀντιδόσεις. or exchanges of fortunes, (of which, see note on Phil. I. p. 17.) and by allowing exemptions to persons in certain circumstances; yet both these expedients must have occasioned delays, and retarded the business of the public. Hence the orator recommends the appointment of the additional eight hundred.

present constitution. And it is my opinion, that of these classes each should be divided into five parts, consisting of twelve persons; ever attending to a just and equal distribution of the richer with the poorer. Thus should our citizens be arranged :—the reason will appear when the whole scheme of the regulation hath been explained.

But our ships; how are they to be appointed? Let their whole number be fixed to three hundred, divided, by fifteenth parts into twenty portions. Of the first hundred, let five [1.] such parts; of the second hundred, five parts; and of the third hundred five, be appointed to each class. Thus shall a fifteenth of the whole be allotted to every class: three ships to each subdivision.

When these establishments are made, I propose, [2.] as the revenue arising from our lands amounts to six thousand talents, that in order to have our funds duly regulated, this sum may be divided into a hundred parts of sixty talents each: that five of these parts may be assigned to each of the twenty great classes; which may thus give severally to each of their divisions a single part of sixty talents.

[3.] So that if we should have occasion for a hundred ships, sixty talents may be granted to each, and twelve trierarchs; if for two hundred, there may be thirty talents assigned, and six trierarchs, to each; if for three hundred, twenty talents may be supplied for each and four trierarchs.

In like manner, my fellow-citizens? upon a due estimate of the stores necessary for our ships, I propose that, agreeably to the present scheme, they should be divided into twenty parts; that one good and effectual part should be assigned to each of the great classes, to be distributed among the small divisions in the just proportion. Let the twelve, in every such division, demand their respective shares; and let them have those ships which it is their lot to provide, thoroughly and expeditiously equipped. Thus may our supplies, our ships, our trierarchs, our stores, be best provided and supplied.—And now I am to lay before you a plain and easy method of completing this scheme.

I say, then, that your generals should proceed to mark out ten dock-yards, as contiguous as may be to each other, and capable of

---

[1.] Of the first hundred, let five, &c.] It should seem from this passage, that each century of the three hundred ships were to be of a different rate and order, by this minute specification of 'five of the first hundred, five of the second, &c.'

[2.] When, and in what manner, this estimate of the lands was made we learn from Polybius, lib. 2, whose words shall be quoted immediately. That the barren lands of Attica should produce such a revenue, [amounting, according to Arbuthnot's computation, to 1,162,500l.] seems wonderful; especially as the lower ranks of citizens held their lands free from all taxation. The soil of Athens itself was celebrated by Homer for its fertility. But this is of little moment, when the barrenness of the Attic territory in general is considered. But what saith Polybius? Τίς γὰρ ὑπὲρ Ἀθηναίων οὐχ ἱστόρηκε, διότι καθ᾽ οὓς καιροὺς μετὰ Θηβαίων εἰς τὸν πρὸς τοὺς Λακεδαιμονίους ἀνέβαινον πόλεμον, καὶ μυρίους μὲν ἐξέπεμπον στρατιώτας, ἑκατὸν δὲ πλήρωσιν τριήρεις, ὅτι τότε κρίναντες ἀπὸ τῆς ἀξίας ποιεῖσθαι τὰς εἰς τὸν πόλεμον εἰσφοράς, ἐτιμήσαντο τήν τε χώραν, καὶ τὴν Ἀττικὴν ἅπασαν, καὶ τάς οἰκίας, ὁμοίως δὲ καὶ τὴν λοιπὴν οὐσίαν. Ἀλλ᾽ ὅμως τὸ σύμπαν τίμημα τῆς ἀξίας ἐνέλιπε τῶν ἑξακισχιλίων διακοσίοις καὶ πεντήκοντα ταλάντοις; 'What historian hath not informed us, that the Athenians at the time when they engaged in war, on the part of Thebes, against the Lacedemonians, sent ten thousand men to the field, and manned a hundred ships; that the Athenians, I say, in order to make a just estimate of the subsidy they might properly grant for this war, then proceeded to a general valuation of the lands of the whole territory of Attica, their houses, and all their effects. And yet the whole valuation fell short of six thousand talents by two hundred and fifty? Which

agrees pretty exactly with this passage of Demosthenes. *Lucchesini.*

[3.] One hundred ships seem to have been the ordinary marine establishment at Athens: and to this the ordinary revenue seems to have been proportioned. When it was necessary to fit out an extraordinary number, the additional charge was answered by an extraordinary taxation on the richer members of the state. The passage before us is indeed concisely expressed, as became a speaker who addressed himself to persons to whom the least hint was sufficient. But the full meaning of it I take to be this: 'If we have occasion but for a hundred ships, the charge of furnishing each may be divided among twelve trierarchs, who are to be supplied, for the expense of this and other preparations, with sixty talents. If for two hundred, these twelve trierarchs must provide two ships; if for three hundred, three. In every case the revenues of the state are to be equally divided amongst them. But the greater the force required, the greater must be the burden on the trierarchs, who are to be taxed for the additional expense, if any such may be required, for fitting out the fleet, and completing the other parts of the intended armament.' This latter part, indeed, is not expressed or insinuated; but I take it to be understood. But if my explanation should not be entirely consonant to the sentiments of the learned reader, who may have the curiosity to examine this part of the oration with accuracy, I must endeavour to screen myself from the severity of his censure, by subscribing to the following ingenious declaration of. Wolfius: 'Whatever is here said of fleets, stores, armaments, and supplies, must, to us, who never saw a fleet or war, and never were conversant in affairs of state, be attended with considerable obscurity.'

containing thirty vessels each. When this is done, they should assign two classes, and thirty ships, to each of these docks. Among these, also, they should divide the tribes and the respective trierarchs; so that two classes, thirty ships, and one tribe, may be assigned to each. Let then each tribe divide its allotted station into three parts, and the ships in like manner. Let these third parts be distributed by lot. Thus shall one tribe preside over one entire division of your shipping; and each third of a tribe take care of one third of such division; and thus shall you know, at all times, first where each tribe is stationed; then, where each third; then, who are the trierarchs; and lastly, the number of your ships. Let affairs be once set in motion after this manner, and, if any thing hath been omitted, (as it is by no means easy to provide accurately for every circumstance,) the execution will itself discover it. And thus may your whole marine, and all its several parts, be uniformly and exactly regulated.

And now, as to money, as to any immediate supplies, sensible, as I am, that the opinion I am now to declare must appear extraordinary, yet I will declare it; for I trust that, when duly weighed, it will be found the only one which reason can recommend; and which must be approved by the event. I say then, that at this time we should not speak at all of money: we have a fund, if occasions call for it; a great, an honourable, and an equitable fund. Should you attempt to raise it now, far from succeeding in such an attempt, you could not depend on gaining it when really wanted. But suspend your inquiries, and you will secure it. What fund is this which now hath no being, yet will be found hereafter? This appears a kind of mystery; but I shall explain it. Cast your eyes round through all this city. Within these walls, Athenians! there are treasures, I had almost said equal to those of all other states. But such is the disposition of their possessors, that if all our speakers were to arise with the most alarming declarations, 'That the king was marching against us; that he was at our gates; that the danger did not admit of any possibility of doubt;' If, with these speakers, as many ministers of heaven were to arise, and pronounce the same declarations as the warning of the gods; so far would these men be from contributing, that they would not even discover their riches; they would not acknowledge the possession of them. But should it once appear, that all those dangers, denounced with so much terror, were really

and in fact impending; where is the wretch that would not give freely, that would not urge to be admitted to contribute? For, who would choose to abandon his life and fortune, to the fury of an enemy, rather than give up a small portion of his abundance, for the safety of himself and all the rest of his possessions? Thus shall we find treasures, when occasions really demand them, but not till then. Let us not therefore inquire for them now. Suppose that we were now strictly to exact the subsidies from all our citizens: the utmost we should raise would be more contemptible than none. Imagine the experiment made; it is proposed to exact a hundredth part of the revenue arising from our lands. Well then; this makes just sixty talents. 'Nay, but we will raise a fiftieth part.' This doubles the sum: we have then one hundred and twenty talents. But what is this, to those hundreds, or those thousands of camels, which they assure us are employed to carry the king's money? But suppose it were agreed to raise a twelfth part, amounting to five hundred talents. This, in the first place, would be too great a burden; and, if imposed, still the fund produced would be insufficient for the war. Let then all our other preparations be completed; but, as to money, let the possessors keep it; and never can they keep it for a nobler public service. When their country calls for it, then shall they freely and zealously contribute.

This, my fellow-citizens! is a practicable scheme; a scheme highly honourable and advantageous, worthy of this state to be reported to the king, and which must strike him with no small terror. He knows, that by three hundred vessels, [1.] of which one hundred only were supplied by us, his ancestors lost a thousand ships. He will hear, that now we have, ourselves, equipped three hundred. He cannot, then, if he hath not lost all reason, he cannot deem it a trivial matter, to make this state his enemy. If from a dependence on his treasures, he is tempted to entertain proud thoughts, he will find this but a vain dependence, when compared with your resources. [2.] They tell us, he is coming with heaps of gold; but when these are once dispersed, he will look for new supplies. Not the richest streams, not the deepest sources, but must, at length, be totally exhausted, when we copiously and constantly drain away their waters. But we, he will be told, have a perpetual resource, in our lands: a fund of six thousand talents. And with what spirit we defend these lands against invaders, his an-

---

[1.] Whoever consults Herodotus will find that Demosthenes is by no means exact in his account either of the Athenian or Persian fleets; but we are not to expect historical precision from the orator. His representations are suited to delight and animate his hearers; and probably his success was too great to give them leisure to attend to any inaccuracy in his account.

[2.] It is just now, the orator hath represented the wealth of Athens as contemptible, that of Persia as magnificent and great. Now, on the contrary, the resources of Persia are neither solid nor permanent: the riches of Athens great and inexhaustible. Various are the instances of this artifice in Demosthenes; which the judicious reader cannot fail to observe without the direction of the annotator

cestors, who fought at Marathon, could best inform him. Let us continue to conquer, and our treasures cannot ever fail.

Nor yet do I think their errors justly founded, who apprehend, that he may employ his gold in raising a large army of mercenaries. I do indeed believe, that in an expedition against Egypt, against Orontes, [1.] or any other barbarians, there are many of the Greeks that would gladly receive his pay : not from any zeal for aggrandizing him; but each in order to obtain such a supply, as might relieve their present necessities. But I never can persuade myself, that any one Greek would assist him to conquer Greece. Whither should he turn after such an event? Would he go and be a slave in Phrygia? He [2.] must know, that, when we take up arms against the Barbarian, we take them up for our country, for our lives, for our customs, for our liberty, and all such sacred rights. Who then could be so base as to sacrifice himself, his parents, the sepulchres of his ancestors, his country to a trifling pittance? Surely, no man!

Nor is it the interest of the Persian, that his mercenaries should subdue the Greeks; for they who can conquer us, must first prove superior to him. And it is by no means his scheme, by destroying us, to lose his own empire. His wishes are to command all; if this cannot be obtained, at least he would secure his power over his own slaves.

If then it be imagined, that the Thebans will unite with him ;—[3.] it is a hard part to speak of Thebes in this assembly : for such is your aversion to this people, that you will not hear the voice of truth itself, if it seems at all to favour them. However, it is the duty of those who debate on great affairs, by no means, and on no pretence whatever, to suppress any argument which may prove of use. —I say, then, that so far are the Thebans from ever, at any time, uniting with the king against the Greeks, that they would freely give the greatest treasures, were they possessed of them, to purchase a fair occasion of atoning for their ancient errors with respect to Greece. But let the Thebans be ever so unhappily disposed, still we must all be sensible, that, if they unite with him, their enemies must necessarily unite with the Greeks. And I trust that the cause of justice, and the friends to this cause, will ever prove superior to traitors, and to all the force of the Barbarian. Let us not then yield to these extravagant alarms, nor rashly brave all consequences, by being first to take up arms.

Nor do I think that any other of the Grecian states should look upon this war with terror. Is there a man among them, who is not sensible, that, (4.) while they regarded the Persian as their common enemy, and maintained a firm union with each other, their fortune was completely happy; but when, by a fatal reliance on his friendship, they were betrayed into contests and dissensions among themselves, their calamities were so great, as to exceed all the imprecations which the most inveterate malice could invent? And shall that man, whom fortune, whom heaven itself pronounces, as a friend, unprofitable : as an enemy, of advantage ;—shall he, I say, be feared ? By no means. Yet, let us have the due regard to ourselves; let us have the due attention to the disorders and suspicions of the rest of Greece ; and let us not incur the charge of injustice. Could we, indeed, with all the

---

[1.] Two of this name are mentioned in history. The first was put to death by the younger Cyrus, on account of a conspiracy. The other, whom Demosthenes points out, was a satrap of Mysia, and served in the army which Artaxerxes sent against Cyprus, under the command of Teribazus. On this occasion he attempted to ruin the reputation of his general, was detected and disgraced; and, in revenge, joined with the rebels of Egypt, Caria, and Phrygia, and headed the army they had raised against the King. But, in hopes of recovering his credit at the Persian court, and of gaining the command of some maritime towns, he betrayed the forces, &c. of the rebels into the hands of the king's lieutenants. History speaks no farther of this Orontes. But, as in this year, the eighth from the time of his revolt, Demosthenes mentions him as an enemy to the Persian, we may conjecture, that his last services had been disregarded, and that he had again taken up arms. *Lucchesini.*

[2.] I cannot persuade myself that there is occasion to point out to the reader the force and pertinency of this argument, although it be elliptically expressed. To be assured of the true signification of the phrase πρὸς τὸν Βάρβαρον, we need but cast our eyes to a sentence a little farther on, ἐκ μὲν γε τῶν ΠΡΟΣ τοὺς ἑαυτοῦ προγόνους πολέμων, 'from the wars waged against his ancestors.'

[3.] The history of both nations accounts for the detestation with which the Athenians are supposed to hear the name of the Thebans: and perhaps it were impossible, that two nations, so different in genius and manners, ever should entertain any sentiments of friendship and esteem for each other. Our orator, however, was far superior to national prejudices. He considered, without partiality, the real interests of his country, whose welfare should be a statesman's passion. Yet, his regard for the people of Thebes was numbered, by Æschines, among his crimes. The error which, he says, they would, if possible, redeem, was their joining with Xerxes in his invasion of Greece. *Francis.*

[4.] The well-known and great events described in the history of Greece, confirm these observations of the orator fully, with respect to all the Grecian states. Yet we may concur with the Italian commentator in supposing, that they had the Lacedemonians particularly in view; to whom they are, indeed, eminently applicable.

12   †

Greeks united firmly on our side, attack him single and unsupported, I would not then suppose that you could be charged with injustice. But, as this is not to be expected, let us be cautious: let us afford him no pretence of appearing to assert the rights of the other Greeks. If we continue quiet, his applications to them will be suspicious: if we are the first to take up arms, he will seem justified by our hostilities, in his attempts to gain their friendship.

Do not then discover to the world the melancholy state of Greece, by inviting those to an alliance, whom you cannot gain; and by engaging in a war, which you cannot support. Be quiet, be resolute, be prepared. Let not the emissaries of Persia report to their king, that Greece and Athens are distracted in their councils, are confounded by their fears, are torn by dissensions. No: let them rather tell him, that, if it were not equally shameful, for the Greeks to violate their honour and their oaths, as it is to him matter of triumph, they would have long since marched against him; and that, if you do not march you are restrained solely by a regard to your own dignity: that it is your prayer to all the gods, that he may be seized with the infatuation, which once possessed his ancestors: and then he would find no defect of vigour in your measures. He knows, that by our wars with his ancestors, this state became happy and powerful; that, by our peaceful demeanour before these wars, we acquired a superiority over the other Grecian states, never more observable than at present. He knows, that the affairs of Greece require some power to be either voluntarily or accidentally the instrument of a general peace; he knows that he himself must prove that instrument, if he once attempts to raise a war; and therefore, these informations will have their due weight and credit.

That I may not longer abuse your patience, I shall repeat the sum of my advice, and then descend.

You should prepare your force against your present enemies: you should use this force against the king, against any power that may attempt to injure you. But never be the first to break through the bounds of justice, either in council or in action. You should be solicitous, not that our speeches, but that our conduct, may be worthy of our illustrious descent. Act thus, and you will serve not yourselves only, but the men who oppose these measures; for they will not feel your resentment hereafter, if they be not suffered to mislead you now. [1.]

[1.] What effect this oration had on the people, we may learn from a passage in the oration for the Rhodians; of which the following is a translation: 'There are some among you who may remember, that at the time when the affairs of Persia were the subject of our consultations, I was the first, the only, or almost the only one, to recommend it as the wisest measure, not to assign your enmity to the king, as the motive of your armament: to make your preparations against your avowed adversaries, but to employ them even against him, should he attempt to injure you. Nor did I urge these things without your full concurrence: they were received with applause.'

THE ORATION FOR THE MEGALOPOLITANS:

PRONOUNCED IN THE ARCHONSHIP OF EUDEMUS, THE FOURTH YEAR OF THE HUNDRED AND SIXTH OLYMPIAD.

INTRODUCTION.

In order to prepare the reader for the perusal of the following oration, it is necessary to recall to his view some of the late important transactions in Greece. He is not to be informed of the flourishing condition of Sparta, after the famous Peloponnesian war; the immoderate ambition of that state, and the war in which the Spartans were consequently involved with Thebes. The conduct and vigour of Epaminondas, the Theban, proved fatal to Sparta, and the battle of Leuctra put an end to the tyrannical dominion which this state had long exercised in Peloponnesus.

Immediately after this battle, several of the Peloponnesian states revolted from the Lacedemonians. The Messenians, their ancient rivals, were restored to their original settlement, by the Theban arms, after many ages of dispersion. The Arcadians and Argives asserted their independency, and, assisted by the Thebans, took up arms against their former sovereigns. The Spartans now seemed on the point of having their ruin completed; they were reduced to fortify their city, whose defenceless condition had been so long their boast; they armed six hundred of their slaves, and sent a deputation to Athens, humbly to solicit the assistance of their old rivals, in this their state of extremity.

The Athenians, who began to conceive a

jealousy of the rising power of Thebes, readily consented to join with the Lacedemonians. Iphicrates was sent, with twelve thousand men, to their relief; and, upon advice received, that Ephaminondas was marching against Lacedemon, at the head of the Thebans, Argives, and Arcadians, Chabrias was despatched, with another reinforcement, to join the Spartans and their confederates.

It is not to the present purpose to mention particularly the several events in the course of this war. It is only necessary to observe, that the Arcadians, in order the better to secure that liberty for which they now contended, determined to collect all their force into one body, brought the detached settlements of their countrymen to a union; and fixed their common residence in a city built by the advice and assistance of Epaminondas (if we may believe Pausanias,) and called Megalopolis, or the great city. This was one considerable barrier against the Lacedemonian power in Peloponnesus; which still subsisted, together with the other equitable regulations of Epaminondas, for securing the liberty of the Peloponnesians.

These were considered, by the Lacedemonians, as so many memorials of their disgrace. And the least respite from the calamities of an unsuccessful war, was sufficient to inspire them with an earnest desire of recovering their ancient power and superiority. Greece was now harassed by the sacred war. Several cities of inferior note had changed their masters, in the course of this quarrel. The re-establishment of peace, and a settlement of the whole nation of Greece, were universally urged as objects highly worthy of the general attention. And now, Archidamus, the king of Sparta, a subtle and designing prince, proposed a plan for this purpose, in appearance advantageous to the whole body, but, in effect, only calculated to restore the superiority of Sparta. He proposed, that, in order to restore the general tranquillity, the several cities should be re-established in the same condition as before the late wars.

This was a scheme which promised some advantage to all the leading states. Oropus, a city on the confines of Bœotia, once commanded by the Athenians, and still claimed as their right, but now possessed by the Thebans, must have returned to its ancient masters. Thespia and Platæa, two eminent cities in Bœotia, that had felt the jealousy and revenge of Thebes, and now lay subverted and depopulated, were, by the same plan, to be restored and fortified. The Phocians were to give up two important acquisitions, gained in the course of the sacred war; the cities of Orchomenus and Coronæa. But these and the other Bœotian cities, were only to acknowledge Thebes, as the principal and leading city in Bœotia, without any absolute submission or dependence, and without any obedience to that jurisdiction which the Thebans claimed and had exercised over them. On the other hand, Peloponnesus was to be reduced to its former state of dependence; the cities of Messenè and Megalopolis were to be destroyed, and their inhabitants dispersed; so as to restore the Spartans to the power of resuming that tyrannical dominion, which they had formerly exercised over their neighbours.

Archidamus began with endeavouring to regain that authority in Peloponnesus, to which the Spartans aspired. A dispute was soon raised between Sparta and Argos, about the boundaries of their dominions. And the king of Sparta, having in vain attempted to succeed, by practising secretly with Nicsostratus, the principal citizen of Argos, determined to have recourse to arms.

The people of Megalopolis were equally concerned in this quarrel. A war was on the point of breaking out in Peloponnesus; each side was assiduous to gain over the other states of Greece. And on this occasion both the Megalopolitans and Lacedemonians sent their ambassadors to Athens: the one to solicit for assistance and support, the other to prevail on the Athenians to continue neuter.

On this occasion was the assembly convened, in which the following oration was delivered. Each state had its partisans in this assembly, and the speakers, on both sides, seem to have delivered their sentiments with the utmost heat and animosity. The orators who opposed the demands of Megalopolis, urged the connexions of Athens with the Lacedemonians, in the Theban war, and the dishonour and inconsistency of arming against their old fellow-soldiers. They represented the old attachment of the Megalopolitans to Thebes, in the most odious and suspicious colours; and declared, that by supporting them and depressing Lacedemon, they would in effect render the Theban power highly formidable, if not irresistible; nor did they forget to urge, that by acquiescing in the attempts of Lacedemon to re-establish its power in Peloponnesus, they themselves would be entitled to the assistance of that state, in order to recover the dominions which had been wrested from them. Through this whole debate, the Athenians seem to have been entirely influenced by motives of policy and convenience. And the reader will find these urged by Demosthenes, with the utmost address and artifice, in favour of the people of Megalopolis, in the following oration.

That this oration was pronounced in the archonship of Theodemus, or Eudemus, we are informed by Dionysius of Hallicarnassus (in Epist. ad. Ammæ.) And this Eudemus was archon, according to Diodorus, in the fourth year of the hundred and sixth Olympiad. In the beginning of the next year the Lacedemonians made their irruption into Arcadia. So that it is probable, that the ambassadors were received at Athens about the latter end of the year, (i. e. a little before the summer solstice, when the Lacedemonians were just preparing to take the field, and the Arcadians threatened with immediate danger.

THE ORATION

FOR THE MEGALOPOLITANS.

Eudemo, Archon.—Olympiad. 106. *An.* 4.

THE speakers on both sides seem to me, ye men of Athens! equally to blame : the partisans of the Arcadians, and the advocates for Lacedemon. Like the deputies of these communities, not like your citizens; to whom their deputations are addressed, they excuse, they inveigh against each other. [1.] This, I say, is to act like deputies; but to speak with a true patriot spirit, to attend entirely to the interest of the state, free from all factious principles; these are their duties, who assume the character of our counsellors. But now, were not their persons known, did they not speak our language, I should have taken

many of them for two distinct people, the one of Arcadia, the other of Lacedemon.

How hazardous a part it is to urge your real interests, is to me apparent; for in this violence of opposition, where you are all alike deceived, as well the favourers of this, as the supporters of the opposite opinion, should a man attempt to point out the just mean between them, and should you prove impatient of direction, he would gratify neither party; he would be calumniated by both. Yet still, I freely choose, if such must be my fate, rather to be thought weakly impertinent, than to suffer any men to mislead you from what I deem most advantageous to the state.' There are other points, of which, if I have your permission, I shall hereafter speak. I now proceed, from principles acknowledged equally by all, to deduce such truths as I think of greatest moment.

There is not a man [2.] who can deny, that it is for the interest of Athens, that both the Lacedemonians, and the Thebans also, should be weak. But, such is the present state of things, (if any conjecture may be formed from the discourses we so often hear,) that, if Orchomenus, [3.] and Thespia, and Platæa, be

---

[1.] This heat and acrimony did not always proceed from conviction and zeal for the public interest. Every city, or community, that solicited any matter in the Athenian assembly, first took care to secure managers and advocates among the popular speakers. If the interposition of these pleaders proved successful, they were sometimes rewarded with a statue erected in the city, whose interest they had supported; sometimes, and indeed more frequently, with a sum of money. Agreements were formally made, and, in some cases, securities given for the payment of this fee. In the oration of Æschines against Ctesiphon, we have one instance of a transaction of this nature, between the city of Oreum, and Demosthenes himself; where the stipulation was so notorious as to appear upon the public records of this city; and so firm and binding, as to oblige the people of Oreum, in a time of their distress, to mortgage their revenues to the orator, as a security for the sum agreed on; and to pay interest, monthly, until the principal could be discharged.

[2.] There is not a man, &c.] Upon this principle it is, that the orator founds all his reasoning. The wars, which these three leading states carried on against each other, were either for acquiring, or supporting, or recovering the sovereignty in Greece. A passion for this pre-eminence constituted the principal part of national virtue and merit. They talked, indeed, of the interest of the whole body of Greece, of an extensive regard and affection to this body, and of the necessity of a just balance of power. Yet in these days of degeneracy, at least, the duty of aggrandizing their own community was frequently made the great law of the morality of statesmen. And this contributed no less to the final ruin of the Grecian states, than their luxury and corruption.'

'Græciæ civitates dum imperare singulæ cupiunt, imperium omnes perdiderunt,' saith Justin. A strict union with each other was necessary, even to the being and support of each. But for extensive dominion, the constitution and circumstances even of the most eminent of their communities were by no means calculated.

[3.] There were two cities in Greece of this name, the one in Arcadia, the other, of which the orator here speaks, in Bœotia, an ancient and illustrious city, to which Thebes was tributary, in the heroic times, until Hercules enabled it to assert its independence. After the battle of Leuctra, the Thebans determined to reduce this rival city to their obedience, but were restrained by the moderation of Epaminondas, who prevailed on his countrymen to admit the people of Orchomenus to their alliance, instead of reducing them to slavery. However, after the battle of Mantinæa, in which this general fell, the Thebans found a pretence for executing their former severe purposes against Orchomenus. Three hundred Orchomenian cavalry had joined with certain Theban exiles, in a conspiracy to overturn the aristocratical constitution of Thebes; and were betrayed by those whom they had agreed to assist. The Thebans, not contented with confining their vengeance to the guilty, seized the city of Orchomenus, put the citizens to the sword, and made slaves of their wives and children. *Lucchesini.*

Of Thespia and Platæa, the reader will find some short account, in the note, p. 35. on the oration on the Peace. The vicinity of these three cities to Thebes, and their hatred to the Thebans, inspired by the remembrance of injuries never to be forgotten, sufficiently explain the assertion of Demosthenes.

repeopled, the Thebans must be weak; that the Lacedemonians, if Arcadia [1.] be reduced to their obedience, and the great city be possessed by them, must once more become powerful. We are therefore to be careful not to suffer these to be great and formidable, before the others are reduced; nor to betray ourselves into greater inconveniences by the strength of Lacedemon, than can possibly be compensated by the weakness of Thebes. Not that we assert, that it is more eligible to have the Lacedemonians our enemies than the Thebans. This is not the point we would support: but that neither of them should have the power of injuring us in any instance; for thus only can our fears be removed, and our security established.

But it will be said, ' Yes! this is indeed a point of utmost moment: Yet it is grievous to make those our allies, against whom we fought at Mantinæa; to unite with them against the very men with whom we then shared the dangers of the field.' Grievous, I confess, it is; but let such delicacy gain some attention among others. Let the parties once agree to live in peace, and we shall not, we need not, send support to the Megalopolitans: our swords shall not then be drawn against our old fellow-soldiers. One party (as they profess) are already in alliance with us, the other are now soliciting our alliance: what have we farther to desire? But what if justice should be violated? if war should be resolved on?

If it be the sole object of debate, whether we should give up the great city to the domi-nion of Lacedemon, or no; let us give it up: I do not contend against it, though it be not just: let us not arm against those who once shared with us the dangers of the field. But as we are all convinced, that, if once masters of this city, they will instantly attack Messenè; let any one of those, who have been so severe on the Megalopolitans, arise and say, what conduct he would recommend to us on such an emergency. They are silent. But you are not to be informed, that whether they should urge us or dissuade us, we should be obliged to send succours, both by those sacred oaths which engage us to Messenè, [2.] and by our interest, which requires that this city should subsist. Consider, therefore, with yourselves, which would be the noblest and most benevolent procedure, to begin your opposition to the encroachments of Lacedemon, by the defence of the Megalopolitans, or that of the Messenians. In the one case, you will appear attentive only to the safety of the Arcadians, and to the solid establishment of that tranquillity, for which you have exposed yourselves to the dangers and the toils of war. In the other, all mankind must see, that in defending Messenè, you act, not so much from principles of equity, as from your fears of Lacedemon. Our designs and actions should be just; but we should be careful that, at the same time, they may also prove conducive to our interest. [3.]

It is urged, by those who have spoken on the other side, that we should endeavour to regain Oropus. But, should we now make those our enemies, who would assist us in this de-

---

[1.] The subversion of the Lacedemonian power seems to have been not so much the effect of the defeat at Leuctra, as of the revolt of their allies in Peloponnesus, and particularly of the Arcadians. It was not difficult for a warlike nation to have reassembled and reinforced its troops, after such an engagement. Nor could the Thebans have ventured to pursue their victory so far, as even to threaten Sparta with slavery, unless they had been assisted by the Arcadians. Hence, both the Thebans and Athenians ever courted the alliance of the Peloponnesians, and cultivated their friendship with the greatest assiduity. And hence the orator is justly warranted to observe, that the power of Lacedemon must rise to a formidable pitch, by the reduction of the Arcadians, who, by the extent of their territory and the strength of their towns, were, next to Sparta, evidently the most considerable of the Peloponnesian states. *Lucchesini.*

[2.] The Lacedemonians, mortified and incensed at the re-establishment of Messenè, refused to include this state in the general peace which was made after the battle of Mantinæa; and when the Thebans were once involved in the Phocian war, determined to seize the opportunity of oppressing those Peloponnesians who had united with their rivals. Hostilities were declared against the Messenians: this people applied for succour to the Athenians, who engaged to defend them against invasions, though they refused to assist them in any offensive measures. This seems to have been the engagement to which the orator refers.

[3.] The reasoning in this passage may possibly deserve to be opened and illustrated somewhat farther than can be done by a simple detail of historical facts. It is one of the numberless instances of our orator's accommodating his style and manner of address to the quickness and liveliness of his countrymen; and complimenting their understandings, by leaving something to be supplied by them. The purport of his argument seems to be this. ' Sooner or later we must oppose the attempts of Lacedemon, to extend our sovereignty. Our own interest requires it, as well as our regard to equity, and the general interest of Greece. To both we owe the due attention, and it should be our care to make them coincide: while the Arcadians are supported, the Lacedemonians cannot be supposed sufficiently powerful to become an object of terror: our interposition, therefore, in favour of the Arcadians, will be regarded as the pure effect of public spirit. But, if the Lacedemonians be first suffered to reduce Arcadia, and the Athenians then begin to oppose their farther progress, the motives of equity and public spirit may, indeed, still be pleaded, but those of self-interest must necessarily be supposed to have had the greater influence.'

sign, we must forfeit all hopes of their assistance. It is my opinion, too, that we should attempt to regain Oropus. But, that Lacedemon will now become our enemy, if we unite with those Arcadians who sue for our alliance; they of all men, never should [1.] assert, who persuaded us to support the Lacedemonians in the time of their distress. For, when the whole body of the Peloponnesians was ready to unite with us ; when they called on us to lead them against the Lacedemonians, the very men, who now urge this objection, persuaded you to reject their overtures, [2.] (which forced them to apply to Thebes, then their sole resource,) and to expend your treasures, and endanger your persons, in defence of Lacedemon.—Surely, you could not have acted with such spirit, to save this people, had you been fairly told, that, when once saved, no restraint must be prescribed to their desires, no bounds to their injustice : else they would retain no sense of that safety which we gave them. Let it then be supposed, that our forming an alliance with the Arcadians be ever so repugnant to the views of the Lacedemonians: still, that gratitude which they owe to this state for their preservation, at a time when they were threatened with the utmost dangers, should far outweigh any resentment they may conceive, from our opposing their injustice. And can they then deny us their assistance to regain Oropus ? This would prove them the most abandoned of mankind. No! by the gods, I cannot suspect them of such baseness!

I hear it also urged, and am surprised at the objection, that, by this alliance with the Arcadians, and by the measures now proposed, the state must contradict its former conduct, and thus lose its credit. To me, Athenians! the very contrary seems manifest. And why ? Because it cannot be denied, that, in defending the Lacedemonians, in granting the like defence to Thebes, in former times, and, lately, in saving the Euboeans, [3.] and then admitting them to an alliance, we have uniformly pursued one and the same design.—And, what is this? The protection of the injured.—And, if this be so, the charge of inconsistency must be urged, not against us, but those who refuse to adhere to justice. Affairs have changed, by means of those whose ambition is unbounded. This state hath not changed.

It appears to me, that the Lacedemonians are now acting a subtle and insidious part. They say, that the Eleans [4.] ought to have a portion of Triphylia; the Phliasians, Tricaranus; some others of the Arcadians, the territories which are theirs: and we, Oropus. Not that they wish to see each of us in possession of our rightful dominions. Far from it! Such public-spirited sentiments are new to them. They but affect this zeal for the support of all in the recovery of their several interests; that, when they themselves marched against Messenè, all may arm in their cause, and cheerfully join with them; or else appear to act unjustly, who had their concurrence in regaining their particular claims; and yet refuse to grant them the like returns of friendship. It is my opinion in the first place, that, without subjecting any part of Arcadia to the power of the Lacedemonians, Athens will regain Oropus : that these people will themselves support our claim, if they have the least re-

---

[1.] They, of all men, never should, &c.] Because these men then reasoned from the necessity of preserving a due balance of power, and preventing any one state from becoming formidable. The resentment of the party to be opposed, they then considered as of no weight against so cogent an argument. The same argument was now urged with equal force and propriety, in favour of the Arcadians. They could not, therefore, urge an objection now, which, in a case exactly parallel, they had affected to despise.

[2.] The history of this fact, as described by Xenophon, does not exactly agree with this passage, unless supplied and illustrated by the narration of Diodorus. After the battle of Leuctra, the Athenians offered liberty to all the states of Peloponnesus. The Mantineans, thus encouraged, determined to fortify their city, but were opposed by the Lacedemonians, who first remonstrated by their deputies, and then took up arms. Many of the Arcadians themselves refused to give up their authority over some of their dependent cities. This produced a war between the Lacedemonians, Tegeans, and their allies, on one part; and the Mantineans, and the principal Arcadian states on the other. The Mantineans and Arcadians were victorious: ' Yet still,' saith

Diodorus, (lib. 15. an. 4. Olym. 102.) ' they dreaded the weight of Sparta, and could not venture, by themselves, to carry on the war. They, therefore, gained over the Argians and Eleans, and sent an embassy to the Athenians, inviting them to unite in the confederacy against the Spartans. But, as they could gain no attention at Athens, they had recourse to the Thebans, and prevailed on them to join in a league against Lacedemon.' This extract from Diodorus throws sufficient light on the present passage. *Lucchesini.*

[3.] In saving the Euboeans.] At the time when the Thebans had gained possession of a part of the island, with an intent of destroying the Athenian power in Euboea. See note, [1.] p. 13. on Phil. I.

[4.] That the Eleans, &c.] Triphylia was a district on the sea-coast, situated between Elis and Messenè. Certain Arcadian exiles had seized Lasseio, its principal city, and delivered it to the Eleans. This produced a war, in which Triphylia so often changed its masters, that the right to it became doubtful. The Arcadians, however, prevailed at length, and now possessed several cities in this district.— Tricaranus had been taken from the Phliasians, by the Argives, some time after the battle of Leuctra.

gard to justice: and, that there are others [1.] to support it, who think that Thebes should not be suffered to possess the rights of others. But, were it evident, that unless we permit the Lacedemonians to overturn all Peloponnesus, we never can be able to obtain this city, I should think it more eligible (if I may so speak) absolutely to resign our pretensions to Oropus, than to abandon Messenè and Peloponnesus to the Lacedemonians. It is not in this particular alone, that we are to attend to the conduct of Lacedemon.—But, I suppress those thoughts which are now starting. I only say, we are, in many instances, exposed to danger. [2.] As to the actions of the Megalopolitans against this state, during their connexion with the Thebans, it is absurd to urge these now as criminal. It is absurd, I say, when they are inclined to form a strict union with us, that so they may redeem their former conduct, by doing us effectual service, maliciously to seek for all pretences to defeat such favourable intentions; and not to consider, that the greater zeal and ardour they are proved to have discovered for the interest of Thebes, the greater and the juster should be your resentment against those who deprived the state of such confederates. (For your protection they first solicited, before their application to the Thebans.) These are the wretched arguments of men, who wish that these people should unite with other states.

From all the judgment I can form, on the most mature reflection, I am persuaded, (and there are many here who agree with me in this opinion,) that, if the Lacedemonians are once masters of Megalopolis, Messenè must certainly be in danger. Should they gain this city also, I say, we must form an alliance with the Thebans. And, it will be much more noble, much more advantageous, at once to take those allies of the Thebans to our protection, and vigorously to oppose the ambition of Lacedemon; than to refuse them that protection, because allies to the Thebans; to abandon them to their oppressors; and thus be forced to save Thebes itself from ruin; nay, to involve this our own state in danger. For I cannot think it a matter of no consequence to Athens, that the Lacedemonians should be masters of Megalopolis, and resume their ancient greatness: while, even now, I see them draw the sword, not to defend their state from wrong, but to regain that sovereign power which they formerly enjoyed. And what were their designs, [3.] when they enjoyed this power, you can better say than I; and must, therefore, feel the juster and the stronger apprehensions.

I would gladly ask our speakers, those who express such aversion to Thebes, and those who declare themselves the enemies of Lacedemon; whether in these, their particular resentments, they be actuated by a regard to you, and to your interests; or, whether they severally hate the Thebans, for the sake of the Lacedemonians; and the Lacedemonians, from their affection to the Thebans. If, for their sakes, they have lost their reason, and are each unworthy of our attention: if for our interest; whence this unnecessary zeal for their favourite states? It is possible, very possible, to humble the Thebans, without aggrandizing the Lacedemonians. This may be easily effected, as I shall now endeavour to convince you.

It is well known that men are, to a certain degree, obliged by shame, to adhere to justice, even where their inclinations are averse. They affect to appear strenuous against every injurious attempt; especially, when, in any instance, they have suffered by such attempts. Here we find the great cause of all disorders, the origin of all calamities, in this want of a sincere, disinterested regard to justice. To avoid this danger, therefore, in our attempts to reduce the power of Thebes, let us declare, that Thespia, and Orchomenus, and Platæa, must be restored: let us exert ourselves for this purpose, and call on others to assist us. Thus shall our true regard to equity, our real patriotic spirit, be displayed in this generous concern for the restoration of ancient cities. But, at the same time, let us not abandon Messenè and Megalopolis to the power of their oppressors. Let us not, under the pretence of serving the Thespians and Platæans, look on with unconcern, whilst cities now in being, already filled with inhabitants, are rased to their foundations. If we show this equal regard to justice, there is not a state in Greece but will readily unite with us, to wrest from the Thebans their unjust acquisition. If not, this people must necessarily oppose our endeavours to restore the cities; an event which they must justly regard as their own destruction; and, in our own affair, [4.] the attempt must prove ineffectual. And what, in

---

[1.] There are others, &c.] The Phocians Thessalians, and Corinthians, who were now engaged against the Thebans in the sacred war.

[2.] The objections on the other side were: 'Shall we arm against the Lacedemonians, our fellow-soldiers in the Theban war!' And 'shall we assist the Arcadians, who drew their swords against us at Mantinæa?' Both very popular, and likely to influence the assembly. The speaker seems particularly to dread the latter: he states it in gentle and extenuating terms: his answer hath as much art and liveliness as force; and he appears not at all inclined to dwell long, or particularly, on this point.

[3.] The sovereignty of Lacedemon is to be dated from the destruction of Athens by Lysander, in the first year of the ninety-fourth Olympiad, a considerable time before the birth of Demosthenes, but within the memory of some citizens: at least, the consequences of this important event must have been remembered by numbers in the assembly.

[4.] Our own affair.] That is, the recovery of Oropus.

truth, can be expected, if we are ever suf-fering cities, now in being, to be destroyed; and demanding, that cities, long since ruin-ed, should be restored?

It hath been urged in this debate, by those who have spoken with the greatest appearance of reason, that these people should take down the public monuments [1.] of their treaty with Thebes, if they mean to be real allies to this state. On the other side, it is alleged, that it is not such monuments, but interest, which they regard as the essential cause of friend-ship: that they must look on those as their real allies, who will grant them their assis-tance.

But, however sincerely they may thus pro-fess, this is my opinion; that you should de-mand, both that these monuments be taken down, and that Lacedemon be obliged to peace. If either of these demands be rejected, we should then unite with that party which hath acquiesced. For if, when they are al-lowed to live unmolested, the Megalopolitans should still adhere to their connexions with the Thebans, they must then discover to the world, that they were influenced by the hopes conceived from the superiority of Thebes; not by motives of equity. If, on the other hand, when the Megalopolitans have, with real faith and sincerity, formed an alliance with us, the

Lacedemonians should still refuse to live in peace, it must be manifest, that all this their solicitude is not, that Thespia may be restored, but that, while the Thebans are embroiled in this war, they must seize the opportunity of reducing all Peloponnesus.

I am surprised at some persons, who express dreadful apprehensions, at the allies of The-bes becoming enemies to Lacedemon; yet, should Lacedemon subdue these people, see no danger in such an event; especially, when we have the experience of past times to as-sure us, that the Thebans have ever used those allies [2.] against the Lacedemonians; the Lacedemonians, when their masters, have ever employed them against us. It is, there-fore, seriously to be considered, that should you now refuse to admit the Megalopolitans to your alliance, they must either be subvert-ed and dispersed; and then the Lacedemo-nians, at once, become powerful; or they must escape the danger, (as we sometimes see strange and unexpected events;) and, then, with good reason, they must become firm as-sociates to the Thebans: but, if we accept of these their overtures, they must then owe and acknowledge their preservation to this state.

But let us turn our thoughts from their for-tunes and their dangers, and fix our attention on the Thebans and Lacedemonians. Should

---

[1.] *The public monuments, &c.*] In the original, Τὰς ΣΤΗΛΑΣ καθελεῖν τὰς πρὸς Θη-βαίους. It was the custom in Greece, that the treaties of the several states, and the conditions of these treaties, should be inscribed on co-lumns, which were erected, and, while the treaties subsisted, were preserved in the most public and frequented places, as in the scenes of their great games, where the whole nation was collected at particular seasons, and there had an opportunity of being witnesses of the terms agreed on. The observance of these was, in some sort, a matter of national concern, and came under the cognizance of the great council of Amphictyons. That the contract-ing powers themselves might have the monu-ments of their public acts continually in view, the like columns were erected in the most con-spicuous places of their cities. Thus we learn from Thucydides, (l. 18.) that, when the Athe-nians and Lacedemonians had concluded a truce for fifty years, in the tenth year of the famous Peloponnesian war, it was provided, that the columns on which the treaty was in-scribed, should be erected in such places as have been mentioned. Στήλας δὲ στῆσαι 'Ολυμ-πίασι, καὶ Πυθοῖ, καὶ 'Ισθμῷ, καὶ ἐν 'Αθήναις ἐν πό-λει, καὶ ἐν Λακεδαίμονι 'Αμυκλαίῳ. Pausanias ob-serves that in his days, many of these co-lumns were preserved in the Olympian temple, and particularly that which was the monu-ment of the treaty concluded between the Athenians, Argians, and Mantinæans, in the twelfth year of the Peloponnesian war.

[2.] *By those allies*, the orator undoubtedly means not the Arcadians only, but the whole body of the Peloponnesian states. And what

he observes of these states, is fully confirmed by history. To mention only the more famous battles fought between the Thebans and Athe-nians, it appears, that the former were not as-sisted by the Peloponnesians in their first un-successful engagement at Tanagra; (An. 4. Ol. 80.) in the second, when they were victo-rious; (An. 2. Ol. 83.) or in the third, when they were again conquered; (An. 1. Ol. 89.) or in their victory at Delium, in the following year. On the other hand, after the battle of Leuctra, the Thebans were joined by the Ar-cadians in their invasion of Sparta, (An. 3. Ol. 102.) and the next year entered the territory of Lacedemon, in conjunction with the Arca-dians, Argives, and Eleans. But the Lacede-monians were assisted by their Peloponnesian allies, in all their wars with the Athenians. In the great Peloponnesian war, ' the confeder-ates of the Lacedemonians were,' (said Thu-cydides, lib. II. 9.) ' all the Peloponnesians that dwelt within the Isthmus, except the Ar-gives and Achæans, who had attachments to each of the contending parties.' Λακεδαιμονίων μὲν οἱ ξύμμαχοι, Πελοποννήσιοι μὲν οἱ ἐντὸς 'Ισθμοῦ πάντες, πλὴν 'Αργείων, καὶ 'Αχαιῶν. Τούτοις δ' ἐς ἀμφοτέρους φιλία ἦν.

Many other instances, to the same purpose, might be produced from history. But should it be objected to the assertion of the orator, that, at the battle of Mantinæa, some of the Pe-loponnesians united with the Thebans against the Athenian powers, the answer is obvious, that the Athenians were not the objects of this confederacy; that it was formed against the Spartans, to whom Athens served but as an auxiliary. *Lucchesini.*

this war prove fatal to the Thebans, (as our interest requires,) still the power of the Lacedemonians will be duly circumscribed, whilst they have the Arcadians on their borders, ever ready to arm against them. But, suppose the Thebans should prove superior to their dangers, should still defend their country, and should not fall before their enemies; yet must they be the less powerful, if on our side we be strengthened by allies, to whom we ourselves gave being. At all events, therefore, the interest of the state demands, that we should not abandon the Arcadians; that, if preserved, they should not seem to owe their preservation to themselves; they should not owe it to any others; but that it should be the act of the Athenians.

And now, my fellow-citizens! I call the gods to witness, that I have spoken, not from private affection, not from particular resentment to either party, but from a regard to what I deem the real interest of my country. This, then, is my opinion; that you should not abandon the people of Megalopolis; no, nor any weaker state to the power of the stronger. [1.]

[1.] It does not appear from history that this oration had the due effect. Whether the prospect of recovering Oropus had greater influence than the more liberal and less confined policy of Demosthenes; or, whether the present circumstances and connexions of the Athenians prevented them from acting in favour of the Megalopolitans; certain it is, that they did not exert themselves on this occasion, in defence of the liberty of Peloponnesus. The quarrel was carried on, for some short time. The Lacedemonians had generally the advantage; but soon found it necessary to end the war by a truce with the people of Megalopolis.

THE ORATION FOR THE LIBERTY OF THE RHODIANS:

PRONOUNCED IN THE ARCHONSHIP OF THESSALUS, THE SECOND YEAR OF THE HUNDRED AND SEVENTH OLYMPIAD.

INTRODUCTION.

AN attempt made (in the hundred and fifth Olympiad) to reduce the states of Chios, Cos, and Rhodes, to a dependency on Athens, produced the war, well known by the name of 'the social war;' which was, for three years, supported by the Athenians, on one side: and on the other by the Chians, Coans, and Rhodians, assisted by the Byzantines, and by Mausolus, king of Caria; which prince, (or rather his wife Artemisia, who governed in his name,) was the principal agent in fomenting this quarrel. Their fears of the Persian arms obliged the Athenians to give a peace to the confederates, in which it was expressly stipulated, that they should be free and independent. So that, in effect, these states triumphed over their adversary; whose concessions were extorted by necessity, and who, of consequence, harboured all the resentment of disappointed ambition against their opponents.

The people of Rhodes, who had engaged warmly in this confederacy, had formerly been indebted to Athens for assistance, in defence of their popular form of government, against the favourers of aristocracy; who, on their part, had been supported by the Lacedemonians. The peace, now concluded, promised to put an end to those civil commotions and revolutions to which the state of Rhodes had been exposed. But the enterprising genius of Artemisia, who now reigned in Caria, prompted her to attempt the conquest of Rhodes. The king of Persia favoured her design against an island, which, by its situation, commanded the Ægean sea, and rendered the passage into Greece secure and easy; and which he justly expected to gain from the Carian princess, by treaty, or by arms, with less umbrage to the Greeks than any direct attack would give.

As a step previously necessary to this design, the aristocratical faction was, partly by the gradual influence of secret practices, and partly by force, established in the government of Rhodes: which they proceeded to exercise in an oppressive and tyrannical manner. The people, whose liberties were thus overturned, saw no resource in their distress, but to apply to the generosity of Athens, their ancient protector. Ambassadors were despatched to implore the assistance of the great defenders of liberty; and, in the assembly convened on this occasion, the following oration was delivered in favour of the people of Rhodes.

Their cause laboured under many difficulties. They had defied the people whose protection they were soliciting: and were now the objects of their resentment.—Their late opposition was considered, at Athens, as the effect, not of a zeal for liberty, but of ingratitude and pride, of perverseness and insolence, which were represented as a part of their national character. No speaker could venture to oppose these sentiments, which afforded those who spoke against the Rhodians ample matter for invective. It was well known that the Persian king interested himself in favour of the reigning party at Rhodes. The danger of irritating this prince had been, by Demosthenes himself, strongly urged upon other occasions. So that, not only the passions and

13   †

prejudices of the assembly, but policy also, pleaded powerfully against the present demand of the Rhodians. In these circumstances, they required an able, artful, and insinuating advocate: and such they found in our orator.

———

THE ORATION

FOR THE LIBERTY OF THE RHODIANS.

Thessalo, Archon.—Olympiad. 107. *An.* 2.

WHEN affairs, like these, become the subjects of our debates, it is my opinion, Athenians, that a general liberty of speech should be allowed to all in this assembly. [1.] Not that I have ever thought it difficult to point out the measures fittest to be pursued; for (to speak my thoughts plainly) you seem of yourselves sufficiently apprized of these. But to prevail on you to pursue them; there is the difficulty. For when any thing hath been resolved; when it hath been confirmed by your voices, we are just as far from carrying it into execution, as if it had never been resolved.

One particular there is, eminently distinguishable amongst all those favours which we owe to Heaven. I mean, that they who, not long since, prompted by their insolence, appeared in arms against us, now rest all their hopes of safety on this state. An event which should inspire us with the greatest satisfac-

tion. For, by a just and proper conduct upon this occasion, we shall, by our actions, gloriously and nobly refute the calumnies of our traducers. The Chians, and the Byzantines, and the Rhodians, accused us of dangerous designs against them; and, from this pretence, conspired to raise the late war against us. But it will now appear that Mausolus, [2.] the great author and conductor of this war—he who affected such zeal for the interest of the Rhodians,—is the very person who deprived them of their freedom; that the Chians and the Byzantines, [3.] who then professed to be their allies, have refused to assist them when distressed: but that you, the great objects of their apprehensions, prove to be the people, of all others, to whom alone they are indebted for protection. When this is once made manifest to the world, such must be the sentiments with which you shall inspire the people of every community, that they will regard your friendship as the pledge of their security. And surely you cannot enjoy greater happiness than such a universal confidence and affection.

It is with surprise I find the very persons who urged us to oppose the king [4.] in defence of the Egyptians, now deterring us, by the apprehensions of his displeasure, from engaging in the affairs of Rhodes: and this, when it is well known that the Rhodians are really Greeks; the others, of the number of this prince's subjects.

There are some among you who may re-

———

[1.] This exordium seems to have been founded on some particular circumstances of the assembly, or some difficulties, which Demosthenes was obliged to encounter, before he could obtain an audience. The assembly of the people at Athens was necessarily subject to the inconveniences attending all popular meetings. Clamour, tumult, and contention frequently disturbed it; especially, when the point in debate was of an important kind; or the popular leaders divided; and, by interest or principle, prompted to support their different opinions and parties, with zeal and ardour. Sometimes (as we learn from some passages in Æschines) the leaders on one side took occasion to seize the gallery, from whence the speakers addressed themselves to the people, and, by open violence, prevented any one from taking his place there, who was not a friend to the measures which they recommended. Sometimes the magistrates, who presided in the assembly, either thought it necessary, for the preservation of peace and order, or were induced by private motives, to exert their authority, and to circumscribe that liberty of speech, for which the constitution of Athens had so scrupulously provided. Hence, frequently arose a tumultuous mixture of acclamation, opposition, loud and vehement commanding, and earnest expostulation, which formed a scene fitted to discourage and terrify an unexperienced or dastardly speaker: a scene for which Demosthenes prepared

himself, by declaiming on the sea-shore, amidst the roaring of the waves.

[2.] This passage seems to intimate that measures had been taken to establish the aristocracy at Rhodes, during the lifetime of Mausolus. The queen, who is said to have directed and governed her husband, probably recommended, and made some progress in the execution of a design, which was crowned with complete success in her own reign.

[3.] It was, probably, the fear of Artemisia's power which prevented the Chians and Byzantines from assisting their friends the Rhodians to overturn the usurpation. Otherwise, the Chians, whose government was republican, must have exerted themselves to secure the like constitution to their allies. *Lucchesini.*

[4.] When Artaxerxes engaged in the war with Nectanebus, king of Egypt, both parties applied to the Greeks for assistance: the Persian was refused; but such numbers of Grecian mercenaries engaged in the service of Nectanebus, that he was enabled to detach four thousand of these to the assistance of the Sidonians. And probably the greater part of these forces were Athenians: as the inveterate resentment of this people to the Persians prompted them to take all means of opposing them, which were not absolutely inconsistent with treaties. *Lucchesini.*

member that, at the time when the affairs of Persia were the subject of our consultations, I was the first, I think the only, or almost the only one, to recommend it as the wisest measure, not to assign your enmity to the king, as the motive of your armament: to make your preparations against your avowed adversaries; but to employ them even against him, should he attempt to injure you. Nor did I urge these things without your full concurrence. You received them with applause. [1.] On this present occasion, my sentiments are exactly consonant to what I then proposed. And were I a subject to the king, were I called to be his counsellor, to him I should suggest the very measures I now recommend to you; to fight for his own dominions, if attacked by any of the Greeks; never to indulge an extravagant ambition of making foreign conquests. If, on your part, ye men of Athens! it be resolved to give up all those cities to the king, which he may reduce to his obedience, by surprising and deceiving some members of the several cities; it is a resolution I can by no means praise. But, if ye be persuaded, that, in the cause of justice, ye should, on all occasions, boldly draw the sword, and encounter every difficulty; in the first place, such occasions will occur more rarely, the more you are possessed with this persuasion; and then, it must be acknowledged, that such sentiments are worthy of this state.

That I recommend nothing new, in moving you to give liberty to the Rhodians; that you will do nothing new, if my counsels should prevail; may appear from one instance of our former conduct, which proved of important service. It may be remembered, Athenians! that you once sent out Timotheus, to assist Ariobarzanes. [2.] It was expressly prescribed in his commission, that he should not proceed to any infringement of our treaty with the king. He saw that Ariobarzanes had openly revolted from his master. He saw that Samos was held by Cyprothemes, and his Persian garrison; and that Tigranes, the king's own lieutenant, had placed them in this city. To Ariobarzanes, therefore, he refused assistance: Samos he invested, and restored to freedom. And to this day, we never were involved in any war on this account. For there is a material difference between these two motives of war; the enlargement of dominion, and the defence of rightful possessions. When an invasion is to be repelled, the contest is supported to the utmost; not so for the objects of ambition. Men will, indeed, attempt to gratify this passion, if permitted; but, if opposed, they do not charge the opposition as injurious. Nor do I think that Artemisia will act contrary to these principles, if the state should interpose in the affairs of Rhodes.—Hear me for a moment, and judge whether my reasons be well-founded or invalid.

[1.] The approbation of the people, he affects to consider as a full proof of the justness of these his sentiments. 'If they be then just, the king must adopt them; no other can be recommended to him. And if his conduct is to be guided by such principles, he cannot be provoked to take up arms against the Athenians, by their interposition in favour of the liberty of Rhodes, (a Grecian state.) It must be equally his interest not to oppose the Athenians, where his own kingdom is not immediately attacked, as it is for the Athenians not to give unnecessary umbrage to him. Such delicacy and caution must be acknowledged just and necessary, but are quite different from a supine inattention to all his motions; and an abject concession of all the conquests he may be prompted to make, however injurious to Greece. Such conduct would not only be dishonourable but impolitic. While, on the contrary, vigour and resolution, prudently directed, instead of involving them in war, must awe their enemies, and preserve them in peace and security.'—This seems to be the sum of the present argument. And the judicious will probably forgive the attempt to open and illustrate particular passages, as the sentiments, in this oration especially, are delivered with such liveliness and rapidity, that a reader, not strictly attentive, is oftentimes in danger of losing the full view of our orator.

[2.] The time and circumstances of this expedition do not seem necessary for illustrating the argument of Demosthenes, as he himself hath distinctly explained the particulars necessary for his purpose. However, the reader whose curiosity may prompt him to seek for farther information, has here a fuller account from the Italian commentator.—There is no doubt, but that Timotheus was sent on this expedition in the second, or in the beginning of the third year of the hundred and fourth Olympiad: because, in this year, Ariobarzanes, together with some other satraps on the sea-coast, Mausolus, and Tachus king of Egypt, revolted from Artaxerxer. The rebellion of Ariobarzanes was probably unknown to the Athenians at this time. The design of the expedition was, to establish this satrap in the government of Phrygia, which he had seized on the death of Mithridates, by his own authority: though possibly he might have assured the Athenians that he had acted by the king's commission. Hence was Timotheus sent to support him with instructions, however, to commit no infringement of the treaties subsisting between Athens and the Persian. And as this general could not, consistently with these instructions, pursue the intended expedition in favour of Ariobarzanes, it was not without good reason that he chose to employ his forces in the relief of Samos; which was under the jurisdiction of Athens, and unjustly seized by the king's lieutenants, in order to facilitate his operations against the rebels on the sea-coast. Nor was it at all prudent for the Athenians to suffer the Persians to possess an island, from whence they might readily pass over into Greece.

I think, then, that if all the king's attempts in Egypt had been crowned with effectual success, Artemisia would have exerted her utmost efforts to reduce Rhodes to his subjection; not from an affection to the king, but in order to bind him, by a signal favour, should he extend his dominions to her neighbourhood; that, in return, he might admit her to the strictest connexions of friendship. But, since he hath acted, [1.]—as fame reports; since he hath been unsuccessful in all his attempts; she must suppose (and it is in fact the case) that this island can be of no other use to him, but as a citadel, to awe her kingdom, and to control her motions. So that, in my opinion, she would rather that we were in possession of the island, (provided that this did not appear to be the act of Artemisia,) than that he should gain it. Nor would she assist him in such an attempt; at least, not with sincerity and vigour. As to the king, how he may act on any emergency, I do not pretend to say. But, that it highly imports this state to have it known explicitly, whether he means to assert any claim to Rhodes or

no; this I firmly maintain. If he should, our consultations are not to be confined to the Rhodians; our concern must be for ourselves, and for all the Greeks.

[2.] Yet, were these Rhodians, who now possess the city, strong enough to maintain their possession, I should not have advised you to grant them aid: no, though they should make you the most magnificent promises. For I find, that in order to dissolve the free government, they first seduced some citizens of their party; and then the moment they had gained their purpose, they drove out those very citizens. And they who have been false to both parties, cannot, I presume, prove faithful allies to this state.

These things I never should have urged, had I only considered the interest of Rhodes. I have no public [3.] attachment to this state; no particular connexion with any of its citizens; or, were I engaged by both these ties, in this assembly I should be influenced only by the interest of my country. As to these Rhodians, if one may so speak who pleads for their protection, I rejoice at what hath

---

[1.] We learn from Diodorus, (lib. 16.) that in the present year, when this oration was delivered, Ochus had not penetrated as far as Egypt: but led his army against Sidon; which city being betrayed by Mentor, and Tennes its king, was set on fire, and reduced to ashes by the inhabitants. From hence the Persians marched, the next year, into Egypt, where they at first met with some sinister accidents, (a considerable part of the army being lost in morasses, though in the conclusion they were enabled to conquer Nectanebus at Pelusium, and to reduce him to the utmost extremity. Thus the assertion of Demosthenes seems not reconcilable to history. But it must not be forgotten, that a passionate eagerness for intelligence was a distinguishing part of the character of the Athenians; which, we must suppose, was frequently gratified by rumours and advices invented to please them, and artfully or credulously propagated. Something of this kind might have happened at present: and agreeable news from the Persian camp, whether believed by the orator or no, might have been assumed as certain, without any scruple, to answer the present purpose.

[2.] At first glance, it may occur to the render to ask, how it comes, that Demosthenes, who pleads for the restoration of the popular state, here seems to speak in favour of the reigning party. And though the commentators, &c. take no notice of any difficulty in this passage, it may not be deemed impertinent to endeavour to illustrate its purport and connexion.—Demosthenes hath endeavoured to prove that the king, however he may favour or support the aristocracy at Rhodes, yet will not consider the interposition of the Athenians, in defence of the liberty of that island, as an act of hostility against him; and that neither he, nor Artemisia, will oppose

them. 'Not that I pretend,' saith the orator, 'to ascertain what the king's designs are, or what measures he may pursue. But if he should assert any direct claim to the dominion of Rhodes, his treaty with the Greeks is broken: we and all Greece are threatened. The question is no longer how the Rhodians shall be governed: the island must be defended for our own sake, whatever party may prevail there. But, in such a case, it is the interest of Greece, not that of the aristocratical faction at Rhodes, which should be considered; and however warrantable, and just, and prudent, a vigorous defence of the island would then be; yet still, nothing but necessity, nothing but the certainty of its falling into the power of the Persian, without our assistance, could induce me to recommend the granting that assistance. If the reigning party could by themselves defend the island, they do not merit, nor should they be favoured with, our interposition; but, if not, our own and our nation's interests require, that we should defeat the designs of the Persian against Rhodes, even though this party should reap the immediate advantage.

[3.] I have no public, &c.] The citizens of the more eminent states in Greece had it sometimes in their power to confer favours on inferior communities; and these in return expressed their gratitude by declaring that such persons should, at any time during their residence among them, be entitled to entertainment at the public expense. In like manner, favours conferred and received by particular persons entitled them to the rights of private hospitality from each other. These were declarations of the most strict and inviolable friendship; and the least neglect or violation of this hospitality was accounted a crime of the most heinous nature.—The expressions in the original are founded on these customs.

happened : that the men who could not bear that we should regain our just rights, have now lost their own liberty : and they, who might have united upon terms of equality with the Greeks, and with us, the best of Greeks, chose to admit barbarians [1.] and slaves into their citadel, and to become their abject vassals. I had almost said, that these things must prove of use to them, if you vouchsafe your aid. In a course of prosperity, I know not whether they would ever have returned to reason; for they are Rhodians.[2.] But now, taught by experience that perverse folly is the cause of numberless calamities, they may possibly entertain sentiments more just and prudent for the future. And this, I apprehend, would be no small advantage to them. Let us then endeavour to avert their ruin: let us not harbour ancient resentments: let it be remembered that you yourselves have oftentimes been deceived by those who entertained designs against the state : and yet, on none of these will ye confess that punishment should be inflicted.

Let it also be considered, that you, my fellow-citizens, have waged many wars against states, both of popular and oligarchal governments. Of this you are not to be informed : but, perhaps, you have never once reflected, what were the causes of your several wars with each. With popular states [3.] your wars arose from particular complaints, which could not be decided in a national council; or from disputes about districts and boundaries; or from the love of glory or preeminence. But of your wars with oligarchies, [4.] there were different causes: with these you fought, for your constitution, for your liberty. So that I should not scruple to avow my opinion, that it would be better for us to be at war with all the states of Greece, provided [5.] that they enjoyed a popular government, than to be in friendship with them all, if commanded by oligarchies. For, with free states, I should not think it difficult to conclude a peace whenever ye were inclined; but with oligarchal governments, we could not even form a union, to be relied on. For, it is not possible that the few can entertain a sincere affection for the many; or the friends of arbitrary power, for the men who choose to live in free equality.

[1.] By Barbarians and slaves, he means the forces of Artemisia, which she sent to the assistance of the aristocratical faction; and which they kept in the citadel for their defence. *Lucchesini*—The admission of these forces into Rhodes is ascribed by Vitruvius to a stratagem of an extraordinary nature. He tells us, the Rhodians held a private intelligence in Halicarnassus, the capital of Caria; and hoped that the inhabitants would willingly unite with them, in order to shake off the yoke of a woman. In these expectations they sent a fleet thither. But Artemisia, having discovered the plot, ordered the inhabitants to range themselves under their walls, and to receive the Rhodians as their expected deliverers. Deceived by this appearance, the Rhodians landed, and left their ships deserted. They were surrounded, and cut to pieces. Artemisia, who had ordered her galleys to fall down some canals which communicated with the port, and to seize their ships, now set sail in the Rhodian fleet, and appeared before their island. It was supposed by the people of Rhodes, that their own army was returned victorious; and the Carians were masters of their fortress before the fatal mistake was perceived.

[2.] They are Rhodians.] Homer calls the Rhodians ὑπερηφάνους, insolent. And to this day they are said to be distinguished by the same fault, though now reduced to the extremity of slavery. *Lucchesini*.

[3.] I imagine that the orator had here in view the expeditions against the Corinthians and Syracusans. With the former, the Athenians contended about boundaries and territory; particular causes of complaint, but especially ambition, prompted them to wage war against the latter. And the government both of Corinth and Syracuse was regularly democratical. *Lucchesini*.

[4.] By oligarchies, the orator means the Bœotians and Megareans, but principally the Lacedemonians. *Lucchesini*.

[5.] With all the states of Greece, provided, &c.] To this the orator subjoins a reason, which makes the assertion appear less extraordinary: 'If attacked by all, it is true, the contest could not be supported, yet no terms of accommodation would be imposed that would alter or destroy our constitution. But no peace could secure the freedom of the only democratical state. The enemies of liberty, however apparently reconciled, must ever hate and fear, and at length destroy it.'—As I have taken the liberty to translate this passage in a manner different from that of the commentators and interpreters, it will be necessary fairly to quote the original at large. Ὥστε ἔγωγε οὐκ ἂν ὀκνήσαιμι εἰπεῖν μᾶλλον ἡγεῖσθαι συμφέρειν, δημοκρατουμένους τοὺς Ἕλληνας ἅπαντας πολεμεῖν ὑμῖν, ἢ ὀλιγαρχουμένους φίλους εἶναι.——Δημοκρατουμένους τοὺς Ἕλληνας hath been generally taken as equivalent to τοὺς τῶν Ἑλλήνων δημοκρατουμένους, &c. and the original understood as containing this assertion: 'It would be more eligible that all the republics in Greece should be at war with us, than that we should be in alliance with all the oligarchies. The learned in the Greek language will determine whether, in order to warrant this interpretation, the form of the sentence in the original should not have been τοὺς δημοκρατουμένους, Ἕλληνας, instead of δημοκρατουμένους τοὺς, &c. But, not to insist on grammatical niceties, it is submitted to the reader, who attends to the history and circumstances of Greece, whether to be at war with the free states, that is, the states of Peloponnesus, or to be in alliance with the oligarchies, that is (principally) the states of Lacedemon and Bœotia, be two particulars so necessarily in-

I am surprised that none among you should conceive, that if the Chians, and the Mitylenæans, [1.] and now the Rhodians, are to be subjected to a few; I had almost said, if all mankind are to be thus enslaved, our constitution must be threatened with danger. It is surprising that none among you should reflect, that if this form of policy be established in every place, it is not possible that our free government should be suffered to continue. For it must then be certain, that none others but the Athenians can arise to restore affairs to their original state of freedom. And those whom men regard as dangerous, they must ever labour to destroy. In every other case, they who act unjustly are enemies only to those whom their injustice hath immediately affected; but they who subvert free states, and reduce them to the power of a few, are to be deemed the common enemies of all the zealous friends of liberty. And justice too demands, ye men of Athens, that you, who enjoy a popular government, should discover the same concern for the misfortunes of other free states, which you yourselves would expect from them, if at any time (which Heaven avert!) the like misfortunes should oppress you. It may be said, indeed, that the Rhodians are deservedly distressed; but this is not a time for such objections. Let the prosperous ever show the tenderest solicitude for the unhappy; since none can say what may be their own future fortune.

I have heard it frequently observed in this assembly, that, when the state was in its deepest distress, there were not wanting friends to concert measures for its restoration. Of this I shall, at present, briefly mention but one instance, I mean that of the Argives. [2.] And I should be sorry that we, whose distinguished character it is to protect the wretched, should appear inferior to the Argives in this particular. They, though seated on the borders of Lacedemon, witnesses of the uncontrolled power of this city, both by sea and land; yet, could not be diverted, could not be deterred from expressing their affection to the Athenians. When ambassadors came from Lacedemon, to demand some Athenian exiles who had taken refuge at Argos, they declared by a decree, that unless these ambassadors departed from their city, before the setting sun, they should be accounted enemies. And would it not be shameful, my countrymen, that the populace of Argos should, in such times as these, defy the terror of the Lacedemonian power and sovereignty; and yet, that you, who are Athenians, should be terrified by a barbarian; nay, by a woman? The Argives might have justly pleaded, that they had oftentimes been conquered by the Lacedemonians. But you have frequently proved victorious over the king; never were once defeated, either by his slaves or by himself. Or, if the Persian boasts to have obtained any advantage over us, he owes it to those treasures which he lavished on the corrupt traitors and hirelings of Greece. If ever he hath prevailed, by these means hath he prevailed. Nor have such successes proved of real use. No: we find that, at the very time when he was endeavouring to depress this state, by the help of Lacedemon, [3.] his own dominions were exposed to the dangerous attempts of Clearchus and Cyrus. Thus were his avowed attacks ever unsuccessful; his secret practices attended with no real advantage.

There are men among you, who frequently affect a disregard of Philip, as if beneath their attention, but of the king express the most terrible apprehensions, as of an enemy truly dangerous to those whom he may determine to attack. If then we are never to oppose the one, because weak, and to make unbounded concessions to the other, because formidable, against whom, my countrymen, are we to draw our swords?

---

compatible,[*] as to oblige the Athenians to choose one or the other. If it be said that it is sufficient to suppose that particular quarrels might arise, in which a union with Sparta and Bœotia, would prevent the free states from attacking the Athenians; and the rejecting this union might encourage them to the attack; in such case, I suspect that the orator never could have advised his countrymen to engage singly in a war, as the most eligible measure, which, by weakening each party, would render both an easier prey to those who are supposed (from the nature of their constitution) to be their common enemies. And such advice would still be more unaccountable, should it be supposed, that in consequence of rejecting the alliance of Sparta and Bœotia, these states would unite with the enemies of Athens.

[1.] From this passage it seems not improbable, that the designs of the Persian had extended farther than to Rhodes; and that he had by his power of influence lately made alterations in the state and government of these inferior islands, which the embarrassed condition of the Athenians, and their attention to the motions of the Macedonian king, might have prevented them from opposing.

[2.] This instance of the magnanimity of the Argives must have been particularly agreeable to the assembly, as the form of government at Argos was, like that of Athens, republican. The memory of this noble and generous act hath been passed over by historians. But we have it here preserved, enlivened, and enforced, by the most vivid colouring, and the utmost strength of expression. *Lucchesini.*

[3.] In the first year of the 94th Olympiad, the Lacedemonians became masters of Athens, and there established the thirty tyrants. In the fourth year of the same Olympiad, Cyrus took up arms against his brother Artaxerxes. So that between these two events, but a small interval of time intervened; which sufficiently warrants the assertion of the orator *Lucchesini!*

There are men, too, most powerful in pleading for the rights of others, in opposition to your demands. To these I would make one request; that they should endeavour to display an equal zeal in the defence of your rights, against your adversaries. Thus shall they be the first to show a real regard to justice. It is absurd to urge its precepts to you, if they themselves pay no deference to its authority. And, surely, a member of this state cannot pretend to a regard for justice, who seeks industriously for every argument against us, never for those which may be urged in our favour. Consider, I conjure you, why, among the Byzantines, there is no man to inform them, that they are not to seize Chalcedon, [1.] which is really the king's; which you some time possessed; but to which they have no sort of claim: that they should not attempt to reduce Sylembria to their subjection, a city once united in alliance with us: that in assuming a power of determining the boundaries of the Sylembrian territory, the Byzantines violate their oaths, they infringe those treaties which say expressly, that this people shall be governed by their own laws. Why, during the life of Mausolus, or since his death, hath no one been found to inform Artemisia, that she is not to possess herself of Cos, of Rhodes, of many other Grecian states, which the king, who was master of them, ceded by treaty to the Greeks; and for which the Greeks of those days encountered many dangers, supported many noble contests? Or, were these things thus urged to both; that they would have any influence, is by no means probable.—I, on my part, see no injustice in reinstating the people of Rhodes; but, even if it were not strictly just, yet, when I view the actions of others, I think it my duty to recommend this measure. And why? Because, if all others confined themselves within the bounds of justice, it would be shameful, that you, Athenians, should be the only people to transgress. But, when every other state seeks all opportunities of acting injuriously, that you alone should give up every advantage from pretended scruples, and nice distinctions of right; this is not justice, but cowardice.

In effect, indeed, we find men proportion their claims of right to their present power. Of this I shall mention one example, well known to all. There are two treaties [2.] on record, between the Greeks and the king; that which our state concluded, which is the subject of universal praise; and this latter, made by the Lacedemonians, which was condemned as odious and dishonourable. In these treaties, the rights of either party were by no means defined in the same manner; 'and no wonder,' for, in civil society, the rights of individuals are determined by the laws, with the same equal and common regard to the weak and to the strong. But, in political and national transactions, the powerful ever prescribe the bounds of right to the weaker. You assume the character of arbitrators and defenders of justice: be careful ♦ then to preserve such power as may give due weight and effect to your determinations. And this will be done by showing that the Athenians are the general patrons and protectors of liberty.

Sensible, indeed, I am, and with good reason, that it is not without the utmost difficulty that you can execute any purposes of moment. All others have but one contest to maintain, that against their avowed enemies: when they have once conquered these, they enjoy the fruits of their conquest without farther opposition. But you, Athenians! have a double contest to support. Like others, you have your open enemies; but you have enemies still more dangerous and alarming; you have those of your own citizens to subdue,

---

[1.] Chalcedon.] This city of Bithynia, after various vicissitudes of fortune, had been given up to the king of Persia, by the peace of Antalcidas. But now it appears to have been exposed in the invasions of the Byzantines, as well as Sylembria, a maritime town in the neighbourhood of Byzantium. *Lucchesini.*

[2.] The passage, as here translated, plainly points out the two most famous treaties concluded between the Greeks and Persians; the one, by Cimon the Athenian (An. 3. Olymp. 77;) the other, by Antalcidas the Lacedemonian (An. 2. Olymp. 98.) The first was made immediately after the final overthrow of the Persian forces, both by sea and land. By this treaty it was provided, that all the Grecian cities in Asia should be free and independent; and that no Persian ship of war should presume to sail to the westward of the Cyanæan and Chelidonian islands: that is, to approach so near as to give the least umbrage or alarm to the Greeks: terms, which plainly supposed the superiority of Greece, and are, accordingly, represented by historians as highly honourable to this nation. The latter treaty, on the contrary, was dictated by the Persians, and the weakness and disorders of the Greeks obliged them to accept of it. By this, the Grecian colonies of Asia, together with some of the islands, were formally given up to the power and jurisdiction of the Persian king. And historians have not restrained their indignation at the meanness and ignominy of these concessions.

The interpreters and commentators have indeed rendered this passage in another manner. But, without entering into controversy, the translator submits the pertinency and propriety of the present interpretation to the judgment of the learned reader; by no means confident, yet not without hopes of his concurrence. And, should he happen to be more fortunate, in some particular instance, than his predecessors or associates in the same labour, he esteems it a matter which warrants no sort of triumph or exultation.

who, in this assembly, are engaged against the interests of their country. And, as they are ever strenuous in their opposition to all useful measures, it is no wonder that many of our designs are frustrated. Perhaps, those emoluments which their corruptors hold forth to tempt them, may be the inducement to many, boldly to aspire to the rank of ministers and public counsellors. But still you yourselves may be justly blamed. For it is your part, Athenians! to entertain the same sentiments with regard to the rank of civil duty, as to that of battle. And what are these sentiments? He who deserts the post assigned him by the general, you pronounce infamous, [1.] and unworthy to share the common rights of an Athenian citizen. In like manner, he who, in our civil polity, abandons the station assigned by our ancestors, and attempts to establish the power of the few, should be declared unworthy to speak in this assembly. Do you think it necessary to bind our allies by an oath, to have the same friends and the same enemies with us, in order to be assured of their attachment? And shall those ministers be deemed truly loyal, who are certainly and evidently devoted to the service of our enemies?

But, what might be urged in accusation against them, what might be urged with severity against you, it is by no means difficult to find. By what counsels, by what conduct, the present disorders of our state may be removed; this is the great point of difficulty. Nor is this, perhaps, the time to enlarge on every particular. Exert yourselves on the present occasion; endeavour to render your designs effectual, by an advantageous execution; and then, your other interests may, perhaps, gradually wear a fairer aspect.

It is, therefore, my opinion, that you should engage in the affairs of this people with the utmost vigour; and act as becomes the dignity of Athens. Think with what joy you attend to those who praise your ancestors, who display their achievements, and recount their trophies. And think, that your ancestors erected these trophies, not that the view might barely strike you with admiration; but that you might imitate the virtues of the men who raised them. [2.]

[1.] In the Olynthiac orations, we find Demosthenes complaining, that the severity of the ancient military laws had been considerably relaxed. And this passage furnishes us with a remarkable instance of such relaxation. For, by the original laws and constitutions of Athens, it was declared a capital offence for any citizen to fly, or to desert from his post. Even he who cast away his shield was punished with death. If any man lost it by accidental neglect he was bound to pay a fine of five hundred drachmæ. *Lucchesini.*

[2.] From the succeeding oration, we learn, that the address and energy which Demosthenes exerted in favour of the people of Rhodes were by no means effectual. The times in which he lived were distracted and corrupted; his country not well disposed, nor indeed possessed of force sufficient to support the general cause of liberty. The assembly in which he spoke was (if we except some extraordinary cases of immediate danger) ever governed by party. The citizens came together, not to deliberate on the public interests, but to support a faction, already determined, and resolved in what manner to give their voices; and armed against the power of truth. It is no wonder, therefore, that we find the most consummate eloquence, the justest, the strongest, and the most animated representations, in so many instances unsuccessful.

THE ORATION ON THE REGULATION OF THE STATE:

PRONOUNCED IN THE ARCHONSHIP OF THEOPHRASTUS, THE FIRST YEAR OF THE HUNDRED AND TENTH OLYMPIAD.

INTRODUCTION.

THE contests between the Macedonians and Athenians (to which we owe the most valuable remains of Demosthenes) have been explained in the former volume of the Philippic orations. The reader is not now to be informed, at what time, and with what success, king Philip attempted to reduce Perinthus and Byzantium. When he found himself obliged to raise the siege of Byzantium, he is said to have turned his arms against Scythia.

The Athenians, who were elated by the least appearance of good fortune, considered this as a flight. They were fired with the imagination of an enemy, that had so long proved formidable and successful, defeated in his designs, and ,this, principally, by the counsels and arms of Athens; retiring before their general Phocion, and forced from all attempts on Greece, to retrieve the honour of his arms, in parts remote and barbarous. This they considered as the happy moment for pursuing their advantages, and for reducing that ambition to just and equitable bounds, which was now, for the first time, severely mortified and disappointed.

In order to render the hostilities now meditated more formidable and effectual, the Athenians began seriously to reflect on the causes of past misfortunes, and seemed resolved to reform those 'corruptions and abuses, which had disgraced their constitution, and weakened their power.

The oppressions and severe exactions, of which their allies and dependent states had lately found particular occasion to complain, and to which the necessity of their affairs had contributed, as well as the avarice of their commanders, naturally determined them to reflect on the necessity of making some effectual provision for the payment of their armies: and this as naturally determined the honest and faithful counsellors to resume the consideration of that old, scandalous abuse, the 'Theatrical distributions.' Of these the reader hath been sufficiently informed in the 'Notes' and 'Introductions' of the Olynthiac orations.

An assembly was therefore convened, to consider of the most eligible methods to provide for the public exigencies, in the least burdensome and most effectual manner; and particularly to consider of the expediency of restoring their theatrical funds to the service of the army; a point which their misguided decrees had rendered so dangerous to be proposed. On this occasion was the following oration delivered; in which the orator resumes his favourite subject, with his usual spirit, yet with sufficient caution: points out the corruptions of his countrymen, with their causes and consequences: and describes both the ancient and present state of Athens; Athens uncorrupted, illustrious, and fortunate; and the same state degenerated and disgraced;

with all the honest severity and indignation of a patriot.

In this oration no mention is made of Philip or his designs, of the late transactions in Greece, of the late advantages or disgraces of the Athenian arms. The orator confines himself entirely, and directs the attention of his hearers, to the points immediately under consideration. And we find that these afforded him sufficient room for the exertion of his abilities.

THE ORATION ON THE REGULATION OF THE STATE.

Theophratus, Archon.— Olympiad. 110. *An.* 1.

MEN OF ATHENS!

[1.] As to this money, and the affairs, at this time, proposed to the assembly, it appears to me, that a speaker may, without danger, espouse either side. By condemning those who thus distribute and exhaust the public treasure, he may gain their esteem, who regard this custom as injurious to the public; or, by assenting, and encouraging these distributions, he may recommend himself to their favour, whose necessities prompt them to demand these public aids. By neither party is the interest of the state considered. Their approbation, or their condemnation of this custom, is influenced entirely by their several circumstances of indigence or affluence. I, on my part, shall neither oppose nor recommend it. But this I would entreat you seriously and maturely to consider, that the money, now the subject of debate, is of little moment; but the custom which it hath produced, [2.] of great

---

[1.] The fatal consequences of lavishing the public revenues, on spectacles and entertainments, had been long and severely experienced. Yet still numbers were found in the assembly, who, from private motives, either of interest, or to recommend themselves to the lower part of the citizens, pleaded in favour of this abuse, and found plausible arguments to urge in its favour. These, and their opposers, seem to have already debated the present point, with considerable heat and violence; and to have been supported by their respective partisans, not with that decorum or temper which, perhaps, are sometimes found in less numerous assemblies. Hence, the appearance of moderation in this exordium: which, in the present disposition of the people, was probably necessary in order to obtain the orator an audience. And it may, in general, be observed, that although the eloquence of Demosthenes be commonly, and very justly, compared to the irresistible lightning, storm, or torrent; yet such similitudes are not to be understood too strictly: for, on all necessary occasions, he appears a consummate master of the gentle arts of insinuation.

He thunders and lightens indeed; yet, sometimes (if the allusion be warrantable,) 'half his strength he puts not forth.' Nor, in effect, does he ever give a free and full course to his energy, until he has prepared his hearers to receive the impression.

[2.] I have here endeavoured to express what I take to be the intent and meaning of the orator, from comparing the passage with others of the like import, in the Olynthiac orations. To propose to the assembly that the theatrical money (as it was called) should be applied to other purposes, was, by the law of Eubulus, declared a capital offence. Demosthenes therefore advises, not that this money should be alienated to the payment of their armies; but, that all citizens should receive their distributions as usual; yet, at the same time, discharge all their respective offices, whether civil or military, without farther salary or pay: and, that such only as had thus discharged, or were ready to discharge, these offices, should be entitled to the public distributions. The two proposals are, in effect and reality, the same, but different in form: and this difference was sufficient for eluding

14   †

consequence. If, then, these distributions be established, for those who have first respectively discharged their public offices; far from injuring, you will do the most essential service both to your country and to yourselves. But if a feast, or any other like pretence, be sufficient for demanding these sums; if the mention of any farther conditions be rejected with impatience; beware, lest all your regulations, how specious, how promising soever, may hereafter prove erroneous.

This I now declare as my opinion (let me not be interrupted by clamour; but hear, and then determine)—That, as we are now convened about receiving these distributions, so should an assembly be appointed to consider of a general regulation of the state, and particularly of a provision for our military affairs: and every citizen should discover not only a just attention to all useful measures, but a just alacrity to carry them into execution; that so, my countrymen, our hopes of good success may depend upon ourselves, instead of being amused with reports of this or that man's exploits. Let all the public treasures; let all the 'funds for which private fortunes are now so uselessly exhausted; let all those resources, which our allies afford, be equitably distributed, and effectually applied: by the soldier, to his support in time of action; by the man who hath passed the age of military duty, as a recompense for his services in the administration of justice. Let the duties of the field be discharged by yourselves, duties too important to be intrusted to others; let your armies be composed of citizens: thus let them be paid and provided. So shall they go on with vigour and success: [1.] so shall your general really command his forces; and so shall your occupation be no longer to conduct the trials of your officers, nor the result of all your measures prove

but this—an accuser,[2.] an impeachment, and a criminal.

What then may be expected 'from the measures now proposed?' First, that the attachment of our allies will be secured, not by garrisons, but by making their and our interests the same; then, that our generals, attended by their troops of foreigners, will [3.] no longer harass our confederates by their depredations, without once daring to face the enemy (a conduct by which all emoluments have centred in these generals, but which hath loaded the state with odium and disgrace.) On the contrary, by leading out an army composed of citizens, they shall inflict that severity on our enemies, hitherto directed against our friends and allies.

But, besides these, there are other affairs which demand your personal service. A war in our own country must certainly be better supported by an army of our own citizens: and for other purposes such an army is absolutély necessary. Were it consistent with your character, to sit down inactive, without the least concern or interest in the affairs of Greece, I should then use a different language. But, now, you affect the dignity of supreme commanders and umpires in Greece: but yet, the forces to defend and to preserve this superiority, you have not yet prepared, nor are solicitous to prepare. No! by your indolence and insensibility the people of Mitylene [4.] have lost their liberty; by your indolence and insensibility the people of Rhodes have lost their liberty.—But these, it may be said, were our enemies.—Yet we should regard oligarchies as much more the objects of our aversion (merely on account of their constitution) than free states can be from any cause.

But I have wandered from my purpose. My advice is this: That you should be arranged in your classes; and that, by one and

---

the severity of the law. See Note 2. p. 26. Olynth. II.

[1.] In the Philippic orations we find notice frequently taken of the misconduct of the Athenian generals, in employing their forces not conformably to their instructions, but in expeditions neither appointed nor approved by their country. This Demosthenes ever affects to ascribe principally to disobedience and want of discipline in the foreign forces, and to the necessities of the general, which obliged him to procure, by arms, that provision for his soldiers, which the state neglected to supply. See note 4. p. 14, on Philip. I.

[2.] An accuser, &c.] In the original— 'Such a man, the son of such a man, hath impeached such a person: Ὁ δεῖνα τοῦ δεῖνος, τὸν δεῖνα εἰσηγγειλεν. Alluding to the usual form of the bill or motion preferred to the assembly, or to the judges, upon such occasions.—I have here chosen to adhere to the interpretation of Wolfius; as sufficiently warranted by the original, as most pertinent, and certainly most spirited.

[3.] When the Athenians sent to collect their tribute from the dependent islands, they

frequently employed an admiral, attended with such a navy as proved both a burden and a terror to the islanders. When Phocion was appointed to sail with twenty ships on such an occasion, 'Why such a force?' said this humane Athenian; 'If I am to meet enemies, it is insufficient; if I am sent to friends, a single vessel will serve.' And even those allies who found themselves obliged to implore the assistance of the Athenians against their enemies, frequently experienced more miserable effects from the oppression and rapine of their auxiliaries, than from the arms of their assailants. So notorious and odious was the avarice of Chares, that when he led an army to the relief of Byzantium (a little before the date of this oration,) the Byzantines shut their gates against him.

[4.] This change of the government at Mitylene, as it could not convey any instruction to posterity, hath been passed over in silence, by all the ancients except Demosthenes: so that we are ignorant of the manner in which it was effected. (And how far the Athenians were really to blame in not preventing it.) *Lucchesini.*

the same regulation, you should be entitled to receive, and obliged to act. Of these things I have spoken upon former occasions; and explained the manner in which our infantry, our cavalry, in which those who are exempt from military service, may be all duly regulated, and all receive their stipends fully. But, that which of all things gives me the most melancholy apprehensions, I shall here declare without disguise. Many, and noble, and important, are the objects which should command your attention. Yet no man hath the least respect to any one of them; all attend solely to the wretched pittance [1.] you distribute. Such a pittance then, they must confess, is adequate to their desert. But a just attention to the objects I have mentioned, must have consequences more valuable than all the wealth of Persia :—the exact regulation and appointment of a state like this, possessed of so great an infantry, of such a navy, of such a cavalry, of such revenues.

But, wherefore do I mention these things? For this reason: There are men shocked at the thoughts of obliging all our citizens to serve in war; but there are none, who do not readily acknowledge, that it is of the utmost moment to the state, to be duly regulated and perfectly provided. It is your part, therefore, to begin here; and to allow a full freedom of speech to those who would urge the importance of this point in its full force. If you be convinced, that this is the proper time for considering of the necessary provisions, you may command them when called to action. But, should you imagine that such considerations may more properly be deferred to some future

occasion; then must ye be reduced to give up the time of execution to the necessary preparations.

It may have been already asked, Athenians! (not by the majority of this assembly, but by certain persons, who would burst with vexation should these measures be pursued,) 'What real advantage have we derived from the speeches of Demosthenes? He rises when he thinks proper: he deafens us with his harangues: he declaims against the degeneracy of present times: he tells us of the virtues of our ancestors: he transports us by his airy extravagance: he puffs up our vanity; and then sits down.'—But, could these my speeches once gain an effectual influence upon your minds, so great would be the advantages conferred upon my country, that, were I to attempt to speak them, they would appear to many as visionary. Yet, still I must assume the merit of doing some service, by accustoming you to hear salutary truths. And, if your counsellors be solicitous for any point of moment to their country, let them first cure your ears, for they are distempered; and this, from the inveterate habit of listening to falsehoods, to every thing rather than your real interests.

Thus it lately happened—(Let no man interrupt me: let me have a patient hearing,) —that some persons broke into the treasury. The speakers all instantly exclaimed, 'Our free constitution is overturned: our laws are no more.' And now, ye men of Athens! judge, if I speak with reason. They who are guilty of this crime, justly deserve to die; but, by such offenders, our constitution is not overturned. Again, some oars [1.] have been sto-

---

[1.] To the wretched pittance, &c.] Literally, 'to the two Oboli:' that is '2d. 2q. the sum distributed to the poorer citizens for their support, and for the purchase of their seats in the theatre. And small as this largess was, yet, as the number of such citizens was great, and as the distribution seems to have been made daily, the treasury must have been considerably exhausted by it. Nor are we warranted to suppose, that the people always confined their demands to this sum. Entertainments, processions, and religious ceremonies, afforded pretences for still farther demands.

[2.] Some oars, &c.] We cannot well suppose, that the depredations made in the naval stores were really so slight and inconsiderable, as they are represented in these extenuating terms. A design had lately been concerted, of a very momentous and alarming nature, and an attempt made on the naval stores at Athens, which Demosthenes himself laboured, with the utmost zeal, to detect and punish. A man named Antipho had been, for some time, considered as an Athenian citizen; till, by an examination of the registers, he was found to be really a foreigner; was accordingly deprived of all the privileges of a native, and driven, with some ignominy, from the city. Enraged at this disgrace, he went off to Philip, and to him proposed to steal

privately into Athens, and to set fire to the arsenal. The Macedonian, who was neither delicate in the choice of his instruments, nor in the means of distressing his enemies, listened readily to the proposal of this hireling, and by bribes and promises encouraged him to the attempt. Antipho repaired to Athens, and was lodged in the port, ready to put his enterprise in execution, when Demosthenes, who received timely intimation of this black design, flew to the Piræus, and seized and dragged the delinquent before an assembly of the people. Here the clamours of the Macedonian party were so violent, that the accusation was slighted, and Antipho dismissed without the formality of a trial. He departed, triumphing in his escape, to pursue his designs with greater confidence and security. But the court of Areopagus, whose peculiar province it was, to take the cognizance of all matters of treason against the state, caused him to be again seized and examined. Torture forced from him a full confession of his guilt; and sentence of death was passed and executed upon him.—This account we have from the oration on the Crown. And the detection of so dangerous a design might have quickened the vigilance of the people, and exasperated their resentment against any the least attempts made on their military stores.

len from our arsenal.—'Stripes and tortures for the villain; our constitution is subverted!' This is the general cry. But what is my opinion? This criminal, like the others, hath deserved to die: but, if some are criminal, our constitution is not therefore subverted. There is no man who dares openly and boldly to declare, in what case our constitution is subverted. But I shall declare it. When you, Athenians! become a helpless rabble, without conduct, without property, without arms, without order, without unanimity; when neither general, nor any other person, hath the least respect for your decrees; when no man dares to inform you of this your condition, to urge the necessary reformation, much less to exert his efforts to effect it—'then is your constitution subverted.' And this is now the case.

But, O my fellow-citizens! a language of a different nature hath poured in upon us; false, and highly dangerous to the state. Such is that assertion, that in your tribunals is your great security; that your right of suffrage is the real bulwark of the constitution. That these tribunals are our common resource in all private contests, I acknowledge: but, it is by arms we are to subdue our enemies, by arms we are to defend our state. It is not by our decrees that we can conquer. To those, on the contrary, who fight our battles with success, to those we owe the power of decreeing, of transacting all our affairs, without control or danger. In arms, then, let us be terrible; in our judicial transactions, humane.

If it be observed, that these sentiments are more elevated than might be expected from my character, the observation, I confess, is just. Whatever is said about a state of such dignity, upon affairs of such importance, should appear more elevated than any character. To your worth should it correspond, not to that of the speaker. And now I shall inform you why none of those, who stand high in your esteem, speak in the same manner. The candidates for office and employment go about soliciting your voices, the slaves of popular favour. To gain the rank of general, is each man's great concern; not to fill this station with true manlike intrepidity. Courage, if he possesses it, he deems unnecessary; for thus he reasons: he has the honour, the renown of this city to support him; he finds himself free from oppression and control; he needs but to amuse you with fair hopes: and thus

he secures a kind of inheritance in your emoluments. And he reasons truly. But, do you yourselves once assume the conduct of your own affairs; and then, as you take an equal share of duty, so shall you acquire an equal share of glory. Now, your ministers and public speakers, without one thought of directing you faithfully to your true interests, resign themselves entirely to these generals. Formerly you divided [1.] into Classes, in order to raise the supplies: now the business of the Classes is to gain the management of public affairs. The orator is the leader; the general seconds his attempts; the Three Hundred are the assistants on each side; and all others take their parties, and serve to fill up the several factions. And you see the consequences: this man gains a statue; this amasses a fortune; one or two command the state; while you sit down unconcerned witnesses of their success; and, for an uninterrupted course of ease and indolence, give them up those great and glorious advantages which really belong to you.

And now consider what was the conduct of our ancestors in these particulars (for, if we would be taught how to act with dignity, we need not look to other countries for examples; we have had them in our own state.) To Themistocles, who commanded in the sea-fight at Salamis; [2.] to Miltiades, the general at Marathon; to many others, who surely never did such services as our present generals, they never once erected a brazen statue. These men were never such darling favourites; never were deemed superior to their fellow-citizens. No, by the gods! the Athenians of those days never would give up their share in the honour of any noble action. Nor is there a man that will say, the sea-fight of Themistocles, at Salamis, but of the Athenians: not the engagement at Marathon, by Miltiades, but by the state. But now we are perpetually told, that Timotheus took Cocyra; that Iphicrates cut off the detachment; that Chabrias gained the naval victory at Naxos. Thus, you seem to resign all your share in these actions, by those extravagant honours which you heap upon your generals.

Such was the noble conduct of our ancestors in rewarding citizens; and such is your mistaken conduct. But of honouring foreigners what have been the methods? To [3.] Menon the Pharsalian, who supplied us with

---

[1.] Formerly you divided, &c.] See Note 3. on Olynth. I, p. 23.

[2.] Who commanded in the sea-fight at Salamis, &c.] These are the very expressions of the original; and although the common metonymical phrase ['Who gained the victory at Salamis'] might appear less uncouth, and be more familiar to a modern ear, yet I should have thought it unpardonable in the translation, as it is a mode of speaking which Demosthenes studiously avoids. And, indeed, had he been betrayed into it, he must have

exposed himself to all the ridicule of his acute and observant audience: for, in the very next sentence, he condemns it as highly derogatory to the honour of his country.

[3.] This war at Eion, near Amphipolis, I am bold to assert, was the same with that so particularly described by Thucydides, in the eighth, ninth, and tenth years of the Peloponnesian war; when the Lacedemonians, under the command of Brasidas, opposed the Athenians in this country; although the historian, who confined himself to the transactions of

twelve talents of silver, in our war at Eion, near Amphipolis, and reinforced us with two hundred horsemen, of his own dependents, our ancestors never voted the freedom of our city, but only granted certain immunities. [1.] And in earlier times, Perdiccas, who reigned in Macedon [2.] at the time of the barbarian's invasion, who fell on the barbarians in their retreat from the slaughter of Platæa, and completed the ruin of the king, they never voted the freedom of the city; they but granted him immunities : thoroughly persuaded that the honour of being a citizen of Athens was too exalted, too illustrious, to be purchased by any services. But now, my countrymen, it is exposed to common sale : the most abandoned of mankind, the slaves [3.] of slaves are admitted to pay down the price, and at once obtain it. And such difference of conduct doth not arise from this, that you are naturally less excellent than your ancestors ; but from those truly noble sentiments which they were accustomed to entertain, and which you have lost. For it is not possible that men, engaged in low and grovelling pursuits, can be possessed with great and generous thoughts. Just as those, who act with dignity and honour, cannot harbour any mean and abject thought. Whatever be their course of conduct, such must men's sentiments ever prove.

And now, let us take one general view of the actions performed by our ancestors, and by ourselves ; that, by such comparison, we may learn to excel ourselves. Five-and-forty years did they govern Greece with general consent. More than ten thousand talents did they collect

---

greatest importance, makes no mention of this assistance afforded to the Athenians by Menon the Pharsalian. This Menon I take to be the same with the Thessalian of that name, who, in the fourth year of the ninety-fourth Olympiad, led a body of forces to the assistance of Cyrus, against his brother Artaxerxes, according to Diodorus and Xenophon. The circumstances of his supplying the Athenians with money, and giving them a body of horse, exactly agree to two particulars in the character of that Menon whom Xenophon describes : that it was his custom to court the friendship of the powerful, that they might screen him from the punishment due to his infamous practices ; and that he constantly kept in his service a large body of forces ready to act as he directed. *Lucchesini.*

[1.] Certain immunities.] A manner of doing honour to these men, which, at the same time, expressed a high sense of the dignity of their own city. For it supposed that these eminent personages might find it necessary to take up their residence for some considerable time at Athens, as ' sojourners.' And, in order to understand the nature of these immunities, we must attend to the situation of those Μέτοικοι, or sojourners. So were those foreigners called, who settled at Athens, by permission of the Areopagus. Here they were allowed to follow their occupations, without disturbance ; but had no share in the government ; were not intrusted with public offices, nor voted in the assembly. They were obliged to the performance of certain duties ; as in the festival celebrated in honour of Minerva, called Panathenæa, the men were obliged to carry the σκάφαι, or little ships, which were the signs of their foreign extraction, while the women bore the ὑδρίαι, vessels of water, and the σκιάδια, umbrellas, to defend the free women from the weather. This last custom, indeed, was introduced in the insolence of the Athenian prosperity, after the defeat of the Persians. Besides this, the men paid an annual tribute of twelve drachmæ. The women, who had no sons, paid six. Such as had sons that paid, were excused. And this tribute was exacted not only of those that dwelt in Athens, but of all that settled themselves in any town of Attica. This tribute, by the interposition of Themistocles, was, for a time, remitted ; but seems to have been restored in consequence of his disgrace : and, upon any failure of payment, the delinquent was liable to be seized, and sold as a slave. —Such of these sojourners as had been remarkably serviceable to the public, were honoured, by edict, with an immunity from all impositions and duties, except such as were required of the free-born citizens. Hence this honour was called Ἰσοτέλεια, and Ἀτέλεια, (the expression of the text.) To foreigners of eminence, such immunities might have extended even to an exemption from certain duties, to which citizens themselves were obliged. For immunities of this kind were frequently granted, so as to occasion complaints and remonstrances.

[2.] Perdiccas, who reigned in Macedon, &c.] According to Herodotus, Alexander, the son of Amyntas, was king of Macedon at the time of the Persian war. And therefore we may suppose, with the Italian commentator, that this Perdiccas was one of the royal family, and governed one of those districts into which Macedon was divided in the earlier times. Nor are we to wonder, that this action of the Macedonian has been passed over in silence by the historians, as it was not very considerable, when compared with the great events of the Persian war.

[3.] The slaves, &c.] The freedom of the city was, by the constitution of Athens, conferred only by the voices of the people, nor was their act valid, unless confirmed in a subsequent assembly by the votes of more than six thousand Athenians, by ballot (as we learn from the oration of Demosthenes against Neæra ;) but now their poverty had made them much less delicate. And we learn from Athenæus, that they had about this time conferred the freedom of their city (this compliment, in former times, scarcely vouchsafed to kings and potentates) on two men whose only pretence of merit was, that their father had been famous for improving the art of cookery. Such a scandalous prostitution of their honours fully justifies all the severity of Demosthenes.

into our treasury. Many and noble monuments did they erect, of victories by land and sea, which are yet the objects of our applause. And be assured, that they erected these, not to be viewed in silent wonder, but that you might be excited to emulate the virtues of those who raised them. Such was their conduct. Say then, can we, though seated thus securely above all opposition, boast of any actions like these? Have we not lavished more than one thousand five hundred talents on every Grecian state that pleaded their distress; and all to no purpose? Have we not exhausted all our private fortunes, all the revenues of our state, all we could exact from our confederates? The allies which we gained by arms, have they not been given up in our treaties?—Yes! in these particulars, it is granted, that our ancestors excelled us; but there are others in which we are superior.—Far from it!—Shall we pursue the comparison? The edifices they have left to us, their decorations of our city, of our temples, of our harbours, of all our public structures, are so numerous and so magnificent, that their successors can make no addition. Look round you to their vestibules, their arsenals, their porticoes, and all those honours of our city, which they transmitted to us. Yet, were the private habitations of the men of eminence, in those times, so moderate, so consonant to that equality, the characteristic of our constitution, that, if any one of you knows the house of Themistocles, of Cimon, of Aristides, of Miltiades, or of any of the then illustrious personages, he knows that it is not distinguished by the least mark of grandeur. But now, ye men of Athens! as to public works, the state is satisfied, if roads be repaired, if water be supplied, if walls be whitened, if any trifle be provided. Not that I blame those who have executed such works. No! I blame you who can think so meanly as to be satisfied with such fruits of their administration. Then, in private life, of the men who have conducted our affairs, some have built houses, not only more magnificent than those of other citizens, but superior to our public edifices; others have purchased and improved an extent of land greater than all their dreams of riches ever presented to their fancies.

And here lies the great source of these errors. Formerly, all power and authority were in the people. Happy was it for any individual, if they vouchsafed him a share of honours, employments, or emoluments. But now, on the contrary, individuals are masters of all advantages, are directors of all affairs; whilst the people stand in the mean rank of their servants and assistants; fully satisfied, if these men vouchsafe to grant them some small share of their abundance.

To such a state have we been reduced by these means, that if a man were to peruse your decrees, and then distinctly to examine your actions, he could not persuade himself, that the same people had been authors of both. Witness the decrees you made against the accursed Megareans, [1.] who had possessed themselves of the consecrated ground; that you would march out, that you would oppose them, that you would not permit such sacrilege. Witness your decrees about the Phliasian exiles; [2.] that you would support them; that you would not abandon them to their assassins; that you would call on those of the Peloponnesians who were inclined to unite with you in their cause. These were all noble declarations; these were just; these were worthy of our state. Not so the execution. Thus your decrees serve but to discover your hostile dispositions; your enemies never feel their effects. The resolutions of your assembles fully express the dignity of your country; but that force which should attend these resolutions, you do not possess. It is, in my opinion, your only alternative (and let it not raise your indignation;) either to entertain sentiments less elevated, and to confine your attention to your own affairs, or to arm yourselves with greater force. If this assembly were composed of the inhabitants of some obscure and contemptible islands, I should advise you to think less highly. But, as you are Athenians, I must urge you to increase your force. For it is shameful, O my countrymen! it is shameful to desert that rank of magnanimity, in which our ancestors have placed us. Could we descend to such a thought, it would be impossible to withdraw our attention from the affairs of Greece. We

---

[1.] This instance of the impiety of the Megareans, of whom Demosthenes here affects to speak with so much detestation, probably happened about the time, and was the occasion of the embassy of Anthemocritus, of whom mention is made in Philip's letter to the Athenians. *Lucchesini.*

[2.] As this affair is not mentioned in history, and but slightly hinted at by Demosthenes, it requires some pains to investigate it. The Phliasians had ever been in open or secret enmity with the Argives; while the one endeavoured to support their independency, the other, to reduce their city, which they regarded as part of their own territory. In the third year of the hundred and first Olympiad, certain Phliasians who had been banished, formed a conspiracy with some kinsmen

who still continued in the city, in order to betray it to the Argives. It was attacked vigorously by night, and the enemy, with the utmost difficulty, repelled. This attempt exasperated each party, and produced various quarrels and hostilities. And whether these were suspended or continued down to the date of this oration, it seems to admit of no doubt, that the Argives and Arcadians, supported by the king of Macedon, made war on the Phliasians, restored the exiles, and drove out those citizens who had opposed their interest; and that these citizens, thus oppressed and expelled, implored the assistance of the Athenians, and received those magnificent promises and decrees which the orator here mentions. *Lucchesini.*

have ever acted greatly and nobly; those who are our friends it would be scandalous to desert; our enemies we cannot trust; nor must we suffer them to become powerful. In a word, we see in this city, that the men who have engaged in the public administration, even when they wish to retire, cannot resign their charge. This is your case; you are the ministers in Greece.

This, then, is the sum of what hath now been offered. Your speakers never can make you either bad or good; you can make them whatever you please. You are not directed by their opinions; for they have no opinion, but what your inclinations dictate. It is your part, therefore, to be careful that your inclinations be good and honourable. Then shall all be well. Your speakers either must never give pernicious counsels; or, must give them to no purpose; when such counsels have no longer any influence in this assembly. [1.]

[1.] These representations of Demosthenes were so far successful, that, early in the following year, the assembly repealed that scandalous law of Eubulus, which denounced death against any person who should propose the alienation of the theatrical appointments; and the orator himself had the honour of introducing a decree for applying them to the military service; to which the people consented, when it was to late too derive any considerable advantages from this reformation.

THE FIRST OF THE SUSPECTED ORATIONS;

VIZ.

ON THE HALONESUS:

PRONOUNCED IN THE ARCHONSHIP OF SOSIGENES, THE THIRD YEAR OF THE HUNDRED AND NINTH OLYMPIAD.

INTRODUCTION.

IT was not originally my intention to have translated either of the following orations : nor is it from any alteration in my opinion, but from a deference to that of others, that I have presented this, 'on the Halonesus,' to the English reader, in order to give him an opportunity of comparing it with the others, and of judging for himself, whether it is to be admitted among the genuine remains of our orator, or to be rejected as unworthy of his abilities, although apparently received and quoted by the ancient critics.

This oration takes its title from an island called Halonesus, which one Sostratus, a pirate, had some time since take from the Athenians, and which Philip, having driven out this pirate, now claimed as his property. This was regarded, at Athens, as an infraction of the treaty lately concluded (of which some account hath been given in the Introduction to the 'Oration on the Peace:) and, together with some other transactions of the Macedonian prince, produced complaints and jealousies amongst the Athenians, which were deemed, by their rival, of too much consequence to be

neglected. Python, one of his most able partisans, was despatched to Athens, to obviate all objections to the sincerity and integrity of his conduct.

In order to corroborate the representations of this ambassador, Philip found it expedient to write a letter to the Athenians; which, although addressed immediately to this people, was intended as a kind of manifesto to all Greece. This letter, among other pieces of the same kind, which might have done honour to the abilities of the Macedonian, is unhappily lost to posterity; but the general contents of it are distinctly pointed out in the following oration, which contains a regular and methodical answer to this letter.

THE

ORATION ON THE HALONESUS.

Sosigenes, Archon.—Olympiad. 109. *An.* 3.

MEN of Athens! [1.] it is by no means reasonable, that the complaints, which Philip

[1.] The oration, as hath been already observed, plainly points out to us the several allegations, and apologies for Philip's conduct, contained in the letter which occasioned the present debate. And this exordium as plainly shows, that, to these allegations, the writer added some strong remonstrances, against the severity and indecency with which some speakers in the assembly had, on many occasions, treated the character of the king of Macedon; and demanded that some restraint should be laid on their insolence. The author of the oration, artfully enough, considers this as an attempt to control that freedom of speech and debate, which was the sacred right of every, even the meanest, citizen. It was the

urges against those speakers who assert your rights, should deprive us of the liberty of enforcing the true interests of our country. Grievous, indeed, would be the case, if the freedom of our public debates were to be at once destroyed by a letter sent from him. It is my present purpose, first, to examine the several allegations mentioned in this letter; then shall we proceed to the other particulars urged by his ambassadors.

Philip begins with speaking of the Halonesus: this island he declares, is his; that he presents it to us as a free gift; that we have no rightful claim to it; nor hath he injured our property, either in acquiring or in keeping possession of it. Such were his professions at the time when we were sent on our embassy to Macedon: that he had won this island from the pirates who had seized it, and was, therefore, justified in keeping his acquisition. But, as this plea hath no support from truth and justice, it is not difficult to deprive him of it. The places, seized by pirates, are ever the property of some others: these they fortify, and from thence make their excursions. But the man who punishes their outrages, and drives them out, cannot reasonably allege, that the possessions, which these pirates unjustly wrested from the rightful proprietors, must instantly devolve to him. If this be suffered, then, if some pirates should seize a part of Attica, or of Lemnos, or of Imbros, or of Scyros, and if any power should cut them off, the places which they had seized, though our undoubted property, must continue in his possession, whose arms chastised these pirates. Philip is himself sensible of the weakness of this plea. There are others equally sensible of this: but it is imagined easy to impose on you by means of those who are administering our affairs agreeably to the wishes of the Macedonian; who promised him, and are now performing this service. Yet he cannot but know, that we must come into possession of this island, in whatever terms our transaction may be expressed, whether you accept it, or resume it. [1.] Why then should he not use the fair and equitable term, and restore it; rather than adhere to that word which proves his injustice, and pretend to present it as a gift? Not that he may be supposed to confer a benefit upon us (such benefits are ridiculous,) but that he may demonstrate to all Greece, that the Athenians think themselves happy in owing their maritime dominions to the favour of the Macedonian. O my countrymen! let us not descend to this.

As to his proposal of submitting this contest to umpires, it is the language of derision and mockery. It supposes, in the first place, that we, who are Athenians, could, in our dispute with one sprung from Pella, descend to have our title to the islands determined by arbitration. And if our own power, the power to which Greece owes its liberty, cannot secure us the possession of these places: if umpires are to be appointed, if we are to commit our cause to them; if their votes are absolutely to decide our rights, and if they are to secure to us these islands (provided [2.] that they be influenced by Philip's gold;) if such, I say, be your conduct, do ye not declare, that ye have resigned all your power on the continent? Do ye not discover to the world, that no attempt can possibly provoke you to oppose him; when for your maritime dominions, whence Athens derives its greatest power, you have not recourse to arms, but submit to umpires?

He farther observes, that his commissioners have been sent hither to settle a cartel of com-

---

privilege, as we may call it, of the assembly, and therefore is with propriety asserted, previous to the consideration of any other particular.

[1.] Accept it, or resume it.] ''Αν τε λάβητε, ἂν τ' ἀπολάβητε. This was a distinction suggested and asserted by Demosthenes, as we learn from a passage in the oration of Æschines against Ctesiphon, where it is ridiculed as frivolous and litigious. But (as Mons. Tourreil observes on that passage) the Athenians had most important reasons to examine which of these two terms they used in their convention with Philip. For, according to the choice of one or the other term, their right to the Halonesus was established or destroyed. The king of Macedon consented to put them in possession of the island; he declared that he would give it to them. If then the Athenians were to answer that they accepted of it (as a gift or favour,) by this they must acknowledge, that Philip was the rightful proprietor of the island. It was therefore insisted that this prince should declare that he restored it; while the Athenians, on their part, declared that they renewed it; which plainly implied that the Macedonians had usurped their right, and that they were truly and justly entitled to the Halonesus. Yet however reasonable and necessary such precision may appear, and particularly in transactions with a prince of so much address and artifice as Philip, yet the ridicule of Æschines had some effect. And, 'a man who disputes about the words, giving or restoring,' became a proverbial phrase to express a person of an obstinate adherence to nice and frivolous distinctions. The comic poets did not a little contribute to introduce this proverb into fashion. Athenæus quotes a number of fragments, in which we find that Alexis, Anaxilas, and Timocles, employed it to heighten the humour and pleasantry of their performances: and Athenæus himself makes use of it, in the beginning of the sixth book.

[2.] Provided, &c.] Æschines asserts, in the oration against Ctesiphon, that, in the present debate, Demosthenes declared that no impartial arbitrators could be found in Greece, so general had been the influence of corruption.—If Demosthenes was really the author of this oration, we must suppose that the assertion of his rival was founded on the insinuation contained in the passage here quoted.

merce; [1.] and, that this shall be confirmed, not when it hath received the sanction of your tribunal, as the law directs, but when it hath been returned to him. Thus would he assume a power over your judicature. His intention is to betray you into unguarded concessions, to have it expressly acknowledged in this cartel, that you do not accuse him of injuring the state by his outrageous conduct, with respect to Potidæa; that you confirm his right both of seizing and possessing this city. And yet those Athenians who had settled in Potidæa, at a time when they were not at war with Philip, when they were united with him in alliance; when the most solemn engagements subsisted between them, when they had the utmost reliance on Philip's oaths, were yet despoiled by this prince of all their possessions. And now, he would have you ratify this his iniquitous procedure, and declare that you have suffered no injury, that you have no complaints to urge against him. For, that the Macedonians have no need of any cartels in their commerce with the Athenians, former times afford sufficient proof. Neither Amyntas, the father of Philip, nor any of the other kings of Macedon, ever made these cartels with our state, although our intercourse was much greater in those days than now: for Macedon [2.] was then subject to us, it paid us tribute; and then, much more than now, did we frequent their markets, and they enjoy the advantages of ours; nor were the tribunals to which affairs of commerce might be brought, settled in so regular a manner as at present. As these are opened once in each month, they make all cartels between two countries, so far removed from each other, quite unnecessary. And, as these were not agreeable to ancient usage, it is by no means prudent to establish them now; and thus to subject men to the inconvenience of a voyage from Macedon to Athens, or from us to Macedon, in order to obtain justice. The laws of each country are open; and they are sufficient for the decision of all controversies. Be assured, therefore, that by this cartel, he means but to betray you into a resignation of all your pretensions to Potidæa.

As to the pirates, he observes, that justice requires that we should act in concert with him, in order to guard against those who infest the seas. By this, he in effect desires, that we should resign to him the sovereignty of the seas, and acknowledge, that, without Philip's aid, we are not able to secure a navigation free and unmolested. Nor is this his only scheme. He would have an uncontrolled liberty of sailing round, and visiting the several islands, under the pretence of defending them from pirates: that so he may corrupt the inhabitants, and seduce them from their allegiance to us. Not contented with transporting his exiles to Thasus, [3.] under the conduct of our commanders, he would gain possession of the other islands, by sending out his fleets, to sail in company with our admirals, as if united with us in the defence of the seas. There are some who say, that he hath no occasion for a maritime power: yet he, who hath no occasion to secure such a power, prepares his ships for war, erects his arsenals, concerts his naval expeditions, and, by the vast expense bestowed upon his marine, plainly shows that it is the grand object of his attention. And can you think, ye men of Athens! that Philip could desire you to yield to him this sovereignty of the seas, unless he held you in contempt? unless he had firm reliance on the men whose services he determined to purchase? the men who, insensible to shame, live for Philip, not for their country; who vainly fancy they have enriched their families by the bribes received from him; when these bribes are really the prices for which they have sold their families.

And now, with respect to the explanation of the articles of the peace, which the ambassadors, commissioned by him, submitted to our determination, (as we insisted only on a point universally acknowledged to be just, that 'each party should enjoy their own dominions,') he denies, that ever his ambassadors were commissioned to make, or ever did make, such a concession: so that his partisans must have persuaded him, that you have utterly forgotten the declarations made publicly in the assembly. But these of all things cannot

---

[1.] A cartel of commerce.] The word thus rendered [συμβολα,] is explained by lexicographers, as denoting (among many other particulars) certain conventions [συνθηκας] settled between two states, as a rule for the decision of all differences which might arise in their commercial intercourse with each other. The particular nature, force, effects, and consequences, of such conventions, the translator cannot take on him to explain distinctly; nor, of consequence, the force and propriety of the speaker's argument in this passage.

[2.] I do not remember to have met with any particular account of Macedon being at any time tributary to Athens, but in Demosthenes. Eurydice, the mother of Philip, was indeed obliged to implore the protection

of Iphicrates the Athenian. *Wolfius.*

Tourreil, in his notes on the second Olynthiac oration, dates the period of the Macedonians being in this tributary state, from the establishment of the Athenian colony at Amphipolis, under Agnon the son of Nicias (about forty-eight years before the Peloponesian war,) to the fifth or sixth year of this war, when Brasidas, the Lacedemonian, drove the Athenians from the frontiers of Macedon. But this is no more than the conjecture of the critic, founded on the authority of the present passage.

[3.] This must have happened immediately after their treaty with Macedon, before they found any reason to complain of the insidious conduct of Philip with respect to this treaty.

possibly be forgotten. For, in the very same assembly, his ambassadors arose, and made these declarations; and, in consequence of them, the decree was instantly drawn up. As then the recital of the decree immediately succeeded the speeches of the ambassadors, it is not possible that you could have recited their declarations falsely. This then is an insinuation not against me, but against the assembly; as if you had transmitted a decree, containing an answer to points never once mentioned. But these ambassadors, whose declarations were thus falsified, at the time when we returned our answer in form, and invited them to a public entertainment, never once rose up, never once ventured to say, 'Men of Athens, we have been misrepresented; you have made us say, what we never said :' but acquiesced, and departed.

Recollect, I entreat you, the declarations of Python, who was at the head of this embassy; the man who then received the public thanks of the assembly. They cannot, I presume, have escaped your memory. And they were exactly consonant to Philip's present letter. He accused us of calumniating Philip; he declared, that you yourselves were to be blamed; for, when his master was endeavouring to do you service, when he preferred your alliance to that of any other of the Grecian states, you defeated his kind intentions, by listening to sycophants; who wished to receive his money, and yet loaded him with invectives: that when those speeches were repeated to him, in which his reputation was so severely treated, and which you heard with such satisfaction, he naturally changed his determination, as he found that he was regarded as devoid of faith, by those whom he had resolved to oblige. He desired, that the men who spoke in this assembly, should not declaim against the peace; which certainly was not to be broken; but that, if any article was amiss, it should be amended, in which we might be assured of Philip's entire concurrence. But that, if they continued their invectives, without proposing any thing by which the treaty might be confirmed, and all suspicions of his master removed, then no attention should be given to such men. You heard these declarations of Python; you assented; you said that they were just; and just they certainly were. But, by these professions, it was by no means intended to give up an article [1.] of the treaty so essential to his interest; to give up what all his treasures had been expended to obtain: no; he had been taught by his instructors, of this place, that not a man would

dare to propose any thing contradictory to that decree of Philocrates, by which we lost Amphipolis. I, on my part, Athenians! never have presumed to propose any thing illegal. I have, indeed, ventured to speak against the decree of Philocrates, because it was illegal. For this decree, by which Amphipolis was lost, contradicted former decrees, by which our right to this territory was asserted. This then was an illegal decree which Philocrates proposed. And, therefore, he, who had the due regard to our laws in all that he proposed, could not but contradict a decree so inconsistent with our laws. By conforming to the ancient legal acts of this assembly, I showed the due attention to the laws, and, at the same time proved that Philip was deceiving you; that he had no intention of amending any article of the treaty; that his sole purpose was to destroy the credit of those speakers who asserted the rights of their country.

It is then manifest, that, having first consented to this amendment of the treaty, he now recalls his concession. He insists, that Amphipolis is his; that you have acknowledged it to be his, by the very words of your decree, which declare, that he shall enjoy his own possessions. Such was, indeed, your declaration: but not that Amphipolis was Philip's. For a man may possess the property of others; nor can possession infer a right, since it is frequently acquired by unjust usurpation. So that his argument is no more than an idle sophistical equivocation. He insists particularly on the decree of Philocrates: but he forgets his letter to this state, at the time when he laid siege to Amphipolis; in which, he directly acknowledged that Amphipolis belonged to you, and declared that his intention in attacking this city, was to wrest it from the then possessors, who had no claim to it, and to vest it in the Athenians, who were the rightful sovereigns. Well, then! The men who were in possession of this city before Philip's conquest, usurped our right: but when Philip had reduced it, did our right cease at once? Did he but recover his own dominions? When he reduced Olynthus also, when he subdued Apollonia, when he gained Pallene, did he but recover his own dominions?—When he makes use of such evasion, can you think that he is at all solicitous to preserve a decent semblance of reason and justice? No; he treats you with contempt, in presuming to dispute your title to a city, which the whole nation of Greece, which the Persian king himself, by the most authentic declarations, acknowledged to be ours.

[1.] An article, &c.] That is, to give up Amphipolis, which was claimed on each side by virtue of that clause, which declared, that the contracting powers should keep all their several dominions. Philip was now in possession of this city. The right of the Athenians had been at first asserted in the congress held for settling the terms of the peace; but this point was afterward given up. Yet now we find it was revived; at least, that the speakers who opposed the Macedonian interest, endeavoured to persuade the people, that the cession lately made was illegal, and that the general clause should be explained in favour of the Athenian claim to Amphiplios.

Another amendment of the treaty which we contended for, was this; that all the Greeks, not included in the peace, should enjoy their liberty and their laws: and that, if invaded, they should be defended by all the confederating parties. For this, I say, we contended; sensible that justice and humanity required, not only that we and our allies, and Philip and his allies, should enjoy the advantages of the peace, but that those who were neither allies to Athens, nor to Macedon, should by no means lie exposed to the oppression of any powerful invader. That they also should derive security from the peace; and that we should in reality lay down our arms, and live in general friendship and tranquillity. This amendment his letter confesses to be just; you hear that he accepts it. And yet hath he overturned the state of the Pheræans; he hath introduced his garrison into the citadel; certainly that they may enjoy their own laws. His arms are directed against Ambracia. Three cities in Cassopia, Pandosia, Bucheta, and Elatia, all Elean colonies, hath he invaded with fire and sword, and reduced to the vassalage of his kinsman Alexander. [1.] Glorious proofs of his concern for the liberty and independence of the Greeks!

As to those promises of great and important service, which he was perpetually lavishing on the state, he now asserts, that I have belied and abused him to the Greeks: for that he never once made such promises. So devoid of shame is he, who declared in his letter, which still remains upon record, that he would effectually silence his revilers, when an accommodation was once obtained; by the number of good offices he would confer upon us, and which should be particularly specified, whenever he was assured of such an accommodation. These his favours, then, were all provided, and ready to be granted to us when the peace should be concluded; but when this peace was once concluded, all his favours vanished. How great havoc hath been made in Greece, you need not be informed. His letters assure us of his gracious intentions to bestow large benefits upon us. And now see the effect of his promises. He refuses to restore our dominions, he claims them as his own. And, as to granting us any new dominions, they must not be in this country. No; the Greeks might else be offended. Some

other country must be sought for, some foreign land must furnish such grants.

As to those places which he seized in time of peace, in open violation of his engagements; as he hath no pretence to urge, as he stands convicted manifestly of injustice, he says, that he is ready to submit these points to the decision of an equal and common tribunal. But they are points, which, of all others, need no decision. A fair computation of time determines the cause at once. We all know in what month, and on what day, the peace was made. We all know, too, in what month, and on what day, Serrium, Ergiske, and the Sacred Mount were taken. The nature and manner of these transactions are no secret. Nor is there need of a tribunal in a point so evident as this, that the peace was made one month before these places were seized.

He asserts, that he hath returned all your prisoners that were taken. Yet there was one prisoner, a man of Carystus, [2.] bound to this city by all the strictest ties, for whose liberty we sent no less than three deputations. Such was Philip's desire to oblige us, that he put this man to death: nay, refused to restore his body for interment.

It is also worthy of attention to consider what was the language of his letters with respect to the Chersonesus, and to compare it with his present actions. All that district which lies beyond the Forum, he claims as his own, in defiance of our pretensions, and hath given the possession to Apollonides the Cardian. And yet the Chersonesus is bounded not by the Forum, but by the altar of Jupiter of the Mountain, which lies in mid-way between the elm, and the chalky shore, where the line was traced, for cutting through the Chersonesus. [3.] This is evident, from the inscription on the altar of Jupiter of the Mountain, which is in these terms:

Here, Jove's fair altar, rais'd by pious hands,
Adorns, at once, and marks the neighb'ring lands:
On this side, lo, yon chalky cliffs display'd !
On that, the elm extends its awful shade;
Whilst, in midway, e'en Heav'n's great monarch deigns
To point the bound'ries, and divide the plains.

This district then, whose extent is known to

7. ⸱ ⸱ ⸱ ⸱ ⸱ ⸱ ⸱ /x. ⸱ ⸱ ⸱

[1.] This Alexander was the brother of Olympias, Philip's wife, and had been placed on the throne of Epirus by the interest and power of the Macedonian. The three cities here called Elean colonies, might have possibly been thus disposed of, with the consent of Elis, where the power and influence of Philip were in effect absolute.

[2.] Wolfius is inclined to think, that this was the name of the prisoner. But I have chosen to translate the passage in this manner, as there was a town in the island of Euboea known by the name of Carystus. The

name or the country of this man are, indeed, circumstances of no moment; and should there be a mistake in the translation, the learned reader can scarcely find it worth while to detect or to censure it.

[3.] A work which Philip had promised to execute at his own expense (as is mentioned in the second Philippic) for the convenience and expedition of commerce, which was frequently interrupted by the length of time spent in doubling Mount Athos, and sailing round the Chersonesus; or by contrary winds.

many in this assembly, he claims as his property; part of it he himself enjoys, the rest he gives to his creatures: and thus he deprives us of our most valuable possessions. But he is not content with wresting from us all the lands which lie beyond the Forum: his letter directs us to come to a judicial decision of any controversy we may have with the Cardians who lie on this side of the Forum; with the Cardians, I say, who have presumed to settle in our lands. We have, indeed, a controversy with these men; and judge ye, whether the subject be inconsiderable. The lands, where they have settled, they claim as their just property, and deny our title. The lands that we enjoy, they declare are unlawfully usurped; that they themselves are the rightful proprietors; and that their right was acknowledged by a decree proposed by your own citizen Calippus, of the Pænean tribe. He did, indeed, propose such a decree; for which he was, [1.] by me, impeached of an illegal proceeding; but you suffer him to escape; and thus was your title to these lands rendered disputable and precarious. But, if you can submit to a judicial decision of your disputes with the Cardians, what should prevent the other inhabitants of the Chersonesus from demanding the like trial?

With such insolence doth he treat you that he presumes to say, that, if the Cardians refuse to be determined by a judicial process, he will compel them. As if we were not able to compel even the Cardians to do us justice. An extraordinary instance this of his regard to Athens.

Yet there are men among you who declare, that this letter is very reasonable; men much more deserving of your abhorrence than Philip. His opposition to this state is actuated by the love of glory and power; but citizens of Athens, who devote themselves, not to their country, but to Philip, should feel that vengeance which it must be your part to inflict with all severity, unless your brains have forsaken your heads, and descended to your heels. [2.] It remains, that I propose such an answer to this so reasonable letter, and to the declarations of the ambassadors, as may be just and advantageous to the state. [3.]

[1.] The author of this oration affirms, that Calippus was impeached by him of violating the laws. But it is certain, that Hegesippus, and not Demosthenes, was the author of this impeachment. *Libanius.*

[2.] This remarkable passage, which has been so much censured by critics, is here translated pretty exactly, without any attempt to soften the boldness and severity of the original. And it is left to the reader to compare with the expressions of greatest freedom, in those remains of Demosthenes which are confessedly genuine. Æschines has, indeed, recorded some expressions of our author, equally rude and disgusting: such was his threat, 'that he would sow up Philip's mouth with a bull-rush, &c.' But it is certain, that in all his addresses to the assembly, even where he censures and inveighs with the greatest freedom and severity, he still discovers a remarkable attention to decorum; and sometimes tempers his reproof with the most artful and delicate flattery.

[3.] The deputies, who presented Philip's letter, seem to have been dismissed without any satisfactory answer. And, by the eagerness with which the people now listened to the leaders who opposed the Macedonian interest, it appeared plainly, that the influence of Philip's partizans was declining. So that Demosthenes judged it a favourable opportunity to prefer an accusation against his rival Æschines, for fraud and corruption in his late conduct of the treaty concluded with Philip; which produced the two orations on the subject of their embassy.

THE SECOND OF THE SUSPECTED ORATIONS:

Entitled

ON THE TREATY WITH ALEXANDER.

INTRODUCTION.

THE death of Philip, king of Macedon, was an event, at first, judged fatal to the interest of that kingdom; which gave the Athenians hopes of recovering their superiority, and encouraged them to form some confederacies against his successor, whose spirit and abilities were not yet completely discovered.

It is not here necessary to recount the actions of this prince, on his accession to the throne. It may be sufficient to observe, that a treaty had been concluded by his father with the Greeks, and was by him confirmed; in which it was provided, that the laws, privileges, and liberties, of the several states, should be secured and confirmed. But such engagements are seldom found sufficient to restrain a violent youthful ambition. The Macedonian was soon emboldened to discover his contempt of this treaty, by acting in several instances contrary to its articles. The

Athenians, who still retained some remains of their ancient spirit, resented these his infractions. An assembly was convened to take the treaty into consideration, and to determine on the proper method of procedure, in consequence of Alexander's conduct. On this occasion was the following oration delivered, which contains a distinct specification of the several instances of violation, now complained of.

Critics seem willing to ascribe this oration to Hegesippus, or to Hyperides. It is observed, that the style is diffuse, languid, and disgraced by some affected phrases; and that the whole composition by no means breathes that spirit of boldness and freedom which appears in the orations of Demosthenes. But these differences may possibly be accounted for, without ascribing it to another author. Dejection and vexation, a consciousness of the fallen condition of his country, despair and terror at the view of the Macedonian power, might have naturally produced an alteration in the style and manner of the orator's address. A great epic genius, when in its decline, is said, by Longinus, to fall naturally into the fabulous. In like manner, a great popular speaker, when hopeless and desponding, checked and controlled by his fears, may find leisure to coin words, and naturally recur to affected expressions, when the torrent of his native eloquence is stopped. Nor is the oration now before us entirely destitute of force and spirit. It appears strong and vehement, but embarrassed. The fire of Demosthenes sometimes breaks forth through all obstacles, but is instantly allayed and suppressed, as if by fear and caution. The author, as Ulpian expresses it, speaks freely, and not freely: he encourages the citizens to war, and yet scruples to move for war in form; as if his mind was distracted between fear and confidence.

In a word, I regard the Oration on the Treaty with Alexander, as the real work of Demosthenes, but of Demosthenes dejected and terrified, willing to speak consistently with himself, yet not daring to speak all that he feels. It may be compared to the performance of an eminent painter, necessarily executed at a time when his hand or his eyes laboured under some disorder, in which we find the traces of his genius and abilities obscured by many marks of his present infirmity.

ON THE

TREATY WITH ALEXANDER.

WE should by all means, Athenians! concur with those who so strenuously recommend an exact adherence to our oaths and treaties, if they really speak their sentiments; for nothing is so becoming the character of free states, as a strict attention to honesty and justice. Let not these men, therefore, who urge the necessity of this attention, embarrass our councils by harangues, which their own actions contradict. Let them submit to an examination; if their sentiments are approved, they will for the future influence the assembly; if not, let them give place to those whose opinions of our rights may seem more consonant to truth. Thus shall you determine, either to submit quietly to your wrongs, and esteem their author as your friend; or to prefer the cause of justice to all other considerations, and to make such provisions for your interest, with speed and vigour, as none can possibly condemn. The very terms of our treaty, and of those oaths by which the general peace was ratified, must, upon the first inspection, show who are the transgressors. This I shall briefly prove in the most essential articles.

Suppose this question asked, what event, Athenians, could most effectually excite your resentment? You would answer, an attempt to destroy your liberty. Should the family of Pisistratus now revive; and should any man attempt to reinstate them in their former power, ye would at once take up arms, and brave all dangers, rather than submit to these masters. Or, if you should submit, you would be reduced to the condition of purchased slaves; nay, to a worse condition: for no master wantonly kills his slave; but those who are under the power of tyrants we see every day destroyed without the shadow of law, and exposed to insults still worse than death, in the persons of their wives and children.

Well, then, in open violation of his oaths, of the express terms of the general peace, hath Alexander reinstated the family of Philiades in Messenè. In this hath he acted from a regard to justice? or, from his own arbitrary principles, in open contempt of you, and of his engagements with the Greeks?— If, then, an attempt to introduce arbitrary power into Athens would excite your utmost indignation, would rouse you to maintain the treaty; you ought not to be indifferent, you ought not to neglect this treaty, when, in equal violation of its sacred purport, other states are oppressed by the like power. Nor should they, who so strenuously recommend to you to adhere to your engagements, leave those uncontrolled, who have, on their part, violated them in a manner so notorious. Such violation cannot be suffered, if you have the due regard to justice. For it is expressly declared in our treaty, that he who should act as Alexander hath now done, should be deemed an enemy to all included in the peace: that all should take up arms against him, and against his dominions. If then we have the least regard to these our declarations, we are to consider him as our enemy, who hath restored this family. 'But,' say the favourers of these tyrants, 'the sons of Philiades governed in Messenè before this treaty was concluded; and therefore were they restored by Alexander.' This is a ridiculous allegation; the tyrants of Sestos, established long before our treaty, were expelled from Antissa, and Eresus; and this form of government declared to be in itself unjust and oppressive. It cannot then be a matter of indifference, that Messene be exposed to the like oppression.

Besides, it is provided, in the very first article of the treaty, that the 'Greeks shall enjoy their freedom and their laws; and if their freedom and their laws were the first point secured, what assertion can be conceived more absurd, than that he, who reduces them to slavery, is not guilty of any violation of this treaty? If then, Athenians! you would adhere to your oaths and your engagements, if you have a regard to justice (and this, as I have observed, is the advice of your speakers,) it is incumbent on you to take up arms, to collect your allies, and to declare hostilities against those who have really violated the peace. Have you, when some fair occasion offered, pursued your interest with vigour, even though not induced by the motive of supporting justice? And now, when justice, and a fair occasion, and your own interest, all conspire to rouse you, what other season do you wait for, to assert your own liberty and that of Greece?

I am now come to another point of right, resulting from this treaty. It is expressly provided, that, if any persons should subvert the constitutions subsisting in each state, at the time of ratifying the peace, they should be deemed enemies to all included in the treaty. Consider then, Athenians! that the Achæans of Peloponnesus, at that time, enjoyed democratical governments. Yet, of these, the Macedonian hath subverted the constitution of Pellæne, by expelling most of its citizens: their fortunes he distributed among his domestics, and Chæron, the wrestler, the established tyrant of the city. In this treaty were we included, which thus directs, that they who act in this manner shall be regarded as enemies. Shall we not then regard them as enemies, pursuant to the tenor of those engagements, by which we are all equally obliged? Or, can any of those hirelings of the Macedonian, those whose riches are the wages of their treason, be so abandoned as to forbid it? They cannot plead ignorance of these things; but, to such a pitch of insolence have they arrived, that, guarded, as it were, by the armies of the tyrant, they dare to call on us to adhere to oaths already violated; as if perjury were his prerogative: they force you to subvert your own laws, by releasing those who stood condemned at our tribunals; and, in various other instances, drive you to illegal measures. Nor is this surprising. For they, who have sold themselves to the enemies of their country, cannot have the least regard to law, the least reverence for oaths. The names of these, and but the names, serve them to impose on men who come to this assembly for amusement, not for business: and never once reflect, that their present indolence must prove the cause of some strange and terrible disorders.

Here, then, I repeat what I at first asserted, that we should agree with those who recommend an adherence to the general treaty. Unless they suppose, that, in recommending this adherence, they do not of consequence declare, that no act of injustice should be committed; or, imagine it yet a secret, that arbitrary power hath been established in the place of popular governments, and that many free constitutions have been subverted. But, such a supposition is utterly ridiculous. For these are the very terms of the treaty: 'the directors and guarantees, appointed for the general security, shall take care that, in the several states included in this peace, there shall be no deaths or banishments contrary to the laws established in each society; no confiscations, no new divisions of land, no abolition of debts, no granting freedom to slaves, for the purposes of innovation.' But, far from preventing these things, these men themselves contribute to introduce them. And what punishment can be equal to their guilt, who are the contrivers of these evils in the several states, which were deemed of such consequence, as to demand the united care of the whole body to prevent them?

I shall now mention another point, in which this treaty is infringed. It is expressly provided, that 'no flying parties shall make excursions from any of the cities included in the treaty, and commit hostilities on any other of the confederated cities; and that whatever people should thus offend, are to be excluded from the alliance.' But so little doth the Macedonian scruple to commit hostilities, that his hostilities are never suspended; nor are any free from them, that he can possibly infest. And much more flagrant are his later hostilities, as he hath, by his edict, established tyrants in different places; in Sicyon, his master of exercises. If, then, we should conform to the treaty, as these men insist, the cities guilty of these actions should be excluded from the confederacy. If the truth must be concealed, I am not to declare, that these are the Macedonian cities. But if, in defiance of the truth, those traitorous partizans of Macedon persevere in urging us to observe the general treaty, let us concur with them, (their advice is just and equitable:) and, as this treaty directs, let us exclude those from the alliance, who have been thus guilty; and consider of the measures necessary to be pursued against people so insolent and aspiring, whose schemes and actions are thus invariably criminal, and who treat their solemn engagements with contempt and ridicule. Why will they not acknowledge that these consequences are just? Would they have every article that opposes our interest confirmed? every article that favours us erased? Are these their notions of justice? If any part of our engagements provides for the interest of our enemies, in opposition to this state, are they to contend for that? But if, by any other part, our rights and interests are secured against our enemies, are all their utmost efforts to be directed against this?

To convince you still more clearly, that none of the Greeks will accuse you of infringing this treaty, but will acknowledge it as an obligation, that you have arisen singly to detect those who really infringed it, I shall run over a few of its numerous articles. One article is thus expressed: 'the uniting parties shall all have the full liberty of the seas. None shall molest them, or seize their vessels, on pain of being regarded as the common enemy.' And now, my fellow-citizens, it is notoriously evident to you all, that the Macedonians have done these things. To such a pitch of lawless insolence have they proceeded, as to seize the ships of Pontus, and send them into Tenedos. Every pretence was invented to detain them; nor were they at last released, before we had decreed to equip one hundred ships, to send them instantly to sea, and had actually appointed Menestheus to command them.

When such and so many are the outrages committed by others, is it not absurd that their friends in this assembly should not endeavour to prevail on them to change their conduct, instead of advising us to adhere to engagements so totally neglected on the other side? As if it were expressly provided, that one party might transgress when they pleased, and that the other should not resist. And could the Macedonians have acted a more lawless and a more senseless part, than to have so far abandoned all regard to their oaths, that they had well-nigh forfeited their sovereignty of the seas? [1.] Nay, they have indisputably forfeited this right to us, whenever we are disposed to assert it. For they are not to expect, that no penalty is to be incurred from violating the treaty, because they have, for some time past, discontinued their violations. No; they should rather be well pleased, that they have hitherto enjoyed the advantage of our indolence, and total aversion to maintain our rights.

Can any thing be conceived more mortifying, than that all other people, Greeks and Barbarians, should dread our enmity; but that these men, of sudden affluence, should make us contemptible, even to ourselves, by seducing and forcing us to their purposes? As if they had the conduct of affairs at Abdera, or Maronæa, [2.] not at Athens. But while they are depressing their own country, and aggrandizing its enemies, they do not consider, that, by prescribing the rules of justice in a manner so totally unjust they, in effect, acknowledge that their country is irresistible; for this is tacitly to confess, that, if we have a due attention to our interests, we shall easily subdue our enemies. And in this they rightly judge. For, let us take care to maintain a superiority at sea; let us but take care of this, and we shall effectually secure noble accessions to our present land force: especially, if fortune should so far favour us, as to crush the men now guarded by the armies of tyrants; if some of them should perish, and others discover their insignificance.

These then have been the infractions of the Macedonian, with respect to maritime affairs; besides the others already mentioned. But we have just now seen the most extravagant instance of the pride and insolence of his people, in daring to sail into the Piræus, manifestly contrary to the treaty concluded with us. Nor, is this their infraction the less criminal, because but one ship of war presumed to enter our harbour. It plainly appears, that this was an experiment, whether we might not prove so inattentive, as to suffer them hereafter to come in with more; and that, in this, as well as other instances, they renounce all regard to decrees and conventions. For, that they meant gradually to introduce, and to habituate us to such encroachments, appears from this, that he who then put in, with his ship (which together with his convoy should have been destroyed,) demanded liberty to build small vessels in our port. For this proves that their purpose was, not to obtain the privilege of entering our harbour, but to gain the absolute command of it. It cannot be alleged, that this demand was made, because the materials for building ships are in plenty at Athens, (for they are brought hither from great distances, and procured with difficulty;) and, that they are scarce at Macedon, (where they are sold at the cheapest rates to any that will purchase.) No: they were in hopes to gain the power of building and loading vessels in our port; a power expressly denied by treaty; and thus gradually to proceed to other enormities. In such contempt have they been taught to hold you, by their instructors in this city, who direct their whole conduct; and thus are they persuaded, that this state is irrecoverably lost in indolence, incapable of providing for its interest; and utterly regardless, whether the actions of a tyrant be conformable to his treaty, or no.

To this treaty I advise you to adhere: in that sense, I mean, which I before explained. And the experience of my age warrants me to assure you, that your rights will be thus as-

---

[1.] The maritime force of Macedon seems to have been, even at this time, scarcely greater than that of Athens, notwithstanding all the attention of Philip to increase and improve it. For we shall immediately find the orator recommending to his countrymen, to maintain a superiority at sea. But this sovereignty of the seas, which is here acknowledged to belong to the Macedonians, seems to have been the consequence of the treaty made with Philip, immediately after the battle of Chæronea, in which the Athenians were obliged to give up the dominion of the islands, and Samos was declared the bound of their territories and jurisdiction.

[2.] Abdera or Maronæa.] Two cities of small consequence in Thrace. 'The understanding of an Abderite,' was a proverb to express a remarkable deficiency in point of genius and acuteness; though this despised city had produced Democritus, a philosopher of no small reputation in Greece.

serted, without the least offence to others; and the occasions, favourable to your interests, most effectually improved. These {are the terms of the treaty; we must act thus, ' if we would be included.' They, then, who act differently, are not to be included. And, therefore, let us now, if ever, refuse to pay an abject submission to the directions of others. Else, must we renounce the memory of those ancient and illustrious honours, which we of all other people can most justly boast:—If you command me, Athenians! I shall now move you in form, pursuant to the tenor of our engagement, to declare war against those who have violated the treaty.

THE ORATION OF DINARCHUS AGAINST DEMOSTHENES.

INTRODUCTION.

THE reader is here presented with a translation of a performance which we find, in some editions, annexed to the public orations of Demosthenes. It is an artful, spirited, and virulent invective against him, when, in the decline of life, he had fallen into disgrace, and the displeasure of his countrymen. The occasion of it is distinctly recounted by Plutarch; who informs us, that some time after the famous contest about the crown, in which Demosthenes gained so complete a triumph over his rival Æschines, one Harpalus, who had been in the service of Alexander, fled to Athens, with the remains of an immense fortune, which had been dissipated by his luxury; and there sought refuge from the anger of his master, whose severity towards his favourites alarmed and prompted him to this flight. The orators received his money, and laboured to gain him the protection of the state. Demosthenes, on the contrary, urged to his countrymen the danger of exposing themselves to an unnecessary and unjustifiable war, by entertaining this fugitive. Harpalus, however, found means to soften his severity, by a present of a magnificent vase, accompanied with twenty talents. And, when it was expected that Demosthenes would have exerted his abilities, in the assembly, against Harpalus, he pleaded indisposition, and was silent. This is the sum of Plutarch's account. But Pausanias, who seems to have conceived a more favourable opinion of the integrity of Demosthenes, observes, as a proof of his innocence, that an authentic account was sent to Athens, after the death of Harpalus, of all the sums distributed by him in this city, and of the persons to whom each was paid; and that, in this account, no mention was at all made of Demosthenes, although Philoxenus, who procured it, was his particular enemy, as well as Alexander. But, however this may be, the rumour of Harpalus's practices, and the report of the corruption of Demosthenes in particular, raised a considerable ferment at Athens. Demosthenes strenuously asserted his innocence, and proposed, that the council of Areopagus should proceed to a strict inquiry into this distribution, supposed to have been made by Harpalus; declaring his readiness to submit to their sentence, whatever it might be. Contrary to his expectations, the report of the Areopagus condemned him. In vain did he represent this report, as the effect of the malicious practices and contrivance of his enemies. He was brought to his trial; Stratocles managed the prosecution; in which he was assisted by Dinarchus, who, though he gave a favourable testimony to the character of Demosthenes on a subsequent occasion (in the oration against Aristogiton,) yet now inveighed against him, with the utmost virulence, in the following oration.

THE ORATION

Of DINARCHUS AGAINST DEMOSTHENES.

THIS your minister, Athenians! who hath pronounced sentence of death upon himself, should he be convicted of receiving any thing from Harpalus; this very man hath been clearly convicted of accepting bribes from those whom, in former times, he affected to oppose with so much zeal. As Stratocles hath spoken largely upon this subject, as many articles of accusation have been anticipated, as the counsel of Areopagus hath made a report on this inquiry, so consonant to equity and truth; a report, confirmed and enforced by Stratocles, who hath produced the decrees enacted against these crimes; it remains that we, who are now to speak (who are engaged in a cause of more importance than ever came before this state,) should request the whole assembly, first, that we obtain your pardon, if we should repeat some things already urged, (for here our purpose is, not to abuse your patience, but to inflame your indignation;) and, secondly, that you may not give up the general rights and laws of the community, or exchange the general welfare, for the speeches of the accused. You see that, in this assembly, it is Demosthenes that is tried: in all other places, your own trial is depending. On you men turn their eyes, and wait with eagerness, to see how far the interest of your country will engage your care: whether you are to take upon yourselves the corruption and iniquity of these men; or, whether you are to manifest to the world a just resentment against those who are bribed to betray the state.

This last is fully in your power. The assembly hath made a fair decree, [1.] The citizens have discovered their desire to detect those speakers, whoever they may be, who, to the disgrace and detriment of the community, have presumed to receive gold from Harpalus. Add to this, that you yourself, Demosthenes, and many others, have moved in form, that the council, agreeably to ancient usage, should enter into an inquiry whether any persons had been thus guilty. The council hath made this inquiry; not that your instances were wanting to remind them of their duty; or, that they wished to sacrifice the truth, the trust reposed in them, to you: but from a full persuasion (as the Areopagites have expressed) of the influence of such practices on all our counsels and transactions; and a firm resolution never to plead the danger of being exposed to calumny, when they were to detect the man who attempted to bring disgrace and danger on his country.

And, although the dignity and propriety of this procedure have received the approbation of the people, Demosthenes has recourse to complaints, to appeals, to malicious accusations, now that he finds himself convicted of receiving twenty talents of gold. Shall then this council, on whose faith and justice we rely, even in the important case of premeditated murder: to whom we commit the vengeance due to this crime; who have an absolute power over the persons and lives of our citizens; who can punish every violation of our laws, either by exile or by death: shall this council, I say, on an inquiry into a case of bribery, at once lose all its authority? 'Yes; for the Areopagus hath reported falsely of Demosthenes.' Extravagant and absurd! What! report falsely of Demosthenes and Demades, against whom even the truth seems scarcely to be declared with safety? You, who have in former times moved that this council should take cognisance of public affairs, and have applauded their reports; you, whom this whole city hath not been able to restrain within the bounds of justice; hath the council reported falsely against you? Why then did you declare to the people, that you were ready to submit to death, if condemned by the report of this council? Why have you availed yourself of their authority, to take off so many of your citizens? Or, whither shall we have recourse; to whom shall we intrust the detection of secret villany? if you, notwithstanding all your affected regard to our popular government, are to dissolve this council; to whose protection our lives have been intrusted; to whose protection our liberty and our constitution have oftentimes been intrusted; by whose protection that person of thine hath been preserved (for, as you pretend, it hath frequently

been attempted,) to utter these calumnies against them; to whose care we have committed our secret archives, on which the very being of our state depends.

But it is just, it is just I say, that the council should meet with those returns of calumny. For I shall freely speak my sentiments. One of these two methods should they have pursued: either instantly have entered into the first inquiry relative to the three hundred talents, sent hither by the king of Persia, as the people directed; and then this monster would have been punished, his accomplices in corruption detected, and all his traitorous practices, by which Thebes was betrayed to ruin, being clearly laid open, an ignominious death would have freed us from him; or, if you were inclined to pardon this crime in Demosthenes, and thus to propagate the race of corrupted hirelings within your city, this discovery of your sentiments should have determined them not to enter into any inquiry, or information of the money received by Demosthenes. For now, when the council of Areopagus had nobly and equitably proceeded to a full detection of this man, and his accomplices; when, regardless of the power of Demosthenes and Demades, they have adhered inviolably to truth and justice; still, Demosthenes goes round the city, utters his invectives against this council, and boasts of his services, in those speeches, which you shall hear him instantly use, to deceive the assembly.—'It was I who gained you the alliance of Thebes!'—No! You it was who ruined the common interest of both states. 'I drew out the forces of Chæronea!' —No, you were the only person who there fled from your post.—'For you have I engaged in several embassies.' And what would he do, what would he demand, had these his negotiations been successful; when, having ranged through the world, only to involve us in such calamities and misfortunes, he expects to be rewarded with a liberty of receiving bribes against his country, and the privilege of speaking and of acting in this assembly as he pleases? To Timotheus, who awed all Peloponnesus by his fleet; who gained the naval victory at Corcyra over the Lacedemonians; who was the son of Conon, the man who restored liberty to Greece; who gained Samos, and Methone, and Pydna, and Potidæa, and, besides these, twenty cities more; you did not admit those important benefits, which he conferred upon us, to have any weight against the integrity of your tribunals, against those oaths by which we were engaged in pronouncing sentence. No: you imposed on him a fine of one hundred talents, because that he had, by his own acknowledgment, received money from the Chians and the Rhodians. And, shall not this outcast, this Scythian, [2.] (for

[1.] A fair decree.] That is, a decree committing the cognisance of the crimes alleged against Demosthenes, &c. to the court of Areopagus.

[2.] A term of reproach, which the enemies of Demosthenes frequently made use of. His grandfather (by his mother's side) had, in the time of his exile, married a woman of Scythia.

my indignation will not be restrained,) whom not one man, but the whole body of the Areopagus, hath, on full inquiry, declared guilty of receiving bribes; declared an hireling, and fully proved to be a corrupted traitor to his country; shall he not be punished with that severity which may serve as an example to others? He, who hath not only been detected in receiving money from the king, but hath enriched himself with the spoils of the state; and, now, could not even be restrained from sharing the vile wages which Harpalus here distributed.

And can the negotiations of Demosthenes, at Thebes, be deemed equivalent to the smallest part of the noble actions of Timotheus? Who can refrain from laughter to find you patiently attending, while he presumptuously displays his pretended services, and dares to compare them with those of Timotheus, and of Conon? Actions worthy of our state, worthy of the glory of our ancestors, disdain all comparison with those of an abandoned wretch. Here I shall produce the decree enacted against Timotheus, and then return to my subject.—Read!

The Decree.

Such was this citizen, (Demosthenes) that he might reasonably have expected pardon and favour from his fellow-citizens of those days. Not in words, but actions, did he perform important services to his country. His principles were steady, his conduct uniform, not various and changeable like yours. He never made so unreasonable a request to the people, as to be raised above the laws. He never required that those who had sworn to give sentence justly, should break through that sacred tie; but submitted to stand condemned, if such was the judgment of his tribunal. He never pleaded the necessity of times; nor thought in one manner, and harangued in another. And shall this miscreant live, who, besides his other numerous and heinous crimes, hath abandoned the state of Thebes to its destruction, when, for the preservation of that state, he had received three hundred talents from the king of Persia? For, when the Arcadians marched to the Isthmus, refused to treat with the ambassadors of Antipater, and received those of the unfortunate Thebans, who, with difficulty gained access to them by sea, appeared before them in the form of wretched suppliants, declared that their present motions were not intended to dissolve their connexions with Greece, or to oppose the interest of that nation; but to free themselves from the intolerable yoke of Macedonian tyranny, from slavery, from the horrid insults to which freemen were exposed; when the Arcadians were disposed to assist them, when they commiserated their wretched state, when they discovered that, by the necessities of the times alone, they had been obliged to attend on Alexander, but that their inclinations were invariably attached to Thebes and to the liberties of Greece; when Astylus, their mercenary general, demanded (as Stra-

tocles hath informed you) ten talents for leading a reinforcement to the Thebans, when the ambassadors applied to this man, who they well knew had received the king's money, requested, besought him to grant such a sum for the preservation of the state;—then did this abandoned, this impious, this sordid wretch (when there was so fair a prospect of saving Thebes,) refuse to part with ten talents out of all the vast treasures which he received; insensible to the affecting consideration, urged by Stratocles, that there were those who would give as great a sum to divert the Arcadians from this expedition, and to prevent them from assisting Thebes.

Has then Greece but slight, but common injuries to urge against Demosthenes, and his sordid avarice? Hath the man, so highly criminal, the least pretence to mercy? Do not his late and former offences call for the severest punishment? The world will hear the sentence you are this day to pronounce. The eyes of all men are fixed upon you, impatient to learn the fate of so notorious a delinquent. You are they, who, for crimes infinitely less heinous than his, have heavily and inexorably inflicted punishments on many. Menon was by you condemned to death, for having subjected a free youth of Pallene to his servile offices. Themistius, the Amphidnæan, who had abused a Rhodian woman, that performed on the harp in the Eleusinian ceremonies, was by you condemned to death. The same sentence you pronounced upon Euthymachus, for prostituting a maiden of Olynthus. And now hath this traitor furnished all the tents of the barbarians with the children and wives of the Thebans. A city of our neighbours and our allies hath been torn from the very heart of Greece. The plougher and the sower now traverse the city of the Thebans, who united with us in the war against Philip. I say, the plougher and the sower traverse their habitations; nor hath this hardened wretch discovered the least remorse at the calamities of a people, to whom he was sent as our ambassador: with whom he lived, conversed, and enjoyed all that hospitality could confer; whom he pretends to have himself gained to our alliance; whom he frequently visited in their prosperity, but basely betrayed in their distress. Our elder citizens can inform us, that, at a time when our constitution was destroyed; when Thrasybulus was collecting our exiles in Thebes, in order to possess himself of Phyle; when the Lacedemonians, now in the height of power, issued out their mandate, forbidding all states to receive the Athenians, or to conduct them through their territories; this people assisted our countrymen in their expedition; and published their decree, so often recited in this assembly, 'that they would not look on with unconcern, should any enemy invade the Athenian territory.' Far different was the conduct of this man who affects such attention to the interests of our allies (as you shall soon hear him boast.) The very money which he received to preserve this people from ruin, he refused to part with. Let these things sink deep into your minds. Think on the calamities which arise from traitors; let the wretched fate of the Olynthians and the Thebans teach you to make the just provision for your own security. Cut off the men, who are ever ready to sell the interests of their country for a bribe, and rest your hopes of safety upon yourselves and the gods. These are the means, Athenians, the only means of 'reforming our city; to bring offenders of eminence to justice, and to inflict a punishment adequate to their offences. When common criminals are detected, no one knows, no one inquires their fate. But the punishment of great delinquents commands men's attention; and a rigid adherence to justice, without regard to persons, is sure to meet with due applause.—Read the decree of the Thebans—Produce the testimonies—Read the letter.

The Decree. The Testimonies. The Letter.

He is a corrupted traitor, Athenians; of old a corrupted traitor! This is the man who conducted Philip's ambassadors from Thebes to this city; who was the occasion of putting an end to the former war; who was the accomplice of Philocrates, the author of the decree for making peace with Philip, for which you banished him; the man who hired carriages for the ambassadors that came hither with Antipater; who entertained them: and introduced the custom of paying obsequious flattery to the Macedonians. Do not, O Athenians! do not suffer this man, whose name is subscribed [1.] to the misfortunes of this state, and all the states of Greece, to escape unpunished; when Heaven hath been so far favourable to us, that one of these pests of our community is driven from the city, the life of the other forfeited to the state, let us not obstinately reject these favours; let the men, most eminently guilty, bear the load of our offences; so may we form happy presages of our future fortune. For what occasion should we reserve this man? When may we hope that he will prove of advantage to us? I call on this assembly: I call on all those who attend this trial: say, in what affairs hath he engaged, either private or public, that he hath not ruined. [2.] Did he not enter the house of Aristarchus, and there concert his designs? and did he not (the fact is well known) force this Aristarchus from the city loaded with the infamous imputation of contriving the mur-

der of Nicodemus? And such a friend did he find in Demosthenes, that he regarded him as his evil genius, as the author of all his misfortunes. But I must pass over his private conduct, for the time will not admit of a minute detail. From the moment that he first began to direct our affairs, hath any one instance of good fortune attended us? Hath not all Greece, and not this state alone, been plunged in dangers, calamities, and disgrace? Many were the fair occasions which occurred to favour his administration; and all these occasions, of such moment to our interests, did he neglect. When any friend to his country, any useful citizen, attempted to do us service, so far was this leader, who is impatient to boast of his great actions, from co-operating with such men, that he instantly infected them with the contagion of his unhappy conduct. Charidemus went over to the king of Persia, resolved to approve himself our friend, not by words, but actions; and to purchase security for us, and for the Greeks, by his own dangers. This man went round the public places, framed his speeches, and pretended to a share in these transactions. Then came the severe reverse of fortune; all our expectations were utterly defeated. Ephialtes sailed out; he hated Demosthenes: yet, from necessity, admitted him to share in his councils.—The fortune of the state destroyed him. Euthydicus assumed the conduct of public affairs; he professed himself a friend to Demosthenes.—He perished. You know these things much better than I: shall not then the experience of the past direct your judgment of the future? Can any services be expected from him? Yes; the service of forming contrivances in favour of our enemies, on some critical emergency. Such was the time when the Lacedemonians had encamped, when the Eleans united with them, when they were reinforced with ten thousand mercenaries; Alexander said to be in India; all Greece inflamed with indignation at the ignominious state to which traitors had reduced every community; impatient of distress, and earnest for relief. In this conjuncture, who was the man, Demosthenes, that had the direction of our councils? In this perilous conjuncture (not to mention other like occasions,) did you, whom we shall hear expressing the utmost indignation at the present fallen state of Greece: did you propose any decree? Did you assist us with your counsels? Did you supply us with your treasures? Not at all! You were employed in ranging

[1.] Is subscribed, &c.] That is, who was the author of all those decrees which were purposely contrived to bring on these misfortunes. The name of the person who proposed any Ψηφισμα, or decree, to the assembly, was always affixed to it. And the expression in the original is supposed to allude to this custom.

[2.] This sentence, in the original, is somewhat embarrassed; but I have endeavoured to express the general purport of it. Nico-

demus, a native of Aphidna, had been found dead, with his eyes torn out. As he was known to have been a friend to Eubulus who was in the party that opposed Demosthenes, the suspicion of this murder fell on the orator, who was said to have persuaded Aristarchus, a youth with whom he was connected in friendship, to commit it. Aristarchus was publicly accused, and fled to avoid the consequences. *Dem. Orat. in Mid.*

through the city, providing your whisperers, forging letters; * * [1.] the disgrace of his illustrious country, was then seen trimly decked with his rings, indulging in effeminacy and luxury amidst the public calamities; borne through our streets in his sedan, and insulting the distresses of the poor. And can we expect future services from him, who hath neglected all past occasions of serving us? O goddessMinerva! O Jupiter protector! May our enemies ever have such counsellors and leaders!

Men of Athens! do you yet remember the actions of your ancestors? They, when the state was threatened with many and great calamities, encountered dangers for your safety, in a manner worthy of their country, worthy of their free condition, worthy of their reputation. I shall not here engage in a long detail of our most early times; of the actions of Aristides and Themistocles, who fortified our city, and brought in such immense tributes, the free and voluntary contributions of the Greeks. Let us confine ourselves to the actions performed a little before our own days, the actions of Cephalus, of Thraso, of Heliodorus, of other great men; some of whom are yet alive. When the citadel of Thebes was possessed by the Lacedemonian forces, [2.] they assisted those exiles who attempted to rescue their country; they braved, the dangers of war, and gave liberty to a neighbouring state that had long been subjected to slavery. Cephalus was the man, whose decree roused our fathers to this expedition; who, in defiance of the Lacedemonian power, of the hazards of war, of the danger of advising measures whose event was precarious, proposed the resolution, that the Athenians should march out, and support the exiles who had now possessed themselves of Thebes. And our fathers did issue forth: in a few days the Spartan garrison was forced out; the liberty of Thebes restored; and the conduct of this state approved worthy of our ancestors. These were counsellors, Athenians! these were leaders, worthy of you and of your country: not such miscreants as those, who never did, never can prove useful to the public: attentive only to the preservation of their own vile persons, to amassing their sordid gains; who render their country more inglorious than themselves; who now, when evidently convicted of bribery, practise all their arts to deceive you, and expect, amidst their baseness, to find credit and security in the fruits of their avarice. Let their long course of iniquity, at length, meet the just punishment. Let them die; their own sentence hath condemned them.

Is it not scandalous, Athenians! that your opinion of the guilt of Demosthenes should depend only on our representations? Do you not know that he is a corrupted traitor, a public robber, false to his friends, and a disgrace to the state? What decrees, what laws have not been made subservient to his gain? There are men in this tribunal, who were of the Three Hundred, when he proposed the law relative to our trierarchs. [3.] Inform those who stand near you, how, for a bribe of three talents, he altered and new modelled this law, in every assembly: and, just as he was feed, inserted or erased clauses. Say, in the name of Heaven! Think ye, O men of Athens, that he gained nothing by his decree, which gave Diphilus the honours of public maintenance, and a statue? Was he not paid for obtaining the freedom of our city to Chærephilus, and Phidon, and Pamphilus, and Philip, and such mean persons as Epigenes and Conon? Was it for nothing he procured brazen statues to Berisades, and Satyrus, and Gorgippus, those detested tyrants; from whom he annually receives a thousand bushels of corn: although he is ready to lament the distress of his fortune? Was it for nothing he made Taurosthenes an Athenian citizen, who enslaved his countrymen: and together with his brother Callias, betrayed all Eubœa to Philip? whom our laws forbid to appear in Athens, on pain of suffering the punishment of those who return from exile. [4.] Such a man this friend to our constitution enrolled amongst our citizens. These and many other instances, in which he hath prostituted our honours, can be proved by authentic evidence. And could he, who gladly descended to small gains, resist the temptation of so great a sum as twenty talents? Six months hath the Areopagus been engaged, in their inquiry into the conduct of Demosthenes, Demades, and Cephisophon. And was all this time wasted only to make a false and unjust report? The whole body of our citizens, and of the Greeks, now fixed their eyes upon you (as I before observed,) impatient for the result of this day's business: earnest to be informed whether corruption may expect its just punishment, or fear no control; whether the authority of our tribunals is to be confirmed, or destroyed, by the sentence passed upon Demosthenes; a man whose public conduct hath long since called for severe vengeance; who is obnoxious to all the curses ever denounced within this city; who hath sworn falsely by the tremendous furies, and all the divinities whose names are sacred in the Areopagus; who hath been devoted to destruction in every assembly, as he is convicted of bribery, and hath dealt insidiously with his

---

[1.] This passage is supposed to be imperfect in the copies.

[2.] See Plutarch, in the Life of Pelopidas.

[3.] This was the law, of which Demosthenes speaks in the oration on the crown; by which every citizen was bound to contribute

to the expense of the navy, in proportion to his fortune, instead of just paying one-sixteenth part of the expense of one ship, whatever might be his circumstances.

[4.] In the original, 'from banishment by sentence of the Areopagus.'

country, in defiance of the awful execration; [1.] Whose declarations are ever different from his private sentiments; who gave to Aristarchus the most shocking and nefarious advice. If there be any punishment due to perjury and villany, surely he must this day, this moment, feel its utmost weight.—Ye judges, hear the execrations.

The Execrations.

And now, ye judges, so prone to falsehood and absurdity is Demosthenes, so devoid of shame, so insensible to his conviction, to the awful purport of these execrations, that, as I am informed, he presumes to urge against me, that I was once condemned by the Areopagus, and that I am guilty of the greatest inconsistency, in first objecting to the authority of this council, in my own case, and now founding my accusation against him on their authority. Thus, in order to deceive certain persons, hath he framed a tale utterly false and groundless. But that he may not deceive you by this insinuation, that you may be assured that the Areopagus never did, never can condemn me; but that I was, indeed, treated injuriously by one wicked man, on whom you inflicted the just punishment of his guilt; I shall first briefly state this affair, and then return to my allegations against Demosthenes.

There are two methods in which the Areopagus may proceed to an indictment against any person. And what are these? By entering into an inquiry, either of their own mere motion and pleasure, or by direction of the popular assembly. There is no other way. If, then, thou darest to assert, monster as thou art, that the proceedings against me were in consequence of the assembly's direction, produce the decree, name my accusers, as I have done in the present case; shown the decree, by which the council was directed to enter into this inquiry, and produced the accusers chosen by the people, who have so fully displayed thy guilt. If this can be done in my case, I am ready to submit to death. But if you allege, that the Areopagus proceeded against me of its own motion, produce some members of the council to attest this, as I shall to attest the contrary. The man, like you, an abandoned traitor, who so falsely charged both me and the council, I impeached before the five hundred, convicted of being suborned by Timocles to conduct the prosecution against me, and prevailed on his judges to punish with due severity.—Take the evidence which I produced in this cause, whose truth and validity were never questioned, and which I shall now produce; read

The Evidence.

Nor is it at all wonderful, Athenians! that when Pistias, a member of the Areopagus, accused me of injustice; (falsely charging both me and the council,) truth should for a while be borne down; and that his malicious accusations should gain some credit against a man whose infirmities and retired life rendered him unable to make the necessary defence. But now, when the whole body of the Areopagus hath solemnly pronounced, that Demosthenes hath been guilty of accepting twenty talents, in contempt of his duty, and the good of his country; when this your popular leader, on whom all your hopes were fixed, is convicted of clandestinely receiving bribes! shall the laws, shall justice, shall truth, have less weight than the speeches of Demosthenes? Shall the calumnies he utters against the council prevail against the whole force of evidence? The council, saith he, hath frequently indicted persons of illegal proceedings, who have been acquitted on a fair trial, and, in some cases, scarcely a fifth part of the judges concurred with the Areopagus. But such cases are easily accounted for. This council takes cognisance of all crimes whatever, which are either referred to them by you, or belong immediately to their own jurisdiction; and, in such proceedings, they do not act like you (let not my freedom give offence,) who are frequently influenced by pity, rather than directed by justice; but, in whatever cases our laws are violated, they consider only the evidence, and indict the guilty; well knowing that if slight offences are neglected, men will be habituated and imboldened to proceed to greater. Hence are their indictments returned to you, against several delinquents [2.] of the inferior kind. These, when brought to trial, you acquit; not from the least suspicion of this council's integrity, but because you are inclined to mercy, rather than to rigour; and deem the punishment prescribed by the letter of the law too great for their offences. In these cases, Demosthenes, were the declarations of the council false? By no means! And yet, in these and other cases, have you acquitted those whom they declared guilty. Thus, when the Areopagus was directed to inquire, whether Polyeuctus had gone to Megara, and held an intercourse with our exiles, and to report their determination; they reported that he had gone thither. Accusers were chosen; he was brought to a trial; you acquitted him, although he confessed that he had gone to Megara, to Nicophanes, who married his mother. For you thought it no such heinous offence that he had held an intercourse with his own father-in-law,

---

[1.] The awful execration.] Which was pronounced by the herald, on the opening of every assembly, against those who should act or speak to the prejudice of the community.

[2.] Particular instances of these are mentioned in the text: but, as they cannot be interesting to the English reader, I have chosen the general expression. The same liberty hath been taken in this oration, in sometimes omitting names and circumstances, which could not give either light or beauty to the translation.

when in exile and distress, and had assisted him to the utmost of his power. In this case, Demosthenes, no objection lay to the proceedings of the council: these were acknowledged to be just. Yet was Polyeuctus acquitted by his judges: for the Areopagus is only to consider, and declare the fact; but the criminal, as I have observed, was deemed worthy of the mercy of his tribunal. And are we, from such cases, to conclude, that no credit is due to the declarations of the Areopagus, by which you and your accomplices are charged with corruption? Show your judges, if you can, that your case is at all similar to those I have hinted at: that the guilt of bribery deserves mercy; and, then, you may expect mercy. But what saith the law? In other pecuniary matters, it directs that the injurious party shall be fined in twice the value of his fraudulent gains. In the case of bribery, two different punishments are prescribed: the first is death, that the example of the delinquent may serve as a terror to others; the second, a fine, tenfold of the bribe received, that they who proceed to such enormities, may be disappointed in their sordid hopes of gain.

To this do you object, that all the persons, thus declared guilty by the Areopagus, confessed that their judgment was fair and equitable, but that you have objected to their determination? No: you are the only person who have solicited to be judged by their sentence. You yourself preferred the decree, by which you are now condemned: you made the whole assembly a witness to your concessions: you yourself directed that death should be your punishment, if the council declared that you had received any part of those treasures which Harpalus brought hither; you yourself have moved, in former cases, that the Areopagus should have jurisdiction over all our citizens, should proceed, agreeably to our ancient laws, to punish all delinquents. To this council, which you now call an oligarchical faction, did you implicitly resign this whole city. By your decree, which acknowledged its authority, were two Athenians, the father and the son, delivered to the executioner: by your decree, was a descendant of our great deliverer, Harmodius, cast into chains: the decision of the Areopagus condemned Antipho [1.] to torture and death: in obedience to its authority, and in execution of its just sentence, did you banish Archinus from the city as a traitor. And do you attempt to invalidate this authority in your own case? Is this just? Is this consonant to our laws?

On you, ye judges, I denounce the vengeance of the tremendous goddesses who possess this land, of the heroes of our country, of Minerva our patroness, of all our other guardian divinities, if ye suffer this corrupted traitor to escape, whom the state hath given into your hands; whose counsels have ruined our fortune, defeated our hopes, betrayed us to our assailants;

whom our enemies wish to live, convinced that he must prove our destruction; whose death our friends regard as the only event which can raise us from this fallen state; and for whose just punishment they, therefore, breathe their warmest wishes, their most fervent prayers to the gods. To these gods I too pour out my petitions, that they may save the Athenians, who now see their children, their wives, their honour, all that they account valuable, exposed to danger.

What shall we say, ye judges, to those who stand waiting the event of this cause, if, (which Heaven avert!) the craft of this impostor should deceive you? When we depart from this tribunal, with what face can each of you enter under his own roof, if you dismiss this traitor, whose roof was polluted by his corrupt gains? And, if you pronounce that council void of credit and authority, which we have hitherto regarded as highly awful and august, what hopes, my countrymen, (Oh! consider this,) what hopes can we conceive, on any perilous emergency, if we teach men to despise the danger of receiving bribes against their country? and, if an assembly, the guardians of their country on such emergencies, be branded with disgrace?

Let us suppose the case, that, agreeably to the decree of Demosthenes, Alexander should, by his ambassadors, demand the gold which Harpalus brought hither: that, to confirm the sentence of the Areopagus, he should send back the slaves, and direct us to extort the truth from them. What should we then say? would you, Demosthenes, then move for a declaration of war? you, who have so nobly conducted our former wars? And, if such should be the resolution of the assembly; which would be the fairer procedure, to take that money to ourselves, which you secreted, in order to support our war; or to load our citizens with taxes, to oblige our women to send in their ornaments, to melt down our plate, to strip our temples of their offerings, as your decree directed? Though, from your houses in the Pyræus, and in the city, you yourself contributed just fifty drachmæ: and nobly have your twenty talents repaid such bounty. Or, would you move that we should not declare war; but that we should agreeably to your decree, return the gold, conveyed hither, to Alexander? In this case, the community must pay your share. And, is this just, is this equal dealing, is this constitutional, that our useful citizens should be taxed to glut your avarice? that men of avowed property should contribute; while your property lies concealed, notwithstanding you have received one hundred and fifty talents, partly from the king's, partly from Alexander's treasure; all carefully secreted, as you justly dread the consequences of your conduct? that our laws should direct that every public speaker, every leader of our forces, should recommend himself to the confidence of the public, by educating children, and by possessing land within our territory, nor assume the direction of our affairs until he had given these pledges of his

[1.] See note 1. Orat. XIV. p. 98, on the Oration for the Regulation of the State.

fidelity; and that you should sell your patrimonial lands, and adopt the children of strangers, to elude the force of laws and oaths? that you should impose military service on others? you who basely fled from your own post?

To what causes, Athenians! is the prosperity or the calamity of a state to be ascribed? To none so eminently as to its ministers and generals. Turn your eyes to the state of Thebes. It subsisted once; it was once great; it had its soldiers and commanders. There was a time (our elder citizens declare it, and on their authority I speak,) when Pelopidas led the 'sacred band;' when Epaminondas and his colleagues commanded the army. Then did the Thebans gain the victory at Leuctra; then did they pierce into the territories of Lacedemon, before deemed inaccessible; then did they achieve many and noble deeds. The Messenians they reinstated in their city, after a dispersion of four hundred years. To the Arcadians they gave freedom and independence; whilst the world viewed their illustrious conduct with applause. On the other hand, at what time did they act ignobly, unworthy of their native magnanimity? When Timolaus called himself Philip's friend, and was corrupted by his gold; when the traitor Proxenus led the mercenary forces collected for the expedition to Amphissa; when Theagenes, wretched and corrupt, like this man, was made commander of their band; then did these three men confound and utterly destroy the affairs of that state, and of all Greece. So indisputably true it is, that leaders are the great cause of all the good and all the evil that can attend a community. We see this in the instance of our own state: reflect, and say, at what time was this city, great and eminent in Greece, worthy of our ancestors, and of their illustrious actions? When Conon (as our ancient citizens inform us) gained the naval victory at Cnidos; when Iphicrates cut off the detachment of the Lacedemonians; when Chabrias defeated the Spartan fleet at Naxos; when Timotheus triumphed at the sea-fight near Corcyra. Then, Athenians! then it was that the Lacedemonians, whose wise and faithful leaders [1.] whose adherence to their ancient institutions had rendered them illustrious, were reduced so low, as to appear before us like abject suppliants, and implore for mercy. Our state, which they had subverted, by means of those who then conducted our affairs, once more became the sovereign of Greece: and no wonder, when the men, now mentioned, were our generals; and Archinus and Cephalus our ministers. For what is the great security of every state and nation? Good generals and able ministers.

Let this be duly and attentively considered,

and let us no longer suffer by the corrupt and wretched conduct of Demosthenes. Let it not be imagined, that we shall ever want good men and faithful counsellors. With all the generous severity of our ancestors, let us exterminate the man whose bribery, whose treason, are evidently detected; who could not resist the temptation of gold; who hath involved his country in calamities the most grievous: let us destroy this pest of Greece; let not his contagion infect our city; then may we hope for some change of fortune, then may we expect that our affairs will flourish. Attend, Athenians! while we read the decree proposed by Demosthenes, this friend to liberty, in the midst of our public disorders, immediately after the engagement of Chæronea. Hear also the Oracle of Dodona, the voice of Dodonæan Jove himself (for long since have we been warned to guard against leaders and ministers.)—First read the Oracle.

The Oracle.

Now read this fine decree.

Part of the Decree.

He is a friend to liberty indeed, who issues out his mandate for our citizens to take up arms; himself, spiritless and dastardly; who, if displeased at any of his countrymen, orders them to the post of toil and labour; and assumes, in every instance, a despotic power of acting as he pleases.—Now read the rest.

The rest of the Decree.

You hear, ye judges, that the ambassadors are all named in the decree. But the instant this man was informed of the battle of Chæronea, and that Philip was preparing to invade us, he procured himself to be nominated an ambassador, that he might fly from the danger which threatened us; and, with a shameless insensibility to the distresses of his country, did he then secrete eight talents of the public money, while other citizens were freely contributing to the necessities of the state from their own fortunes. Such was this minister, and such the occasions, the only occasions, he ever took of going abroad; the first, immediately after the engagement, when he fled from the danger of his country; the second, when, protected by his office of chief inspector of the solemnities, [2.] he went to Olympia, to confer with Nicanor. A man worthy to be intrusted with the interests of his country, worthy to be regarded as our great resource in time of danger; who when his fellow-citizens are called forth to meet their enemies, flies

---

[1.] The word ἡγεμών seems to have been sometimes used, by the orator, as a general term, signifying not only commanders in war, but popular leaders and ministers.

[1.] 'Αρχιθεωρίας. The name of their office who went as deputies to offer sacrifices, &c.

at the most famous temples, or (as in the present case) to attend at the public games. The scenes of such solemnities were exempt from all hostilities, and the persons of the Θεωροί and 'Αρχιθεωροι were sacred and inviolable.

from his post, and hides himself at home; when the danger is at home, and his aid demanded here, pretends that he is an ambassador and runs from the city. When there was a real occasion for an embassy, to induce Alexander to peace, he refused to move one step from home; but when it was once reported that this prince was so favourably disposed toward us, as to permit those to return whom his power had banished, and that Nicanor [1.] had come to Olympia, then did he offer his services, as inspector of the solemn rites. Such is this man's conduct: if we are to take the field, he is confined at home; if this be the scene of duty, he is an ambassador; if really sent on an embassy, we find him a fugitive. [2.]

Attend to these decrees of Demosthenes, which empower the Areopagus to inquire into such corrupt practices, when he himself, and when other citizens were accused; and by comparing cases so exactly parallel, convince yourselves of the infatuation of Demosthenes.

A Decree.

Did you, Demosthenes, propose this decree? You did: it cannot be denied. Was the report of the Areopagus decisive in this case? It was. Were the delinquents punished with death? They were: your decree had its due weight: it cannot be denied. Now, read that decree which Demosthenes preferred against Demosthenes. Attend, ye judges!—He hath detected, he hath informed against Demosthenes (this is the fact, in one word:) and upon himself hath he justly pronounced the sentence of death. And now, when he is consigned over to you, judges, selected from the body of our citizens, sworn to obey the laws and resolutions of the assembly; how will you proceed? Will you impiously defy the vengeance of the gods? Will you violate all that is accounted just and sacred among men? O, no! my countrymen! by no means! Grievous and scandalous it would be, if other citizens, not more unworthy, not more criminal than Demosthenes, should be destroyed by his decrees; whilst he himself, convicted by himself, and by his own decree, should despise you and your laws, and triumph in his impunity. This very council, this place, these laws, this very speaker, were the causes of all the severity which hath been, or may be felt, by other delinquents. The same speaker hath, in the presence of the popular assembly, committed the decision of his own cause to the same council. You were witnesses of this, of the compact which he made with his country.

He drew up the decree, by which he is condemned: he deposited it with the mother of the gods, the guardian of all our public acts and laws. It would be impious to rescind it; to invoke the gods as witnesses to the integrity of your decisions; and to decide in opposition to those facts which the gods have sanctified. Neptune, when condemned by this council, in his contest with Mars, submitted to its decision. The tremendous Furies witnesses, of its sentence in the cause of Orestes, of the sanctity and integrity of its judgment, have fixed their residence in this council. And how will you proceed, you who affect the character of consummate piety? Shall the wicked arts of Demosthenes prevail on you to invalidate its authority? No, Athenians! your wisdom cannot suffer it. You are this day to give sentence, in no ordinary or trivial cause. You are to determine the safety of your country: you are to pronounce sentence on corruption, on those wicked practices which involve the world in calamity. If, then, you now exert yourselves to the utmost, exterminate those criminals, and correct the shameless eagerness of receiving bribes: then (if Heaven so pleases) you shall enjoy prosperity; but if you permit your public speakers to sell you, such negligence must prove the ruin of your country.

In our popular assembly, Demosthenes proposed (as a thing indispensably required by the rules of justice,) that all the treasure, brought into Attica by Harpalus, should be seized and kept for Alexander. But say, how shall we keep this treasure, if you secrete your twenty talents, if another secures his sum, if Demades is to have his ample portion, if the rest are to possess their several shares, as specified in the report? Sixty-four talents are declared to be the amount of such distributions. And which is the nobler and the juster procedure; to intrust the whole to the state, until the people shall have come to some fair determination; or to suffer our orators and some generals to divide the spoil? To intrust it to the public, must in my opinion be universally acknowledged just and reasonable; that it should be possessed by private persons, can never be pretended.

Many, and various, and inconsistent, are the allegations, which you shall hear this man urge, ye judges! For he knows, that heretofore you have always suffered him to amuse you with airy hopes and false representations; nor ever retained the memory of his promises longer than whilst he was delivering them. If, then, the state is to be still loaded with the baseness and accursed fortune of Demosthenes, I can only say, that whatever

---

[1.] Nicanor was the agent of Alexander, sent to the public games to proclaim his master's kind intentions to the Greeks.

[2.] Plutarch informs us (in his Life of Demosthenes) that the orator was appointed, with some other Athenians, to go on an embassy to Alexander, immediately after the destruction of Thebes, in order to conclude a treaty with this prince: and that, when he had proceeded so far as Citheron, he began to reflect seriously on the danger of the Macedonian's resentment, and returned home in a fit of terror. So far his accuser's allegations are confirmed by history.

may be the event, we must submit. But, if we still retain the due regard to our country, if we still retain the just abhorrence of wicked and corrupted men, if we would redeem our fortune, and form happy presages of futurity, we must be deaf to the entreaties of this abandoned impostor; we must not suffer his artful tears, and insidious supplications, to prevail upon us. Which of you, O Athenians! is so credulous, who so inconsiderate, who so inexperienced in all past and present affairs, as to expect, that a state, reduced from such grandeur to its present ignoble condition (from what cause or what fortune I shall not say,) a state, that now finds its distresses aggravated, and its dangers increased, by the corrupt practices of its citizens, loaded with odious imputations, obliged to justify his conduct, to obviate the suspicion of having received money which some individuals have secreted; that such a state, I say, can still be saved, by the services of such a man? Why should I mention the numerous instances of his false and inconsistent conduct? How, at one time, he insisted and proposed, that no divinity should be admitted, but such as descended to us from ancient tradition; and the next moment declared, that the people should not contend with Alexander, about his claim of divine honours? How, when he himself was in danger of a trial, he impeached Callimedon of conspiring with the exiles at Megara to destroy our constitution; and then, at once, withdrew his impeachment? How, in the assembly lately convened, he procured and suborned a witness to testify, that a design was formed against our stores, but never preferred a decree; only alarmed us with these informations, just to serve the present purpose?—Of all these things you have been witnesses.

He is, indeed, my countrymen, an impostor and a profligate; no true Athenian; as all his conduct and transactions declare. What ships of war were provided for the state, in his administration, as in that of Eubulus? What conveniences or buildings for our marine? When did he, by any decree, or any law, regulate our cavalry? What force, either by land or sea, did he provide, when so many fair occasions offered, after the fatal engagement at Chæronea? What offerings did he deposite in our citadel, to grace the shrine of our patroness? What edifices hath he erected in our port, in our city, or in our territory? None. And shall this man, who, in war, hath proved a coward, in his civil conduct, useless; who hath never once attempted to oppose or control the traitorous enemies of the state; who hath wavered, and changed, and deserted the service of the people; shall this man find mercy? No. If you are wise, if you have a generous regard for yourselves and for your country, embrace this happy opportunity; deliver to the hand of justice those public speakers whose corruption hath disgraced the state, and guard against that danger, which the gods, by their sacred oracles, have frequently denounced; the danger to be apprehended from leaders and counsellors. Hear the words of this Oracle. Read!

The Oracle.

[1.] But how can we have one mind, how can we all conspire to the general interest, if our ministers and leaders are suffered to desert that interest for a bribe? If you and all the people are to see your native soil, your religion, your children, your wives, exposed to the danger of utter ruin; while they form their iniquitous schemes in concert; affect to be severe, and to inveigh against each other in public; but in private all conspire and concur in one design, that of deceiving and abusing your credulity?—What is really the conduct of a minister true to the community, and sincerely an enemy to those who act and speak against its interest? Or, what is said to have been the regular tenour of their conduct who lived before your time, Demosthenes and Polyeuctes, when the state was involved in no distress? Did they not bring criminals to justice? Did they not impeach? Did they not prosecute them for illegal practices? Where is the instance, in which you have imitated this conduct, you who affect such veneration for the people, who tell us, that our security depends wholly on their determinations? Did you commence any prosecutions against Demades, when his administration had been so repeatedly and enormously illegal? Did you endeavour to control any of those his actions, purposely calculated to oppose our interest? No; not one! Did you impeach him, when his conduct had, in many instances, violated our decrees and laws? Never! No; you suffered his statue to be erected in our city; you suffered him to obtain the honour of public maintenance, as if equal in merit to the descendants of Harmodius and Aristogiton. On what occasion hath the people ever experienced your affections? When have they felt the good effects of your force and energy, as public speakers? Is it then you boast this energy, when you deceive them, when you can gain their attention to your servile flattery? 'No resource can you find abroad: your only refuge is in their kindness.'—First, you should have approved yourselves zealous in opposing those whose counsels are repugnant to the people's interest; then might you expect some credit, when you declare, that your only refuge is in the kindness of the people. But your de-

---

[1.] It appears plainly, that this oracle concluded with recommending unanimity, so as to form a connexion with this passage, in which, probably, the very words of the oracle are repeated.

17   †

clarations are false; you have secured your resources abroad, vying with each other in abject flattery of those who, confessedly, devote themselves to the service of Alexander: who, confessedly, have shared those bribes which the council hath thus detected and condemned. You, Demosthenes, in particular, have had your interview with Nicanor, in the presence of all Greece: you have been at Olympia; you have consulted the god. 'Thus it is plain that you are in no danger from abroad.' Yet you represent your condition as truly pitiable, traitor and hireling as you are, vainly imagining that your wicked artifices shall deceive; and that you shall escape the punishment due to your offences. Thus have you proved more shameless and abandoned than Demades himself. He, indeed, did not disguise his guilt; he confessed that he had received, and would receive gold. But then he did not presume to show his face in public; he did not dare to object to the report of the council: though he never moved that the sentence of the council should be decisive in his case; never condemned himself to die, if adjudged guilty of bribery by the council. But such was your dependance on your fair speeches, such was your contempt of the simplicity of your countrymen, that you thought it easy to persuade your judges, that in your case only the Areopagus had reported falsely; against you alone, their sentence had been unjust. But who can admit of such a thought?

And now, my fellow-citizens, consider how you are to act. The people have returned to you an information of a crime lately committed. Demosthenes stands first before you, to suffer the punishment denounced against all whom this information condemns. We have explained his guilt, with an unbiassed attention to the laws. Will you then discover a total disregard of all these offences? Will you, when intrusted with so important a decision, invalidate the judgment of the people, of the Areopagus, of all mankind? Will you take upon yourselves the guilt of these men? Or, will you give the world an example of that detestation in which this state holds traitors and hirelings, that oppose our interests for a bribe? This entirely depends on you. You, the fifteen hundred chosen judges, have the safety of our country in your hands. This day, this sentence you are now to pronounce, must establish this city in full security, if it be consonant to justice; or must entirely defeat all our hopes, if it gives support to such iniquitous practices. Let not the false tears of Demosthenes make an impression on your minds; nor sacrifice our rights and laws to his supplications. Necessity never forced him to receive his share of this gold: he was more than sufficiently enriched by your treasure. Necessity hath not forced him, now, to enter on his defence; his crimes are acknowledged; his sentence pronounced by himself. The sordid baseness, the guilt of all his past life,

have, at length, brought down vengeance upon his head. Let not then his tears and lamentations move you. It is your country that much more deservedly claims your pity; your country, which his practices have exposed to danger; your country, which now supplicates its sons, presents your wives and children before you, beseeching you to save them, by punishing this traitor: that country, in which your ancestors, with a generous zeal, encountered numberless dangers, that they might transmit it free to their posterity; in which we find many and noble examples of ancient virtue. Here fix your attention. Look to your religion, the sacred rites of antiquity, the sepulchres of your fathers; and give sentence with an unshaken integrity. When Demosthenes attempts to deceive and abuse you, with his tears and wailings, then turn your eyes to the city, reflect upon its former glory, and consider whether Demosthenes hath been reduced to greater wretchedness, by the city; or the city, by Demosthenes. You will find that he, from the time that he was intrusted with our affairs, rose, from the condition of a writer of speeches, and hired pleader for Ctesippus and Phormio, to a state of affluence superior to all his countrymen: from obscurity, from a birth ennobled by no ancestry, he arose to eminence: but, that the city hath been reduced to a condition utterly unworthy of its ancient illustrious honours.

Despising then·the entreaties, the false artifices of this man, let justice and integrity be your only objects. Consider the good of your country, not that of Demosthenes. This is the part of honest upright judges. And should any man arise to plead in favour of Demosthenes, consider, that such a man, if not involved in the same guilt, is at least disaffected to the state; as he would screen those from justice who have been bribed to betray its interests; as he would subvert the authority of the Areopagus, on which our lives depend, and confound and destroy all our laws and institutions. But should any orator or general arise to defend him, in hopes to defeat an indictment by which they themselves must be attacked, suffer them not to speak: consider that they have been accomplices in entertaining and conveying Harpalus away. Consider, that these men do really speak against their country, and are the common enemies of our laws and constitution. Silence such insidious advocates. If the facts alleged be false, let that be proved. And, especially, let your indignation fall on him who foolishly relies on his power of speaking; who, when evidently convicted of receiving bribes, adds to his guilt, by attempting to practise his artifice upon you. Inflict that punishment upon him, which the honour of our country and your own honour demands. Else, by one vote, by one sentence, will you bring down all their guilt upon yourselves and on the people, who have, or may be convicted of corruption; and you yourselves will condemn that ill-judged lenity which now suffers them to escape, when it is no longer in your power to prevent the fatal consequences.

Thus have I endeavoured to discharge my part of this prosecution. I have assisted without regard to any consideration, but that of justice, and the interest of the state. I have not deserted the cause of my country, nor sacrificed the trust reposed in me by the people, to private favour. I but request that your sentence may be directed by the same principles. And now let those speak, who are to succeed me in this prosecution. [1.]

[1.] The former part of the Philippic orations was closed with a brief account of the overthrow of Grecian liberty by the arms of Macedon. The addition of the oration of Dinarchus to the present collection, affords an occasion of deducing the history of our orator himself, from his public administration, down to the fatal period of his life. A short time before he had been loaded with the imputation of having suffered himself to be corrupted by Harpalus, he had a fair occasion of explaining the general tenour of his public conduct: and, on this occasion (I mean his contest with Æschines about the crown,) the people gave a full and ample testimony to the wisdom and integrity of his counsels, to his patriotic zeal, and indefatigable ardour, in the service of his country.

Yet his character, great and splendid as it certainly was, had yet one fault, which obscured and disgraced its lustre, that of too passionate a regard for money. And the indelicate means to which he descended, of acquiring riches, diverted the attention of severe observers from the noble purposes to which he applied them. Faction must have contributed to increase the clamour which the suspicion of his avarice excited. And both might have conspired to give credit to the late accusation of his enemies. The testimony of Pausanias (as mentioned in the introduction to the oration of Dinarchus) affords a very strong presumption of his innocence in this case. His own steady appeal to the justice of his country, his forwardness in promoting an inquiry into the private practices of Harpalus, and the zeal which he expressed for detecting those who had been really guilty of receiving his money, seem to be no indications of his own guilt; unless it be supposed, that he had arrived to a pitch of consummate hypocrisy, and even of folly. The sentence of the Areopagus, indeed, condemned him; but this sentence would have had more weight, had we any authentic evidence that, amidst all the corruption and degeneracy of Athens, this council still maintained its purity and integrity. A private man (as Dinarchus himself declares) found means to corrupt one Areopagite. The Macedonian faction might with equal ease have corrupted the whole council; and, although the authority of this council afforded a plausible and popular argument to our orator's accusers, yet the people did not always pay an implicit deference to their authority. The other persons who were, on this occasion, pronounced guilty by the Areopagus, were, when brought to trial, acquitted by their judges, though Demosthenes was condemned in the first heat and violence of the public resentment.

In consequence of his condemnation he was committed to prison, until he should pay the fine of fifty talents imposed upon him. The disgrace of his sentence operated so powerfully on his bodily frame, that he grew impatient and unable to endure the rigour of confinement, and, by the connivance of his keepers, found means to escape, and to fly from the city. He chose Trœzene for his residence; where he lived for some time, in a gloomy and dejected state of exile; frequently turning his face towards Attica (saith Plutarch,) and bursting into tears, and constantly warning the youth who visited him, not to meddle in political affairs.

Whilst Demosthenes continued in this melancholy state, the Greeks, impatient of subjection, and still possessed with hopes of recovering their ancient glory, took the advantage of Alexander's absence, and began to concert measures for reducing the Macedonian power and recovering their own independence. The satraps of Asia encouraged them in these dispositions; and Leosthenes, an Athenian of eminence, was soon made commander of a large body of forces that had been dismissed from the service of the Macedonians; and was supplied by his country with all necessaries for the vigorous prosecution of war. In the midst of these preparations, advice was received of Alexander's death, which increased the hopes and animated the efforts of the Greeks. The Athenians in particular, despatched their ambassadors to the several states, to urge them to embrace this happy opportunity, and to take up arms for the recovery of their liberty. The states paid the utmost attention to these remonstrances, collected their forces, marched under the command of Leosthenes, gained some advantages over the Macedonians, pressed forward into Thessaly, defeated Antipater, the governor of Macedon, and blocked him up in Lamia, where their general Leosthenes was unfortunately slain, as he was visiting the works, and directing the siege with the fairest prospect of success.

During these commotions in Greece, Demosthenes, though an exile, could not remain an unconcerned spectator. A zeal for opposing the progress of the Macedonian power had ever been his strongest passion. He still retained the same violent impressions; and, transported to find his countrymen now full of that spirit which his life had been spent in raising, he attended the Athenian deputies from city to city, assisting and supporting their remonstrances. He was strenuously opposed by Pytheas, an Athenian, who had revolted to Antipater. These two partisans happened to meet in Arcadia, where the heat of their opposition was inflamed to a considerable degree of passion and animosity. 'When-

THE ORATIONS

Of ÆSCHINES AND DEMOSTHENES ON THE CROWN.

INTRODUCTION.

THROUGH the whole progress of that important contest which Athens maintained against the Macedonians, Demosthenes and Æschines had ever been distinguished by their weight and influence in the assemblies of their state.

They had adopted different systems of ministerial conduct, and stood at the head of two opposite parties, each so powerful as to prevail by turns, and to defeat the schemes of their antagonist. The leaders had, on several occasions, avowed their mutual opposition and animosity. Demosthenes, in particular,

---

ever,' said Pytheas, 'we see asses milk brought into a family, we conclude that it is distempered; just so, when Athenian ambassadors are introduced into any city, we may presume that it labours under disorders.' 'True,' replied Demosthenes, 'and as asses' milk is ever brought into a family to restore its health; so the Athenians never send ambassadors to any city, but to put an end to the disorders which oppress it.'

The liveliness of this answer had more effect than all the pathetic remonstrances and entreaties of Demosthenes. It delighted the imaginations, and flattered the vanity of his countrymen. We may well suppose, that their condemnation had been violent and precipitate, when so slight an incident was sufficient to reconcile him to their favour. He was instantly recalled; a ship was despatched to convey him home; and no sooner did he land at the Piræus, than he found himself surrounded by the whole body of his fellow-citizens, and congratulated by their united acclamations.

The fine formerly imposed upon him, could not indeed be remitted; but an expedient was found to elude the law. It had been usual to assign a sum of money to the person who was intrusted to provide for the celebration of a festival in honour of Jupiter the Saver. To this office Demosthenes was appointed, and, for the performance of it, the people assigned him fifty talents, the sum in which he had been condemned.

But Demosthenes did not long enjoy his present triumph. A considerable reinforcement, which Antipater received from Asia, enabled him to prosecute the war with new vigour against the confederated Greeks, whom he defeated at Cranon, in Thessaly. Each state was now forced, by a prompt submission, to recommend itself to the mercy of the conqueror. The severest terms were imposed on the Athenians. Their form of government was changed to an oligarchy; they were obliged to receive a Macedonian garrison; and Antipater demanded that ten of their public speakers (in which number Demosthenes was included,) should be given up to his vengeance. Alexander had made the like demand, and the Athenians bravely refused to comply. But now Demosthenes found them by no means inclined to protect him. He, therefore, fled from the city: and his fickle countrymen, with a shameful servile adulation to the conqueror

condemned him to death. He gained Calauria, an obscure island; and there took sanctuary in the temple of Neptune. But he was quickly pursued to the place of his retirement, by Archias, one of the principal instruments of Antipater's revenge, attended by a party of soldiers. This Archias, who had formerly been a tragedian, appeared before Demosthenes, affected to commiserate his condition, and gave him hopes of pardon and security. To this he replied with a cold contempt: 'You never could affect me on the stage, nor can your promises make the least impression.' When Archias began to speak in more peremptory and menacing terms; 'Now,' said Demosthenes, 'you pronounce the very dictates of the Macedonian oracle; before, you but acted a part. I desire but a moment's respite, that I may send some directions to my family.' He then retired and seemed employed in writing for a while: Archias and his soldiers drew near, and found him with his head bowed down and covered. They imputed his behaviour to timidity and unmanly terror, and pressed him to rise. The great Athenian had now completely executed his fatal purpose: and perceiving that the poison he had taken, by this time had seized his vitals, he uncovered his head, and fixing his eyes on Archias, 'Now,' said he, 'you need not scruple to act the part of Creon in the tragedy, and cast out this corpse unburied.' (Alluding to a speech in the Antigone, of Sophocles, in which Creon orders that the body of Polynices should be exposed to dogs and birds of prey.) 'O gracious Neptune!' continued Demosthenes; 'I will not defile thy temple; while I yet live, I retire from this holy place, which Antipater and the Macedonians have not left unpolluted.' He then rose, and desired to be supported; but, as he passed by the altar, in a feeble and trembling pace, he sunk down and expired with a groan.

Thus died Demosthenes, at the age of sixty years. His countrymen, ever wavering and inconsistent in their conduct, regretted the death of that man whom they had basely given up to destruction; and, by the honours which they paid to his memory, seemed desirous to efface the stain of their ingratitude.

Among other honours paid to their illustrious citizen, his statue was erected in the city, with an inscription on its base, to the following purport:

had brought an impeachment against his rival, and obliged him to enter into a formal defence of his conduct, during an embassy at the court of Macedon. His resentment was confirmed by this desperate attack; and his success, in bearing up against it, encouraged him to watch some favourable opportunity for retorting on his accuser.

The defeat at Chæronea afforded this opportunity. The people in general were, indeed, too equitable to withdraw their confidence from Demosthenes, although his measures had been unsuccessful. But faction, which judges, or affects to judge, merely by events, was violent and clamorous. The minister was reviled, his conduct severely scrutinized, his errors aggravated, his policy condemned, and he himself threatened with inquiries, trials, and impeachments. The zeal of his partisans, on the other hand, was roused by this opposition; and they deemed it expedient to procure some public solemn declaration in favour of Demosthenes, as the most effectual means to silence his accusers.

It was usual with the Athenians, and, indeed, with all the Greeks, when they would express their sense of extraordinary merit, to crown the person so distinguished with a chaplet of olive interwoven with gold. The ceremony was performed in some populous assembly, convened either for business or entertainment; and proclamation was made in due form, of the honour thus conferred, and the services for which it was bestowed.

To procure such an honour for Demosthenes, at this particular juncture, was thought the most effectual means to confound the clamour of his enemies. He had lately been intrusted with the repair of the fortifications of Athens, in which he expended a considerable sum of his own, over and above the public appointment, and thus enlarged the work beyond the letter of his instructions. It was therefore agreed, that Ctesiphon, one of his zealous friends, should take this occasion of moving the senate to prepare a decree [to be ratified by the popular assembly] reciting this particular service of Demosthenes, representing him as a citizen of distinguished merit, and ordaining that a 'golden crown' (as it was called) should be conferred upon him. To give this transaction the greater solemnity, it was moved that the ceremony, should be performed in the theatre of Bacchus, during the festival held in honour of that god, when not only the Athenians, but other Greeks, from all parts of the nation, were assembled to see the tragedies exhibited in that festival.

The senate agreed to the resolution. But before it could be referred to the popular assembly for their confirmation, Æschines, who

had examined the whole transaction, with all the severity that hatred and jealousy could inspire, pronounced it irregular and illegal, both in form and matter: and without delay assumed the common privilege of an Athenian citizen, to commence a suit against Ctesiphon, as the first mover of a decree repugnant to the laws, a crime of a very heinous nature in the Athenian polity.

The articles on which he founds his accusation are reduced to these three.

I. Whereas every citizen, who has borne any magistracy, is obliged, by law, to lay a full account of his administration before the proper officers; and that it is expressly enacted, that no man shall be capable of receiving any public honours, till this his account hath been duly examined and approved; Ctesiphon hath yet moved that Demosthenes should receive a crown, previously to the examination of his conduct in the office conferred upon him, and before the passing of his accounts.

II. Whereas it is ordained that all crowns conferred by the community of citizens shall be presented and proclaimed in their assembly, and in no other place whatsoever; Ctesiphon hath yet proposed that the crown should be presented and proclaimed in the theatre.

III. Whereas the laws pronounce it highly penal for any man to insert a falsehood in any motion or decree; Ctesiphon hath yet expressly declared, as the foundation of this his decree, that the conduct of Demosthenes hath been ever excellent, honourable, and highly serviceable to the state; a point directly opposite to the truth.

The two former of these articles he endeavours to establish by an appeal to the laws and ordinances of Athens. Here he was obliged to be critical and copious, which may render the first parts of his pleading not so agreeable to an English reader, as that in which he enters into the public transactions of his country, and the ministerial conduct of his adversary.

The prosecution was commenced in the year of the fatal battle of Chæronea. But the final decision of the cause had been suspended about eight years; and this interval was full of great events, to which each of the speakers frequently alluded.

It was the first care of Alexander, on his accession to the throne, to undeceive those among the Greeks, who, like Demosthenes, had effected to despise his youth. He instantly marched into Peloponnesus, and demanded the people of that country to accept him as commander of their forces against Persia. The Spartans alone sullenly refused. The Athenians, on their part, were intimidated, and

---

If with a sage and martial soul inspir'd,
Thine arm had conquer'd, as thy counsels fir'd,
Greece then had braved the Macedonian
    sword,
Nor bow'd, submissive, to her conqu'ring
    lord.

An inscription, which, possibly, may, without presumption, be pronounced defective, in point of delicacy, as it professes to do honour to Demosthenes, but, at the same time, keeps in full view the great and notoriously exceptionable part of his character.

yielded to his demand with greater expressions of reverence and submission than they had ever paid to his father.—He returned to Macedon to hasten his preparations, where he found it necessary to march against his barbarous neighbours, who were meditating a descent upon his kingdom. His conflicts with these people occasioned a report to be spread through Greece, that the young king had fallen in battle. The Macedonian faction were alarmed: their opposers industriously propagated the report, and excited the Greeks to seize this opportunity to rise up against a power which had reduced them to a state of ignominious subjection. The Thebans, unhappily, yielded to such instances, took arms, and slaughtered the Macedonian garrison that had been stationed in their citadel.

But this insolence and cruelty did not long remain unpunished. Alexander suddenly appeared before their gates, at the head of his army, and in a few days became master of their city, where he executed his vengeance with fire and sword. The miserable state of desolation and captivity to which the Thebans were thus reduced, is attributed, in the following oration, to the pernicious counsels and machinations of Demosthenes, and displayed in the most lively and pathetic terms.

Nor did this extraordinary instance of rigour fail of its intended effect. The Greeks were astonished and confounded. The Athenians thought it expedient to send a deputation of their citizens, to congratulate the king of Macedon on his late successes. Demosthenes was one of the persons chosen to execute this commission; but, conscious of the resentment which his well known zeal against the Macedonian interest must have merited from Alexander, he deserted the other deputies while they were on their journey, and returned precipitately to Athens. Nor, indeed, were his apprehensions groundless: for, although the address was graciously received, yet the king took this occasion of complaining, in a manner which marked his superiority, of those factious leaders among the Athenians, to whom he affected to impute all the calamities of Greece, from the battle of Chæronea to the destruction of Thebes. He demanded that several of the public speakers, and Demosthenes among the rest, should be delivered up to the power of the Amphictyonic council, there to abide their trial, and to meet the punishment due to their offences. This was in effect to demand that they should be delivered into his own hands. The Athenians were in the utmost consternation; but found means to deprecate his resentment, and prevail upon him to be satisfied with the banishment of Charidemus, one of his most distinguished opposers: who accordingly repaired to the court of Darius, where his sage counsel, that the Persian should avoid an engagement with Alexander, provoked the haughty and capricious tyrant to put him to death.

During Alexander's famous expedition into Asia, and the progress of his stupendous victories, Greece enjoyed a sort of calm, and the Athenians found leisure to decide the contest between their rival statesmen. The parties now appeared before a number of judges, probably not less than five hundred, and these chosen from the citizens at large; men of lively and warm imaginations, and of all others most susceptible of the impressions made by the force and artifice of popular eloquence. The partisans of each side crowded round, to assist and support their friend; and the tribunal was surrounded, not only by the citizens of Athens, but by vast numbers from all parts of Greece, curious to hear two so celebrated speakers, upon a subject so engaging as the late national transactions, and to be witnesses of the decision of a cause, which had been, for some years, the object of general attention and expectation.

THE ORATION

OF ÆSCHINES AGAINST CTESIPHON.

You see, Athenians! what forces are prepared, what numbers formed and arrayed, what soliciting through the 'assembly, by a certain party; and all this, to oppose the fair and ordinary course of justice in the state. As to me, I stand here in firm reliance, first on the immortal gods, next on the laws, and you; convinced that faction never can have greater weight with you than law and justice.

It were to be wished, indeed, that the presidents of our senate, and of our popular assembly, would attend with due care to the order of their debates; that the laws ordained by Solon, to secure the decency of public speaking, might still preserve their force; that so, our elder citizens might first arise in due and decent form (as these laws direct,) without tumult or confusion; and each declare in order the salutary counsels of his sage experience; that, after these, our other citizens who choose to speak, might severally, and in order, according to their ages, propose their sentiments on every subject. Thus, in my opinion, would the course of government be more exactly regulated; and thus would our assemblies be less frequently engaged in trials. But now, when these institutions, so confessedly excellent, have lost their force; when men propose illegal resolutions, without reserve or scruple; when others are found to put them to the vote, not regularly chosen to preside in our assemblies, but men who have raised themselves to this dignity by intrigue; when, if any of the other senators on whom the lot of presidency hath fairly fallen, should discharge his office faithfully, and report your voices truly, there are men who threaten to impeach him, men who invade our rights, and regard the administration as their private property; who have secured their vassals and raised themselves to sovereignty; who have suppressed such judicial procedures as are founded on established laws, and, in the decision of those appointed by temporary decrees, consult their passions; now, I say, that most sage and virtuous proclamation is no longer heard : ' Who is disposed to speak, of those above fifty years old ?' and then, ' Who of the other citizens in their turns ?' Nor is the indecent license of our speakers any longer restrained by our laws, by our magistrates ; [1.] no, nor by the presiding tribe, which contains a full tenth part of the community.

If such be our situation, such the present circumstances of the state,—and of this you seem convinced ; one part alone of our polity remains (as far as I may presume to judge :) prosecutions [2.] of those who violate the laws. Should you suppress these ; should you permit them to be suppressed ; I freely pronounce your fate ; that your government must be gradually and imperceptibly given up to the power of a few. You are not to be informed, Athenians ! that there are three different modes of government established in the world ; the monarchical, the government of the few, and the free republic. In the two former, the administration is directed by the pleasure of the ruling powers ; in free states, it is regulated by established laws. It is then a truth, of which none should be ignorant, which every man should impress deeply on his mind ; that when he enters the tribunal, to decide a case of violation of the laws, he that day gives sentence on his own liberties. Wisely therefore hath our legislator prescribed this, as the first clause in the oath of every judge : ' I will give my voice agreeably to the laws ;' well knowing, that when the laws are preserved sacred in every state, the freedom of their constitution is most effectually secured. Let these things be ever kept in memory, that your indignation may be kindled against all those whose decrees have been illegal. Let not any of their offences be deemed of little moment, but all of the greatest importance ; nor suffer your rights to be wrested from you, by any power ; neither by the combinations of your generals, who, by conspiring with our public speakers, have frequently involved the state in danger ; nor by the solicitations of foreigners, who have been brought up to screen some men from justice, whose administration hath been notoriously illegal. But as each man [3.] among you would be ashamed to desert from his post in battle ; so think it shameful to abandon the post this day assigned to you by the laws, that of guardians of the constitution.

Let it also be remembered, that the whole body of our citizens have now committed their state, their liberties, into your hands. Some of them are present, awaiting the event of this trial ; others are called away to attend on their private affairs. Show the due reverence to these ; remember your oaths and your laws ; and if we convict Ctesiphon of having proposed decrees illegal, false and detrimental to the state, reverse these illegal decrees, assert the freedom of your constitution, and punish those who have administered your affairs in opposition to your laws, in contempt of your constitution, and in total disregard of your interest. If, with these sentiments impressed upon your minds, you attend to what is now to be proposed, you must, I am convinced, proceed to a decision just and religious, a decision of the utmost advantage to yourselves, and to the state.

As to the general nature of this prosecution, thus far have I premised, and, I trust, without offence. Let me now request your attention to a few words about the laws relative to persons accountable to the public which have been violated by the decree proposed by Ctesiphon.

In former times there were found magistrates of the most distinguished rank, and intrusted with the management of our revenues, who, in their several stations, were guilty of the basest corruption, but who, by forming an interest with the speakers in the senate, and in the popular assembly, anticipated their accounts by public honours, and declarations of applause. Thus, when their conduct came to a formal examination, their accusers were involved in great perplexity, their judges in still greater. For many of the persons thus subject to examination, though convicted on the clearest evidence, of having defrauded the public, were yet suffered to escape from justice : and no wonder. The judges were ashamed that the same man, in the same city, possibly in the same year, should be publicly honoured in our festivals ; that proclamations should be made, ' that the people had conferred a golden crown upon him, on account of his integrity and virtue ;' that the same man, I say, in a short time after, when his conduct had been brought to an examination, should depart from the tribunal, condemned of fraud. In their sentence, therefore, the judges were necessarily obliged to attend, not to the nature of those offences, but to the reputation of the state.

[1.] By our magistrates.] In the original, ' by the Prytanes, nor by the Proedri.' Of which officers some account hath been already given, in the Introduction to the first Philippic Oration translated.

[2.] Prosecutions, &c.] These any citizen might commence against the author of any decree or public resolution, which he deemed of pernicious tendency, or repugnant to the established laws. The mover of any new law was also liable to the like prosecution. And this was necessary in a constitution like that of Athens, where all decisions were made in large and tumultuous assemblies. Here, a few

leaders might easily gain an absolute authority, and prevail upon the giddy multitude to consent to any proposition whatever (if enforced by plausible arguments,) unless they were restrained by the fear of being called to account for the motions they had made, and the resolutions passed at their instances.

[3.] As each man, &c.] To perceive the whole force and artifice of this similitude, the reader is to recollect, that, at the battle of Chæronea, Demosthenes betrayed the utmost weakness and cowardice ; a matter of great triumph to his enemies, and a constant subject of their ridicule.

Some of our magistrates [1.] observing this, framed a law, (and its excellence is undeniable,) expressly forbidding any man to be honoured with a crown, whose conduct had not yet been submitted to the legal examination. But, notwithstanding all the precaution of the framers of this law, pretences were still found of force sufficient to defeat its intention. Of these you are to be informed, lest you should be unwarily betrayed into error. Some of those who in defiance of the laws have moved, that men who yet stood accountable for their conduct should be crowned, are still influenced by some degree of decency (if this can with propriety be said of men who propose resolutions directly subversive of the laws:) they still seek to cast a kind of veil upon their shame. Hence are they sometimes careful to express their resolutions in this manner, 'that the man whose conduct is not yet submitted to examination, shall be honoured with a crown, when his accounts have first been examined and approved.' But this is no less injurious to the state; for by these crowns and public honours is his conduct prejudged, and his examination anticipated: while the author of such resolutions demonstrates to his hearers, that his proposal is a violation of the laws, and that he is ashamed of his offence. But Ctesiphon (my countrymen) hath at once broken through the laws relative to the examination of our magistrates; he hath scorned to recur to that subterfuge now explained: he hath moved you to confer a crown upon Demosthenes, previously to any account, to any examination of his conduct; at the very time while he was yet employed in the discharge of his magistracy.

But there is another evasion, of a different kind, to which they are to recur. These offices, say they, to which a citizen is elected by an occasional decree, are by no means to be accounted 'magistracies,' but 'commissions' or 'agencies.' Those alone are magistrates, whom the proper officers [2.] appoint by lot in the temple of Theseus, or the people elect by suffrage in their ordinary assemblies; such as generals of the army, commanders of the cavalry, and such like; all others are but commissioners, who are but to execute a particular decree. To this their plea I shall oppose your own law, a law enacted from a firm conviction, that it must at once put an end to all such evasions. In this it is expressly declared, that all offices whatever, appointed by the voices of the people, shall be accounted magistracies. In one general term the author of this law hath included all. All hath he declared 'magistrates,' whom the 'votes of the assembly have appointed:' and particularly 'the inspectors of public works.'—Now Demosthenes inspected the repair of our walls, the most important of public works.—'Those who have been intrusted with any public money for more than thirty days.' 'Those who are entitled to preside in a tribunal.' [3.]—But the inspectors of works are entitled to this privilege. What then doth the law direct? That all such should assume, not their 'commission,' but their 'magistracy,' having first been judicially approved (for even the magistrates appointed by lot are not exempted from this previous inquiry, but must be first approved, before they assume their office.) These are also directed by the law to submit the accounts of their administration to the legal officers, as well as every other magistrate. And for the truth of what I now advance, to the laws themselves do I appeal.—Read

The Laws.

Here then you find that what these men call commissions or agencies, are declared to be magistracies. It is your part to bear this in memory, to oppose the law to their presumption; to convince them that you are not to be influenced by the wretched sophistical artifice, that would defeat the force of laws by words; and that the greater their address in defending their illegal proceedings, the more severely must they feel your resentment. For the public speaker should ever use the same language with the law. Should he at any time speak in one language and the law pronounce another; to the just authority of law should you grant your voices, not to the shameless presumption of the speaker.

To that argument on which Demosthenes

[1.] In the original, NOMOΘΕΤΗΣ τις, i. e. One of those who were appointed to revise the laws, and to propose the amendment or abrogation of such as were found inconvenient, as well as such new laws as the public interest seemed to demand. See note 6. on the Second Olynthiac, p. 25.

[2.] The proper officers.] In the original, Thesmothetæ, i. e. the six inferior archons, who were called by this general name, while each of the three first had his peculiar title.

[3.] There was scarcely any Athenian at all employed in public business, but had some sort of jurisdiction annexed to his office. Inferior suits and controversies were thus multiplied, and found perpetual employment for this lively meddling people; who were trained from their youth, and constantly exercised in the arts of managing and conducting suits at law. This was their favourite employment, and became the characteristic mark of an Athenian. 'I saw,' saith Lucian, (in Icaro-Menip.) ' the Egyptian tilling his ground, the Phœnician at his traffic, the Cilician robbing, the Spartan under the lash, and the Athenian at his law-suit.'—And this suggests the real value of that compliment which Virgil is supposed to pay this people, in that well-known passage, 'Orabunt causas melius, &c.' Critics have discovered in it 'dishonesty, affected contempt' of eloquence, 'invidious detraction' from the merit of Cicero, &c. And yet it seems to amount to no more than an acknowledgment of their superior skill in legal forms and pleadings, and the arts of litigation.

relies, as utterly unanswerable, I would now briefly speak.—This man will say, 'I am director of the fortifications. I confess it. But I have expended of my own money, for the public service, an additional sum of one hundred minæ, and enlarged the work beyond my instructions; for what then am I to account? Unless a man is to be made accountable for his own beneficence.'—To this evasion you shall hear a just and good reply.—In this city, of so ancient an establishment, and a circuit so extensive, there is not a man exempted from account, who has the smallest part in the affairs of state. This I shall show, first in instances scarcely credible. Thus, the priests and priestesses are by the laws obliged to account for the discharge of their office: all in general, and each in particular; although they have received no more than an honorary pension, and have had no other duty but of offering up their prayers for us to the gods. And this is not the case of single persons only, but of whole tribes, as the 'Eumolpidæ,' [1.] the 'Ceryces,' and all the others. Again, the trierarchs [2.] are by the law made accountable for their conduct; although no public money hath been committed to their charge; although they have not embezzled large portions of their revenue, and accounted but for a small part; although they have not affected to confer bounties on you, while they really but restored your own property: no; they confessedly expended their paternal fortunes to approve their zealous affection for your service; and not our trierarchs alone, but the greatest assemblies in the state, are bound to submit to the sentence of our tribunals. First, the law directs, that the council of Areopagus shall stand accountable to the proper officers, and submit their august transactions to a legal examination: thus our greatest judicial body stands in perpetual dependance upon your decisions. Shall the members of this council then be precluded from the honour of a crown?—Such has been the ordinance from times the most remote.—And have they had no regard to public honour?—So scrupulous is their regard, that it is not deemed sufficient that their conduct should not be notoriously criminal, their least irregularity is severely punished; a discipline too rigorous for our delicate orators. Again; our lawgiver directs that the senate of Five Hundred shall be bound to account for their conduct: and so great diffidence doth he express of those who have not yet rendered such an account, that in the very beginning of the law it is ordained, 'that no magistrate who hath not yet passed through the ordinary examination, shall be permitted to go abroad.'—But here a man may exclaim, 'What! In the name of Heaven, am I, because I have been in office, to be confined to the city? —Yes, and with good reason;' lest when you

have secreted the public money, and betrayed your trust, you might enjoy your perfidy by flight. Again; the laws forbid the man who hath not yet accounted to the state, to dedicate any part of his effects to religious purposes, to deposit any offering in a temple, to accept of any adoption into any family, to make any alienation of his property; and to many other instances is the prohibition extended. In one word, our lawgiver hath provided that the fortunes of such persons shall be secured as a pledge to the community, until their accounts are fairly examined and approved. Nay, farther; suppose there be a man who hath neither received nor expended any part of the public money, but hath only been concerned in some affairs relative to the state; even such a one is bound to submit his accounts to the proper officers. 'But how can the man, who hath neither received nor expended, pass such accounts?' The law hath obviated this difficulty, and expressly prescribed the form of his accounts. It directs that it shall consist of this declaration: 'I have not received, neither have I disposed of any public money.' To confirm the truth of this, hear the laws themselves.

The Laws.

When Demosthenes therefore shall exult in his evasion, and insist that he is not to he accountable for the additional sum which he bestowed freely on the state, press him with this reply; 'It was then your duty, Demosthenes, to have permitted the usual and legal proclamation to be made: Who is disposed to prosecute? and to have given an opportunity to every citizen that pleased to have urged on his part, that you bestowed no such additional sum; but that, on the contrary, having been intrusted with ten talents for the repair of our fortifications, you really expended but a small part of this great sum. Do not assume an honour to which you have no pretensions; do not wrest their suffrages from your judges; do not act in presumptuous contempt of the laws, but with due submission yield to their guidance. Such is the conduct that must secure the freedom of our constitution.'

As to the evasions on which these men rely, I trust that I have spoken sufficiently. That Demosthenes really stood accountable to the state, at the time when the men proposed his decree; that he was really a magistrate, as manager of the theatrical funds; a magistrate, as inspector of the fortifications; that his conduct in either of these offices had not been examined, had not obtained the legal approbation, I shall now endeavour to demonstrate from the public records. Read, in whose archonship, in what month, on what day, in what assembly Demosthenes was chosen into the office of manager of the theatrical funds. So shall it

---

[1.] Eumolpidæ, &c.] Families (so called from their founders, Eumolpus and Ceryx,) who had an hereditary right of priesthood.

[2.] The trierarchs.] See note on Philip. I. p. 17.

18

†

appear that, during the execution of this office, the decree was made, which conferred this crown upon him.—Read!

The Computation of the Times.

If then I should here rest my cause, without proceeding farther, Ctesiphon must stand convicted; convicted, not by the arguments of his accuser, but by the public records. In former times, Athenians, it was the custom that the state should elect a comptroller, who, in every presidency of each tribe, was to return to the people an exact state of the finances. But by the implicit confidence which you reposed in Eubulus, the men who were chosen to the management of the theatrical money, executed this office of comptroller (I mean before the law of Hegemon was enacted,) together with the offices of receiver, and of inspector of our naval affairs; they were charged with the building of our arsenals, with the repair of our roads; in a word, they were intrusted with the conduct of almost all our public business. I say not this to impeach their conduct, or to arraign their integrity; I mean but to convince you, that our laws have expressly directed, that no man yet accountable for his conduct in any one office, even of the smallest consequence, shall be entitled to the honour of a crown, until his accounts have been regularly examined and approved: and that Ctesiphon hath yet presumed to confer this honour on Demosthenes, when engaged in every kind of public magistracy. At the time of this decree he was a magistrate as inspector of the fortifications, a magistrate as intrusted with public money: and, like other officers of the state, imposed fines, and presided in tribunals. These things I shall prove by the testimony of Demosthenes and Ctesiphon themselves. For, in the archonship of Chærondas, on the 22d of the month Thargelion, was a popular assembly held, in which Demosthenes obtained a decree, appointing a convention of the tribes on the second of the succeeding month; and on the third, his decree directed still farther, that supervisors should be chosen, and treasurers from each tribe, for conducting the repairs of our fortifications. And justly did he thus direct; that the public might have the security of good and responsible citizens, who might return a fair account of all disbursements.—Read these decrees!

The Decrees.

Yes!—But you will hear it urged in answer, that to this office of inspector of the works he was not appointed in the general assembly, either by lot or suffrage. This is an argument on which Demosthenes and Ctesiphon will dwell with the utmost confidence. My answer shall be easy, plain, and brief; but first I would premise a few things on this subject. Observe, Athenians! Of magistracy there are three kinds. First, those appointed by lot or by election. Secondly, the men who have managed public money for more than thirty days, or have inspected public works. To these the law adds another species, and expressly declares, that all such persons as, in consequence of a regular appointment, have enjoyed the right of jurisdiction, shall, when approved, be accounted magistrates. So that, should we take away the magistrates appointed by lot or suffrage, there yet remains the last kind, of those appointed by the tribes, or the thirds, of tribes, or by particular districts, to manage public money; all which are declared to be magistrates from the time of their appointment. And this happens in cases like that before us, where it is a direction to the tribes to make canals, or to build ships of war. For the truth of this, I appeal to the laws themselves.— Read!

The Law.

Let it be remembered, that, as I have already observed, the sentence of the law is this; that all those appointed to any office by their tribes shall act as magistrates, when first judicially approved. But the Pandionian tribe hath made Demosthenes a magistrate, by appointing him an inspector of the works; and for this purpose he hath been intrusted with public money to the amount of near ten talents. Again, another law expressly forbids any magistrate, who yet stands accountable for his conduct, to be honoured with a crown. You have sworn to give sentence according to the laws. Here is a speaker who hath brought in a decree for granting a crown to a man yet accountable for his conduct. Nor hath he added that saving clause, 'When his accounts have first been passed.' I have proved the point of illegality from the testimony of your laws, from the testimony of your decrees, and from that of the opposite parties. How then can any man support a prosecution of this nature with greater force and clearness?

But farther: I shall now demonstrate that this decree is also a violation of the law, by the manner in which it directs that this crown shall be proclaimed. The laws declare, in terms the most explicit, that, if any man receives a crown from the senate, the proclamation shall be made in the senate-house; if by the people, in the assembly: never in any other place.—Read this law!

The Law.

And this institution is just and excellent. The author of this law seems to have been persuaded, that a public speaker should not ostentatiously display his merits before foreigners; that he should be contented with the approbation of this city, of these his fellow-citizens; without practising vile arts to procure a public honour. So thought our lawgiver. What are the sentiments of Ctesiphon?—Read his decree!

The Decree.

You have heard, Athenians, that the law directs, in every case where a crown is granted by the people, that the proclamation shall be made in presence of the people, in the Pnyx, in full assembly : never in any other place. Yet Ctesiphon hath appointed proclamation to be made in the theatre : not contented that the act itself should violate our laws, he hath presumed to change the scene of it. He confers this honour not while the people are assembled, but while the new tragedies are exhibiting; not in the presence of the people, but of the Greeks ; that they too may know on what kind of man our honours are conferred.

And now when the illegal nature of this decree is so incontestably established, the author, assisted by his confederate, Demosthenes, hath yet recourse to subtleties in order to evade the force of justice. These I must explain ; I must so guard you against them, that you may not be surprised by their pernicious influence.—These men can by no means deny, that our laws expressly direct that a crown conferred on any citizen by the people shall be proclaimed in the assembly, and in no other place. But, to defend their conduct, they produce a law relative to our festivals : of this they but quote a part, that they may more effectually deceive you : and thus recur to an ordinance by no means applicable to the case before us. Accordingly they will tell you, there are in this state two laws enacted relative to proclamations. One is, that which I have now produced, expressly forbidding the proclamation of a crown granted by the people to be issued in any other place but the assembly. The other, say they, is contrary to this : it allows the liberty of proclaiming a crown so conferred, in the theatre, when the tragedies are exhibited, 'provided always that the people shall so determine by their voices.' On this law it is (thus will they plead) that Ctesiphon has founded his decree. To this artifice I shall oppose your own laws, my assistants, [1.] my constant reliance, through the whole course of this prosecution. If this be so : if such a custom hath been admitted into our government ; that laws repealed are still allowed to hold their place amidst those in full force ; that two, directly contradictory to each other, are enacted on the same subject ; what shall we pronounce on that polity, where the laws command and forbid the very same things ? But this is by no means the case ; and never may your public acts be exposed to such disorder ! The great lawgiver to whom we owe our constitution was not inattentive to guard against such dangers. It is his express direction, that, in every year, our body of laws shall be adjusted by the legal inspectors, in the popular assembly ;

and if, after due examination and inspection, it shall appear, that a law hath been enacted contradictory to a former law; or that any one, when repealed, shall still hold its place among those actually in force ; or that any more than one have been enacted on the same subject; that in all such cases, the laws shall be transcribed and fixed up in public on the statues of our heroes; that the presidents shall convene the assembly, shall specify the authors of these several laws, and that the proper officers shall propose the question to the people, that they may by their voices repeal some, and establish others; that so one single law, and no more, may remain in force on one subject. To prove this,—Read the laws !

The Laws.

If then the allegations of these men were just ; and that in reality there were two different laws relative to proclamations ; it seems impossible but that the inspectors must have detected this ; the president of the assembly must have returned them to their respective authors ; and the one or other must have been repealed ; either that which grants the power of proclaiming, or that which denies it. But since nothing of all this appears, these men must stand convicted of asserting what is not only false, but absolutely impossible.

The source, from whence they derive this falsehood, I shall here explain; when first I have premised, on what occasion these laws were enacted relative to proclamations in the theatre.—It hath been the custom in this city, during the performance of the tragedies, that certain persons made proclamation, not of an act ordained of the people, but some, of a crown conferred upon them by their tribe, or sometimes by their district; of others it was thus notified, that they granted freedom to their slaves, to which they called on the Greeks as witnesses, and (which was the most invidious case) some persons, who had obtained the honours of hospitable reception in foreign states, used their interest to gain a proclamation, importing that such a community, as that of Rhodes for instance, or of Chios, conferred a crown upon them, on account of their virtue and magnanimity. And this they did, not as men honoured by the senate or by the people, in consequence of your concession, by virtue of your suffrage, and with a due acknowledgement of your favour, but merely on their own authority, without any decree of yours. By these means it happened, that the audience, and the managers, and the performers, were disturbed : and the men who obtained proclamations in the theatre, were really more honoured than those on whom the people conferred crowns. These had a place assigned for receiving

---

[1.] My assistants.] The strict import of the original expression is, ' my counsel,' or ' my advocate.' So that, by a bold figure, the laws are represented, as personally present, supporting the cause of Æschines, pleading on his side, detecting the fallacy and prevarication of his adversary. *Tourreil.*

these honours, the assembly; in no other place could proclamation be made: the others displayed their honours in the presence of all the Greeks. The one obtained their crowns from your decree, by your permission: the others, without any decree. One of our statesmen, observing this, established a law by no means interfering with that which respects persons crowned by the people; by no means tending to render this invalid: for it was not the assembly that was disturbed, but the theatre: nor was it his intention to contradict laws already established: our constitution forbids this. No: the law I mean solely regards those who are crowned, without a decree of the people, by their tribe or district, those who give freedom to their slaves; those who receive crowns from foreigners; and it expressly provides, that no person shall make their slaves free in the theatre; no person shall be proclaimed as honoured with a crown by their tribe, by their district, or by any other people whatsoever, (these are the words of this law,) on pain of infamy to the herald who shall make such proclamation.

Since then it is provided, that those crowned by the senate shall be proclaimed in the senate-house: those by the people, in the assembly: since it is expressly forbidden that men crowned by their districts, or by their tribes, shall have proclamation made in the theatre; that no man may indulge an idle vanity, by public honours th is clandestinely procured: since the law directs still farther, that no proclamation shall be made by any others, but by the senate, or by the people, or by the tribes, or by the districts respectively: if we deduct all these cases, what will remain but crowns conferred by foreigners? That I speak with truth, the law itself affords a powerful argument. It directs that the golden crown, conferred by proclamation in the theatre, shall be taken from the person thus honoured, and consecrated to Minerva. But who shall presume to impute so illiberal a procedure to the community of Athens? Can the state, or can a private person be suspected of a spirit so sordid, that, when they themselves have granted a crown, when it hath been justly proclaimed, they should take it back again and dedicate it? No. I apprehend that such dedication is made, because the crown is conferred by foreigners; that no man by valuing the affection of strangers at a higher rate than that of his country, may suffer corruption to steal into his heart. But when a crown hath been proclaimed in the assembly, is the person honoured bound to dedicate it? No, he is allowed to possess it; that not he alone, but his posterity, may retain such a memorial in their family, and never suffer their affections to be alienated from their country. Hence hath the author of the law farther provided, that no proclamation shall be made in the theatre of any foreign crown, unless the people shall so direct by their decree; so the community, which is desirous of granting a crown to any of our citizens, may be obliged to send ambassadors and solicit your permission, and the person crowned shall owe less gratitude to those who confer this honour, than to you, by whose permission it is proclaimed. For the truth of this, consult the laws themselves.

The Laws.

When these men therefore insidiously alleged, that the law hath declared it allowable to confer a crown, by virtue of a decree of the assembly, remember to make this reply: 'True, if such a crown be offered by any other state; but if it be the gift of the Athenian people, the place of conferring it is determined. No proclamation is to be made but in the assembly.' Wrest and torture this clause, 'and in no other place whatever,' to the utmost; still you can never prove that your decree hath not violated the laws.

There remains a part of this my accusation, on which I must enlarge with the greatest care; that which respects the pretence on which he hath pronounced this man worthy of the crown. These are the words of his decree: 'And the herald shall make proclamation in the theatre, in presence of the Greeks, that the community of Athens hath crowned him, on account of his virtue and magnanimity; and (what is still stronger) for his constant and inviolable attachment to the interest of the state, through the course of all his counsels and administration.' And, from henceforward, I have but to lay before you a plain simple detail; such as can give you no trouble in forming your determination. For it is my part, as the prosecutor, to satisfy you in this single point, that the praises here bestowed on Demosthenes are false: that there never was a time in which he commenced faithful counsellor, far from persevering in any course of conduct advantageous to the state. If this be proved, Ctesiphon must at once stand justly condemned; for all our laws declare, that no man is to insert any falsehood in the public decrees. On the other hand, it is incumbent on the defendant to prove the contrary. You are to determine on the several allegations. Thus then I proceed.

To enter into a minute examination of the life of Demosthenes, I fear might lead me into a detail too tedious. And why should I insist on such points, as the circumstances of the indictment for his wound, brought before the Areopagus, against Demomeles his kinsman, and the gashes he inflicted on his own head? Or why should I speak of the expedition under Cephisodotus, and the sailing of our fleet to the Hellespont, when Demosthenes acted as a trierarch; entertained the admiral on board his ship; made him partaker of his table, of his sacrifices and religious rites; confessed his just right to all those instances of affection, as an hereditary friend: and yet when an impeachment had been brought against him which affected his life, appeared as his accuser? Why, again, should I take notice of his affair with Midias; of the blows which he received in his office of director of the entertainments; or, how, for the sum of thirty minæ, he compounded this insult, as well as the sentence which the people pronounced against Midias in the theatre? These and the like particulars, I determine to pass over; not that I would betray the cause of justice; not that I would recommend myself to favour by an affected tenderness; but lest it should be objected, that I produce facts true indeed, but long since acknowledged and notorious. Say then, Ctesiphon; when the most heinous instances of this man's baseness are so incontestably evident, that his accuser exposes himself to the censure not of advancing falsehoods, but of recurring to facts so long acknowledged and notorious, is he to be publicly honoured, or to be branded with infamy? And shall you, who have presumed to form decrees equally contrary to truth and to the laws, insolently bid defiance to the tribunal, or feel the weight of public justice?

My objections to his public conduct shall be more explicit. I am informed that Demosthenes, when admitted to his defence, means to enumerate four different periods, in which he was engaged in the administration of affairs. One, and the first of these (as I am assured,) he accounts, that time in which we were at war with Philip for Amphipolis. [1.] And this period he closes with the peace and alliance which we concluded, in consequence of the decree proposed by Philocrates, in which Demosthenes had equal share, as I shall immediately demonstrate. The second period he computes from the time in which we enjoyed this peace, down to that day when he put an end to a treaty that had, till then, subsisted: and himself proposed the decree for war. The third, from the time when hostilities were commenced, down to the fatal battle of Chæronea. The fourth is this present time.

After this particular specification, as I am informed, he means to call upon me, and to demand explicitly, on which of these four periods I found my prosecution? and at what particular time I object to his administration, as inconsistent with the public interest? Should I refuse to answer, should I attempt the least evasion or retreat, he boasts that he will pursue me, and tear off my disguise; that he will haul me to the tribunal, and compel me to reply. That I may, then, at once confound this presumption, and guard you against such artifice, I thus explicitly reply; before these your judges, before the other citizens, spectators of this trial, before all the Greeks who have been solicitous to hear the event of this cause (and of these I see no small number, but rather more than ever yet known to attend on any public trial,) I thus reply, I say, that on every one of these four periods, which

you have thus distinguished, is my accusation founded. And if the gods vouchsafe me their assistance; if the judges grant me an impartial hearing; and, if my memory shall faithfully recall the several instances of your guilt; I am fully confident that I shall demonstrate to this tribunal, that the preservation of the state is to be ascribed to the gods, and to those citizens who have conducted our affairs with a truly patriot and well tempered zeal; and, that all our calamities are to be imputed to Demosthenes as their real author. And, in this charge, I shall observe the very same method, which, as I am informed, he intends to use. I shall begin with speaking of his first period; then proceed to the second and the third in order; and conclude with observations on present affairs. To that peace then I now go back, of which you, Demosthenes, and Philocrates were the first movers.

You had the fairest opportunity (Athenians) of concluding this first peace in conjunction with the general assembly of the Greeks, had certain persons suffered you to wait the return of our ambassadors, at that time sent through Greece to invite the states to join in the general confederacy against Philip; and, in the progress of these negotiations, the Greeks would have freely acknowledged you the leading state. Of these advantages were you deprived by Demosthenes and Philocrates, and by the bribes which they received in traitorous conspiracy against your government. If, at first view, this assertion should seem incredible to any in this tribunal, let such attend to what is now to be advanced, just as men set down to the accounts of money a long time since expended. We sometimes come from home, possessed with false opinions of the state of such accounts. But when the several sums have been exactly collected, there is no man of a temper so obstinate as to dissemble, or to refuse his assent to the truth of that which the account itself exhibits. Hear me, in the present cause, with dispositions of the same kind. And if, with respect to past transactions, any one among you who hath come hither possessed with an opinion, that Demosthenes never yet appeared as advocate for the interest of Philip, in dark confederacy with Philocrates; if any man, I say, be so persuaded, let him suspend his judgment, and neither assent nor deny, until he hath heard, (for justice requires this.) And, if I shall obtain your attention to a brief recital of these periods, and to the decree which Demosthenes and Philocrates jointly proposed; if the fair state of truth itself shall convict Demosthenes of having proposed many decrees in concert with Philocrates, relative to the former peace and alliance; of having flattered Philip and his ambassadors with a most abandoned and shameful servility;

[1.] Of the several periods, and, indeed, all the political conduct of these contending statesmen, the translator hath already given the best account in his power, particularly in the 'History of the Life and Reign of Philip.' To attempt to illustrate the historical transactions here mentioned or alluded to, by large notes, would only be to repeat what he hath already laid before the public.

of having precipitated our negotiations without waiting the return of our deputies : and forced the people into a separate peace, without the concurrence of the general convention of the Greeks; of having betrayed Cersobleptes, king of Thrace, the friend and ally of this state, into the hands of Philip; if I shall clearly prove these points, I make but this reasonable request, that in the name of Heaven, you would concur with me, that, during the first of these four periods, his administration hath been by no means excellent. I shall proceed in such a manner, that you may accompany me without any difficulty.

Philocrates proposed a decree, by which Philip was admitted to send hither his heralds and ambassadors to treat about a peace and an alliance. This decree was accused as a violation of the law : the time of trial came : Lycinus, who had first moved for this trial, now appeared as prosecutor : Philocrates entered on his defence ; in this he was assisted by Demosthenes ; and Philocrates escaped. Then came the time in which Themistocles was archon. During his magistracy, Demosthenes obtains a seat in the senate, as a member of that body, without any [1.] immediate right or any reversionary title, but by intrigue and bribery ; and this in order to support Philocrates with all his power and interest, as the event itself discovered. For Philocrates prevailed still farther, so as to obtain another decree, by which it was resolved to choose ten deputies, who should repair to Philip, and require him to send hither ambassadors, with full powers to conclude a peace. Of these Demosthenes was one. At his return to the city, he applauded the treaty ; his report was exactly consonant with that of the other deputies ; and he alone, of all the senators, moved that we should proceed to a solemn ratification of the treaty with Philip's ministers.

Thus did he complete the work which Philocrates began. The one allows these ministers to repair to Athens ; the other ratifies the negotiation.—What I am now to observe, demands your utmost attention. Through the course of this treaty, the other deputies (who upon a change of affairs, were exposed to all the malignity of Demosthenes,) had scarcely any transactions with the ministers of Macedon. The great agents were Demosthenes and Philocrates, and with good reason ; for they had not only acted as deputies, but had also been authors of the decrees which secured these important points ; first, that you should not wait the return of the ambassadors, sent to unite the Greeks against Philip; that you should conclude this treaty separately, and not in conjunction with the Greeks ; secondly, that you should resolve not only to conclude a peace, but an alliance with Philip ; that if any of the states preserved a regard for us, they might at once be confounded with despair, when, at the very time that you were prompting them to war, they found you not only concluding a peace, but entering into a strict alliance with the enemy : and, lastly, that Cersobleptes should be excluded from the treaty ; that he should be denied a share in this alliance and this peace, at the very time when his kingdom was threatened with an immediate invasion.

The prince, whose gold purchased these important points, is by no means to be accused. Before the treaty was concluded, and previously to his solemn engagements, we cannot impute it as a crime, that he pursued his own interests. But the men, who traitorously resigned into his hands the strength and security of the state, should justly feel the severest effects of your resentment. He then, who now declares himself the enemy of Alexander ; Demosthenes, who at that time was the enemy of Philip ; he, who objects to me my connexions of friendship with Alexander, proposed a decree utterly subversive of the regular and gradual course of public business, by which the magistrates were to convene an assembly on the 8th of the month Elaphebolion, a day destined to the sacrifices and religious ceremonies in honour of Æsculapius, when the rites were just preparing. And, what was the pretence for choosing this solemn festival, on which no assembly hath ever been remembered ? 'In order,' saith he, 'that if ambassadors should arrive from Macedon, the people may, as soon as possible, deliberate on sending their deputies to Philip.' Thus, before the ambassadors had yet appeared, an assembly was secured to favour them : you were at once precluded from all the advantages which time might produce ; and your transactions fatally precipitated, that you might conclude this treaty separately, not in conjunction with the Greeks, on the return of your ambassadors. After this, the ministers of Philip arrived at Athens ; ours were still abroad, labouring to stir up the Greeks against Macedon. Then did Demosthenes obtain another decree, by which it was resolved, that you should take into consideration, not only a peace, but an alliance ; and this (without waiting for the return of your ambassadors,) immediately after the festivals of Bacchus, on the 18th day of the month. For the truth of this, I appeal to the decrees.

The Decrees.

After these festivals, our assemblies were accordingly convened. In the first was the general resolution of our allies publicly read ; the heads of which I shall here briefly recite. They, in the first place, resolved, that you should proceed to deliberate only about a peace.

[1.] Without any, &c. i. e.] Not chosen by lot into the office of a senator, nor appointed conditionally, to fill the place of another ou whom the lot had fallen, but who might die, or whose character might not be approved, upon the scrutiny previously necessary to a citizen's entering into any public office or station.

Of an alliance not one word was mentioned; and this not from inattention, but because they deemed even a peace itself rather necessary than honourable. In the next place, they wisely provided against the fatal consequences of the corruption of Demosthenes; for they expressly resolved still farther, that 'it shall and may be lawful for any of the Grecian states whatever, within the space of three months, to accede in due form to this treaty, to join in the same solemn engagements, and to be included in the same stipulations.' Thus were two most important points secured. First, an interval of three months was provided for the Greeks, a time sufficient to prepare their deputations: and, then, the whole collected body of the nation stood well affected and attached to Athens; that, if at any time the treaty should be violated, we might not be involved in war single and unsupported. These resolutions are themselves the amplest testimony to the truth of my assertions.

The Resolutions of the Allies.

To these resolutions, I confess that I gave my voice, as did all the speakers in the first assembly. And the people in general rose with a firm persuasion, that a peace indeed should be concluded; but that, as to an alliance, it would be most expedient to postpone the consideration of this, on account of the invitations sent through Greece, as this should be the act of the whole nation. Night intervened; and the next morning we were again assembled. But now Demosthenes had taken care to secure the gallery, and to exclude all those who might speak against his measures: he declared, that all the proceedings of the day before must be utterly ineffectual, unless the Macedonian ministers could be persuaded to concur; that he, on his part, had no conception of a peace distinct from an alliance; We ought not, said he, (I well remember his expression,) which the odiousness of both the speaker and of the term itself hath impressed deeply upon my mind,)we ought not to rend the alliance from the peace; we ought not to wait the dilatory proceedings of the Greeks; but at once determine either to support the war alone, or to make a separate peace. He concluded with calling up Antipater to the gallery; he proposed some questions to him which had been previously concerted between them, and, to which he instructed him in such a reply, as might effectually defeat the interest of the state. Thus the deliberation ended, in the full establishment of those measures to which the importunity of Demosthenes extorted your consent, and which were confirmed in form by the decree of Philocrates.

Nothing now remained, but to make an absolute resignation of Cersobleptes and the Thracian territories. And this they effected on the 26th of the same month, before that Demosthenes had proceeded on the second embassy appointed for the solemn ratification of the treaty. For this hater of Alexander, this foe to Philip, this your public speaker, went twice on an embassy to Macedon, although he needed not to have once accepted of this charge: he who now urges you to spurn with contempt at the Macedonians; he, I say, having taken his place in the assembly, I mean, that which was convened on the 26th; he, whose intrigues procured him the dignity of a senator, betrayed Cersobleptes into the hands of Philip, with the assistance of his confederate Philocrates. For this Philocrates surreptitiously inserted in his decree, that decree which Demosthenes proposed in form, the following clause among many others; 'that the several representatives of the allies shall be bound to enter into solemn ratifications of the peace with the ministers of Philip on this very day.' But Cersobleptes had no representatives then present: and therefore he who moved that the representatives should then swear to the treaty, by direct consequence excluded Cersobleptes from the treaty, who had not been at all represented in this assembly. To prove the truth of this, read the authors of this decree, and the name of the president who proposed it.

The Decree.

THE PRESIDENT.

A noble institution this, a truly noble institution, Athenians, this exact preservation of our public records! Thus they remain unalterable, and never change from one to the other party, with our variable politicians; but, whenever we are pleased to resort to them, afford us ample satisfaction as to the real characters of those, who, after a long course of baseness, affect to be thought men of worth and excellence on any change of circumstances.

It remains that I produce some instances of his abandoned flattery. For one whole year did Demosthenes enjoy the honour of a senator; and yet, in all that time, it never appears that he moved to grant precedency to any ministers: for the first, the only time, he conferred this distinction on the ministers of Philip; he servilely attended to accommodate them with his cushions and his carpets; by the dawn of day he conducted them to the theatre; and, by his indecent and abandoned adulation, raised a universal uproar of derision. When they were on their departure toward Thebes, he hired three teams of mules, and conducted them in state into that city. Thus did he expose his country to ridicule. But, that I may confine myself to facts, read the decree relative to the grant of precedency.

The Decree.

And yet this [1.] abject, this enormous flat-

[1.] And yet this, &c.] The reader may not be displeased with the following account of this transaction from Plutarch, together with the reflections of the biographer:—

terer, when he had been the first that received advice of Philip's death, from the emissaries of Charidemus, pretended a divine vision, and, with a shameless lie, declared that this intelligence had been conveyed to him, not by Charidemus, but by Jupiter and Minerva. Thus ho dared to boast, that these divinities, by whom he had sworn falsely in the day, had condescended to hold communication with him in the night, and to inform him of futurity. Seven days had now scarcely elapsed, since the death of his daughter, when this wretch, before he had performed the usual rites of mourning, before he had duly paid her funeral honours, crowned his head with a chaplet, put on his white robe, made a solemn sacrifice, in despite of law and decency; and this when he had lost his child, the first, the only child that had ever called him by the tender name of father. I say not this to insult his misfortunes; I mean but to display his real character. For he who hates his children, he who is a bad parent, cannot possibly prove a good minister. He who is insensible to that natural affection which should engage his heart to those who are most intimate and near to him, can never feel a greater regard to your welfare than to that of strangers. He who acts wickedly in private life, cannot prove excellent in his public conduct; he who is base at home, can never acquit himself with honour when sent to a strange country in a public character. For it is not the man, but the scene that changes.

By what fortunate revolution he hath been enabled to assume a new character (for I now come to the second period;) whence it is, that Philocrates, for the same conduct in which he was equally concerned, hath been impeached and condemned to exile, while Demosthenes supports his station, and maintains the power of impeaching others; and by what means this abandoned wretch hath been enabled to plunge you into such calamities; these are points which merit your peculiar attention.

When Philip, then, had possessed himself of Thermopylæ by surprise; when, contrary to all expectation, he had subverted the cities of the Phocians; when he had raised the state of Thebes to a degree of power too great (as

we then thought) for the times, or for our interest; when we were in such consternation that our effects were all collected from the country, and deposited within these walls; the severest indignation was expressed against the deputies in general, who had been employed in the negotiation of the peace; but principally, and above all others, against Philocrates and Demosthenes; because they had not only been concerned in the deputation, but were the first movers and authors of the decree for peace. It happened, at this juncture, that a difference arose between Demosthenes and Philocrates, nearly on the same occasion which you yourselves suspected must produce animosities between them. The ferment which arose from hence, together with the natural distemper of his mind, produced such counsels, as nothing but an abject terror could dictate, together with a malignant jealousy of the advantages which Philocrates derived from his corruption. He concluded, that by inveighing against his colleagues, and against Philip, Philocrates must inevitably fall; that the other deputies must be in danger; that he himself must gain reputation; and, notwithstanding his baseness and treachery to his friends, he must acquire the character of a consummate patriot. The enemies of our tranquillity perceived his designs; they at once invited him to the gallery, and extolled him as the only man who disdained to betray the public interest for a bribe. The moment he appeared, he kindled up the flame of war and confusion. He it was, Athenians, who first found out the Serrian fort, and Doriskum, and Ergiske and Murgiske, and Ganos, and Ganides, places whose very names were hitherto utterly unknown; and such was his power in perverting and perplexing, that if Philip declined to send his ministers to Athens, he represented it as a contemptuous insult on the state; if he did send them, they were spies, and not ministers; if he inclined to submit his disputes with us to some impartial mediating state, no equal umpire could be found, he said, between us and Philip. This prince gave us up the Halonesus. But he insisted that we should not receive it, unless it was declared, not that he resigned, but 're-stored:' thus cavilling about syllables. And,

---

' Demosthenes, having received private information of Philip's death, in order to inspirit his countrymen, appeared in the senate with an air of gayety, pretending to have seen a vision, which promised some good fortune to the Athenians. Immediately after, arrives an express with a full account of this event. The people in a transport of joy sacrifice to the gods, for the good tidings, and decree a crown to Pausanias. On this occasion Demosthenes appeared in public, with a chaplet on his head, and in splendid attire, although it was but the seventh day from the death of his daughter, as Æschines observes, who discovers his own want of firmness and elevation, by reproaching him on this account as devoid of natural affection. As if tears and lamentations were the infallible signs of tenderness and sensibility, he objects to him that he bore his misfortunes with composure. I do not say that it was right to wear chaplets, and to offer sacrifices, upon the death of a prince who had used his good fortune with so much moderation. It was rather base and ungenerous to pay him honours, and enroll him among their citizens, when alive; and, when he had been killed, to break out into such extravagances, to insult over his dead body, and to sing hymns of joy, as if they themselves had performed some great exploit. But I can by no means condemn Demosthenes, for leaving it to the women to mourn over the misfortunes of his family, and exerting himself in what he deemed the service of his country upon this emergency.' *Plut. in Vit. Demosth.*

to crown all his conduct, by paying public honours to those who had carried their arms into Thessaly and Magnesia under the command of Aristodemus, in direct violation of the treaty, he dissolved the peace, and prepared the way for calamity and war.

Yes, but by the alliance of the Euboeans and the Thebans, did he (for thus he boasts) surround our city with walls of brass and adamant. But the truth is, Athenians, that in these transactions he committed no less than three most enormous offences, of which you are utterly uninformed. Although I am impatient to come to that grand article, the alliance of the Thebans, yet, for the sake of order, I must begin with that of the Euboeans.

You, my countrymen! had received many and great injuries from Mnesarchus the Chalcidian, the father of Callias and Taurosthenes (the man whom he hath now presumed, for the sake of a wretched bribe, to enroll among the citizens of Athens,) and also from Themison the Eretrian, who, in time of profound peace, wrested Oropus from you. Yet you consented to bury all this in oblivion, and, when the Thebans had invaded Euboea, in order to enslave the cities, within five days you appeared in their defence, with a powerful armament; and, before thirty days had yet elapsed, you obliged the Thebans to capitulate, and to evacuate the island. Thus absolute masters of Euboea, you reinstated its cities and communities in all their privileges; you generously and equitably relied on their faith, and thought it highly unjust to retain the memory of ancient animosities, when they implicitly resigned themselves to your honour. Yet to these important obligations the people of Chalcis did by no means make the due returns. On the contrary, when you had passed into Euboea, to assist Plutarch, at first indeed you were received with all the appearances of friendship; but when once we had advanced beyond Tamynas, and passed the eminence named Cotylaeum, Callias now perceiving that we had encamped in a dangerous situation, from whence it was impossible to disengage ourselves but by a victory, and where we could receive no reinforcement either by sea or land; this Callias, I say, on whom Demosthenes, having received his bribes, so freely lavishes his applause, collected an army from all quarters of Euboea, which he reinforced with a detachment sent in by Philip: while his brother Taurosthenes, he who so graciously salutes and smiles upon every citizen, brought down his band of mercenaries from Phocis, and both advanced with a firm purpose to destroy us. And, had not the same deity graciously interposed to save our army, and had not all our forces, both infantry and ca-

valry, performed extraordinary acts of valour at the Hippodrome of Tamynas, and after a complete victory obliged the enemy to lay down their arms, the state must have been exposed to a defeat the most disgraceful. For a defeat is not of itself the greatest of calamities; but, when that defeat is the consequence of an engagement with dishonourable enemies, then the calamity is doubled.

Yet, notwithstanding this treatment, you were again reconciled to these people. And Callias, now restored to your favour, preserved appearances for a little time, but soon returned with extraordinary violence to his natural dispositions. His pretence was, to form a convention of the Euboean states at Chalcis; his real design, to fortify the island against us, and to secure to himself a sovereignty of peculiar importance. And, hoping to prevail on Philip to assist him in this design, he went over to Macedon; was constantly in Philip's train, and came to be regarded as one of those who are styled his companions. But, having forfeited this prince's favour by his offences, he was obliged to fly; and, having rendered himself obnoxious at Thebes, he retired from that city also; and thus his course of conduct, more uncertain and variable than the Euripus that flows by his native habitation, involved him in the resentment both of the Thebans and of Philip. In the midst of his confusion and perplexity, when an army was actually preparing to march against him, he saw but one resource left, and this was to prevail on the Athenians, by acknowledging him as their confederate, to enter into solemn engagements to defend him if attacked by any enemy: and it was evident he must be attacked, unless you were to prevent it. Possessed with this design he sent hither his deputies, Glaucetes Empedon, and Diodorus, so distinguished in the race, [1.] who came with airy hopes for the people, but with money for Demosthenes and his associates. And three material points there were, for all of which he then bargained; first, that he should not be disappointed of our alliance: for if the Athenians were to remember his former offences, and to reject him as a confederate, he had but one melancholy alternative, either to fly from Chalcis, or to suffer himself to be taken and put to death; with such formidable powers were both Philip and the Thebans now preparing to surround him. In the second place, the manager and mover of this alliance was to contrive (and for this gold was liberally bestowed) that the Chalcidians should not be obliged to attend the convention held at Athens. The third point was, that they should be excused from paying their contributions. Nor was Callias defeated in any one

---

[1.] In the race.] In the original, 'the runner in the long race.' And whatever air of ridicule the speaker affects to throw upon this accomplishment, the foot-race, it is well known held a distinguished rank among the athletic exercises of Greece. The common course was a stadium, or 625 feet. Sometimes the racers returned back again, performing what was called δίαυλος, or the 'double course.' But the δολιχοδρόμος (as Diodorus is here styled) was the man who could continue his career for twelve stadia or more.

of these schemes. No. [1.] This Demosthenes, this foe to tyrants, as he calls himself, this man whom Ctesiphon declares a faithful minister, betrayed the most critical interests of the state, and by his decree obliged us to take up arms, on every occasion, in defence of the Chalcidians. This was the purport, though not the formal style of the decree: to secure his point in the most delicate and least offensive manner, he artfully changed a single phrase, and ordained that the Chalcidians should take up arms, if on any occasion the Athenians should be attacked. But as to the acknowledgement of our superiority in the general convention; as to obliging the confederates to pay their subsidies, the great support of war; these articles he entirely gave up; he who disguises the basest actions by the most honourable names: whose importunity obliged you to declare, that you were resolved to send assistance to any of the Greeks that needed it: but that you must suspend all farther engagements of alliance; which should be formed only with those whose good offices you at first had experienced. To prove the truth of my assertions, I produce the instrument of Callias, the treaty of alliance, and the decree.

The Decree.

Nor is it his most heinous offence, that he hath sold our interests, our rights of precedency, and our subsidies; what I have now to produce must be acknowledged still more enormous. For such a pitch of insolence and extravagance did Callias proceed, and to such sordid corruption did Demosthenes descend, he whom Ctesiphon hath thus applauded, that they contrived, in your presence, in your view, in the midst of your attention, to defraud you of the contributions from Oreum, and of those from Eretria to the amount of ten talents. And, when the representatives of these states had appeared in Athens, they sent them back to Chalcis, to assist in what was called the convention of Euboea. By what means, and by what iniquitous practices, they effected this, will deserve your serious regard.

I am then to inform you, that Callias was now no longer satisfied to negotiate with us by his emissaries; he appeared in person: he rose up and addressed himself to the assembly, in a speech concerted by Demosthenes. He told us that he was just arrived from Peloponnesus, where he had been lately employed in settling the subsidies which each city was to pay, in order to support a war against Philip; the whole amounting to a hundred talents. He distinguished the sums to be paid by each state. The contributions of all the Achaeans and Megaraeans he raised at sixty talents; those of the cities of Euboea at forty talents; a sum, as he observed, sufficient to maintain a formidable armament, both by sea and land. Many other

Grecian states were ready to join in this supply, so that there would be no deficiency either in money or in forces. These were the effects of his public negotiations: but he had besides carried on some secret transactions which were not to be explained; of these some of our own citizens were witnesses: and then he called on Demosthenes by name, and required him to confirm this by his testimony. With a face of gravity and importance, Demosthenes then arose; bestowed the most extravagant applause on Callias; and pretended to be well acquainted with his secret transactions. He declared himself ready to report the success of his own embassy to Peloponnesus, and of that to Acarnania. The sum of all was this, that, by his means, the whole body of the Peloponnesians, and all the Acarnanians, were ready to march against Philip; that the amount of their several contributions would be sufficient to complete an armament of one hundred ships of war, ten thousand infantry, and one thousand horse: that to these were to be added the domestic forces of each state: from Peloponnesus more than two thousand heavy-armed foot, and from Acarnania the same number: that all these states had freely resigned the chief command to you, and that their preparations were not fixed to some distant time, but were to be completed by the 16th of the month Anthesterion, as by his direction and appointment, the states were to hold their convention at Athens, at the time of full moon. For in these cases the man acts a distinguished and peculiar part. Other boasters, when they advance their falsehoods, are careful to express themselves in vague and obscure terms, from a just dread of being detected. But Demosthenes, when he would obtrude his impostures, first adds an oath to his lie, and imprecates all the vengeance of Heaven on his own head. And then, if he is to assure us of events, which he knows will never be, he has the hardiness to assign their particular times; if to persuade us that he has negotiated with those he never saw, he enters into a distinct detail of their names; thus insinuating himself into your confidence, and imitating the natural and explicit manner of those who speak truth; so that he is doubly an object of detestation, as he is base and false, and as he would confound all the marks of truth and honesty.

When he had finished, he presented a decree to the secretary, longer than the Iliad, more frivolous than the speeches which he usually delivers, or than the life which he hath led; filled with hopes never to be gratified, and with armaments never to be raised. And while he diverted your attention from his fraud, while he kept you in suspense by his flattering assurances, he seized the favourable moment to make his grand attack, and moved that ambassadors should be sent to Eretria, who should entreat the Eretrians (because such entreaties were mighty necessary) not to send their contributions of five talents to Athens, but to intrust it to Callias; again he ordained

[1.] See History of the Life of Philip, book iv. sec. 2.

that ambassadors should be appointed to repair to Oreum, and to prevail on that state to unite with Athens in strict confederacy. And now it appeared, that through this whole transaction he had been influenced by a traitorous motive; for these ambassadors were directed to solicit the people of Oreum also, to pay their five talents, not to you, but to Callias. To prove the truth of this, read the decree,—not all the pompous preamble, the magnificent account of navies, the parade and ostentation; but confine yourself to the point of fraud and circumvention, which were practised with too much success by this impious and abandoned wretch, whom the decree of Ctesiphon declares to have persevered, through the course of all his public conduct, in an inviolable attachment to the state.

The Decree.

Here is a grand account of ships and of levies, of the full moon, and of conventions. Thus were you amused by words; while in fact, you lost the contributions of your allies, you were defrauded of ten talents.

It remains that I inform you of the real motive which prompted Demosthenes to procure this decree; and that was a bribe of three talents; one received from Chalcis by the hands of Callias; another from Eretria by Clitarchus, the sovereign of this state; the third paid by Oreum; by which means the stipulation was discovered; for, as Oreum is a free state, all things are there transacted by a public decree. And as the people of this city had been quite exhausted in the war with Philip, and reduced to the utmost indigence, they sent over Gnosidemus, who had once been their sovereign, to entreat Demosthenes to remit the talent; promising, on this condition, to honour him with a statue of bronze, to be erected in their city. He answered their deputy, that he had not the least occasion for their paltry brass; that he insisted on his stipulation; which Callias should prosecute. The people of Oreum, thus pressed by their creditor, and not prepared to satisfy him, mortgaged their public revenues to Demosthenes for this talent, and paid him interest at the rate of one drachma [1.] a month for each mina, until they were enabled to discharge the principal. And to prove this, I produce the decree of the Oreitans. Read!

The Decree.

Here is a decree, Athenians, scandalous to our country. It is no small indication of the general conduct of Demosthenes, and it is an evidence of the most 'flagrant kind, which must condemn Ctesiphon at once. For it is not possible, that he who hath descended to such sordid bribery can be that man of consummate virtue, which Ctesiphon hath presumed to represent him in his decree.

[2.] And now I proceed to the third of these periods; which was indeed the fatal period, distinguished by the calamities in which Demosthenes involved all Greece as well as his own city by his impious profanation of the Delphian temple, and by the iniquitous and oppressive treaty in which he engaged us with the Thebans. But first I must speak of his offences toward the gods.

There is a plain, Athenians, well known by the name of Cyrrha, and a port now called the devoted and accursed. This tract the Cyrrhæans and Acragallidæ inhabited, a lawless people, whose sacrilegious violence profaned the shrine of Delphi and the offerings there deposited, and who presumed to rebel against the Amphictyonic council. The Amphictyons in general, and your ancestors in particular (as tradition hath informed us,) conceived the justest resentment, and addressed themselves to the oracle, in order to be informed by what punishment they might suppress these outrages. The priestess pronounced her answer, that they were to wage prepetual war againts the Cyrrhæans and Acragallidæ, without the least intermission, either by day or night; that they were to lay waste their lands, and to reduce their persons to slavery; that their possessions were to be set apart from all worldly purposes, and dedicated to the Pythian Apollo, to Diana, to Latona, and to Minerva; and that they were not to cultivate their lands, nor to suffer them to be cultivated. In consequence of this oracle, the Amphictyons decreed, and Solon the Athenian was the first mover of this decree (the man so eminent for making laws, and so conversant in the arts of poesy and philosophy,) that they should take up arms against these impious men, in obedience to the divine commands of the oracle. A sufficient force being accordingly raised by the Amphictyons, they reduced these men to slavery, demolished their harbour, razed their city, and consecrated their district, as the oracle directed. And to confirm these proceedings, they bound themselves by an oath, that they would never cultivate this consecrated land, nor suffer others to cultivate it: but that they would support the rights of the god, and defend this district thus consecrated, with their persons and all their power. Nor were they contented to bind themselves by an oath conceived in the usual form; they enforced it by the addition of a most tremendous imprecation. Thus it was expressed: 'If any shall violate this engagement, whether city, or private person, or community, may such violators be devoted to the vengeance of Apollo, of Diana, of Latona, and of Minerva; may their lands never yield their fruits; may their women ne-

---

[1.] At the rate of one drachma, &c.] i. e. at the rate of about twelve per cent. per ann. See Life of Philip, b. iv. sect. 2.

[2.] The reader will find a detail of this whole important transaction, and of its momentous consequences on the interest of Greece, in the fifth book and first section of the history above mentioned.

ver bring forth children of the human form, but hideous monsters: may their herds be accursed with unnatural barrenness; may all their attempts in war, all their transactions in peace be ever unsuccessful! may total ruin for ever pursue them, their families, and their descendants! and may they never (these are the very terms) appease the offended deities, either Apollo, or Diana, or Latona, or Minerva; but may all their sacrifices be for ever rejected!' To confirm the truth of this, let the oracle be read; listen to the imprecations, and call to mind the oath by which your ancestors were engaged, in conjunction with the other Amphictyons.

The Oracle.

Still shall these tow'rs their ancient pride
    maintain;
Nor force, nor valour, e'er their rampart gain;
Till Amphitritè, queen of azure waves,
The hallow'd lands of sov'reign Phœbus
    laves;
Till, round his seat, her threat'ning surges
    roar,
And burst tumult'ous on the sacred shore.

The Oath.

THE IMPRECATION.

Yet, notwithstanding these imprecations, notwithstanding the solemn oath, and the oracle, which to this day remain upon record, did the Locrians and the Amphissæans, or to speak more properly, their magistrates, lawless and abandoned men, once more cultivate this district, restore the devoted and accursed harbour, erect buildings there, exact taxes from all ships that put into this harbour, and, by their bribes, corrupt some of the pylagoræ who had been sent to Delphi, of which number Demosthenes was one. For, being chosen into this office, he received a thousand drachmæ from the Amphissæans, to take no notice of their transactions, in the Amphictyonic council. And it was stipulated still farther, that, for the time to come, they should pay him at Athens an annual sum of twenty minæ, out of their accursed and devoted revenues; for which he was to use his utmost efforts, on every occasion, to support the interest of the Amphissæans in this city; a transaction which served but to give still farther evidence to this melancholy truth, that, whenever he hath for med connexions with any people, any private persons, any sovereign magistrates, or any free communities, he hath never failed to involve them in calamities the most deplorable. For, now, behold how Heaven and fortune asserted their superior power against this impiety of the Amphissæans!

In the archonship of Theophrastus, when Diognetus was iëromnemon, you chose, for pylagoræ, Midias (that man, who on many accounts I wish were still alive,) and Thrasycles; and with these was I joined in com-

mission. On our arrival at Delphi, it happened, that the iëromnemon Diognetus was instantly seized with a fever, and that Midias also shared the same misfortune. The other Amphictyons assembled: when some persons, who wished to approve themselves the zealous friends of this state, informed us, that the Amphissæans, now exposed to the power of the Thebans, and studious to pay them the most servile adulation, had introduced a decree against this city, by which a fine of fifty talents was to be imposed on the community of Athens, because we had deposited some golden shields in the new temple, before it had been completely finished, which bore the following, and a very just, inscription:

'By the Athenians: taken from the Medes and Thebans, when they fought against the Greeks.'

The iëromnemon sent for me, and desired that I should repair to the Amphictyons, and speak in defence of the city, which I had myself determined to do. But, scarcely had I begun to speak, on my first appearance in the assembly, (where I rose with some warmth, as the absence of the other deputies increased my solicitude,) when I was interrupted by the clamours of an Amphissæan, a man of outrageous insolence, who seemed a total stranger to politeness, and was perhaps driven to this extravagance by some evil genius. He began thus:—'Ye Greeks, were ye possessed with the least degree of wisdom, ye would not suffer the name of the Athenians to be mentioned at this time; ye would drive them from the temple, as the objects of divine wrath.' He then proceeded to take notice of our alliance with the Phocians, which the decree of Crobylus had formed; and loaded the state with many other odious imputations, which I then could not hear with temper, and which I cannot now recollect but with pain. His speech inflamed me to a degree of passion, greater than I had ever felt through my whole life. Among other particulars, on which I shall not now enlarge, it occurred to me to take notice of the impiety of the Amphissæans, with respect to the consecrated land which I pointed out to the Amphictyons, from the place where I then stood, as the temple rose above the Cyrrhæan plain, and commanded the whole prospect of that district. 'You see,' said I, 'ye Amphictyons, how this tract hath been occupied by the people of Amphissa; you see the houses and factories they have there erected. Your own eyes are witnesses, that this accursed and devoted harbour is completely furnished with buildings. You yourselves know, and need not any testimony, that they have exacted duties, and raised large sums of wealth, from this harbour.' I then produced the oracle, the oath of our ancestors, and the imprecation by which it was confirmed; and made a solemn declaration, that, 'for the people of Athens, for myself, for my children, and for my family, I would support the rights of the god, and maintain the consecrated land, with all my might and power; and thus rescue my country from the guilt of sacrilege.—Do you, ye Greeks,' thus did I proceed, 'determine for yourselves as ye judge proper. Your sacred rites are now prepared; your victims stand before the altars; you are ready to offer up your solemn prayers for blessings on yourselves and on your countries;—but, O! consider with what voice, with what front, with what confidence can you breathe out your petitions, if ye suffer these sacrilegious men, thus devoted and ac- cursed, to escape with impunity. The im- precation is not conceived in dark or doubtful terms. No: the curse extends not only to these impious profaners, but to all those who suffer their profanation to pass unrevenged. These are the very words with which the awful and affecting form is closed: May they, who permit them to escape unpunished, never offer up an acceptable sacrifice to Apollo, or to Diana, or to Latona, or to Minerva; but may all their devotions be rejected and abhorred!'

When I had urged these and many other particulars, I retired from the assembly: when a considerable clamour and tumult arose among the Amphictyons; and the debate was now no longer about the shields which we had dedi- cated, but about the punishment due to the Amphissæans. Thus was a considerable part of that day wasted, when at length a herald arose, and made proclamation, That all the inhabitants of Delphi, above the age of sixteen, both slaves and freemen, should the next morn- ing, by sunrise, assemble in the adjoining plain, called 'the plain of victims,' with spades and mattocks; and by another proclamation it was ordained, that the representatives of the several states should repair to the same place, to sup- port the rights of the god, and the consecrated land; and that, if any representatives should disobey this summons, their state was to be excluded from the temple, as sharing in the sacrilege, and involved in the imprecation. The next day we accordingly repaired to the place appointed, from whence we went down to the Cyrrhæan plain; and having there de- molished the harbour, and set fire to the build- ings, we retired. During these transactions, the Locrians of Amphissa, who are settled at the distance of sixty stadia from Delphi, as- sembled in arms, and fell upon us with their whole force; and, had we not with difficulty gained the town, by a precipitate flight, we must have been in danger of total destruction. On the succeeding day, Cattyphus, who acted as president of the council, summoned a 'con- vention' of the Amphictyons; so they call an assembly formed not only of the representatives, but of all who came to offer sacrifice, or consult the oracle. In this convention, many accusa- tions were urged against the Amphissæans, and much applause bestowed on our state. The whole debate was closed with a resolution, by which the iëromnemons were directed to repair to Thermopylæ, at a time appointed, previously to the next ordinary assembly, with a decree prepared for inflicting the due punish-

ment on the Amphissæans, for their sacrile- gious offences against the god and the conse- crated land, and for their outrage on the Am- phictyons. To prove the truth of this, I pro- duce the resolution itself.

The Resolution.

And when at our return we reported this resolution, first in the senate, and then in the assembly of the people; when we had made a full relation of all our transactions to the people, and the whole state determined to act agreeably to the dictates of piety;·when De- mosthenes, from his private connexions with Amphissa, laboured to defeat this purpose, and his iniquitous practices were by me clearly detected, in your presence; when he found it impossible to defeat the interests of his country by a public opposition, he had recourse to secret management in the senate. There, having first taken care to exclude all private citizens, he gained a resolution (by taking advantage of his inexperience who moved it,) which he pro- duced to the popular assembly; and this reso- lution he contrived to be confirmed by the voices of the people, and to be made their decree, at a time when the assembly was actually ad- journed, when I was absent (else I never should have suffered it,) and when the people were dismissed from their attendance. The purport of the resolution was this: 'That the iëromnemon and pylagoræ, who should at any time be deputed by the Athenians to execute these offices, should repair to Thermopylæ and to Delphi, at the times appointed by our an- cestors.' This was speciously expressed, but it concealed the basest purpose, which was, to prevent our deputies from attending the extra- ordinary council at Thermopylæ, necessary to be held before the next stated day of assem- bly.

But there was another clause in this resolu- tion, still plainer and more virulent. It direct- ed, that the iëromnemon and pylagoræ, who should, at any time, be appointed by the Athe- nians, were to have no sort of intercourse with this extraordinary council, either in word, or deed, or decree, or any transaction whatever. 'To have no sort of intercourse.' What is the intent of this? Shall I declare the truth, or shall I speak to please you? The truth by all means; for, by consulting only your gratification, in all that is here delivered, hath the state been reduced to its present con- dition. The real purpose, therefore, of this clause is: that we should renounce all regard to the oath by which our ancestors were en- gaged, to the awful imprecation, and to the oracles of the god.

Agreeably to this resolution, we stayed at home, while all the other deputies assembled at Thermopylæ, except those of one people, whose name I cannot bear to mention; (and never may any Grecian state suffer calamities in the least like theirs!) In this assembly, it was resolved to undertake a war against the Amphissæans; and Cattyphus, the Pharsalian, who then presided in the assembly, was appointed general. Nor was Philip, at this time, in Macedon, no, nor in any part of Greece, but removed as far as Scythia, he who, Demosthenes presumes to say, was by me brought down upon the Greeks. In the first expedition, when the Amphissæans were at their mercy, they treated them with the utmost moderation; and, for their most heinous offences, they only imposed a fine, which was to be paid to the god by a time appointed; removed the most notoriously criminal and principal authors of the sacrilege; and restored those who had been banished on account of their scrupulous regard to religion. But, when this fine was not discharged; when the principal offenders were recalled home; and the innocent and religious men whom the Amphictyons had restored, were once more expelled; then was the second expedition made against the Amphissæans, a considerable time after, when Philip was on his return from the Scythian expedition. And now, when the gods presented you with the sovereign command in this holy war, by the corruption of Demosthenes were you deprived of that honour.

And did not the gods warn us of our danger? did they not urge the necessity of vigilance, in a language scarcely less explicit than that of man? Surely never was a state more evidently protected by the gods, and more notoriously ruined by its popular leaders. Were we not sufficiently alarmed by that portentous incident in the mysteries, the sudden death of the initiated? Did not Amyniades still farther warn us of our danger, and urge us to send deputies to Delphi to consult the god? And did not Demosthenes oppose this design? Did he not say, the Pythian priestess was inspired [1.] by Philip, rude and brutal as he is, insolently presuming on that full power to which your favour raised him? And did he not at last, without one propitious sacrifice, one favourable omen to assure us of success, send out our armies to manifest and inevitable danger? Yet, he lately presumed to say, that Philip did not venture to march into our territories, for this very reason, because his sacrifices had not been very propitious. What punishment, therefore, is due to thy offences, thou pest of Greece? If the conqueror was prevented from invading the territories of the vanquished by unpropitious sacrifices, shouldst thou, who, without the least attention to futurity, without one favorable omen, hast sent our armies to the field, shouldst thou be honoured with a crown for those calamities, in which thou hast involved the state, or driven from our borders with ignominy?

And, what can be conceived surprising or extraordinary, that we have not experienced? Our lives have not passed in the usual and natural course of human affairs; no, we were born to be an object of astonishment to posterity. Do we not see the king of Persia, he who opened a passage for his navy through mount Athos, who stretched his bridge across the Hellespont, who demanded earth and water from the Greeks; he who, in his letters, presumed to style himself sovereign of mankind, from the rising to the setting sun; now no longer contending to be lord over others, but to secure his personal safety? Do not we see those crowned with honour and ennobled with the command of the war against Persia, who rescued the Delphian temple from sacrilegious hands? Hath not Thebes, our neighbouring state, been in one day torn from the midst of Greece? And, although this calamity may justly be imputed to her own pernicious counsels, yet we are not to ascribe such infatuation to any natural causes, but to the fatal influence of some evil genius. Are not the Lacedemonians, those wretched men, who had but once slightly interfered in the sacrilegious outrage on the temple; who, in their day of power, aspired to the sovereignty of Greece; now reduced to display their wretchedness to the world, by sending hostages to Alexander, ready to submit to that fate which he shall pronounce upon themselves and on their country; to those terms which a conqueror, and an incensed conqueror, shall vouchsafe to grant? And, is not this our state, the common refuge of the Greeks, once the great resort of all the ambassadors from the several cities, sent to implore our protection as their sure resource, now obliged to contend, not for sovereign authority, but for our native land? And, to these circumstances have we been gradually reduced from that time when Demosthenes first assumed the administration. Well doth the poet Hesiod pronounce on such men, in one part of his works, where he points out the duty of citizens, and warns all societies to guard effectually against evil ministers. I shall repeat his words; for I presume we treasured up the sayings of poets in our memory when young, that, in our riper years, we might apply them to advantage.

When one man's crimes the wrath of Heav'n provoke,
Oft hath a nation felt the fatal stroke.
Contagion's blast destroys, at Jove's command,
And wasteful famine desolates the land.
Or, in the field of war, her boasted powers
Are lost; and earth receives her prostrate towers.
In vain in gorgeous state her navies ride:
Dash'd, wreck'd, and bury'd in the boist'rous tide.

Take away the measure of these verses, consider only the sentiment, and you will fancy that you hear, not some part of Hesiod, but a prophecy of the administration of De-

---

[1.] Was inspired, &c.] Demosthenes'expressed this by an artificial phrase (the priestess Philippized,) on which the adversary founds his charge of rudeness and brutality.

mosthenes; for true it is, that both fleets and armies, and whole cities, have been completely destroyed by his administration; and, in my opinion, neither Phryrondas, nor Eurybatus, nor any of those most distinguished by their villanies in former times, have been equal to this man in the arts of imposture and deceit; this man, who (hear it, O earth; hear it, all ye gods, and all of human race who have the least regard to truth!) dares to meet the eyes of his fellow-citizens, and shamelessly assert, that the Thebans were induced to the confederacy with us not by the conjuncture of their affairs, not by the terror which possessed them, nor yet by our reputation; but by the negotiations of Demosthenes. True it is, that before this time we sent many ambassadors to Thebes, all of them united with that state in the strictest connexions. First we sent our general Thrasybulus, a man highest above all others in the confidence of the Thebans: after him, Thraso, on whom the Thebans conferred the honours of hospitality: then again, Leodamas, nothing inferior to Demosthenes in the powers of eloquence, and in my opinion a much more pleasing speaker: Archidemus, another powerful speaker, whose attachment to Thebes had exposed him to considerable danger: Aristophon, the popular leader, who had long incurred the censure of being in his heart a Bœotian. Add to these, Pyrandrus, the public speaker, who is yet alive. And yet not one of these was ever able to prevail on them to unite in alliance with our state. I know the cause: but I must not insult their calamities.—The truth is (as I conceive) that when Philip had wrested Nicæa from them, and delivered it to the Thessalians; when he had transferred the war from Phocis to the very walls of Thebes, that war which he had before repelled, from the territories of Bœotia; and when, to crown all, he had seized, and fortified, and fixed his garrison in Elatæa, then did their fears of approaching ruin force them to apply to Athens: and then did you march out and appear at Thebes with all your power, both of infantry and cavalry, before Demosthenes had ever proposed one syllable about an alliance. For it was the times, present terror, and the necessity of uniting with you, which then brought you to Thebes; not Demosthenes.

And let it be observed, that in these his negotiations he committed three capital offences against the state. In the first place, when Philip made war on us, only in name, but in reality pointed all his resentment against Thebes (as appears sufficiently from the event, and needs not any farther evidence,) he insidiously concealed this, of which it so highly concerned us to be informed; and pretending that the alliance now proposed was not the effect of the present conjuncture, but of his negotiations, he first prevailed on the people not to debate about conditions, but to be satisfied that the alliance was formed on any terms: and, having secured this point, he gave up all Bœotia to the power of Thebes, by inserting this clause in the decree, that, if any city should revolt from the Thebans, the Athenians would grant their assistance to such of the Bœotians only as should be resident in Thebes: thus concealing his fraudulent designs in specious terms, and betraying us into his real purposes, according to his usual practice: as if the Bœotians, who had really laboured under the most grievous oppression, were to be fully satisfied with the fine periods of Demosthenes, and to forget all resentment of the wrongs which they had suffered.—Then, as to the expenses of the war, two thirds of these he imposed on us who were the farthest removed from danger, and one third only on the Thebans; for which, as well as all his other measures, he was amply bribed. And with respect to the command, that of the fleet, he indeed divided between us; the expense he imposed entirely on Athens, and that of the land-forces (if I am to speak seriously, I must insist upon it,) he absolutely transferred to the Thebans; so that, during this whole war, our general Stratocles had not so much authority as might enable him to provide for the security of his soldiers. And here I do not urge offences too trivial for the regard of other men. No. I speak them freely; all mankind condemns them; and you yourselves are conscious of them; yet will not be roused to resentment. For so completely hath Demosthenes habituated you to his offences, that you now hear them without emotion or surprise. But this should not be; they should excite your utmost indignation, and meet their just punishment, if you would preserve those remains of fortune which are still left to Athens.

A second and a much more grievous offence did he commit in clandestinely taking away all authority of our senate, all the jurisdiction of our popular assembly, and transferring them from Athens to the citadel of Thebes, by virtue of that clause which gave the magistrates of Bœotia a share in all councils and transactions. And such an uncontrolled power did he assume, that he rose publicly in the assembly, and declared that he would go as ambassador whither he himself thought proper, although not authorized by your commission; and, if any of the generals should attempt to control him, he declared (as a warning to our magistrates to acknowledge his sovereign power, and as a means of accustoming them to implicit submission) that he would 'commence a suit for establishing the pre-eminence of the speaker's gallery over the general's pavilion;' for that the state had derived more advantages from him in this gallery, than ever it had gained from the generals in their pavilions. Then, by his false musters in the contract for the foreign troops, he was enabled to secrete large sums of the money destined to the military service. And by hiring ten thousand of these troops of the Amphisseans, in spite of all my remonstrances, all my earnest solicitations in the assembly, he involved the state in the most perilous difficulties, at a time when the loss of these foreign troops had left us unprepared to encounter dangers. What think you was at this time the object of Philip's most ardent wishes? Was it not that he might attack our domestic forces separately, and our foreign troops at Amphissa separately, and thus take advantage of the general despair into which the Greeks must sink at such an important blow? And now Demosthenes, the great author of these evils, is not contented that he escapes from justice; but if he be denied the honour of a crown, expresses the highest indignation: nor is he satisfied that this crown should be proclaimed in your presence; but, unless all Greece be made witness of his honours, he complains of the grievous injury. And thus we find, that, when a disposition, naturally base, hath obtained any considerable share of power, it never fails to work the ruin of a state.

I am now to speak of a third offence, and this still more heinous than the others. Philip by no means despised the Greeks: was by no means ignorant (for he was not devoid of all sense) that by a general engagement he must set his whole power to the hazard of a day; he was well inclined to treat about an accommodation, and was on the point of sending deputies for this purpose, while the Theban magistrates, on their parts, were alarmed at the approaching danger, with good reason. For it was not a dastardly speaker, who fled from his post in battle, that presented it to their thoughts, but the Phocian war, that dreadful contest of ten years, which taught them a lesson never to be forgotten. Such was the state of his affairs, and Demosthenes perceived it: he suspected that the Bœotian chiefs were on the point of making a separate peace, and would receive Philip's gold without admitting him to a share: and deeming it worse than death to be thus excluded from any scheme of corruption, he started up in the assembly, before any man had declared his opinion that a peace should, or should not, be concluded with Philip, but with an intent of warning the Bœotian chiefs, by a kind of public proclamation, that they were to allow him his portion of their bribes: he swore by Minerva (whom it seems Phidias made for the use of Demosthenes, in his vile trade of fraud and perjury) that, if any man should utter one word of making peace with Philip, he, himself, with his own hands, would drag him by the hair to prison; imitating in this the conduct of Cleophon, who in the war with Lacedemon, as we are informed, brought destruction upon the state. [1.] But when the magistrates of Thebes paid him no attention, but, on the contrary, had counter-manded their troops when on their march, and proposed to you to consult about a peace, then was he absolutely frantic: he rose up in the assembly; he called the Bœotian chiefs traitors to Greece; and declared that he himself would move (he who never dared to meet the face of an enemy) that you should send ambassadors to the Thebans, to demand a passage through their territory, for your forces, in their march against Philip. And thus through shame, and fearing that they might really be thought to have betrayed Greece, were the magistrates of Thebes diverted from all thoughts of peace, and hurried at once to the field of battle. [2.]

And here let us recall to mind those gallant men, whom he forced out to manifest destruction, without one sacred rite happily performed, one propitious omen to assure them of success; and yet, when they had fallen in battle, presumed to ascend their monument with those coward feet that fled from their post, and pronounced his encomiums on their merit. But O thou, who, on every occasion of great and important action, hast proved of all mankind the most worthless, in the insolence of language the most astonishing, canst thou attempt, in the face of these thy fellow-citizens, to claim the honour of a crown, for the misfortunes in which thou hast plunged thy city? Or, should he claim it, can you restrain your indignation, and hath the memory of your slaughtered countrymen perished with them? Indulge me for a moment, and imagine that you are now not in this tribunal, but in the theatre; imagine that you see the herald approaching, and the proclamation prescribed in this decree, on the point of being delivered: and then consider, whether will the friends'of the deceased shed more tears at the tragedies, at the pathetic stories of the great characters to be presented on the stage, or at the insensibility of their country? What inhabitant of Greece, what human creature, who hath imbibed the least share of liberal sentiments, must not feel the deepest sorrow, when he reflects on one transaction which he must have seen in the theatre; when he remembers nothing else, that on festivals like these, when the tragedies were to be presented, in those times when the state was well governed, and directed by faithful ministers; a herald appeared, and introducing those orphans whose fathers had died in battle, now arrived at maturity, and dressed in complete armour, made a proclamation the most noble, and the most effectual to excite the mind to glorious actions: 'That these youths, whose fathers lost their lives in fighting bravely for their country, the people had maintained to this

---

[1.] Destruction upon the state.] After the battle of Cyzicum, the Spartans offered to conclude a peace with Athens. Their ambassador proposed fair and equitable terms; and the moderate part of the state inclined to an accommodation. But the violent and factious leaders, among whom this Cleophon was distinguished, inflamed the people's vanity by a magnificent display of their late success (as if Fortune, saith Diodorus, had, contrary to her usual course, determined to confine her favours to one party.) And thus the majority were prevailed upon to declare for war. And the event proved fatal.

[2.] See History of Philip, b. v. sect. 2. p. 263.

their age of maturity. That now, having furnished them with complete suits of armour, they dismiss them (with prayers for their prosperity) to attend to their respective affairs; and invite them to aspire to the highest offices of the state.

Such were the proclamations in old times. But such are not now heard. And, were the herald to introduce the person who had made these children orphans, what could he say, or what could he proclaim? Should he speak in the form perscribed in this decree, yet the odious truth would still force itself upon you, it would seem to strike your ears with a language different from that of the herald. It would tell you, that 'the Athenian people crowned this man, who scarcely deserves the name of a man, on account of his virtue, though a wretch the most abandoned: and on account of his magnanimity, though a coward, and a deserter of his post.' Do not, Athenians, I conjure you by all the powers of Heaven, do not erect a trophy in your theatre, to perpetuate your own disgrace; do not expose the weak conduct of your country, in the presence of the Greeks: do not recall all their grievous and desperate misfortunes to the minds of the wretched Thebans; who, when driven from their habitations by this man, were received within these walls; whose temples, whose children, whose sepulchral monuments were destroyed by the corruption of Demosthenes, and the Macedonian gold.

Since you were not personal spectators of their calamities, represent them to your imaginations; think that you behold their city stormed, their walls levelled with the ground, their houses in flames, their wives and children dragged to slavery, their hoary citizens, their ancient matrons, un-learning liberty in their old age, pouring out their tears, and crying to you for pity; expressing their resentment, not against the instruments, but the real authors of their calamities; importuning you by no means to grant a crown to this pest of Greece, but rather to guard against that curse, that fatal genius which evermore pursues him. For never did any state, never did any private persons, conduct their affairs to a happy issue, that were guided by the counsels of Demosthenes. And is it not shameful, my countrymen, that, in the case of those mariners who transport men over to Salamis, it should be enacted by a law, that whoever shall overset his vessel in this passage, even inadvertently, shall never be again admitted to the same employment (so that no one may be suffered to expose the persons of the Greeks to careless hazard,) and yet, that this man, who hath quite overset all Greece,

as well as this state, should be still intrusted with the helm of government?

That I may now speak of the fourth period and thus proceed to the present times, I must recall one particular to your thoughts: that Demosthenes not only deserted from his post in battle, but fled from his duty in the city, under the pretence of employing some of our ships in collecting contributions from the Greeks. But when, contrary to expectation, the public dangers seemed to vanish, he again returned. At first he appeared a timorous and dejected creature; he rose in the assembly, scarcely half alive, and desired to be appointed a commissioner for settling and establishing the treaty. But, during the first progress of these transactions, you did not even allow the name of Demosthenes to be subscribed to decrees, but appointed Nausicles your principal agent. Yet now he has the presumption to demand a crown. When Philip died, and Alexander succeeded to the kingdom, then did he once more practise his impostures. He raised altars to Pausanias, and loaded the senate with the odium of offering sacrifices and public thanksgivings upon this occasion. He called Alexander a Margites, [1.] and had the presumption to assert that he would never stir from Macedon; for that he would be satisfied with parading through his capital, and there tearing up his victims in the search of happy omens. And this, said he, I declare, not from conjecture, but from a clear conviction of this great truth, that glory is not to be purchased but by blood:—The wretch! whose veins have no blood; who judged of Alexander, not from the temper of Alexander, but from his own dastardly soul.

But when the Thessalians had taken up arms against us, and the young prince at first expressed the warmest resentment, and not without reason; when an army had actually invested Thebes, then was he chosen our ambassador; but, when he had proceeded as far as Cithaeron, he turned and ran back to Athens. Thus hath he proved equally worthless, both in peace and in war. But, what is most provoking, you refused to give him up to justice; nor would you suffer him to be tried in the general council of the Greeks. And, if that be true which is reported, he hath now repaid your indulgence by an act of direct treason. For the mariners of the Paralian galley, and the ambassadors sent to Alexander, report (and with great appearance of truth) that there is one Ariston, a Platæan, the son of Aristobulus the apothecary (if any of you know the man.) This youth, who was distinguished by the beauty of his person, lived a long time in the house of Demosthenes. How he was there

---

[1.] A Margites, i. e. a contemptible idiot.] Immediately after the death of Philip, saith Plutarch, the states began to form a confederacy, at the instigation of Demosthenes. The Thebans, whom he supplied with arms, attacked the Macedonian garrison, and cut off numbers of them. The Athenians prepared to join with The bes. Their assemblies were directed solely by Demosthenes, who sent despatches to the king's lieutenants in Asia, to prevail upon them to rise against Alexander, whom he called a boy, and a Margites. *Plut. in Demost.*

employed, or to what purposes he served, is a matter of doubt, and which it might not be decent to explain particularly. And, as I am informed, he afterward contrived (as his birth and course of life was a secret to the world) to insinuate himself into the favour of Alexander, with whom he lived with some intimacy. This man Demosthenes employed to deliver letters to Alexander, which served in some sort to dispel his fears, and effected his reconciliation with the prince; which he laboured to confirm by the most abandoned flattery.

And now observe how this account agrees with the facts which I allege against him. For if Demosthenes had been sincere in his professions; had he really been that mortal foe to Alexander; there were three most fortunate occasions for an opposition, not one of which he appears to have improved. The first was, when this prince had but just ascended the throne; and, before his own affairs were duly settled, passed over into Asia; when the king of Persia was in the height of all his power, amply furnished with ships, with money, and with forces, and extremely desirous of admitting us to his alliance, on account of the danger which then threatened his dominions. Did you then utter one word, Demosthenes? Did you rise up to move for any one resolution? Am I to impute your silence to terror; to the influence of your natural timidity? But the interest of the state cannot wait the timidity of the public speaker. Again, when Darius had taken the field with all his forces, when Alexander was shut up in the defiles of Cilicia, and, as you pretended, destitute of necessaries; when he was upon the point of being trampled down by the Persian cavalry (this was your language;) when your insolence was insupportable to the whole city; when you marched about in state with your letters in your hands, pointing me out to your creatures as a trembling and desponding wretch, calling me the 'gilded victim,' and declaring that I was to be crowned for sacrifice, if any accident should happen to Alexander; still were you totally inactive; still you reserved yourself for some fairer occasion. —But to pass over all these things, and to come to late transactions. The Lacedemonians, in conjunction with their foreign troops, had gained a victory, and cut to pieces the Macedonian forces near Corragus; the Eleans had gone over to their party, and all the Achæans, except the people of Pellene; all Arcadia also, except the 'great city;' and this was besieged, and every day expected to be taken. Alexander was at a distance farther than the pole; almost beyond the limits of the habitable world: Antipater had been long employed in collecting his forces; and the event was utterly uncertain. In this juncture, say, Demosthenes, what were your actions? what were your speeches? If you please, I will come down, and give you an opportunity of informing us. But you are silent. Well, then, I will show some tenderness to your hesitation, and I myself will tell the assembly how you

then spoke. And do you not remember his strange and monstrous expressions? Which you (O astonishing insensibility!) could endure to hear. He rose up and cried, Some men are 'pruning' the city; they are 'lopping' the 'tendrils' of the state; they 'cut through the sinews' of our affairs; we are 'packed up' and 'matted;' they 'thread' us 'like needles.' —Thou abandoned wretch! What language is this? Is it natural or monstrous?—Again, you writhed and twisted your body round the gallery; and cried out as if you really exerted all your zeal against Alexander, 'I confess that I prevailed on the Lacedemonians to revolt; that I brought over the Thessalians and Perrhibæans.' Influence the Thessalians! Could you influence a single village; you who in time of danger never venture to stir from the city, no, not from your own house? Indeed, where any money is to be obtained, there you are ever ready to seize your prey; but utterly incapable of any action worthy of a man. If fortune favours us with some instances of success, then, indeed, he assumes the merit to himself; he ascribes it to his own address; if some danger alarms us, he flies; if our fears are quieted, he demands rewards, he expects golden crowns.

'But all this is granted.' Yet he is a zealous friend to our free constitution. If you consider only his fair and plausible discourses, you may be deceived in this as you have been in other instances. But look into his real nature and character, and you cannot be deceived. Hence it is that you are to form your judgment. And here I shall recount the several particulars necessary to form the character of a faithful citizen, and a useful friend to liberty. On the other hand, I shall describe the man who is likely to prove a bad member of society, and a favourer of the arbitrary power of a few. Do you apply these two descriptions to him, and consider not what he alleges, but what he really is.

I presume, then, it must be universally acknowledged, that these are the characteristics of a friend to a free constitution. First, he must be of a liberal descent, both by father and mother, lest the misfortune of his birth should inspire him with a prejudice against the laws which secure our freedom. Secondly, he must be descended from such ancestors as have done service to the people, at least, from such as have not lived in enmity with them: this is indispensably necessary, lest he should be prompted to do the state some injury, in order to revenge the quarrel of his ancestors. Thirdly, he must be discreet and temperate in his course of life, lest a luxurious dissipation of his fortune might tempt him to receive a bribe in order to betray his country. Fourthly, he must have integrity united with a powerful elocution; for it is the perfection of a statesman to possess that goodness of mind, which may ever direct him to the most salutary measures, together with a skill and power of speaking, which may effectually recommend them to his hearers. Yet, of the two, integrity is to be preferred to eloquence. Fifthly, he must have a manly spirit, that in war and danger he may not desert his country. It may be sufficient to say, without farther repetition, that a friend to the arbitrary power of a few is distinguished by the characteristics directly opposite to these.

And now consider which of them agree to Demosthenes. Let us state the account with the most scrupulous regard to justice. This man's father was Demosthenes of the Pæanian tribe, a citizen of repute (for I shall adhere strictly to truth.) But how he stands as to family, with respect to his mother and her father, I must now explain. There was once in Athens a man called Gylon; who by betraying Nymphæum in Pontus to the enemy, a city then possessed by us, was obliged to fly from his country in order to escape the sentence of death denounced against him, and settled on the Bosphorus, where he obtained, from the neighbouring princes, a tract of land called 'the Gardens;' and married a woman, who indeed brought him a considerable fortune, but was by birth a Scythian. By her he had two daughters, whom he sent hither with a great quantity of wealth; one of them he settled, I shall not mention [1.] with whom, that I may not provoke the resentment of too many; the other Demosthenes, the Pæanian married in defiance of our laws, and from her is the present Demosthenes sprung; our turbulent and malicious informer. So that by his grandfather, in the female line, he is an enemy to the state, for his grandfather was condemned to death by your ancestors. And by his mother he is a Scythian, one who assumes the language of Greece, but whose abandoned principles betray his barbarous descent.

And what hath been his course of life ?—He first assumed the office of a trierarch; and having exhausted his paternal fortune by his ridiculous vanity, he descended to the profession of a hired advocate: but having lost all credit in this employment, by betraying the secrets of his clients to their antagonists, he forced his way into the gallery, and appeared a popular speaker. When those vast sums, of which he had defrauded the public, were just dissipated, a sudden tide of Persian gold poured into his exhausted coffers; nor was all this sufficient; for no fund whatever can prove sufficient for the profligate and corrupt. In a word, he supported himself, not by a fortune of his own, but by your perils. But how doth

he appear with respect to integrity, and force of elocution? Powerful in speaking; abandoned in his manners. Of such unnatural depravity in his sensual gratifications, that I cannot describe his practices; I cannot offend that delicacy to which such shocking descriptions are always odious. And how hath he served the public? His speeches have been plausible; his actions traitorous.

As to his courage, I need say but little on that head. Did he himself deny that he is a coward? Were you not sensible of it, I should think it necessary to detain you by a formal course of evidence. But as he hath publicly confessed it in our assemblies, and as you have been witnesses of it, it remains only that I remind you of the laws enacted against such crimes. It was the determination of Solon, our old legislator, that he who evaded his duty in the field, or left his post in battle, should be subject to the same penalties with the man directly convicted of cowardice. For there are laws enacted against cowardice. It may perhaps seem wonderful, that the law should take cognizance of a natural infirmity. But such is the fact. And why? That every one of us may dread the punishment denounced by law, more than the enemy; and thus prove the better soldier in the cause of his country. The man, then, who declines the service of the field, the coward, and he who leaves his post in battle, are, by our lawgiver, excluded from all share [2.] in public deliberations, rendered incapable of receiving the honour of a crown, and denied admission to the religious rites performed by the public. But you direct us to crown a person, whom the laws declare to be incapable of receiving a crown; and by your decree you introduce a man into the theatre, who is disqualified from appearing there; you call him into a place sacred to Bacchus, who by his cowardice hath betrayed all our sacred places.—But, that I may not divert you from the great point, remember this. When Demosthenes tells you that he is a friend to liberty, examine not his speeches but his actions; and consider not what he professes to be, but what he really is.

And, now that I have mentioned crowns and public honours, while it yet rests upon my mind, let me recommend this precaution. It must be your part, Athenians, to put an end to this frequency of public honours, these precipitate grants of crowns; else they who obtain them will owe you no acknowledgment, nor

---

[1.] I shall not mention, &c.] The name, which Æschines suppresses from motives of policy, Demosthenes hath himself discovered in his oration against Aphobus; where he declares that his mother was daughter to this Gylon, and that her sister married Demochares. This passage must have escaped Plutarch; as he expresses a doubt whether the account here given of the family of Demosthenes be true or false. *Tourreil.*

[2.] From all share, &c.] The original ex-

pression imports, 'from the lustral vessels of our public place of assembling.' These vessels of hallowed water were placed at the entrance of their temples, and the avenues of their forum, for the same purpose to which they are at this day applied in Popish churches. And it was a part of the religious ceremonies performed in their public assemblies, previously to all deliberation, to sprinkle the place, and the people, from those vessels.

shall the state receive the least advantage : for you never can make bad men better; and those of real merit must be cast into the utmost dejection. Of this truth I shall convince you by the most powerful arguments. Suppose a man should ask, At what time this state supported the most illustrious reputation ? in the present days, or in those of our ancestors ? With one voice you would reply, 'In the days of our ancestors.' At what time did our citizens display the greatest merit ? then, or now ? They were then eminent; now much less distinguished. At what time were rewards, crowns, proclamations, and public honours of every kind most frequent ? then, or now ? Then they were rare, and truly valuable ; then the name of merit bore the highest lustre : but now, it is tarnished and effaced ; while your honours are conferred by course and custom, not with judgment and distinction.

It may possibly seem unaccountable, that rewards are now more frequent, yet that public affairs were then more flourishing ; that our citizens are now less worthy, but were then of real eminence. This is a difficulty which I shall endeavour to obviate. Do you imagine, Athenians, that any man whatever would engage in the games held on our festivals, or in any others, where the victors receive a crown, in the exercises of wrestling, or in any of the several athletic contests, if the crown was to be conferred, not on the most worthy, but on the man of greatest interest ? Surely no man would engage. But now, as the reward of such their victory is rare, hardly to be obtained, truly honourable, and never to be forgotten; there are champions found, ready to submit to the severest preparatory discipline, and to encounter all the dangers of the contest. Imagine, then, that political merit is a kind of game, which you are appointed to direct: and consider that, if you grant the prizes to a few, and those the most worthy, and on such conditions as the laws prescribe, you will have many champions in this contest of merit. But, if you gratify any man that pleases, or those who can secure the strongest interest, you will be the means of corrupting the very best natural dispositons.

That you may conceive the force of what I here advance, I must explain myself still more clearly.—Which, think ye, was the more worthy citizen: Themistocles, who commanded your fleet, when you defeated the Persian in the sea-fight at Salamis; or this Demosthenes, who deserted from his post ? Miltiades, who conquered the barbarians at Marathon, or this man ? The chiefs who led back the people from Phylè? [1.] Aristides, surnamed the Just, a title quite different from that of Demosthenes ?—No ; by the powers of Heaven, I deem the names of these heroes too noble to be mentioned in the same day with that of this savage. And let Demosthenes show,

when he comes to his reply, if ever a decree was made for granting a golden crown to them. Was then the state ungrateful ? No : but she thought highly of her own dignity. And these citizens, who were not thus honoured, appear to have been truly worthy of such a state ; for they imagined that they were not to be honoured by public records, but by the memories of those they had obliged ; and their honours have there remained, from that time down to this day, in characters indelible and immortal. There were citizens in those days, who being stationed at the river Strymon, there patiently endured a long series of toils and dangers, and, at length, gained a victory over the Medes. At their return, they petitioned the people for a reward ; and a reward was conferred upon them (then deemed of great importance,) by erecting three Mercuries of stone in the usual portico, on which, however, their names were not inscribed, lest this might seem a monument erected to the honour of the commanders, not to that of the people. For the truth of this I appeal to the inscriptions. That on the first statue was expressed thus :—

Great souls! who fought near Strymon's rapid
   tide ;
And brav'd the invader's arm, and quell'd his
   pride.
Eïon's high tow'rs confessed the glorious
   deed;
And saw dire famine waste the vanquish'd
   Mede.
Such was our vengeance on the barb'rous host;
And such the gen'rous toils our heroes boast.

This was the inscription on the second ;

This the reward which grateful Athens gives !
Here still the patriot and the hero lives!
Here, let the rising age with rapture gaze,
And emulate the glorious deeds they praise.

On the third was the inscription thus :—

Menestheus, hence, led forth his chosen train,
And pour'd the war o'er hapless Ilion's plain.
'Twas his (so speaks the bard's immortal lay,)
To form th' embody'd host in firm array.
Such were our sons—Nor yet shall Athens
   yield
The first bright honours of the sanguine field.
Still, nurse of heroes ! still the praise is thine,
Of ev'ry glorious toil, of ev'ry act divine.

In these do we find the name of the general ? No ; but that of the people. Fancy yourselves transported to the grand portico ; for, in this your place of assembling, the monuments of all great actions are erected full in view. There we find a picture of the battle of Marathon. Who was the general in this battle ? to this question you would all answer, Miltiades. And

---

[1.] From Phylè, i. e.] when Thrasybulus had expelled the thirty tyrants, established by the Lacedemonians in Athens, at the conclusion of the Peloponnesian war.

yet his name is not inscribed. How? Did he not petition for such an honour? He did petition: but the people refused to grant it. Instead of inscribing his name they consented that he should be drawn in the foreground, encouraging his soldiers. In like manner, in the temple of the Great Mother, adjoining to the senate-house, you may see the honours paid to those who brought our exiles back from Phylè. The decree for these honours was solicited and obtained by Archines, one of those whom they restored to the citizens. And this decree directs, first, that a thousand drachmæ shall be given to them, for sacrifices and offerings; a sum which allowed not quite ten drachmæ to each. In the next place, it ordains, that each shall be crowned with a wreath of olive, not of gold. For crowns of olive were then deemed highly honourable; now, those of gold are regarded with contempt. Nor was even this to be granted precipitately, but after an exact previous examination, by the senate, into the numbers of those who had maintained their post at Phylè, when the Lacedemonians and the thirty had marched to attack them, not of those who had fled from their post at Chæronea, on the first appearance of an enemy. And for the truth of this let the decree be read.

The Decree for honouring those who had been at Phylè.

Compare this with the decree proposed by Ctesiphon in favour of Demosthenes, the author of our most grievous calamities.—Read

The Decree of Ctesiphon.

By this decree are the honours granted to those who restored our exiles utterly effaced. If to confer the one was laudable, to grant the other must be scandalous. If they were worthy of their public honours, he must be utterly unworthy of this crown.—But it is his purpose to allege (as I am informed) that I proceed without candour or justice, in comparing his actions with those of our ancestors. In the Olympic games, saith he, Philamon is not crowned because he hath excelled Glaucus the ancient wrestler, but because he hath conquered his own antagonist. As if you did not know that, in these games, the contest is between the immediate combatants; but where political merit is to be honoured, the contest is with merit itself; nor can the herald at all deviate from truth, when he is to make proclamation in the presence of the Greeks. Do not then pretend to say you have served the state better than Patæcion; prove that you have attained to true and perfect excellence; and then demand honours from the people. But, that I may not lead you too far from the subject, let the secretary read the inscription in honour of those who brought back the people from Phylè.

Those wreaths Athenian gratitude bestows
On the brave chiefs, who first, for freedom, rose,
Drove the proud tyrants from their lawless state,
And bade the rescu'd land again be great.

That they had overturned a government repugnant to the laws; this is the very reason here assigned for their public honours. For such was the universal reverence for the laws, at that time, that men's ears were perpetually ringing with this maxim, that, by defeating impeachments against illegal practices, our constitution was instantly subverted. So have I been informed by my father, who died at the age of ninety-five, after sharing all the distresses of his country. Such were the principles he repeatedly inculcated, in his hours of disengagement. By him have I been assured that, at the time when our freedom was just restored, the man who stood arraigned for any violation of the laws received the punishment due to his offence, without respite or mercy. And what offence can be conceived more impious than an infringement of the laws either by word or action?—At that time, said he, such causes were not heard in the same manner as at present. The judges exerted more severity against those who stood impeached, than even the prosecutor. It was then usual for them to interrupt the secretary, to oblige him again to read the laws, and to compare them with the decree impeached: and to pronounce the sentence of condemnation, not on those only who had been convicted of violating the whole tenor of the laws, but even on those only who had deviated from them in one single particle. But the present course of procedure is even ridiculous. The officer reads the indictment; but, as if it were an idle song, or some trivial matter of no concernment to them, the judges turn their attention to some other subject. And thus, seduced by the wiles of Demosthenes, you have admitted a shameful practice into your tribunals; and public justice is perverted; the prosecutor is obliged to appear as the defendant; while the person accused commences prosecutor: the judges sometimes forget the points to which their right of judicature extends, and are forced to give sentence on matters not fairly cognizable on their tribunals; and, if the impeached party ever deigns to enter on his defence, his plea is, not that he is innocent of the charge, but that some other person, equally guilty, hath on some former occasion been suffered to escape. And on this plea Ctesiphon relies with the greatest confidence, as I am informed.

Your citizen Aristophon once dared to boast, that fifty-five times had he been prosecuted for illegal decrees, and as many times had he escaped. Not so Cephalus, our old minister, he whom we deemed the most zealously attached to the constitution. He, on the contrary, accounted it his greatest glory, that, although he had proposed more decrees than any other citizen, yet had he been not once obliged to defend himself against an impeachment. And this was really matter of triumph; for, in his days, prosecutions were commenced, not by the partisans of opposite factions against each other, but by friends against friends, in every case in which the state was injured. To produce an instance of this. Archimus commenced a prosecution against Thrasybulus, on account of a decree for crowning one of those who had returned from Phylè, which, in some circumstances, was repugnant to the laws; and notwithstanding his late important services, sentence was pronounced against him. These were not at all regarded by the judges. It was their principle, that, as Thrasybulus had once restored our exiles, so he in effect drove his fellow-citizens into exile, by proposing any one act repugnant to the laws. But now we have quite different sentiments. Now our generals of character, our citizens whose services have been rewarded by public maintenance, [1.] exert their interest to suppress impeachments; and in this they must be deemed guilty of the utmost ingratitude. For the man who hath been honoured by the state, a state which owes its being only to the gods and to the laws, and yet presumes to support those who violate the laws, in effect subverts that government by which his honours were conferred.

Here then I shall explain, how far a citizen may honestly and regularly proceed in pleading for an offender. When an impeachment for illegal practices is to be tried in the tribunal, the day of hearing is divided into three parts; the first part is assigned to the prosecutor, to the laws, and to the constitution; the second is granted to the accused, and to his assistants. If then sentence of acquittal be not passed on the first question, a third portion is assigned for the consideration of the fine, and for adjusting the decree of your resentment. He then who petitions for your vote, when the fine is to be considered, petitions only against the rigour of your resentment. But he who petitions for your vote upon the first question, petitions you to give up your oath, to give up the law, to give up the constitution; a favour which it is impious to ask; which, if asked, it is impious to grant. Tell these interceders, then, that they are to leave you at full liberty to decide the first question agreeably to the laws: let them reserve their eloquence for the question relative to the fine.

Upon the whole, Athenians, I am almost tempted to declare, that a law should be enacted solely respecting impeachments for illegal proceedings; that neither the prosecutor, nor the accused should ever be allowed the assistance of advocates: for the merits of such

causes are not vague and undetermined. No; they are accurately defined by your laws. As in architecture, when we would be assured whether any part stand upright or no, we apply the rule by which it is ascertained; so in these impeachments we have a rule provided in the record of the prosecution, in the decree impeached, and in the laws with which it is compared. Show, then, in the present case, that these last are consonant to each other, and that you are at once acquitted. What need you call upon Demosthenes? But if you evade the equitable method of defence, and call to your assistance a man practised in craft, in all the wiles of speaking, you then abuse the attention of your judges, you injure the state, you subvert the constitution.

It must be my part effectually to guard you against such evasion. When Ctesiphon rises up, and begins with repeating the fine introduction composed for him; when he winds through his solemn periods without ever coming to the great point of his defence; then remind him calmly and quietly to take up the record of his impeachment, and compare his decree with the laws. Should he pretend not to hear you, do you too refuse to hear him: for you are here convened to attend, not to those who would evade the just methods of defence, but to the men who defend their cause fairly and regularly. And should he still decline the legal and equitable defence, and call on Demosthenes to plead for him, my first request is, that you would not at all admit an insidious advocate, who thinks to subvert the laws by his harangues: that, when Ctesiphon asks whether he shall call Demosthenes, no man should esteem it meritorious to be the first to cry, 'Call him, call him!' If you call him, against yourselves you call him, against the laws you call him, against the constitution you call him. Or, if you resolve to hear him, I then request that Demosthenes may be confined to the same method in his defence, which I have pursued in this my charge. And what method have I pursued? That I may assist your memories: observe, that I have not begun with the private life of Demosthenes; that I have not introduced my prosecution with a detail of misdemeanours in his public conduct; although I could not want various and numberless instances to urge, unless I were totally inexperienced in affairs. Instead of this, I first produced the laws which directly forbid any man to be crowned, whose accounts are not yet passed; I then proved that Ctesiphon had proposed a decree for granting a crown to Demosthenes, while his accounts yet remained to be passed; without any qualifying clause, or any such addition, as, 'when his accounts shall first have been approved:' but in open and avowed contempt of you and of the laws. I men-

***

[I.] By public maintenance.] In the original, 'some of those who have their table in the Prytaneum'—the greatest honour which a citizen could receive for his public services. Such persons then had a natural authority and influence in public assemblies.

tioned also the pretences to be alleged for this procedure, and then recited the laws relative to proclamations, in which it is directly enacted, that no crown shall be proclaimed in any other place but in the assembly only. So that the defendant has not only proposed a decree repugnant in general to the laws, but has transgressed in the circumstances of time and place, by directing the proclamation to be made, not in the assembly, but in the theatre; not when the people were convened, but when the tragedies were to be presented. From these points I proceeded to take some notice of his private life: but chiefly I insist on his public offences.

· It is your part to oblige Demosthenes to the same method in his defence. First, let him speak of the laws relative to magistrates yet accountable to the public; then of those which regard proclamations; and, thirdly, which is the point of greatest moment, let him prove, that he is worthy of this honour. And should he supplicate to be allowed his own method, and should he promise to conclude his defence with obviating the charge of illegality, grant him not this indulgence; know that, in this, he means to engage in a trial of skill with his tribunal. It is not his intention to return at any time to this great point; but as it is a point he can by no means obviate by any equitable plea, he would divert your attention to other matters, that so you may forget the grand article of this impeachment. But as, in athletic contests, you see the wrestlers struggling with each other for the advantage of situation; so, in this contest for the state, and for the method of his pleading, exert the most incessant and obstinate efforts. Suffer him not to wander from the great article of illegality: confine him, watch him, drive him to the point in question; and be strictly guarded against the evasive windings of his harangue.

Should you decline this strict and regular examination of the cause, it is but just that I warn you of the consequences. The impeached party will produce that vile impostor, that robber, that plunderer of the public. He can weep with greater ease than others laugh; and, for perjury, is of all mankind the most ready. Nor shall I be surprised if he should suddenly change his wailings to the most virulent abuse of those who attend the trial; if he should declare, that the notorious favourers of oligarchal power are, to a man, ranged on the side of the accuser, and that the friends of liberty appear as friends to the defendant. But, should he thus allege, his seditious insolence may be at once confounded by the following reply: 'If those citizens who brought back the people from their exile in Phylè, had been like you, Demosthenes, our free constitution had never been established: but they, when the most dreadful calamities were impending, saved the state by pronouncing one single word an amnesty (that noble word, the genuine dictate of wisdom:) while you tear open the wounds of your country, and discover more solicitude for the composition of your harangues than for the interest of the state.'

When this perjured man comes to demand credit to his oaths, remind him of this; that he who hath frequently sworn falsely, and yet expects to be believed upon his oath, should be favoured by one of these two circumstances of which Demosthenes finds neither: his gods must be new, or his auditors different. As to his tears, as to his passionate exertions of voice, when he cries out, 'Whither shall I fly, ye men of Athens? You banish me from the city, and, alas! I have no place of refuge. Let this be your reply; And where shall the people find refuge? What provision of allies? What treasures are prepared? What resources hath your administration secured? We all see what precautions you have taken for your own security: you who have left the city, not, as you pretend, to take up your residence in the Piræus, but to seize the first favourable moment of flying from your country: you who, to quiet all your dastardly fears, have ample provisions secured in the gold of Persia, and all the bribes of your administration.' But, after all, why these tears? Why these exclamations? Why this vehemence? Is it not Ctesiphon who stands impeached? And, in a cause where judges are at liberty to moderate his punishment. You are not engaged in any suit, by which either your fortune, or your person, or your reputation, may be affected. For what then doth he express all this solicitude? For golden crowns; for proclamations in the theatre, expressly forbidden by the law. The man, who, if the people could be so infatuated, if they could have so completely lost all memory, as to grant him any such honour, at a season so improper, should rise in the assembly and say, 'Ye men of Athens, I accept the crown, but approve not of the time appointed for the proclamation. While the city wears the habit of a mourner, let not me be crowned for the causes of her sorrow.' This would be the language of a truly virtuous man:—you speak the sentiments of an accursed wretch, the malignant enemy of all goodness. And, let no man conceive the least fear; (no, by Hercules, it is not to be feared!) that this Demosthenes, this generous spirit, this distinguished hero in war, if disappointed of these honours, shall retire and despatch himself. He who holds your esteem in such sovereign contempt, that he hath a thousand times gashed that accursed head, that head which yet stands accountable to the state, which this man hath proposed to crown in defiance of all law. He, who hath made a trade of such practices, by commencing suits for wounds inflicted by himself; who is so completely battered, that the fury of Midias still remains imprinted on his head:—head did I call it? No, it is his estate. With respect to Ctesiphon, the author of this decree, let me but mention some few particulars. I pass over many things that might be urged, purposely to try, whether you can of yourselves, and without direction, mark out the men of consummate iniquity. I then confine myself to such points as equally affect them both, and may be urged with equal justice against the one and the other. They go round the public places, each possessed with the justest notions of his associate, and each declaring truths which cannot be denied. Ctesiphon says, that for himself he has no fears: he hopes to be considered as a man of weakness and inexperience: but that his fears are all for the corruption of Demosthenes, his timidity and cowardice. Demosthenes, on the other hand, declares, that with respect to himself he hath full confidence, but that he feels the utmost apprehensions from the iniquity of Ctesiphon and his abandoned debauchery. When these, therefore, pronounce each other guilty, do you, their common judges, by no means suffer their offences to remain unpunished.

As to the calumnies with which I am attacked, I would prevent their effect by a few observations I am informed that Demosthenes is to urge, that the state has received services from him, but in many instances hath been injured by me: the transactions of Philip, the conduct of Alexander, all the crimes by them committed, he means to impute to me. And so much doth he rely upon his powerful abilities in the art of speaking, that he does not confine his accusations to any point of administration, in which I may have been concerned; to any counsels, which I may have publicly suggested: he traduces the retired part of my life, he imputes my silence as a crime. And, that no one topic may escape his officious malice, he extends his accusations even to my conduct, when associated with my young companions in our schools of exercise. The very introduction of his defence is to contain a heavy censure of this suit. I have commenced the prosecution, he will say, not to serve the state, but to display my zeal to Alexander, and to gratify the resentment of this prince against him. And (if I am truly informed) he means to ask why I now condemn the whole of his administration, although I never opposed, never impeached, any one part of it separately; and why, after a long course of time, in which I scarcely ever was engaged in public business, I now return to conduct this prosecution.

I, on my part, am by no means inclined to emulate that course of conduct which Demosthenes hath pursued: nor am I ashamed of my own. Whatever speeches I have made I do not wish them unsaid; nor, had I spoken like Demosthenes, could I support my being. My silence, Demosthenes, hath been occasioned by my life of temperance. I am contented with a little: nor do I desire any accession which must be purchased by iniquity. My silence, therefore, and my speaking, are the result of reason, not extorted by the demands of inordinate passions. But you are silent, when you think fittest, not your own sentiments; but whenever you are ordered, and whatever is dictated by those masters whose pay you receive. So that, without the least sense of shame, you boldly assert what in a moment after is proved to be absolutely false. This impeachment, for instance, which is intended not to serve the state, but to display my officious zeal to Alexander, was actually commenced while Philip was yet alive, before ever Alexander had ascended the throne, before you had seen the vision about Pausanias, and before you had held your nocturnal interviews with Minerva and Juno. How then could I have displayed my zeal to Alexander, unless we had all seen the same visions with Demosthenes?

You object to me that I speak in public assemblies, not regularly, but after intervals of retirement. And you imagine it a secret that this objection is founded on a maxim, not of democratical, but of a different form of government. For in oligarchies it is not any man who pleases, but the man of most power, that appears as prosecutor: in democracies, every man that pleases, and when he pleases. To speak only on particular occasions, is a proof that a man engages in public affairs, as such occasions, and as the interests of the public require: to speak from day to day shows, that he makes a trade, and labours for the profit of such an occupation. As to the objection that you have never yet been prosecuted by me, never brought to justice for your offences; when you fly for refuge to such evasions, surely you must suppose that this audience hath lost all memory, or you must have contrived to deceive yourself. Your impious conduct with respect to the Amphissæans, your corrupt practices in the affairs of Eubœa!—some time hath now elapsed since I publicly convicted you of these, and therefore you may perhaps flatter yourself that it is forgotten. But what time can possibly erase from our memory, that, when you had introduced a resolution for the equipment of three hundred ships of war, when you had prevailed in the city to intrust you with the direction of this armament, I evidently proved your fraud, in depriving us of sixty-five ships of this number; by which the state lost a greater naval force than that which gained the victory of Naxos over the Lacedemonians and their general Pollis? Yet so effectual were your artful recriminations to secure you against justice, that the danger fell, not on you, the true delinquent, but on the prosecutors. To this purpose served your perpetual clamours against Alexander and Philip; for this you inveighed against men who embarrass.d the affairs of government:—you, who on every fair occasion have defeated our present interests, and, for the future, amused us with promises. In that my last attempt to bring an impeachment against you, did you not recur to the contrivance of seizing Anaxilus, the citizen of Oreum, the man who was engaged in some commercial transactions with Olympias? Did not your own hand inflict the torture upon him, and your own decree condemn him to suffer death? And this was he, under whose roof you had been received; at whose table you ate and drank, and poured out your libations; whose right hand you clasped in yours; and whom you pronounced your friend and host. This very man you slew; and when all these points were fully proved by me, in presence of the whole city; when I called you murderer of your host,—you never attempted to deny your impiety : no; you made an answer that raised a shout of indignation from the people and all the strangers in the assembly. You said that you esteemed [1.] the salt of Athens more than the tables of foreigners.

I pass over the counterfeited letters, the seizing of spies, the tortures for fictitious crimes, all to load me with the odium of uniting with a faction, to introduce innovations in the state. Yet still he means to ask me, as I am informed, what would be thought of that physician, who, while the patient laboured under his disorder, never should propose the least advice ; but when he had expired, should attend his funeral, and there enlarge upon those methods, which, if pursued, would have restored his health. But you do not ask yourself what must be thought of such a minister as could amuse his countrymen with flattery, while he betrayed their interest at such junctures as might have been improved to their security; while his clamours prevented their true friends from speaking in their cause; who should basely fly from danger, involve the state in calamities the most desperate, yet demand a crown for his merit, though author of no one public service, but the cause of all our misfortunes ; who should insult those men, whom his malicious prosecutions silenced in those times when we might have been preserved, by asking why they did not oppose his misconduct. If this still remains to be answered, they may observe, that, at the time of the fatal battle, we had no leisure for considering the punishment due to your offences : we were entirely engaged in negotiations, to avert the ruin of the state. But after this, when you, not contented with escaping from justice, dared to demand honours ; when you attempted to render your country ridiculous to Greece; then did I arise, and commence this prosecution.

But, O ye gods! how can I restrain my indignation at one thing, which Demosthenes means to urge (as I have been told,) and which I shall explain ? He compares me to the Sirens, whose purpose is not to delight their hearers, but to destroy them. Even so, if we are to believe him, my abilities in speaking, whether acquired by exercise, or given by nature, all tend to the detriment of those who grant me their attention. I am bold to say, that no man hath a right to urge an allegation of this nature against me ; for it is shameful in an accuser not to be able to establish his assertions with full proof. But, if such must be urged, surely it should not come from Demosthenes ; it should be the observation of some military man, who had done important services, but was unskilled in speech ; who repined at the abilities of his antagonist, conscious that he could not display his own actions, and sensible that his accuser had the art of persuading his audience to impute such actions to him as he never had committed. But when a man, composed entirely of words, and these the bitterest and most pompously laboured ; when he recurs to simplicity, to artless facts, who can endure it ? He who is but an instrument, take away his tongue, and he is nothing.

I am utterly at a loss to conceive, and would gladly be informed, Athenians, upon what grounds you can possibly give sentence for the defendant. Can it be because this decree is not illegal ? No public act was ever more repugnant to the laws. Or because the author of this decree is not a proper object of public justice ? All your examinations of men's conduct are no more, if this man be suffered to escape. And is not this lamentable, that formerly your stage was filled with crowns of gold, conferred by the Greeks upon the people (as the season of our public entertainments was assigned for the honours granted by foreigners;) but now, by the ministerial conduct of Demosthenes, you should lose all crowns, all public honours, while he enjoys them in full pomp ? Should any of those tragic poets, whose works are to succeed our public proclamations, represent Thersites crowned by the Greeks, no man could endure it, because Homer marks him as a coward and a sycophant; and can you imagine that you yourselves will not be the derision of all Greece, if this man be permitted to receive his crown ? In former times, your fathers ascribed every thing glorious and illustrious in the public fortune, to the people: transferred the blame of every thing mean and dishonourable to bad ministers. But now, Ctesiphon would persuade you to divest Demosthenes of his ignominy, and to cast it on the state. You acknowledge that you are favoured by Fortune ; and justly, for you are so favoured ; and will you now declare by your sentence that Fortune hath abandoned you ; that Demosthenes hath been your only benefactor ? Will you proceed to the last absurdity, and, in the very same tribunals, condemn those to infamy, whom you have detected in corruption ; and yet confer a crown on him whose whole administration you are sensible hath been one series of corrup-

---

[1.] You esteemed, &c.] The expressions 'salt' and 'tables' were symbols of friendship, familiarity, and affection. So that this declaration imported no more, than that any connexions he had formed abroad were not to interfere with his duty and attachment to the state: a declaration which might well be justified. But his hearers either suspected his sincerity, or were violently transported by that habitual horror which they entertained of every violation of the rights of hospitality.

tion? In our public spectacles, the judges of our common dancers are at once fined, if they decide unjustly; and will you, who are appointed judges, not of dancing, but of the laws, and of public virtue, confer honours not agreeably to the laws, not on a few, and those most eminent in merit, but on any man who can establish his influence by intrigue? A judge who can descend to this leaves the tribunal, after having reduced himself to a state of weakness, and strengthened the power of an orator. For, in a democratical state, every man hath a sort of kingly power, founded on the laws, and on our public acts; but when he resigns these into the hands of another, he himself subverts his own sovereignty. And then the consciousness of that oath, by which his sentence was to have been directed, pursues him with remorse. In the violation of that oath consists his great guilt; while the obligation he confers is a secret to the favoured party, as his sentence is given by private ballot.

It appears to me, Athenians, that our imprudent measures have been attended with some degree of lucky fortune, as well as no small danger to the state. For that you, the majority, have in these times, resigned the whole strength of your free government into the hands of a few, I by no means approve. But that we have not been overwhelmed by a torrent of bold and wicked speakers, is a proof of our good fortune. In former times the state produced such spirits, as found it easy to subvert the government, while they amused their fellow-citizens with flattery. And thus was the constitution destroyed, not by the men we most feared, but by those in whom we most confided. Some of them united publicly with the 'Thirty,' and put to death more than fifteen hundred of our citizens, without trial; without suffering them to know the crimes for which they were thus condemned; without admitting their relations to pay the common rites of interment to their bodies. Will you not then keep your ministers under your own power? Shall not the men, now so extravagantly elated, be sent away duly humbled? And can it be forgotten, that no man ever hath attempted to destroy our constitution, until he had first made himself superior to our tribunals?

And here, in your presence, would I gladly enter into a discussion with the author of this decree, as to the nature of those services, for which he desires that Demosthenes should be crowned. If you allege, agreeably to the first clause of the degree, that he hath sur-

rounded our walls with an excellent intrenchment; I must declare my surprise. Surely the guilt of having rendered such a work necessary, far outweighs the merits of its execution. It is not he who hath strengthened our fortifications, who hath digged our intrenchments, who hath disturbed the tombs of our ancestors, [1.] that should demand the honours of a patriot minister, but he who hath procured some intrinsic services to the state. If you have recourse to the second clause, where you presume to say that he is a good man, and hath ever persevered in speaking and acting for the interest of the people, strip your decree of its vain-glorious pomp; adhere to facts; and prove what you have asserted. I shall not press you with the instances of his corruption, in the affairs of Amphissa and Euboea. But, if you attempt to transfer the merit of the Theban alliance to Demosthenes, you but impose on the men who are strangers to affairs, and insult those who are acquainted with them, and see through your falsehood. By suppressing all mention of the urgent juncture, of the illustrious reputation of these our fellow-citizens, the real causes of this alliance, you fancy that you have effectually concealed your fraud, in ascribing a merit to Demosthenes, which really belongs to the state. And now I shall endeavour to explain the greatness of this arrogance, by one striking example. The king of Persia, not long before the descent of Alexander into Asia, despatched a letter to the state, expressed in all the insolence of a barbarian. His shocking and unmannered license appeared in every part; but in the conclusion particularly, he expressed himself directly, thus: 'I will not grant you gold: trouble me not with your demands; they shall not be gratified.' And yet this man, when he found himself involved in all his present difficulties, without any demand from Athens, but freely, and of himself, sent thirty talents to the state, which were most judiciously rejected. It was the juncture of affairs, and his terrors, and his pressing want of an alliance, which brought this sum; the very causes which effected the alliance of Thebes. You are ever sounding in our ears the name of Thebes, you are ever teasing us with the repetition of that unfortunate alliance: but not one word is ever suffered to escape, of those seventy talents of Persian gold, which you diverted from the public service into your own coffers. Was it not from the want of money, from the want of only five talents, that the foreign troops refused to give up the citadel to the Thebans? Was it not from the want of nine talents of

---

[1.] The tombs of our ancestors, &c.] To understand this, it must be observed that Themistocles, who built these walls, of which Demosthenes was charged with the repair, had ordered that the materials should be instantly collected from all places without distinction, public or private, profane or sacred. 'Quo factum est,' saith Cornelius Nepos, 'ut Atheniensium muri ex sacellis sepulcrisque constaret.' Thus the speaker had a fair opportunity not only for detracting from the merit of his rival, but for converting it into an heinous crime; no less than that of violating those tombs of their ancestors, which had made part of their fortifications.

silver, that, when the Arcadians were drawn out, and all the leaders prepared to march, the the whole expedition was defeated? But you are in the midst of affluence, you have treasures to satisfy your sensuality,—and to crown all—while he enjoys the royal wealth, the dangers all devolve on you.

The absurdity of these men well deserves to be considered. Should Ctesiphon presume to call upon Demosthenes to speak before you, and should he rise and lavish his praises upon himself, to hear him would be still more painful than all you have suffered by his conduct. Men of real merit, men of whose numerous and glorious services we are clearly sensible, are not yet endured when they speak their own praises. But when a man, the scandal of his country, sounds his own encomium, who can hear such arrogance with any temper? No, Ctesiphon, if you have sense, avoid so shameless a procedure; make your defence in person. You cannot recur to the pretence of any inability for speaking. It would be absurd, that you, who suffered yourself to be chosen ambassador to Cleopatra, Philip's daughter, in order to present our condolements on the death of Alexander, king of the Molossi, should now plead such an inability. If you were capable of consoling a woman of another country, in the midst of her grief, can you decline the defence of a decree for which you are well paid? Or is he to whom you grant this crown, such a man as must be totally unknown, even to those on whom he hath conferred his services, unless you have an advocate to assist you? Ask the judges, whether they know Chabrias, and Iphicrates, and Timotheus. Ask for what reason they made them presents, and raised them statues. With one voice they will instantly reply, that to Chabrias they granted these honours, on account of the sea-fight at Naxos; to Iphicrates, because he cut off the detachment of Lacedemonians; to Timotheus, on account of his expedition to Corcyra; and to others, as the reward of those many and glorious services which each performed in war. Ask them again, why they refuse the like honours to Demosthenes; they will answer, because he is a corrupted hireling, a coward, and a deserter. Crown him! would this be to confer an honour on Demosthenes? Would it not rather be to disgrace yourselves, and those brave men who fell in battle for their country? Imagine that you see these here, roused to indignation, at the thoughts of granting him a crown. Hard indeed, would be the case, if we remove [1.] speechless and senseless beings from our borders, such as blocks and stones; when by accident they have crushed a citizen to death;

if, in the case of self-murder, we bury the hand that committed the deed separate from the rest of the body; and yet that we should confer honours on Demosthenes, on him who was the author of the late expedition, the man who betrayed our citizens to destruction. This would be to insult the dead, and to damp the ardour of the living, when they see that the prize of all their virtue is dead, and that their memory must perish.

But to urge the point of greatest moment: should any of your sons demand by what examples they are to form their lives, how would you reply? For you well know that it is not only by bodily exercises, by seminaries of learning, or by instructions in music, that our youth is trained, but much more effectually by public examples. Is it proclaimed in the theatre that a man is honoured with a crown, for his virtue, his magnanimity, and his patriotism, who yet proves to be abandoned and profligate in his life? The youth who sees this is corrupted. Is public justice inflicted on a man of base and scandalous vices, like Ctesiphon? This affords excellent instruction to others. Doth the judge who has given a sentence repugnant to honour and to justice, return home and instruct his son? That son is well warranted to reject his instruction. Advice in such a case may well be called impertinence. Not then as judges only, but as guardians of the state, give your voices in such a manner, that you may approve your conduct to those absent citizens who may inquire what hath been the decision. You are not to be informed, Athenians, that the reputation of our country must be such as theirs who receive its honours. And surely it must be scandalous to stand in the same point of view, not with our ancestors, but with the unmanly baseness of Demosthenes.

How then may such infamy be avoided? By guarding against those, who affect the language of patriotism and public spirit, but whose real characters are traitorous. Loyalty, and the love of liberty, are words that lie ready for every man. And they are more prompt to seize them, whose actions are the most repugnant to such principles. Whenever, therefore, you have found a man solicitous for foreign crowns, and proclamations of honours granted by the Greeks, oblige him to have recourse to that conduct which the law prescribes; to found his pretensions and proclamations on the true basis, the integrity of his life, and the exact regulation of his manners. Should he not produce this evidence of his merit, refuse your sanction to his honours; support the freedom of your constitution, which is now falling from you. Can you reflect without indigna-

---

[1.] If we remove, &c.] Draco the lawgiver had enacted this law for exterminating even such inanimate beings as had occasioned the death of a citizen, in order (as it seems) to inspire a peculiar horror of homicide (the crime most to be guarded against among a people not yet completely civilized.) And it may be proper to observe, that Solon, who abolished the laws of Draco, as too severe, meddled not with those which related to homicide, but left them in full force. *Tourreil.*

tion, that our senate and our assembly are neglected with contempt, while letters and deputations are sent to private houses, not from inferior personages, but from the highest potentates in Asia and in Europe, and for purposes declared capital by the laws? That there are men who are at no pains to conceal their part in such transactions; who avow it in the presence of the people; who openly compare the letters; some of whom direct you to turn your eyes on them, as the guardians of their constitution; others demand public honours as the saviours of their country? While the people, reduced by a series of dispiriting events, as it were to a state of dotage, or struck with infatuation, regard only the name of freedom, but resign all real power into the hands of others. So that you retire from the assembly, not as from a public deliberation, but as from an entertainment, where each man hath paid his club, and received his share.

That this is a serious truth, let me offer something to convince you. There was a man (it grieves me to dwell so often on the misfortunes of the state) of a private station, who, for the bare attempt of making a voyage to Samos, was, as a traitor to his country, put instantly to death by the council of Areopagus. Another private man, whose timid spirit, unable to support the general consternation, had driven him to Rhodes, was not long since impeached, and escaped only by the equality of voices: had but one vote more been given for his condemnation, banishment or death must have been his fate. To these let us oppose the case now before us. A popular orator, the cause of all our calamities, is found guilty of desertion in the field. This man claims a crown, and asserts his right to the honour of a proclamation. And shall not this wretch, the common pest of Greece, be driven from our borders? or shall we not seize and drag to execution this public plunderer, whose harangues enable him to steer his piratical course through our government? Think on this critical season, in which you are to give your voices. In a few days, the Pythian games are to be celebrated, and the convention of Grecian states to be collected. There shall our state be severely censured, on account of the late measures of Demosthenes. Should you crown him, you must be deemed accessories to those who violated the general peace. If, on the contrary, you reject the demand, you will clear the state from all imputation. Weigh this cause maturely, as the interest not of a foreign state, but of your own: and do not lavish your honours inconsiderately: confer them with a scrupulous delicacy; and let them be the distinctions of exalted worth and merit. Nor be contented to hear, but look round you, where your own interest is so intimately concerned, and see who are the men that support Demos-

thenes. Are they his former companions in the chase, his associates in the manly exercises of his youth? No, by the Olympian God; he never was employed in rousing the wild boar, or in any such exercises as render the body vigorous: he was solely engaged in the sordid arts of fraud and circumvention.

And, let not his arrogance escape your attention when he tells you, that, by his embassy, he wrested Byzantium from the hands of Philip; that his eloquence prevailed on the Acarnanians to revolt; his eloquence transported the souls of the Thebans. He thinks that you are sunk to such a degree of weakness, that he may prevail on you to believe that you harbour the very genius of persuasion in your city, and not a vile sycophant. And when, at the conclusion of his defence, he calls up his accomplices in corruption as his advocates, then imagine that you see the great benefactors of your country, in this place from whence I speak, arrayed against the villany of those men: Solon, the man who adorned our free constitution with the noblest laws, the philosopher, the renowned legislator, entreating you, with that decent gravity which distinguished his character, by no means to pay a greater regard to the speeches of Demosthenes than to your oaths and laws: Aristides, who was suffered to prescribe to the Greeks their several subsidies, whose daughters received their portions from the people at his decease; roused to indignation at this insult on public justice, and asking whether you are not ashamed that, when your fathers banished Arthmius the Zelian, who brought in gold from Persia; when they were scarcely restrained from killing a man connected with the people in the most sacred ties, and, by public proclamation, forbade him to appear in Athens, or in any part of the Athenian territory,—yet you are going to crown Demosthenes with a golden crown, who did not bring in gold from Persia, but received bribes himself, and still possesses them. And can you imagine but that Themistocles, and those who fell at Marathon, and those who died at Platæa, and the very sepulchres of our ancestors, must groan, if you confer a crown on this man, who confessedly united with the barbarians against the Greeks?

And, now, bear witness for me, thou Earth, thou Sun, O Virtue and Intelligence, and thou, O Erudition, which teacheth us the just distinction between vice and goodness, I have stood up, I have spoken in the cause of justice. If I have supported my prosecution with a dignity befitting its importance, I have spoken as my wishes dictated; if too deficiently,—as my abilities admitted. Let what hath now been offered, and what your own thoughts must supply, be duly weighed, and pronounce such a sentence as justice and the interests of the state demand.

THE ORATION OF DEMOSTHENES ON THE CROWN. [']

[*] IN the first place, ye men of Athens, I make my prayer to all the powers of heaven, that such affection as I have ever invariably discovered to this state and all its citizens, you now may entertain for me, upon this present trial. And (what concerns you nearly, what essentially concerns your religion and your honour,)—that the gods may so dispose your minds, as to admit me to proceed in my defence, not as directed by my adversary (that would be severe indeed!) but by the laws, and by your oath; in which, to all the other equitable clauses, we find this expressly added— 'each party shall have equal audience.' This imports not merely, that you shall not prejudge, not merely that the same impartiality shall be shown to both; but still farther, that the contending parties shall each be left at full liberty to arrange, [1.] and to conduct his pleading, as his choice or judgment may determine.

In many instances hath Æschines the entire advantage in this cause. Two there are of more especial moment. First, as to our interests in the contest, we are on terms utterly unequal; for they are by no means points of equal import, for me to be deprived of your affections, and for him to be defeated in his prosecution. As to me—but, when I am entering on my defence, let me suppress every thing ominous, sensible as I must be of this, the advantage of my adversary.—In the next place, such is the natural disposition of mankind, that invective and accusation are heard with pleasure, while they who speak their own praises are received with impatience. His, then, is the part which commands a favourable acceptance; that which must prove offensive to every single hearer, is reserved for me. If, to guard against this disadvantage, I should decline all mention of my own actions, I know not by what means I could refute the charge, or establish my pretensions to this honour. If, on the other hand, I enter into a detail of my whole conduct, private and political, I must be obliged to speak perpetually of myself. Here, then, I shall endeavour to preserve all possible moderation; and what the circumstances of the case necessarily extort from me must, in justice, be imputed to him who first moved a prosecution so extraordinary.

I presume, ye judges, ye will all acknowledge, that in this cause Ctesiphon and I are equally concerned; that it calls for my attention no less than his. For, in every case, it is grievous and severe to be deprived of our advantages; and especially when they are wrested from us by an enemy. But to be deprived of your favour and affections, is a misfortune the most severe, as these are advantages the most important. And if such be the object of the present contest, I hope, and it is my general request to this tribunal, that, while I endeavour to defend myself fairly and equitably against this charge, ye will hear me as the laws direct, those laws, which their first author, Solon, the man so tender of our interests, so true a friend to liberty, secured, not by enacting only, but by the additional provision of that oath imposed on you, ye judges, not, as I conceive, from any suspicion of your integrity, but from a clear conviction, that, as the prosecutor, who is first to speak, hath the advantage of loading his adversary with invectives and calumnies, the defendant could not possibly prevail against them, unless each of you, who are to pronounce sentence, should, with a reverend attention to that duty which you owe to heaven, favourably admit the just defence of him who is to answer, vouchsafe an impartial and equal audience to both parties, and thus form your decision on all that hath been urged by both.

As I am, on this day, to enter into an exact detail of all my conduct, both in private life, and in my public administration, here permit me to repeat those supplications to the gods with which I first began, and, in your presence to offer up my prayers, first, that I may be received by you, on this occasion, with the same affection which I have ever felt for this state and all its citizens; and, in the next place, that heaven may direct your minds to that determination which shall prove most conducive to the general honour of all, and most exactly consonant to the religious engagements of each individual.

Had Æschines confined his accusation to those points only on which he founded his impeachment, I too should have readily proceeded to support the 'legality' of the decree. But, as he hath been no less copious upon other subjects, as he hath pressed me with various allegations, most of them the grossest false-

---

[1.] To arrange, &c.] This is a liberty the orator hath accordingly assumed, and most artfully and happily. Under the pretence of guarding against all prepossessions, he first enters into a full detail of public affairs, and sets his own services in the fairest point of view. Having thus gained the hearts of his hearers, then he ventures on the points of law relative to his accounts, &c. And these he soon dismisses, with an affected contempt of his adversary, and a perfect confidence in the merits of his own cause. Then come his objections to the character of the prosecutor, which naturally led him round again to the history of his own administration, the point on which he chiefly relied; and where he had the finest occasions of displaying his own merits, and of loading Æschines and his adherents with the heaviest imputations, as traitors to the state, and malicious enemies to those who were distinguished by their zeal in support of their rights and dignity.

hoods, I deem it necessary, and it is but just, that I first speak a few words of these, that none of you may be influenced by matters foreign to the cause, and no prepossessions conceived against me when I come to the chief point of my defence.

As to all that scandalous abuse which he hath vented against my private character, I mark, on what a plain and equitable issue I rest the whole. If you know me to be such a man as he alleges (for I am no stranger, my life hath been spent among you,) suffer me not to speak, no, though my public administration may have had the most transcendent merit; rise up at once, and pronounce my condemnation. But if you have ever esteemed, if you have known me to be much superior to him, of a family more reputable; inferior to no citizen of common rank, either in character or birth (to say more might seem arrogant and offensive,) then let him be denied all confidence in other matters; for here is a plain proof that he hath equally been false in all; and let me be now favoured with the same regard which I have experienced on many former trials.—Yes, Æschines! depraved as is your heart, your understanding here appears equally depraved! To imagine that I could be diverted from the account of all my political transactions, by turning aside to these your personal scurrilities: I shall not proceed thus: I am not so infatuated; no, I shall first examine all that falsehood and virulence with which you have loaded my administration; and then proceed to those calumnies with which he hath so licentiously abused my private character, if this audience can endure the odious detail.

[1.] To proceed then to the articles on which I am accused. These are many and grievous; some of that kind, against which the laws denounce severe, nay the utmost, punishments. But the whole scheme of this prosecution discovers all the rancour of enmity, all the extravagance, and virulence, and insolence of malice; which, I call the gods to witness, is neither right, nor constitutional, nor just. True it is, that no man should be denied the privilege of appearing and speaking before the people; but this privilege never should be perverted to the purposes of animosity and envy. 'Yet thus hath he abused it.' For, had he really been witness of my crimes against the state, and of crimes so heinous, as he hath now set forth with such theatrical solemnity, he might have resorted to the legal punishments, while the facts were recent; had he seen me acting so as to merit an impeachment, he might have impeached; had I proposed illegal decrees, he might in due form have accused me of illegal decrees: or whatever other crimes his malice hath now falsely urged against me, whatever other instances of guilt he had discovered in my conduct; there are laws against them all, there are punishments, there are legal forms of procedure, which might have condemned me to the severest penalties. Here was his resource. And, did it appear, that he had proceeded thus, that he had thus embraced the legal advantages against me, then had he been consistent in the present prosecution. But now, as he hath deviated from the regular and equitable method; as he hath declined all attempts to convict me, while the facts were recent: and, after so long an interval, hath collected such a heap of calumny, of ribaldry, and scandal; it is evident he but acts a part; while I am the person really accused, he affects the form of proceeding only against this man: while, on the very face of the prosecution, there appears a malicious design against me, he dares not point his malice at the real object, but labours to destroy the reputation of another. So that, to all the other arguments, obvious to be urged, with all the force of truth, in defence of Ctesiphon, I might fairly add one more: That, whatever be our particular quarrels, justice requires that they should be discussed between ourselves; that we ourselves, I say, should support the contest, and not seek for some innocent victim to sacrifice to our animosities. This is the severest injustice. No! he cannot pursue Ctesiphon on my account; and that he hath not directed his impeachment against me, can proceed but from a consciousness that such impeachment could not be supported.

Here then I may rest my cause; as it is natural to conclude from what hath now been offered, that all the several articles of his accusation must be equally unjust, and equally devoid of truth. But it is my purpose to examine them distinctly, one by one; and especially his injurious falsehoods relative to the 'peace' and 'embassy,' where he would transfer the guilt of those actions upon me, which he himself committed, in conjunction with Philocrates. And here, my fellow-citizens, it is necessary, nor is it foreign to the purpose, to recall to your remembrance the state of our affairs in those times: that, together with each conjuncture, ye may have a clear view of each particular transaction.

At that period, then, when the Phocian war broke out (not by my means, for I had no share in public business at that time,) such were, in the first place, the dispositions of this state, that we wished the safety of the Phocians, although we saw the injustice of their conduct; and what calamity soever the Thebans might have suffered would have given us pleasure, as we were incensed, and not without reason and justice, against this people; indeed they had not used their success at Leuctra with moderation. Then Peloponnesus was all divided: those who hated the Lacedemonians were not strong enough to destroy them; nor could the governors, appointed by Lacedemon, maintain their authority in the several

---

[1.] In the common editions of the original, this whole passage is embarrassed and confused. The translator hath followed the arrangement of Dr. Taylor.

cities: but they, and all, were every where involved in desperate contention and disorder. Philip, perceiving this (for it was no secret,) and lavishing his gold on the traitors in the several states, aided the confusion, and inflamed them still more violently against each other. Thus did he contrive to make the faults and errors of other men subservient to his own interests, so as to rise to that height of power which threatened all Greece. And now, when men began to sink under the calamity of a long-protracted war; when the then insolent, but now unhappy Thebans, were on the point of being compelled, in the face of Greece, to fly to you for protection; Philip, to prevent this, to keep the states from uniting, promised a peace to you; to them a reinforcement. What was it, then, which so far conspired with his designs, that you fell into the snare by an error almost voluntary? The cowardice shall I call it? Or the ignorance of the other Greeks? Or rather a combination of both? Who, while you were maintaining a tedious and incessant war, and this in the common cause (as was evident in fact,) never once provided for your support, either by money, or by troops, or by any assistance whatever. This conduct you received with a just and a becoming resentment, and readily listened to the overtures of Philip. Hence were you prevailed on to grant the peace, not by any promises of mine, as he hath falsely asserted. And, it must appear, upon a fair examination, that the iniquity and corruption of these men, in the course of that treaty, have been the real cause of all our present difficulties. But I shall now proceed to a faithful and exact detail of this whole transaction; conscious, that, if any instances of guilt ever so heinous should appear in it, not one can be fairly charged on me.

The first who [1.] ever moved or mentioned a piece was Aristodemus the player. The man who seconded his instances, and proposed the decree, and who, with him, had hired out his services on this occasion, was Philocrates, *your* accomplice, Æschines, not *mine*; no! though you roar out your falsehoods till you burst.—They who united with them in support of this measure (from what motives I shall not now inquire,) were Eubulus and Cephisophon. I had no part in it at all. And though this be really the fact, though it be proved by the evidence of truth itself, yet so abandoned is he to all sense of shame, as to dare not only to assert that I was the author of this peace, but that I prevented the state from concluding it in conjunction with the general assembly of the Greeks.——O thou—by what name can I properly call thee? When thou wert present, when thou sawest me depriving the state of an interest so important, a conjunction of such moment, as thou now describest with so much pomp, didst thou express thy indignation? Didst thou rise up, to explain, to enforce, that guilt of which thou now accusest me? And,

had Philip purchased this my important service of preventing the union of the Greeks, surely it was not thy part to be silent, but to cry aloud, to testify, to inform these thy fellow-citizens. But this was never done: thy voice was never once heard on this occasion.—And, in fact, no embassy was at that time sent to any of the Grecian states; they had all discovered their sentiments long before:—such is the absurdity of his assertions. And, what is still worse, these his falsehoods are principally directed against the honour of our state. For if you called on the other Greeks to take up arms, and at the same time sent out your ministers to Philip to treat for peace, this was the act of an Eurybatus, not the part of this city, not the procedure of honest men. But this is not the fact: no! For what purpose could ye have sent to them at that period? For a peace? They were all at peace. For a war? We were then actually deliberating about the treaty. Upon the whole, therefore, it doth not appear that I was at all the agent, or at all the author, of this first peace: nor can he produce the least reasonable evidence to support those other falsehoods he hath urged against me.

Again, from the time when this state had agreed to peace, examine fairly, what course of conduct each of us adopted. Thus you will clearly see who was Philip's agent upon every occasion; who acted for you, and sought the real interest of his country.

I, on my part, proposed a decree in the senate, that our ambassadors should embark, with all expedition, for such place as they were informed was the present residence of Philip, and receive his oaths of ratification. But they, even after my decree had passed, declined to pay the due obedience. And here, Athenians! I must explain the import and moment of this my decree. It was the interest of Philip, that the interval between our acceding and his swearing to the treaty should be as long, yours, that it should be as short, as possible. And why? You had abandoned all warlike preparations, not only from the day when you had sworn to the peace, but from the moment you had first conceived an expectation of it: he, on the contrary, redoubled his attention to all military affairs, through the whole intervening period; concluding (and it proved a just conclusion,) that whatever places he could wrest from us, previously to his oaths of ratification, he might retain them all securely, and that no one could think of rescinding the treaty upon that account. This I foresaw; I weighed it maturely, and hence proposed this decree, that they should repair to Philip, and receive his oaths, with all expedition; that so he should be obliged to ratify the treaty, while the Thracians, your allies, yet kept possession of those places, the object of this man's ridicule, Serrium, Myrtium, and Ergyskè: not that Philip, by seizing such of them as were most convenient to his purposes, should become master

---

[1.] The first who, &c.] The particulars of this whole negotiation are related at large in the third book of the History of the Life of Philip.

of all Thrace; not that he should acquire vast treasures; not that he should gain large reinforcements, and thus execute all his future schemes with ease.——Here is a decree which Æschines hath never mentioned, never quoted. But, because I moved in the senate, that the ambassadors of Macedon should be introduced, he inveighs against me as highly criminal. What should I have done? Was I to move, that they should not be introduced? The men who came purposely to treat with us! Was I to forbid, that any seats should be appointed for them in the theatre? Why, they might have purchased seats at the common trifling price! Was I to show my concern for Athens by such minute savings, while, like him and his accomplices, I sold our capital interests to Philip? No!——Take my decree, which he, though well acquainted with it, hath passed over in silence. Read!

The Decree.

"In the archonship of Mnesiphilus, on the 19th day of the month Ecatombæon, the Pandionian tribe presiding,—Demosthenes, son of Demosthenes of the Pæanian tribe, proposed the following decree:

"Whereas Philip, by his ambassadors sent to Athens to confer about a peace, hath agreed and concluded on the terms; it is resolved by the senate and people of Athens, in order to the final execution of this treaty, agreeably to the resolutions and conventions of a former assembly, that five ambassadors be chosen from the community of Athens: which ambassadors thus chosen shall depart, and without delay repair to such place as they shall be informed is the place of Philip's residence, and with all possible expedition, mutually receive and take the oaths necessary for ratification of the treaty concluded, as aforesaid, with the people of Athens, including the allies on each side.—The persons chosen into this commission are Eubulus, Æschines, Cephisophon, Democrates, and Cleon."

When, by this decree, I had approved my attachment to the state, not to the interest of Philip, our excellent ambassadors sat down in perfect indifference, three whole months, in Macedon, although, within the space of ten, or rather of three, or four days, they might have arrived at the Hellespont, tendered the oaths, and thus saved the towns before he had reduced them.—For he would not have attempted the least hostility in our presence: or, if he had, we might have refused his ratification, and disappointed his hopes of peace: for he could not have enjoyed both; a peace and his conquests also.

Such was the first instance of Philip's artifice in this negotiation, and of the corruption of these wicked men; for which I then de-

------

[1.] As on a former, &c.] See the Introduction to Philippic I.

nounced, and now and ever must denounce, perpetual war and opposition against these enemies of heaven.—I proceed to point out another, and a still more flagrant instance of iniquity.—When Philip had, in due form, acceded to the treaty, having first possessed himself of Thrace, by means of those ministers who refused obedience to my decree, he bribed them once again not to depart from Macedon, until he had completed his armament against the Phocians; lest a fair report of his designs and preparations should prompt you to issue forth, steer your course to Thermopylæ, as on a former [1.] occasion; and block up the straits of Eubœa with your navy. He resolved that the news of his preparations, and his passage through the straits, should arrive together. And such were his apprehensions, such the violence of his terror, lest, when he had gained the straits, before he had completed the destruction of Phocis, ye should be informed of his motions, resolve to assist this state, and thus defeat his grand design; that he again bribed this wretch, not in conjunction with the other deputies, but now apart, and by himself, to make such representations, and to give you such assurances as effectually ruined all our interests.

And here, my fellow-citizens, I desire, I beseech you to bear in mind, through the whole course of this dispute, that, if Æschines had urged nothing against me foreign to his cause, I too should have confined myself to the great point in contest. But as he hath recurred to every charge, every invective which malice could suggest, it becomes necessary for me to make some short reply to all the several crimes alleged against me,

What then were the declarations which he made at this juncture, and which proved so fatal to our interests? That you ought not to be violently alarmed at Philip's passage through the straits; that the event would answer to your most sanguine wishes, if you but continued quiet: that in two or three days you should hear that he had entered into strict friendship with those who seemed the object of his hostilities, and that he had become their enemy, with whom he now united. 'For it is not words,' said he in all the solemnity of language, 'that form the strict band of friendship, but a similarity of interests. And it is equally the interest of all, of Philip, of the Phocians, and of Athens, to be relieved from the insolence and stupidity of the Thebans.'—And what were the immediate consequences? The unhappy Phocians were speedily destroyed, and their cities razed to their foundations: you, who had relied on his assurances, and continued quiet, were shortly obliged to leave your lands desolate, and collect your property within these walls, while he received his gold. And, still farther, the inveterate hatred of the Thebans and Thessalians fell, with all its weight, on Athens, while Philip's conduct was attended with applause and popularity. To prove these things, read the decree of Callisthenes, and the letter received from Philip,

They both confirm the truth of my assertions. —Read!

The Decree.

"In the archonship of Mnesiphilus on the 21st day of the month of Mæmacterion, in an assembly extraordinary, convened by authority of the generals, prytanes, and senate, at the motion of Callisthenes, it is

"RESOLVED,

"That no citizen of Athens be permitted, on any pretence whatever, to pass the night in the country; but that every man shall confine himself within the city, or the precincts of the Piræus, excepting only such persons as may be appointed to the defence of some post. That every such person shall be obliged to maintain his station, without presuming to absent himself, either by night or day. That whoever refuses to pay due obedience to this resolution and decree, shall incur the penalties ordained for traitors, unless he can allege some necessary cause, to be approved of by the general immediately in command, the treasurer, and the secretary of the senate, who shall have the sole power of judging of such allegations. That all effects now in the country shall be instantly removed; those within the distance of a hundred and twenty stadia, into the city or Piræus; those at any greater distance, to Eleusis, Phyle, Aphidna, Rhamnusium, and Sunium."

Were these the hopes which induced you to conclude the peace? Were these the promises, with which this hireling amused you?—Now read the letter soon afterward received from Philip.

The Letter.

"Philip, king of Macedon, to the senate and people of Athens, health!

"Know ye, that we have passed the straits of Thermopylæ, and reduced Phocis. We have stationed our garrisons in such towns as have submitted and acknowledged our authority. Those which have presumed to resist our force, we have taken by assault, reduced the inhabitants to slavery, and rased their habitations to the ground. But, being informed that you are making dispositions for the support of these people, we, by these presents, recommend to you to spare yourselves the pains of such an ineffectual attempt. Your conduct must certainly appear extremely inequitable and extravagant, in arming against us, with whom you have so lately concluded a treaty. If you have determined to show no regard to your engagements, we shall only wait for the commencement of hostilities, to exert a resolution on our part, no less vigorous and formidable."

You hear how he announces his intention in this letter: how explicitly he declares to his allies, 'I have taken these measures in despite of the Athenians, and to their eternal mortifi-

cation. If ye are wise, then, ye Thebans and Thessalians, ye will regard them as enemies, and submit to me with an entire confidence.' These are not his words, indeed; but thus he would gladly be understood. And by these means did he acquire such an absolute dominion over their affections, that, blind and insensible to all consequences, they suffered him to execute the utmost schemes of his ambition. Hence, all the calamities which the wretched Thebans experience at this day. While he, who was the great agent and coadjutor in procuring this implicit confidence; he, who in this place uttered his falsehoods, and deceived you by his flattering assurances; he it is, who affects a deep concern at the misfortunes of Thebes, who displays them in such pathetic terms; although he himself be the real author both of these and the calamities of Phocis, and of all others which the Greeks have suffered. Yes, Æschines, you must be affected deeply with these events, you must indeed feel compassion for the Thebans: you who have acquired possessions in Bœotia, you who enjoy the fruits of their lands: and I must surely rejoice at their misery; I who was instantly demanded by the man who had inflicted it.

But I have been led insensibly to some particulars, which I may shortly introduce with more propriety. I now return to the proof of my assertion, that the corruption and iniquity of these men have been the real cause of our present difficulties. When Philip had contrived to deceive you so effectually, by means of those who, during their embassy, had sold themselves to this prince, and never reported one word of truth to your assemblies; when the wretched Phocians also had been betrayed, and their cities levelled to the ground;—what followed? The miscreant Thessalians, and the stupid Thebans, regarded Philip as their friend, their benefactor, their saviour: he was every thing with them: nor could they bear a word which tended to oppose these sentiments. On your part, although ye looked with a just suspicion on the progress of affairs, although ye felt the utmost indignation, yet still ye adhered to the treaty: for it was not possible to act, single as ye were. The other Greeks too, equally abused with you, and equally disappointed in their hopes, were yet determined to the same pacific conduct, though Philip, in effect, had long since made war upon them. For when, in the circuit of his expedition, he had destroyed the Illyrians, and the Triballians, and even some Grecian states; when a certain set of men had seized the opportunity of a peace, issued forth from the several cities, and, repairing to Macedon, had there received his bribes (of which number Æschines was one,) then were the real objects of his hostilities discovered, and then was the attack made on the several states. Whether they yet perceived this attack, or no, is another question: a question which concerns not me: I was ever violent in forewarning, in denouncing the danger here, and in every place to which I was deputed. But, in fact, the states were all un-

z 2

sound. Those who had the conduct and ad-ministration of affairs, had been gained by gold: while their private citizens and popular assemblies were either blind to all consequences, or caught by the fatal bait of temporary ease and quiet. And such was the general infatuation that each community conceived, that they alone were to be exempted from the common calamity; nay, that they could derive their own security from the public danger. To this I must impute it, that the many found their inordinate and ill-timed indolence exchanged for slavery: while their statesmen, who imagined that they were selling every thing but themselves, found at length that they had first sold themselves. Instead of friends and guests (so were they styled, while they were receiving their bribes,) now they were called flatterers, enemies to Heaven, and every other odious name so justly merited. For it is not the interest of the traitor that is at all regarded by the man who bribes him; nor, when the purchased service hath been once obtained is the traitor ever admitted into his future confidence. If he were, no man could be happier than the traitor. But this is not the case, my fellow-citizens! How should it? No! Impossible.! When the votary of ambition hath once obtained his object, he also becomes master of his vile agents: and, as he knows their baseness, then, then he detests them; he keeps them at a wary distance; he spurns them from him. Reflect on former events: their time indeed is passed: but men of sense may always find a time to derive instruction from them. Lasthenes was called the friend of Philip, until he had betrayed Olynthus; Timolaüs, until he had destroyed the Thebans; Eudicus and Simo, until they had given him the dominion of Thessaly; then were they driven away with scorn; then were they loaded with every kind of wretchedness; and traitors in disgrace were dispersed through the whole nation. How was Aristratus received at Sicyon? How Perilaüs at Megara? Are they not in abject infamy? And hence it evidently appears, that he who is most vigilant in defence of his country, and most zealous in his opposition to such men, is really a friend to you, Æschines, and your venal, traitorous faction (as his conduct makes it necessary to bribe you;) and that your safety and your gains depend entirely on the number of such patriots, and their obstinate aversion to your counsels.

If left to yourselves, ye must have long since perished.

And now, as to the transactions of those times, I might say more; but I have already said what I deem more than sufficient. To him must it be imputed, who hath disgorged all the foulness of his own iniquity upon me, which it was necessary to wipe away, for the sake of those who were born since the events I speak of. To you, ye judges, the detail must be tedious and disgusting. Before I had uttered one word, you were well informed of his prostitution. He calls it friendship and intimate connexion. Thus hath he just now expressed it—'He who reproaches me with the intimacy of Alexander!' I reproach thee with the intimacy of Alexander! How couldst thou obtain it? How couldst thou aspire to it? I could never call thee the friend of Philip; no, nor the intimate of Alexander. I am not so mad. Unless we are to call those menial servants, who labour for their wages, the friends and intimates of those who hire them. But how can this be? Impossible! No! I formerly called you the hireling of Philip; I now call you the hireling of Alexander; and so do all these our fellow-citizens. If you doubt it, ask them; or I shall ask them for you. Ye citizens of Athens, do you account Æschines the hireling, or the intimate, of Alexander? You hear their answer. [l.]

I now proceed to my defence against the several articles of his impeachment, and to the particulars of my ministerial conduct, that Æschines (although he knows them well) may hear the reasons on which I justly claim the honour of this decree, and might claim still greater honours. Take the impeachment. Read it.

The Impeachment.

"In the archonship of Chærondas, on the 6th day of the month Elaphebolion, Æschines, son of Atrometus, of the Cothocidian tribe, impeached Ctesiphon, son of Leosthenes, of the Anaphlystian tribe, before the archon, of a violation of the laws.

"Forasmuch as he hath been author of an illegal decree, importing, that a golden crown should be conferred on Demosthenes, son of Demosthenes, of the Pæanian tribe; and that proclamation should be made in the theatre, during the grand festival of Bacchus, and the

---

[l.] You hear their answer. Commentators seem surprised at the boldness and the success of this appeal. Some tell us, that the speaker was hurried into the hazardous question by his impetuosity. Some that his friend Menander was the only person who returned the answer he desired. Others, again, that he pronounced falsely on purpose, and that the assembly intended but to correct his pronunciation, when they echoed back the word Μισθωτος hireling. But the truth is, he was too much interested in the present contest, to suffer himself to be really transported beyond the strictest bounds

of prudence and caution; he was too well supported to rely upon a single voice, if such could be at all heard in the assembly; and he had too much good sense to recur to a ridiculous and childish artifice. The assembly, to which he addressed himself, was of a quite different kind from one of our modern courts of law, where order and decorum are maintained. The audience were not at all concerned to suppress the emotions raised in them by the speaker. And Demosthenes had a large party present, who, he was well assured, would return the proper answer loudly.

exhibition of the new tragedies, that the people of Athens had conferred this golden crown upon the said Demosthenes, on account of his virtue, and affectionate attachment to Greece in general, and to Athens in particular; as also, on account of that magnanimity and steady zeal in speaking and acting for the interests of this state, which he hath ever discovered, and still discovers, upon every occasion, to the utmost of his power. All which clauses are false, and repugnant to our laws. As it is enacted,

"First, that no man shall enter false allegations into our public acts.

"Secondly, that no man, yet accountable for any office of trust, shall receive a crown: whereas, Demosthenes was director of the fortifications, and manager of the theatrical funds.

"Lastly, that no crown shall be proclaimed in the theatre during the festival, or dramatic entertainments, but in the senate-house, if the crown be granted by the senate; if by the commons, in the Pynx, and in full assembly.

"The penalty, [1.] fifty talents. The agents, [2.] Cephisophon and Cleon."

Here, you have the several articles of the decree, on which he founds his prosecution. And on these very articles I mean to rest the justice of my cause. I shall take them in the order of this impeachment, and speak to them one by one, without any voluntary omission.—As to the clause of 'that steady zeal in speaking and acting for the interest of this state,' which I have ever discovered, and still discover upon every occasion, to the utmost of my power,' and the honours appointed to me on this account, the decision must depend on my ministerial conduct. From this conduct, duly considered, it will appear whether Ctesiphon hath adhered to truth and propriety in these assertions, or whether they be false.—As to the omission of conferring the crown, 'when my accounts of office should be first passed,' and the appointment of the theatre as the place of proclamation; these points too might be determined by my administration, this might decide whether I be worthy of such an honour and such a publication. Yet I deem it incumbent on me to produce the laws, by which these clauses are fully warranted. So upright and so plain is the scheme of my defence.

I proceed, then, to the particular measures of my administration. And let no man think that I am suspending the discussion of this cause, if I enter into the affairs and counsels of Greece. He who hath attacked this assertion, that 'I have ever spoken and acted for the general interest;' he who expressly accuses it of falsehood; he it is, who makes the account of all my public conduct, all my whole system of administration, immediately pertinent and necessary to this suit. Besides, among the different departments of those who engage in public business, mine was of that nature which attached me more immediately to the interest of Greece. From these I must, therefore, be allowed to deduce my evidence.

As to those conquests and acquisitions which Philip had obtained before I had engaged in the administration, before my appearance as a popular leader, I shall pass them over; for they, by no means (as I conceive,) affect the merits of my cause. As to those various instances in which he found his ambition most effectually restrained, from the very day on which I first entered upon public business, these shall I recall to your thoughts, and freely submit to your judgments. But let this be first premised: one advantage did our adversary enjoy, and this (my fellow-citizens!) of great importance. It was the unhappy fortune of the several Grecian states, not of some only, but equally of all, to supply so vast a provision of traitors, of hirelings, of men devoted by the gods, as was not known in the memory of man. These did Philip engage as his agents and coadjutors, and, by their means, inflamed the animosities which had already torn and distracted the Greeks. Some he deceived; some he gained by bribes; on others he employed all his engines of seduction; and thus rent the nation into many different parties, although all were alike engaged in one common cause, that of uniting against the progress of his power. In such a general dissention of the Grecian states, in such a general blindness, both to the present and to the rising evil, consider, Athenians, what were the measures, what was the conduct, which became this state; And for these let me be brought to a strict account; for I am the man who advised and directed them.

Say then, Æschines, was it our part, in despite of every generous sentiment, every consideration of our dignity, to have taken our station with the Thessalians and Dolopians, to have ranged ourselves on the side of Philip, in order to subvert the dominion of the Greeks, the honours and the conquests of our ancestors? Or, if we were to reject such conduct (and surely none could be more shameful,) was it our part, ours, who had foreseen, who seemed perfectly convinced of the consequences which must arise, unless seasonably prevented, to have proved indifferent spectators, when these consequences had really arisen?

Yes! I would gladly ask the man who appears most severe in his censure of our mea-

---

[1.] The penalty, &c.] The damages, if we may so call them, were laid at such a vast sum as Ctesiphon, if condemned, could by no means discharge: in which case he must have been banished, or branded with infamy: and Demosthenes must probably have shared the same fate; against whom, no doubt, Æschines would

have immediately commenced a second prosecution, with the fairest prospect of success.

[2.] The agents, &c.] These were usually some friends of the contending party, who were employed in summoning the accused, citing witnesses, and other matters of form and legal procedure.

sures, what, in his opinion, was our proper part. Was it the part of those, who were the immediate cause of all the misfortunes and calamities which fell upon the Greeks, as the Thessalians and their associates ? or of those who affected an indifference to all events from views of private interest, as the Arcadians, the Messenians, and the Argives ?—And yet most of these have, in the event, proved greater sufferers than we.

I shall suppose that, after Philip had made all his conquests, he had retired to his kingdom, and there lived in peace, without attempting to molest either his own allies or the other Greeks. Even in this case, some share of censure and reproach must have fallen on those who had refused to arm against him. But when his assaults were equally directed against the dignity, the sovereignty, and the liberty of our whole nation ; nay, against the very being of those states more immediately exposed to his power ; what measures could have been devised more glorious than those which you embraced, and I suggested ?

But let me not wander from my point. What conduct, Æschines, did the dignity of this state demand, when we beheld Philip aiming at the conquest and sovereignty of Greece ? Or what advice should I, her counsellor, have given ; what resolutions should I have proposed : and this, in an assembly of Athenians, the circumstance of most importance ? I, who well knew, that, from earliest times, down to the very day on which I first spoke in public, my country had been incessantly contending for pre-eminence, for honour, and renown ? had expended more blood and treasure, for glory and the interests of Greece, than all the other Grecian states ever had expended for their several private interests ? I, who saw this very prince, with whom we fought for power and empire, with one eye torn out, his neck dislocated, pierced in his arm, maimed in his leg, freely and cheerfully resigning any part of his body which fortune pleased to take, so that he might enjoy the rest with renown and glory ? And let no man presume to say that such elevated sentiments became him who was bred at Pella (a place at that time ignoble and obscure,) as to aspire to the sovereignty of Greece, or to entertain a thought of such a daring purpose : and yet, that you, the citizens of Athens, you who in every assembly, in every theatrical entertainment, find perpetual memorials of the virtue of your ancestors, might descend to such abject meanness, as to resign the liberty of Greece, freely and voluntarily, into the hands of Philip. No! let not the presumptuous assertion be once heard.

The only course then left, and the necessary course, was this ; to defend your just rights

against all his injurious attempts. This course did you instantly pursue, with good reason, and becoming dignity. And in this, I was your counsellor, I was the first mover, during my administration. I confess it. And how should I have acted ? Say, Æschines ; I call on you.—Let all former transactions be forgotten ; Amphipolis, Pydna, Potidæa, Halonesus, I speak not of them. Serrium and Doriscum too, and the storming of Peparethus, and all the other instances in which the state was injured ; let the memory of them be effaced. You say, indeed, that I dwelt invidiously upon them, in order to embroil my country in a war : although the decrees respecting these several places were proposed by Eubulus, and Aristophon, and Diopithes : not by me. No, thou prompt slanderer! nor do I now dwell upon them. But when he had deprived us of Eubœa, when he had erected his fortress to command our whole territory, when he had attacked the Megarians, and possessed himself of Oreum, and rased Porthmus ; when he had distributed his governors through the cities, established Philistides in Oreum ; Clitarchus, in Eretria : when he had reduced the whole Hellespont to his obedience, and laid siege to Byzantium ; when the Grecian cities had, some of them, been subverted by his arms, others forced to received their exiles : in these instances did he act unjustly ? did he violate the treaty, or did he not ? Was it incumbent on some state to rise up against these attempts, or was it not ? If not ; if Greece was to have proved a prey for Mysians [1.] (according to the proverb,) and this, while Athens yet existed, and was witness of her fall ; then was I officious in remonstrating against these transactions : then was the state officious in yielding to my remonstrances ? mine was then the guilt and error of every measure we pursued. But, if the progress of his arms demanded a vigorous opposition, what community but that of Athens should have risen at the call of honour ?—This was the great principle of my administration. I saw the man aspiring to universal dominion— I opposed him : I warned my fellow citizens : I taught them to rise against the ambition of the Macedonian.—And yet the formal commencement of hostilities did not proceed from us. No, Æschines, but from Philip, by his capture of our ships. Produce the decrees, and the letter received from Philip. Read each in order. These, when duly weighed, will enable us to give each transaction to its proper author. Read !

The Decree.

"In the archonship of Neocles : an assembly extraordinary being convened by the generals, in the month of Boedromion ; Eubulus,

[1.] For Mysians, i. e. to the weakest of all people. The proverb is said to have arisen from the distresses of the Mysians in the absence of their king, Telephus, and their helpless state of oppression, when all their neighbours fell upon them, and pillaged the miserable and defenceless people without mercy.

son of Mnesitheus, of the Cyprian tribe, proposed the following *Decree:*

"Whereas the generals have reported to the assembly, that Leodamas, our admiral, together with twenty ships sent under his command to import corn from the Hellespont, has been taken and brought into Macedon by Amyntas, a commander in the service of King Philip; it is decreed, that it shall be the care of the prytanes and generals, that the senate be convened, and ambassadors chosen, who shall repair to Philip, and demand the dismission of the admiral, the vessels, and the soldiers; that they be instructed to declare, that if Amyntas hath in this acted through ignorance, the state of Athens hath no complaints to urge against him; that, if their officer hath in any wise exceeded his commission, they are ready to take cognizance of his offence; and to punish him, as his inadvertence may have merited; but if neither of these be the case, but that this outrage be avowed either by the person who gave, or who received the commission, that the ambassadors shall demand an explanation, and report the same, that the state may determine on proper measures."

And this decree did Eubulus frame; not I. Aristophon proposed the next: then did Hegesippus move for his: then Aristophon again: then Philocrates; then Cephisophon: and then the other speakers; I had no concern in any. —Read the next.

The Decree.

"In the archonship of Neocles, on the last day of the month Boedromion by a resolution of the senate.

"The prytanes and generals having reported the decree of the general assembly, that ambassadors be sent to Philip to demand the restoration of the ships, and that the said ambassadors be furnished with particular instructions, together with a copy of the decree of the assembly:

"The persons hereby chosen into this commission are Cephisophon, Democritus, and Polycrates. Aristophon the Cothocydian moved this resolution, in the presidency of the tribe Hippothoöntis."

As I produce these decrees, so, Æschines, do you produce that particular decree of mine which makes me author of the war. You have not one to show: if you had, it must have made your first and favourite charge. Nay, Philip himself, amidst all his insinuations against others, never once accuses me. Read his own letter to the State.

The Letter.

"Philip, King of Macedon, to the senate and people of Athens, health!

[1.] Here is no mention, &c.] There is indeed no express specification of any person in this letter. But those alluded to were well known. And probably they were the persons

"I have received three of your citizens in quality of ambassadors, who have conferred with me about the dismission of certain ships commanded by Leodamas. I cannot but consider it as an extraordinary instance of weakness, to imagine that I can possibly believe that these ships were destined to import corn from the Hellespont for Lemnos; and that they were not really sent to the relief of the Selymbrians, now besieged by me, and who are by no means included in the treaty of pacification by which we stand mutually engaged. Such were the orders your officer received, not from the people of Athens, but from certain magistrates, and others in no private station, who are by all means solicitous to prevail on the people to violate their engagements, and to commence hostilities against me. This they have much more at heart than the relief of Selymbria, fondly imagining that they may derive advantages from such a rupture. Persuaded as I am, that our mutual interest requires us to frustrate their wicked schemes, I have given orders that the vessels brought in to us be immediately released. For the future let it be your part to remove those pernicious counsellors from the administration of your affairs; and to let them feel the severity of your justice; and I shall endeavour to adhere inviolably to my treaty. Farewell!"

Here is no mention [1.] of Demosthenes, no charge against me. And whence is it, that in all his acrimony against others, he takes not the least notice of my conduct? Because he must have brought his own usurpations full into view, had he mentioned me. On these I fixed, and these I obstinately opposed. I instantly moved for an embassy to Peloponnesus, the moment he entered Peloponnesus. I then moved for an embassy to Eubœa, as soon as he had landed in Eubœa. Then did I propose the expedition (not an embassy) to Oreum, and that to Eretria, as soon as he had stationed his governors in these cities. After this, did I send out those armaments which saved the Chersonesus, and Byzantium, and all our confederates, from which this state derived the noblest consequences, applause, glory, honours, crowns, thanks, from those who had received such important services. And, even of those who had injured us, such as, on this occasion, yielded to your remonstrances, found effectual security; they who neglected them, had only the sad remembrance of your repeated warnings, and the conviction that ye were not only their best friends, but men of true discernment, of a prophetic spirit; for in every instance the event proved exactly consonant to your predictions.

That Philistides would have gladly given the greatest sums to have kept Oreum; that Clitarchus would have given largely to have kept Eretria; that Philip himself would have who had been most active in moving the assembly to exert themselves on this occasion; Eubulus, Aristophon, Philocrates, and Cephisophon.

given largely, that he might possess stations so convenient for annoying us, and that all his other actions should pass unnoticed, all his injurious proceedings unimpeached, cannot be a secret to any man; but least of all to you. You, Æschines, received the deputies sent hither by Clitarchus and Philistides: by you were they entertained. Those whom we drove from us as enemies, as men whose overtures were neither consistent with justice nor with the interest of Athens, were your dearest friends. How false and groundless then are your malicious accusations! You, who say that I am silent when I get my bribe, clamorous when I have spent it.—Your case is different: you are clamorous when you receive your bribe; and your clamours can never cease: unless this day's decision should silence them effectually by the justly-merited infamy.

And when you rewarded these my services with a crown, when Aristonicus proposed his decree, conceived precisely in the very words of this which Ctesiphon hath framed, when proclamation of the honour thus conferred upon me was made in the theatre (for this is the second time I have been thus distinguished,) Æschines, though present, never made the least opposition, never attempted an impeachment.—Take the decree.—Read!

The Decree.

" In the archonship of Chærondas, son of Hegemon, on the 25th of the month Gamelion, the Leontidian tribe then presiding, at the motion of Aristonicus, the following decree was made:

" Whereas Demosthenes, son of Demosthenes of the Pæanian tribe, hath at many times done various and eminent services to the community of Athens, and to many of our confederates; and, at this time, hath by his counsels secured the interests of the state, and particularly restored the liberties of certain cities in Eubœa; as he hath ever uniformly persevered in an unalterable attachment to the state of Athens, and both by words and actions exerted himself to the utmost of his power, in the service of the Athenians and the other Greeks: Be it enacted by the senate and the popular assembly, that public honours shall be paid to the aforesaid Demosthenes; and that he shall be crowned with a golden crown; that the crown shall be proclaimed in the theatre, on the feast of Bacchus, at the time of the performance of the new tragedies; and that the making this proclamation shall be given in charge to the presiding tribe, and to the director of the public entertainments.—This is the motion of Aristonicus of the Phrærian tribe."

And is there a man can say, that this decree brought any of that disgrace upon the state, any of that derision and contempt, which he affirms must happen, if I should obtain this crown? When actions are recent and notorious, if good, they are received with applause; if bad, they meet their punishment. But it is well known, that on this occasion I received marks of public favour; never was censured, never punished. And the consequence is obvious. Down to the period of these transactions, I must have invariably acted for the true interest of the state; for, in all your consultations, my opinions and my measures ever were adopted. These measures I conducted to effectual execution: they were attended with crowns to the state, to me, and to you all; with sacrifices to the gods, and solemn processions, as instances of great success.

And now, when Philip had been driven from Eubœa (yours was the military glory, but the policy, the counsels,—yes! though these my enemies should burst with envy,—were mine,) he raised another engine against this state. He saw that we, of all people, used the greatest quantities of imported grain. Determined to secure this branch of commerce to himself, he passed over into Thrace, and, applying to the Byzantines, then in alliance with him, he first required them to join in a war against us. But when they refused, when they told him (and they told him truth,) that they had not engaged in his alliance for such purposes, he instantly prepared his works, erected his machines, and besieged their city. I shall not say what conduct became us upon this emergency. It is manifest. Who then supported the Byzantines ? Who rescued them from destruction? Who prevented the Hellespont from falling under a foreign power upon this occasion? You, my countrymen. But when I say you, I mean the state. Who spake? Who framed the decrees? Who acted for the state? Who devoted all his powers, wholly and freely, to the public interests? I I!—And how essentially the public interests were advanced by these measures, there need no words to prove. You have facts, you have experience, to convince you. For the war in which we then engaged (besides the glory which attended your arms,) supplied you with all the necessaries of life, in greater plenty, and at cheaper rates, than the present peace, maintained by these good citizens, in opposition to the interests of their country, from their hopes of private advantage. Confounded be their hopes!

Never may they share in these blessings, for which your prayers, ye true friends of Athens, are offered up to Heaven! And O, never may they involve you in the fatal consequences of their machinations! Let them hear the crowns conferred by Byzantium, and those by Perinthus with which our state was honoured upon this occasion.

The Decree of the Byzantines.

" Bosphoricus being iëromnemon, Demagetus, by permission of the senate, drew up the following resolution:

" Whereas the people of Athens have, from the earliest times, persevered in an unalterable affection to the Byzantines, and to their confederates, kinsmen, and the Perinthians; and have lately, when Philip of Macedon invaded and laid waste their territories with fire and sword, and attacked their cities, done them many and signal services; and by a reinforcement of one hundred and twenty ships, with provisions, arms, and soldiers, have extricated us from the utmost dangers, restored our ancient constitution, our laws, and the sepulchres of our fathers; it is therefore resolved, by the people of Byzantium and Perinthus, to grant to the Athenians the right of intermarriage, the freedom of our states, the power of purchasing lands, and the first and most honourable seats in all our public entertainments, in the tholus, in the senate, and in the popular assembly. And that whatever Athenian shall choose to reside in our respective cities, shall enjoy a perfect immunity and exemption from all taxes. And it is farther resolved, that three statues, sixteen cubits high, shall be erected in the port of Byzantium, representing the community of Athens crowned by the Byzantines and Perinthians. And that honorary presents shall be sent to the several general assemblies of Greece, the Isthmian, Nemæan, Olympic, and Pythian, where proclamation shall be duly made of that crown, now by us conferred on the people of Athens; that all Greece may be informed of the magnanimity of Athens, and the gratitude of the Byzantines and Perinthians,"

Read, too, the crowns' conferred by the inhabitants of Chersonesus.

[*The Decree of the Chersonesites.*

" The Chersonesites, inhabitants of Sestos, Eleus, Madytus, and Halonesus, do crown the senate and people of Athens with a golden crown of sixty talents. They also consecrate an altar to Gratitude and the Athenians, on account of the important services conferred by this people on the inhabitants of the Chersonesus, in delivering them from the power of Philip, and in restoring their country, their laws, their liberties, and their religion. Of which the Chersonesites shall ever retain a just and grateful sense, and be ever ready, to the utmost of their power, to return the important obligation.—Thus it was resolved in a full assembly of the senate."

And thus, the measures I concerted, the conduct I pursued, not only saved the Chersonesus and Byzantium, not only foiled the Macedonian in his scheme of commanding the Hellespont, not only gained these public honours to the state, but displayed to all the world the generous sentiments of Athens, and the base perfidiousness of Philip. He, the friend, the ally of the Byzantines, in the face of Greece, besieged their city, (can we conceive a baser, a more abandoned outrage!) You, justly, repeatedly, incensed against them, by injuries received in former times, not only forgot all your wrongs, not only refused to look with indifference upon their danger, but appeared their great deliverers; and, by such transcendent generosity, acquired universal love and glory.—That you have frequently honoured those with crowns, to whom the conduct of

your affairs hath been intrusted, is full well known; but name the citizen if you can, I mean the minister or public speaker, except myself, by whose means the state hath been thus honoured.

I am now to show that all those virulent invectives which he hath thrown out against the Eubœans and Byzantines (invidiously recalling to your view every instance of their former offences,) are merely the effect of malice; not only as his representations have been false, (of this I presume there can be no doubt;) but because we might admit them to be true; and even upon this supposition it will appear that my measures were the measures which your interests demanded. For this purpose, permit me to lay before you, in a few words, one or two instances of the noble conduct of this state. By the most illustrious of their former actions it is, that private men, or public bodies, should model their succeeding conduct.

There was [1.] a time, then, my fellow-citizens! when the Lacedemonians were sovereign masters, both by sea and land: when their troops and forts surrounded the entire circuit of Attica: when they possessed Eubœa, Tanagra, the whole Bœotian district, Megara, Ægina, Cleonè, and the other islands; while this state had but one ship, not one wall. Then did you march to Haliartus; and, not many days after, were your forces once more led to Corinth. And yet the Athenians of these days had many injuries to resent, both from Corinth and from Thebes, by their conduct during the Decelian war. But far were they from harbouring such resentment. Observe then, Æschines; they acted thus, in both these instances, not that they acted for their benefactors, not that they saw no danger in these expeditions. Such considerations never could induce them to abandon those who fled to their protection. No! from the nobler motives of glory and renown, they devoted their services to the distressed. And surely this their determination was just and generous. For death must come to close the period of man's life, into whatever corner one may shrink from the inevitable blow: but the truly brave should draw the sword on all occasions of honourable danger, armed in fair hopes of success, yet still resigned with an equal fortitude to whatever may be decreed by Heaven. Such was the conduct of our ancestors, such the conduct of our elder citizens, who, though the Lacedemonians had been no friends, no benefactors to our state, but had injured us in many and important instances; yet, when the Thebans, flushed with their success at Leuctra, had attempted to destroy them, defeated the attempt; undismayed at the then formidable power of Thebes; determined by the motive of glory, not by the behaviour of those in whose cause they were exposed. And by these actions did you demonstrate to the Greeks, that, whatever injuries Athens may receive, her resent-

[1.] There was, &c.] See note 2, p. 5, on Philippic I.

ment is reserved only for the just occasion; when the being, when the liberty of the injurious party, is once in danger, her wrongs never are remembered, never regarded.

Nor were these the only instances in which such generous principles were displayed. Again, when Thebes [1.] had seduced the Euboeans from their attachment to the state, far from abandoning the island to the consequences of this revolt, far from remembering the injuries received from Themison and Theodorus, in the affair of Oropus, you instantly armed for their relief. And on this occasion did our trierarchs, for the first time, engage voluntarily in the public service; of which number I was one.—But of this hereafter.—And if you acted nobly in thus rescuing the island; still your succeeding conduct was far more noble. When the inhabitants were at your mercy, when you were masters of their cities, you gave up all, with strictest integrity, to the men who had offended you. Nor were their offences once regarded, when they had trusted implicitly to our faith. I might recount ten thousand instances of the same kind; but I pass them over: engagements at sea; expeditions by land; the achievements of ancient times; and our own illustrious actions; all in defence of the liberty and safety of other Grecian states.—And if I saw my country cheerfully engaging in so numerous and so perilous contentions, for the interests of others, when her own interests were in some sort the object of debate, what should I have advised? What measures should I have suggested? To cherish the remembrance of their offences, when these men had accepted our protection? To seek pretences for abandoning all our important interests?—Would not the first brave arm have deservedly stabbed me to the heart, had I thus disgraced the noble actions of my country,—even but in words? For that, in fact, you never could have yielded to such disgrace, I cannot doubt. Had you been in the least inclined, where was the obstacle? Had you not the power? Had you not advisers? Were not these men urgent in their applications? But I must return to those parts of my public conduct, which were subsequent to this period. And, here again, consider what the interest of the state really demanded. I saw the wretched decay to which our marine had been reduced; I saw our richer citizens purchase a total exemption from public taxes, at the expense of a trifling contribution; men of moderate or of small property despoiled and ruined; every opportunity of action lost to the state. I proposed a law, which obliged the rich to act fairly, relieved the poor from their oppressions; and, what was of most consequence, provided for the speedy and effectual execution of all our military operations. I was indicted, on this occasion, for an infringement of our established laws: I appealed to

your justice, as my sole resource; and my accuser had the mortification to find not a fifth of the suffrages in his favour.—What sums of money, think ye, would our richer citizens have given me, they who contribute most largely to the public service, or even they who contribute in the next degree, not to have proposed this law at all; or, at least, to have suffered it to be defeated by affected cavil and delay? Such sums, (my fellow-citizens!) as I am ashamed to mention. And with good reason. By the former law, sixteen of their number were to unite in the discharge of one assessment; so that the proportion of each was almost nothing: and thus they loaded the poor with the public burdens. But by my law, every individual pays in proportion to his fortune: so that he must now equip two ships of war, who by the former assessment was taxed but at the sixteenth part of one. And accordingly they styled themselves not 'trierarchs,' but 'contributors.' They would therefore have given any price, to have been disengaged from the necessity of thus acting justly.—First read the 'Decree' relative to my indictment. Then produce the 'Assessments,' those of the former laws, and that prescribed by mine.

The Decree.

"Polycles being archon. On the 16th of the month Boedromion. The tribe Hippothois presiding.

"Whereas Demosthenes, son of Demosthenes the Pæanian, proposed a law relative to the duty of trierarchs, to be substituted in the place of former laws for regulating assessments, for the navy: and whereas an indictment was brought by Patrocles against the said Demosthenes for an illegal proposal:—Be it remembered, that the prosecutor, not having a fifth of the suffrages in his favour, was condemned in the fine of five hundred drachmæ."

Produce now the first excellent assessment.

"The Trierarchs shall unite in the equipment of one ship, to the number of sixteen men, from the age of twenty-five to forty years. Each to contribute equally to the expense."

Now compare this with the assessment appointed by my law.—Read it.

"Trierarchs shall be taxed according to their fortunes. He who is worth ten talents by valuation, shall fit out one ship; if his fortune be rated higher, he shall be taxed, agreeably to the same proportion, in a higher sum: not exceeding the expense of three ships and a tender. The same proportion also shall be observed in the assessment of those whose fortunes do not amount to ten talents; who are to unite in order to make up the sum necessary for fitting out a ship."

And can this be thought a trivial service to the poor? Or would the rich have given but a trivial sum, to have eluded this equitable mode of taxation?—But I do not magnify my

[1.] When Thebes, &c.] See note 2, p. 5, on Philippic I.

integrity in conducting this transaction. I do not insist on my honourable acquittal. My glory is, that I procured a salutary law, a law approved by experience as highly valuable. For, during the whole course of our late war, in all the armaments conducted agreeably to my regulation, not one trierarch was ever known to petition against the severity of his assessment; not one was known to have fled to sanctuary; not one ever was imprisoned; not a vessel did the state lose abroad; not a vessel was detained here, as unfit for service. But while our former laws subsisted, we were perpetually exposed to all such inconveniences. And they proceeded from our poorer citizens. These were insufficient for the discharge of their assessments; and we were continually feeling the effects of such insufficiency. But by my means were the public burdens transferred from the poorer to our richer citizens, and the business of the state conducted without the least interruption. Permit me, then, to claim some praise on this account at least, that through the course of my public administration I constantly pursued such measures as reflected glory on the state, exalted her renown, and enlarged her power. No sordid envy, no rancour, no malignity, have I ever discovered; no meanness, nothing unworthy of my country. Such was the general tenor of my administration, in the affairs of this city, and in the national concerns of Greece. And no wonder. Here I was never known to prefer the favour of the great to the rights of the people. And, in the affairs of Greece, the bribes, the flattering assurances of friendship which Philip lavished, never were so dear to me, as the interests of the nation.

The only articles, I presume, which now remain for me to speak to, are those of the 'proclamation' and the 'accounts.' For that I have pursued the true interest of the state, that I have on all occasions discovered a warm affection and zealous alacrity in your service, I trust hath been established already, with the clearest evidence. I have indeed omitted the most important parts of my administration, the greatest of my services; both because I deem it incumbent on me to proceed to my defence against the charge of violating the laws; and because I am convinced your own consciences must bear the amplest testimony in my favour, although I should be totally silent as to the other parts of my conduct.

As to what he hath urged with such confusion and embarrassment, about his authentic transcripts of the laws, Heaven is my witness, that I am convinced you could not comprehend it: and, to me, it is, for the most part, utterly unintelligible. But my course shall be more ingenuous and direct. I shall lay before you the plain dictates of truth and equity. Far from asserting that I am not 'accountable' to the public, as he hath repeatedly insinuated and affirmed, I here declare, that through my whole life, I must ever stand accountable for every trust which I have executed, every measure which I have directed. But, for what I have freely expended of my private fortune, in the service of the public, I cannot at any time be liable to account: (observe me, Æschines!) No! nor any other citizen, were he the first of our magistrates. For, where is that law so pregnant with injustice and inhumanity, as to. rob the man of all his merit, whose fortune hath been expended for the state, whose public spirit and munificence have been displayed in some important instance? To expose him to the malice of informers? To give them a power to scrutinize his bounty? There can be no such law! If there be, let him produce it; and I shall submit in silence. No, my countrymen; he cannot!

'But,' saith this sycophant, 'the senate hath conferred public honours on him,' while his accounts were yet to be approved, 'under the pretence of some additional disbursements from his own fortune, when manager of the theatrical funds.'—Not for any part of that conduct which stood 'accountable;' but for those additional disbursements; thou sycophant!— 'But you were director of our fortifications.'— Yes: and on that occasion was entitled to my honours; for I expended more than the state had granted, without charging this addition to the public. Where a charge is made, the accounts must be examined; but where a free gift is conferred, favour and applause are the natural and just returns. This decree of Ctesiphon in my favour is, therefore, strictly warranted. It is a point determined, not by the laws only, but by our constant usage. This I shall readily demonstrate in various instances. In the first place, Nausicles, when at the head of our forces, was frequently honoured with a crown, for his bounty to the state. Then Diotimus, who gave the arms, and Charidemus, also received their crowns. I have another instance before me: Neoptolemus. He was frequently intrusted with public works, and received honours for his additional disbursements. For it would be hard indeed, if the man, invested with some office of authority, should either stand precluded by this office from assisting the state with his private fortune, or find his liberal assistance the object of account and scrutiny, instead of meeting the due returns of gratitude.—To confirm what I have now advanced, produce the decrees made on these occasions.—Read!

A Decree.

"In the archonship of Demonicus, the 26th of the month Boedromion, Callias thus reported the resolution of the senate and people.

"It is resolved, by the senate and people, to confer a crown on Nausicles, the general in command: inasmuch as when two thousand regular forces of Athens were in Imbrus, assisting the Athenian colony in that island, and when by means of the severity of the season, Phialon their agent could not sail thither, and pay the soldiers; the said Nausicles made the necessary disbursements from his own fortune, without any charge to the public in his ac-

23   †

counts—And that proclamation be made of the crown thus granted, during the feast of Bacchus, and the performances of the new tragedies."

A Decree.

"The motion of Callias: agreeably to the report made of the resolution of the senate.

"Whereas Charidemus, commander of the infantry in the expedition to Salamis, and Diotimus, general of horse, when in the engagement at the river, some of our forces had been stripped of their arms by the enemy, at their own private expense furnished the new levies with eight hundred bucklers: it is resolved by the senate and people, that golden crowns be conferred on the said Charidemus and Diotimus: which crowns shall be proclaimed in the grand festival of Minerva, during the gymnastic games and new tragedies; of which the magistrates and managers of the entertainments are to take notice, and cause proclamation to be duly made as aforesaid."

Each of these, Æschines, was bound to account for the office he enjoyed; but the action for which he was honoured, was by no means subject to account. Then why should mine be subject? Surely, I may claim the same treatment with others, in like circumstances. I gave my additional contribution to the public: I was honoured for it; not as a man who stood accountable for this donation. I held a magisterial office; I accounted for my conduct in this office; not for my free bounty.

'True;—but you have acted iniquitously in your office.'—If so, were you not present when my accounts were passed? And why did you not impeach me? But, to convince you that he himself is witness that this crown is not conferred for any part of my conduct really subject to account, take, read this decree of Ctesiphon at large. The clauses unimpeached will show the malice of his prosecution in those he hath attacked.—Read!

The Decree.

"In the archonship of Euthycles, the 29th of the month Pyanepsion: the Oenian tribe presiding. The decree of Ctesiphon, son of Leosthenes the Anaphlystian.

"Whereas Demosthenes, son of Demosthenes, of the Pæanian tribe, in his office of director of the fortifications, expended an additional sum of three talents from his private fortune, which he gave freely to the public: and, when manager of the theatrical funds, increased the general collection, by a voluntary addition of one hundred minæ for sacrifices; be it resolved, by the senate and people of Athens, to grant public honours to the said Demosthenes, on account of his virtue and nobleness of disposition, which he hath, on all occasions, invariably discovered toward the community of Athens: and to crown him with a golden crown: and that proclamation shall be made of this crown thus conferred, in the theatre, during the feast of Bacchus, and the exhibition of the new tragedies; of which the directors of the theatre are to take notice, and cause proclamation to be made as aforesaid."

My free grant of these additional sums is the article not included in your indictment: the honours decreed for this bounty is that on which you found your charge.

You admit that to accept my bounty is no infringement of the laws: you insist that to confer the due returns of favour, on this account, is criminal and illegal. In the name of heaven, what part could the most abandoned, the malignant wretch, odious to the gods, have acted upon this occasion? Must he not have acted thus?

As to the circumstance of making proclamation in the theatre, I shall not mention that many times many thousands have been granted such an honour, or that I myself have been thus honoured on many former occasions. But, is it possible, ye powers! Art thou, Æschines, indeed, so lost to all sense and reason, as to be incapable of apprehending that, to the party who receives the honour, it comes with equal dignity, wherever it be proclaimed? That it is for their sakes who grant it, that their theatre is appointed for the proclamation. For, by this means, the multitude who hear it, are inspired with ardour to approve themselves zealous in the service of their country; and they who give this testimony of their gratitude, share more largely in the public applause, than those who receive it. On this principle was our law enacted. Take up the law itself!—Read it!

The Law.

"In all 'cases, where a crown is conferred on any person by a single district, proclamation shall be made of the said crown, in the particular district so conferring it. Provided always, that, where crowns are granted by the people of Athens, at large, or by the senate, it shall and may be lawful to make proclamation in the theatre during the festival of Bacchus."

Æschines! Dost thou hear? Are not these the very words of our law? 'Provided always, that, where crowns are granted by the people' or the senate,' proclamation shall be made of these. Why then, unhappy man, hath thy malice been thus restless? Why this fictitious tale? Why not recur to medicine, to cure this disorder of thy mind? And feelest thou no shame at a prosecution dictated by envy, not by justice; supported by false recitals of our laws, by imperfect quotations of detached sentences; those laws, which should have fairly and fully been laid before our judges, as they have sworn to decide agreeably to their true tenor? Hence you proceed to delineate the character of a patriot statesman, as if you were giving a model for a statue, and found the piece not conformable to your model; as if words could mark out the patriot statesman, and not his actions and administration. Then comes your clamorous abuse, [1.] vented without distinction or reserve, but suited to you and to your family, not to me. And this (Athenians!)I take to be the true distinction between a vague invective, and a regular prosecution. This is supported by criminal facts, whose penalties the laws have ascertained; that is attended with the rancour which enemies naturally throw out against each other. Our ancestors, I presume, erected these tribunals, not for assembling to indulge our private and personal animosities in mutual scurrility; but to give us occasion of convicting that man fairly, who hath injured the community in any instance. This Æschines must know as well as I. Yet, instead of establishing his evidence, he hath discharged his virulence against me. Nor is it just that he should escape without the due returns of severity on my part. But, before I am involved in the odious task, let me ask him one question. Say, Æschines, are we to deem thee an enemy to Athens. or to me? I presume, to me. And yet, on every occasion, where you had all the advantage of the law, in bringing me to justice (if I had offended,) on passing my accounts, on moving my decrees on former trials, where my conduct was impeached, you were silent. But in a case where all the laws pronounced me innocent, where the procedure hath been regular, where numberless precedents are in my favour, where my conduct, far from discovering any thing of a criminal tendency, appears, in every instance, to have reflected a degree of honour upon my country; in such a case, I say, hast thou chosen to attack me! Beware then, that, while I am the pretended object of thy enmity, thou prove not really the enemy of Athens.

Well then : [2.] since you are all determined on the truly religious and equitable sentence, the virulence this man hath uttered obliges me (I think,) though not naturally fond of invective, to retort his numerous and false assertions, by some necessary remarks upon his character; by showing who he is, and of what family, who so readily begins the hateful work of personal abuse; who presumes to censure some of my expressions, though he himself hath uttered what no man of modest merits

could have ventured to pronounce. No! had one of the awful judges of the shades impeached me, as an Æacus, or a Rhadamanthus, or a Minos; and not this babbling sycophant, this wretched, hackneyed scrivener; he could have used no such language, he could have searched for no such insolent expressions, no such theatrical exclamations, as you have now heard from this man. 'O Earth! and thou Sun! O Virtue!' And again, those pompous invocations,—'Prudence! Erudition! that teachest us the just distinction between good and evil!'—Virtue! thou miscreant! what communion can virtue hold with thee or thine? What acquaintance hast thou with such things? How didst thou acquire it? By what right canst thou assume it? And what pretensions hast thou to speak of Erudition? Not a man of those who really possess it could thus presume to speak of his own accomplishments. Nay, were they mentioned by another, he would blush. But they who, like you, are strangers to it, and yet so stupid as to affect it, do but wound our ears when they utter their presumption, but never acquire the character for which they labour. And here I hesitate, not for want of matter to urge against you and your family, but because I am in doubt where to begin. Shall I first say, how your father Tromes was loaded with his chain and log, when a slave to Elpias, who taught grammar at the temple of Theseus? Or, how your mother, by those marriages daily repeated in her cell near the hero [3.] Calamites, maintained this noble figure, this accomplished actor of third characters? Or, how Phormio, the piper in our navy, the slave of Dion, raised her up from this honourable employment? No! I call the gods to witness, that I fear to mention what is suited to your character, lest I should be betrayed into a language unbecoming my own. Let these things be then buried in silence; and let me proceed directly to the actions of his own life; for the person now before you is not of ordinary rank, but eminent,—yes, as an object of public execration. It is but lately, lately I say, but yesterday, that he commenced at once a citizen and a speaker. By the help of two additional syllables, he transformed his father from Tromes to Atrometus, and dignified his mother with

---

[1.] Your clamorous abuse, &c.] In the original, ωσπερ εξ αμαξης as from a cart. Some derive this proverbial expression from the first rude state of ancient comedy, and find a particular spirit in the allusion, as containing a reflection on the theatrical character of Æschines. But the scholiasts on Aristophanes and Suidas explain the proverb in another manner. They tell us that the Athenian women, when they went in their carriages to the celebration of the Eleusinian mysteries, usually took great liberties in their abuse of each other, and hence the Greek expression τά ἐκ τῶν ἁμαξῶν σκωμματα to signify licentious and indecent ribaldry. It is true the French trans-

lator is extremely shocked at this interpretation, and cannot persuade himself that the Athenian ladies could so far forget the modesty and reserve peculiar to their sex. But it is well if this was the worst part of their conduct, or if they were guilty of no greater transgression of modesty in the course of their attendance on these famous rites.

[2.] Well then, &c.] Here the speaker evidently takes advantage of some acclamations in the assembly, which he affects to regard as the general voice of his judges.

[3.] The hero, &c.] i. e. near the chapel dedicated to this hero, or near the place where his statue was erected,

the stately name of Glaucothea. [1.] And now, observe the ingratitude and malignity of his nature. Though raised by your favour from slavery to freedom, from beggary to affluence; far from retaining the least affection to his country, he hath hired himself to oppose our interests. As to those parts of his conduct, where his disaffection may be at all disputable, I pass them over; but what he evidently and incontestably committed, as an agent to our enemies, this I must recall to view.

—Who knows not the banished Antipho? He who promised Philip to set fire to our arsenal, and, for this purpose, came back to Athens. And when I had seized him in his concealment at the Piræus, when I produced him to the assembly, so effectual was the violence of this railer, so prevalent were hisclamours,—that ' my actions were not to be tolerated in a free government—I insulted the misfortunes of my fellow-citizens—I forced into their houses without authority;'—that this man was suffered to escape unsentenced. And, had not the court of Areopagus been informed of the transaction; had they not perceived your error, an error so dangerous on so critical an occasion; had they not pursued this man; had they not once more seized, and brought him before you, criminal as he was, he must have been snatched from justice, and instead of meeting the punishment due to his offences (thanks to this pompous speaker,) retired in security. But, happily, you gave him the torture, and you punished him with death; a punishment which this his advocate should have suffered. And, so justly did the council of Areopagus conceive of his conduct upon this occasion, that, when influenced by the same error which so often proved fatal to your interests, you had appointed him a pleader for your privileges in the temple of Delos; this council, to whom your appointment was referred, and who were to ratify the nomination, instantly rejected this man as a traitor, and appointed Hyperides to plead. On this occasion were their suffrages given solemnly at the altar: and not one suffrage could this miscreant obtain.

. To prove this, call the witnesses. .

The Witnesses.

┌ " Callias, Zeno, Cleon, and Demonicus, in the name of all the Areopagites, testify in behalf of Demosthenes, that, at the time when the people had chosen Æschines as advocate for the rights of Athens in the temple of Delos, before the Amphictyons, we in full council determined that Hyperides was more worthy to speak for the state. And Hyperides was accordingly commissioned. "

Thus, by rejecting this man, when on the point of proceeding on his commission, and by

substituting another, the council did in effect declare him a traitor and an enemy to Athens. Here then we have a fact which clearly marks the public conduct of this noble personage; such a fact as differs widely from those he hath urged against me. One more there is, not to be forgotten. When Python the Byzantine came on his embassy from Philip; and came attended by commissioners from all the several powers in league with Macedon; as if to expose us, as if to bring witnesses of our injustice; then did I stand forth; and instead of submitting to the insolence of Python, instead of yielding to the torrent of his abuse against the state, I retorted the charge; I supported the rights of Athens. And with such powerful evidence did I demonstrate the injurious conduct of our enemy, that his own confederates were themselves forced to rise, and to confess it. But Æschines was the great coadjutor of this man. He gave testimony against his country; and falsely too. Nor did he stop here. In some time after this transaction, he held and was detected in his intercourse with Anaxinus the spy, at the house of Thraso. And surely the man who holds his private interviews, who confers with an agent of our enemies, is himself a spy, and an enemy to his country. To prove my allegations, call the witnesses.

The Witnesses.

" Celedemus, Cleon, and Hyperides, being duly sworn, testify in behalf of Demosthenes, that, to their knowledge, Æschines repaired to the house of Thraso, at an unseasonable hour of the night, and there held conference with Anaxinus, legally convicted of being Philip's spy. This deposition was signed in the archonship of Nicias, the 3d day of the month Hecatombæon."

Numberless other articles I could urge against him; but I suppress them. For the fact is this : I might display the many instances in which his conduct, during these periods, was equally calculated to serve our enemies, and to indulge his malice against me. But so slight are the impressions which such things make on your minds, that they are not even remembered, much less received with due resentment. Nay, so dangerous a custom hath prevailed, that you have granted full liberty to every man who pleased, to supplant and to malign your faithful counsellor : thus exchanging that real welfare of your country for the pleasure of listening to personal abuse. Hence it is ever easier and less dangerous for the servile tool of our enemies to earn his bribes, than for him to serve the state, who hath attached himself to your interests. That he manifestly supported the cause of Philip, previous to the commencement of hostilities,

---

[1.] Glaucothea.] The original adds, ' who every one knows, was called Empusa, &c.'] i. e. Hag or Spectre.] This, with the cause as-

signed, hath been purposely omitted in the translation.

shocking as it is (yes! I call heaven and earth to witness! for it was an opposition to his country ;) yet forgive him, if you please, forgive him this. But when this prince avowedly made prizes of our ships, when the Chersonesus was plundered by his troops, when he marched in person into Attica, when affairs were no longer doubtful, but the war raged at our very gates; then was this slanderer entirely inactive; no instance of his zeal can this theatrical ranter show, not one decree of any import, great or small, was ever framed by Æschines, in defence of your interests. If he denies this, let him break in upon the time allowed for my defence, and let him produce such decree. No; he cannot! He is therefore necessarily reduced to this alternative. He must acknowledge, either that the measures I proposed on that occasion were not liable to censure, as he himself never offered to suggest any other measures; or that his attachment to our enemies prevented him from directing us to some better course. But was he thus silent, was he thus inactive, when there was an opportunity of injuring his country? On this occasion, no man could be heard, but Æschines.

And, yet, the indulgence of the state may possibly endure the other instances of his clandestine conduct; but one there is, my countrymen! one act of his, that crowns all his former treasons. A subject on which he hath exhausted his whole artifice, in a tedious narrative of decrees about the Locrians of Amphissa, as if to pervert the truth. But this cannot be! impossible; no, nor shall this profusion of words ever wash away the stain of guilt from thy conduct upon this occasion. And here, and in your presence, ye Athenians! I invoke all the deities of heaven, all the divine guardians of our country, and, above all, the Pythian Apollo, tutelary god of Athens: I beseech these powers to grant me safety and prosperity, as I now speak the truth, as I at first publicly spake the truth, from the moment that I found the miscreant engaging in this transaction. For he could not escape my notice : no, I instantly detected him. But, if to indulge my spleen, if from personal animosity, I produce a false charge against him, may these gods blast my hopes of happiness!—But, why this solemnity of imprecation? Why all this vehemence?—The reason is this. We have the authentic records in our archives, which prove my charge : you yourselves remember the transactions clearly : and, yet, I have my fears, that he may be deemed an instrument too mean for such great mischiefs as he hath really effected. This was the case, when he brought down ruin upon the wretched Phocians, by the false assurances which he gave in our assembly. For as to the Amphyssæan war, which opened the gates of Elatæa to our enemy, which gave him the command of the Amphictyonic army, and at once overturned the fortune of Greece; here stands the great agent in this black design, the sole cause of all the grievous calamities

we endured. When I attested this in the assembly; when I exclaimed with all my powers, ' You are bringing an enemy to our gates; yes, Æschines, the whole Amphictyonic body to fall upon us ;' his coadjutors at once silenced me; while others stood confounded at the assertion, and regarded it as a groundless charge, the effect of personal animosity. But, since you were at that time prevented from receiving the important information, attend now my countrymen! hear the true nature of this whole transaction; the secret motives which produced, and the contrivance which effected it. So shall you discover a scheme well concerted, receive new and useful lights into the history of public affairs, and see what deep designs the heart of Philip could conceive.

This prince saw no means of terminating his war with Athens, no resource, unless he were to arm the Thebans and Thessalians against us. No resource, I say; for although the conduct of your generals had been scandalous and unsuccessful, yet the war itself, and the vigilance of our cruisers, had involved him in numberless distresses; as he found it equally impracticable to export the produce of this kingdom, and to supply his own demands by importation. He was not, at that time, superior to us at sea; nor could he penetrate into Attica by land, while the Thessalians refused to follow him, and the Thebans denied him a passage through their territory. Victorious, therefore, as he proved against your generals (such as you employed ;—of that I shall not speak ;) yet, still, the situation of his kingdom, and the circumstances, on each side, reduced him, in the event, to great distress. He knew that his private interest could not obtain the least regard, either from Thebes or Thessaly, as a motive for engaging in hostilities against us; but could he once be admitted to lead their forces in some common cause of theirs, he trusted to the united power of fraud and flattery, and was confident of success. His scheme, then, was this; and observe how well it was concerted ;—to embroil the Amphictyons in a war, by raising dissensions in their general assembly. For, in such a war, he presumed that he should soon be wanted. And, now were he to choose the instrument of this design, either from his own deputies, or from those of his confederates, this must awaken suspicion : the Thebans, and Thessalians, and all the states must be roused to strictest vigilance. But could he obtain an Athenian for his agent, a citizen of that state which avowedly opposed him, this must secure him from detection. Thus he reasoned ; and thus was the event. How then was this point gained? By bribing Æschines. Here stands the man, who seized the advantage of that inattention, that unsuspecting confidence, which you too frequently discover upon such occasions; was proposed as one of our representatives; and, by the few voices of a faction, confirmed in this commission. Thus invested with the august authority of his state, he repairs to the general council; and, regardless of all other concerns, applies himself directly to the service for which he had received his wages. He frames his specious harangues, he delivers his legendary tale of the Cyrrhæan plain, and its consecration; and prevails on the ieromnemons (men unexperienced in the artifices of a speaker, men, whose views never were extended beyond the present moment) to decree that a survey should be had of this district, which the people of Amphissa claimed and occupied as their own; but which this man now asserted to be sacred ground: not provoked by any insolence of the Locrians, by any fine which they imposed upon our state; as he now pretends;—but falsely;—as I shall convince you by one undoubted proof. Unless citation had been regularly issued, it was impossible for the Locrians to have commenced any suit against our state. Who then cited you? Produce the record of this citation. Name the man who can inform us of it: let him appear. No; you cannot. Your pretence therefore is false and groundless.

The Amphictyons, then, having proceeded to the survey of this district, agreeably to his direction, were assaulted by the Locrians, with a violence which had well-nigh proved fatal to them all. Some of the ieromnemons were even made prisoners. And when the ferment became general, and war was denounced against the Amphissæans, Cottyphus was at first chosen to lead the Amphictyonic army. But when some states refused to obey his summons, and those who did obey, refused to act; in the next general council, Philip was appointed to the command. So effectual was the influence of his agents, the old traitors of Thessaly, and those of other states. Nor did their allegations want a fair and specious colour. 'Either we must raise a subsidy,' said they, 'maintain a mercenary army, and fine those people who refuse their quota; or we must choose him general.' Need I say more? He was chosen. His forces were collected with the utmost diligence: he marches, as if toward Cyrrha. But now,—farewell, at once, to all regard either to the Cyrrhæans or the Locrians! He seizes Elatæa. [1.] Had not the Thebans, then, instantly repented, and united with our state, the whole force of this invasion must have fallen, like a thunder-storm, on Athens. But, in this critical conjuncture, they started up and stopped his progress: a blessing which you owe to some gracious divinity, who then defended us; and, under him, to me, as far as one man could be the instrument of such a blessing. Give me the decrees. Produce the date of each transaction. Thus shall you see what infinite confusion this abandoned wretch could raise,

and yet escape unpunished. Read the decrees!

The Decree of the Amphictyons.

"In the pontificate of Clinagoras. At the general assembly of Amphictyons, held in the spring, it is resolved by the Pylagoræ, and the assessors in the said assembly, that, whereas the people of Amphissa continue to profane the consecrated lands, and do at this time actually occupy them by tillage and pasture,—the Pylagoræ and assessors shall repair to the said lands, and determine the boundaries by pillars; strictly enjoining the people of Amphissa to cease from such violation for the future."

Another Decree.

"In the pontificate of Clinagoras, at the general assembly held in the spring. Whereas the people of Amphissa have cantoned out the consecrated lands, have occupied them by tillage and pasture; and, when summoned to desist from such profanation, rose up in arms, and forcibly repelled the general council of Greece, wounding some of the members, and particularly Cottyphus the Arcadian general of the Amphictyons;—It is therefore resolved, by the Pylagoræ, the assessors, and the general assembly, that a deputation shall be sent to Philip, king of Macedon, inviting him to assist Apollo and the Amphictyons, and to repel the outrage of the wretched Amphissæans; and farther, to declare that he is constituted, by all the Greeks, a member of the council of Amphictyons, general and commander of their forces, with full and unlimited powers."

Read now the date of these transactions; for they correspond exactly with the time in which he acted, as our representative.

The Date.

"In the archonship of Mnesithides the sixteenth day of the month Anthesterion."

Give me the letter, which, when the Thebans had refused to concur with him, Philip sent to his confederates in Peleponnesus. This will fully prove that the real motive of this enterprise was studiously concealed; I mean his design against Greece, his schemes against Thebes and Athens; while he affected but to execute the orders of the Amphictyonic council: a pretence for which he was indebted to this man.—Read!

The Letter.

"Philip, king of Macedon, to the magistrates and counsellors of the confederated people of Peloponnesus, health!

(1.) He seizes Elatæa, &c.] Which by its situation commanded the territory of Attica and Bœotia, so as to awe both Thebes and Athens. But we shall immediately learn the policy of this step from Demosthenes himself; and the cause of that dreadful consternation it raised in Athens, which the speaker is just now to paint in such lively colours.

" Whereas the Locri, called Ozolæ, inhabitants of Amphissa, profanely commit outrages on the temple of Apollo in Delphi, and in a hostile manner invade, and make depredations in, the sacred territory; know ye, that we have resolved, in conjunction with you, to assert the rights of the god, and to oppose those impious wretches, who have thus presumed to violate all that is accounted sacred among men. Do you, therefore, meet me in arms at Phocis, with provisions for forty days, within this present month called by us Loüs, by the Athenians Boëdromion, and by the Corinthians Panemus. Such as attend us shall be duly consulted, and all measures pursued with their concurrence; they who refuse obedience to these orders shall be punished. Farewell!"

You see with what caution he keeps his real purpose concealed; how he flies for shelter to the acts of the Amphictyons. And who was the man that procured him this subterfuge? Who gave him such plausible pretences? Who was the great author of all our calamities? Was it not this man?—Yet, mistake me not, Athenians; when our public calamities are the subject of your conversation, say not that we owe them entirely to a single person. No, not to one; let heaven and earth bear witness! but to many abandoned traitors in the several states, in which number he stands distinguished: he, whom, if no regards controlled me, I should not scruple to pronounce the accursed destroyer of persons, places, cities, all that were involved in the general overthrow. For the sower of the seed is surely the author of the whole harvest of mischief. Astonishing indeed it is, that you can behold him, and not instantly turn away with horror from an object so detestable. But this is the effect of that thick cloud, in which the truth has lain concealed.

And thus, from touching slightly on the designs which he pursued against his country, I am led naturally to those measures in which I was myself engaged, in opposition to such traitorous designs. These demand our attention for various reasons; chiefly, because it would be shameful, when I have laboured in your service with indefatigable zeal, to refuse to hear my services recounted.—No sooner then did I perceive the Thebans, I might have said the Athenians also, deceived so effectually by those agents which Philip's gold had secured in each state, as to look with indifference upon an object equally formidable to both, I mean the increasing power of this prince: no sooner did I see them resign all thoughts of guarding against his progress; and, in defiance of their common danger, ready to encounter each other, in mutual enmity; than I roused all my vigilance, exerted my incessant efforts, to prevent such rupture. This I considered as a real service to my country; and not upon my own judgment only: I had the authority of Aristophon and Eubulus to confirm me; men who had ever laboured to effect this scheme of union between the two states, (however violent their opposition upon other points, in this they ever were agreed:) men who, when living, were persecuted by thy abject flattery; yet now, when they are no more, thou presumest to arraign their conduct. So lost art thou to shame! Yes, thou scandal to humanity! for whatever is urged against me, with respect to Thebes, affects their characters much more than mine. They had declared loudly for this alliance long before it was proposed by me.—But I have digressed too far.—When Æschines had effected this Amphissæan war: when his traitorous coadjutors had possessed our minds with animosity against the Thebans; the great secret of that confusion raised among the states was now discovered. Philip marched directly to attack us. And had we not been suddenly awakened to a vigorous exertion of our powers, the danger must have overwhelmed us; so far had these men carried on their desperate design.—But, to form a perfect judgement of the terms on which we then stood with Thebes, consult your own decrees, and the answers received on this occasion.—Take them.—Read!

A Decree.

" In the archonship of Heropythus, on the 25th day of the month Elaphebolion, the Erecthian tribe presiding, the senate and generals came to the following resolution:

" Whereas Philip hath possessed himself of some adjacent cities, and demolished others, and is actually preparing to make an inroad into Attica, (in manifest contempt of his engagements,) and to rescind all his late treaties and obligations, without the least regard to public faith: it is resolved, that ambassadors shall be sent to confer with him, and to exhort him to preserve that harmony, and to adhere to those engagements, which have hitherto subsisted between us: at least, that he may grant the same time to deliberate, and make a truce, till the month Thargelion.—Simus, Euthydemus, and Bulagoras, are elected from the senate for this commission."

Another Decree.

" In the archonship of Heropythus, the last day of the month Munichion:—at the motion of the polemarch:

" Whereas Philip is exerting his most strenuous efforts to alienate the Thebans from us, and prepares to march with all his army to the frontiers of Attica, in direct violation of his treaty now subsisting between us:—It is resolved by the senate and people of Athens, that a herald and ambassadors be sent to him, who shall require and demand a cessation of hostilities, that the people may have an opportunity of deliberating on this exigency; as at present they are inclined to judge that the honour of the state cannot be supported but by an extraordinary and vigorous opposition. Nearchus and Polycrates are chosen for this commission from the senate; and Eunomus from the people, in quality of herald."

Now, read the answer.

Philip's Answer to the Athenians.

" Philip, king of Macedon, to the senate and people of Athens, health !

" How you have been affected towards us from the beginning, we are by no means ignorant : nor of that assiduity with which you have laboured to bring over to your party the Thessalians, the Thebans, and even the Bœotians. As these people had just ideas of their real interests, and have refused to submit to your direction, when you find yourselves disappointed, you send heralds and ambassadors to us, to put us in mind of former treaties : and you demand a truce, although you have in no one instance felt the force of our arms. I, on my part, have admitted your ambassadors to an audience. I agree to your demands, and am ready to grant the cessation which you require, provided that you remove your evil counsellors, and brand them with the infamy which they so justly merit. Farewell !"

The Answer to the Thebans.

" Philip, king of Macedon, to the senate and people of Thebes, health !

" I have received your letter, wherein you take notice of the harmony and peace subsisting between us. I am informed that the Athenians have been assiduous in their solicitations, to prevail upon you to comply with them in those demands which they have lately made. I must confess, I formerly imagined that I had discovered some disposition in your state, to be influenced by their promises, and to acquiesce in their measures : but now I have received full assurances of your attachment to us, and of your resolutions to live in peace, rather than to submit to the guidance of foreign counsels. I feel the sincerest satisfaction, and highly applaud your conduct ; and more particularly as, by your adherence to us, you have in the most effectual manner provided for your interests and safety. Persevere in the same sentiments, and in a short time I hope you will experience their good effects. Farewell !"

Thus, successful in confirming the mutual separation of our states, and elevated by these decrees and these replies, Philip now leads his forces forward, and seizes Elatæa : presuming that, at all events, Athens and Thebes never could unite. You are no strangers to the confusion which this event raised within these walls. Yet permit me to relate some few striking circumstances of our own consternation.—It was evening. A courier arrived, and, repairing to the presidents of the senate, informed them that Elatæa was taken. In a moment some started from supper ; [1.] ran to the public place : drove the traders from their stations, and set fire to [2.] their sheds : Some sent round to call the generals : others clamoured for the trumpeter. [3.] Thus was the city one scene of tumult.—The next morning, by dawn of day, the presidents summoned the senate. The people were instantly collected ; and, before any regular authority could convene their assembly, the whole body of citizens had taken their places above. Then the senate entered ; the presidents reported their advices, and produced the courier. He repeated his intelligence. The herald then asked in form, ' Who chooses to speak ?' All was silence. The invitation was frequently repeated ; still no man rose ; though the generals, though the ordinary speakers, were all present ; though the voice of Athens then called on some man to speak and save her. For surely the regular and legal proclamation of the herald may be fairly deemed the voice of Athens. If an honest solicitude for the preservation of the state had, on this occasion, been sufficient to call forth a speaker ; then, my countrymen, ye must have all arisen and crowded to the gallery : for well I know this honest solicitude had full possession of your hearts. If wealth had obliged a man to speak, the ' Three Hundred' [4.] must have risen. If patriot zeal and wealth united were the qualification necessary for the speaker, then should we have heard those generous citizens, whose beneficence was afterward displayed so nobly in the service of the state ; for their beneficence proceeded from this union of wealth and patriot zeal. But the occasion, the great day, it seems, called not only for a well-affected and an affluent citizen, but for the man who had traced these affairs to their very source ; who had formed the exactest judgement of Philip's motive, of his secret intentions, in this his conduct. He who was not perfectly informed of these, he who had not watched the whole progress of his actions with consummate vigilance ; however zealously affected to the state ; however blest with wealth ; was in nowise better qualified to conceive or to propose the measures, which your interest demanded, on

---

[1.] From supper, i. e. from the table provided at the expense of the public, for such citizens as had been distinguished by their services and merits.

[2.] Set fire to, &c.] Wolfius asks why ? and for what purpose ? The answer, I apprehend, is obvious : To clear the place for an assembly : and in their confusion and impatience they took the speediest and most violent method.

[3.] The trumpeter.] Possibly to summon the assembly on this extraordinary occasion, when there was no leisure nor opportunity for the regular and usual method of convening the citizens.

[4.] The ' Three Hundred,' i. e. the body of richer citizens who were to advance money for the exigencies of the state. See Note I, p. 13, on Olynthiac I.

an occasion so critical. On that day, then, I was the man who stood forth. And the counsels I then proposed may now merit your attention, on a double account; first, to convince you that, of all your leaders and ministers, I was the only one who maintained the post of a zealous patriot in your extremity, whose words and actions were devoted to your service, in the midst of public consternation: and, secondly, to enable you to judge more clearly of my other actions, by granting a little time to this.—My speech then was thus:

"They who are thrown into all this confusion, from an opinion that the Thebans are gained over to the interests of Philip, seem to me entirely ignorant of the present state of affairs. Were this the case, I am convinced ye would now hear, not that he was at Elatæa, but on our very frontier. His intent (I clearly see it,) in seizing this post, is to facilitate his schemes in Thebes. Attend, and I shall now explain the circumstances of that state. Those of its citizens, whom his gold could corrupt, or his artifice deceive, are all at his devotion; those who at first oppose, and continue to oppose him, he finds incapable of being wrought upon. What then is his design? Why hath he seized Elatæa?—That, by drawing up his forces, and displaying his powers upon the borders of Thebes, he may inspire his adherents with confidence and elevation, and strike such terror into his adversaries, that fear or force may drive them into those measures they have hitherto opposed. If then we are resolved, in this conjuncture, to cherish the remembrance of every unkindness we may have received from the Thebans; if we regard them with suspicion, as men who have ranged them on the side of our enemy: we shall, in the first place, act agreeably to Philip's warmest wishes: and then I am apprehensive, that the party who now oppose him may be brought over to his interest, the whole city declare unanimously in his favour, and Thebes and Macedon fall with their united force on Attica.—Grant the due attention to what I shall propose: let it be calmly weighed, without dispute or cavil; and I doubt not but that my counsels may direct you to the best and most salutary measures, and dispel the dangers now impending over the state. What then do I propose?—First, shake off that terror which hath possessed your minds, and, instead of fearing for yourselves, fear for the Thebans; they are more immediately exposed, and must be the first to feel the danger. In the next place, let all those of the age for military service, both infantry and cavalry, march instantly to Eleusis, that Greece may see that you too are assembled in arms; and your friends in Thebes be emboldened to assert their rights: when they are assured, that, as they who have sold their country to the Macedonian, have a force at Elatæa to support them, you too stand prepared to support their antagonists. I recommend it, in the last place, that you nominate ten ambassadors, who, with the generals, shall have full

authority to determine the time and all other circumstances of this march. When these ambassadors shall arrive at Thebes, how are they to conduct this great affair? This is a point worthy your most serious attention.—Make no demands at all of the Thebans: at this juncture it would be dishonourable. Assure them that your forces are ready, and but wait their orders, to march to their support: as you are deeply affected by their danger, and have been so happy as to foresee, and to guard against it. If they are prevailed on to embrace these overtures, we shall effectuate our great purpose, and act with a dignity worthy of our state: but, should it happen that we are not so successful, whatever misfortunes they may suffer, to themselves shall they be imputed; while your conduct shall appear in no one instance, inconsistent with the honour and renown of Athens."

These and other like particulars did I suggest. I came down amidst the universal applause of the assembly, without one word of opposition or dissent. Nor did I thus speak, without proposing my decree in form; nor did I propose my decree, without proceeding on the embassy; nor did I proceed on the embassy, without prevailing on the Thebans. From first to last, my conduct was uniform, my perseverance invariable, my whole powers entirely devoted to repel the dangers then encompassing the state. Produce the decree made on this occasion. Say, Æschines, what character are we to ascribe to you, on that great day? And, in what light am I to be considered? As a Battalus, the odious name your scorn and malice have given me? And you, a hero of no ordinary rank, a dramatic hero, a Cresphontes, a Creon, or an Œnomäus, the character in which your vile performance was punished with such heavy stripes? On that day our country had full proof that I, the Battalus, could perform more worthy services than you, the Œnomäus. You performed no services at all: I discharged the duty of a faithful citizen in the amplest manner.

The Decree.

"In the archonship of Nausicles, the Aiantidian tribe presiding, on the sixteenth day of the month Scirrophorion, Demosthenes, the son of Demosthenes, of the Pæanian tribe, proposed this decree.

"Whereas, Philip, king of the Macedonians, hath, in various times past violated the treaty of peace subsisting between him and the state of Athens, in open contempt of his most solemn engagements, and of all that is esteemed sacred in Greece; possessing himself of cities to which he had no claim or pretensions, reducing some to slavery that were under the Athenian jurisdiction; and this, without any previous injury committed on the part of Athens. And, whereas, he, at this time, perseveres in his outrages and cruelty, imposing his garrisons on the cities of Greece,

24   †

subverting their constitutions, enslaving their inhabitants, and rasing their walls; in some, dispossessing the Greeks, and establishing barbarians; abandoning the temples and sepulchres to their inhuman rage, (actions agreeable to his country and his manners,) insolent in his present fortune, and forgetful of that mean origin from whence he hath arisen to this unexpected power. And, whereas, while the Athenian people beheld him extending his dominion over states and countries like his own, barbarous and detached from Greece, they deemed themselves little affected or injured by such conquests; but now, when Grecian cities are insulted by his arms, or totally subverted, they justly conceive it would be unwarrantable and unworthy of the glory of their illustrious ancestors to look on with indifference, while the Greeks are thus reduced to slavery.—For these reasons, the senate and people of Athens (with due veneration to the gods and heroes, guardians of the Athenian city and territory, whose aid they now implore; and with due attention to the virtue of their ancestors, to whom the general liberty of Greece was ever dearer than the particular interest of their own state,) have resolved:

"That a fleet of two hundred vessels shall be sent to sea, (the admiral to cruise within the streights of Thermopylæ:) That the generals and commanders, both of horse and foot, shall march with their respective forces to Eleusis: That ambassadors shall be sent to the states of Greece; and particularly to the Thebans, as the present situation of Philip threatens their confines more immediately: That these ambassadors shall be instructed to exhort them, not to be terrified by Philip, but to exert themselves in defence of their own liberty, and that of Greece; to assure them, that the people of Athens, far from harbouring the least resentment, on account of any former differences which might have alienated their states from each other, are ready to support them with all their powers, their treasures, their forces, and their arms; well knowing that, to contend for sovereignty among themselves, is an honour to the Greeks; but to be commanded by a foreigner, or to suffer him to wrest from them their superiority, is unworthy of the Grecian dignity, and the glorious actions of their ancestors:—To assure them, that the Athenian people do not look on those of Thebes as aliens, but as kinsmen and countrymen; that the good offices conferred on Thebes, by their progenitors, are ever fresh in their memory, who restored the descendants of Hercules to their hereditary dominions, from which they had been expelled by the Peloponnesian, and, by force of arms, subdued all those who opposed themselves to that illustrious family; who kindly entertained Œdipus and his adherents, in the time of their calamity; and who have transmitted many other monuments of their affection and respect to Thebes:—That the people of Athens, therefore, will not, at this conjuncture, desert the cause of Thebes and Greece; but are ready to enter into engagements, defensive and offensive, with the Thebans, cemented and confirmed by a mutual liberty of intermarriage, and by the oaths of each party tendered and accepted with all due solemnity. The ambassadors chosen on this occasion are Demosthenes, Hyperides, Mnesithides, Democrates, and Callaeschrus."

Here was the foundation laid; here was the first establishment of our interest in Thebes. Hitherto, the traitors had been too successful; and all was animosity, aversion, and suspicion between the cities. But, by this decree, that danger, which hung lowering over our state, was in an instant dissipated like a vapour.—And surely it was the duty of an honest citizen, if he had any better measures to propose, to have declared them publicly, not to have cavilled now. For the counsellor and the sycophant are characters entirely different, in every particular; but in this are they more especially distinguished from each other, that the one fairly declares his opinion previous to the event; and makes himself accountable to those he hath influenced, to fortune, to the times, to the world: while the other is silent when he ought to speak; but when some melancholy accident hath happened, he dwells on this with the most invidious censure. That was the time (I repeat it) for a man sincerely attached to his country, and to truth. Yet, such is my confidence in the abundant merits of my cause, that if any man can, now, point out a better course, nay, if there be any course at all, but that which I pursued, I shall confess myself criminal; for if any more expedient conduct hath been now discovered, I allow that it ought not to have escaped me. But if there neither is, nor was, nor can be, such a conduct pointed out, no, not at this day, what was the part of your minister; was it not to choose the best of such measures as occurred; of such as were really in his power? And this I did (Æschines!) when the herald asked, in due form, 'Who chooses to address the people?' Not 'who will inveigh against things past?' Not 'who will answer for things to come?' In this juncture you kept your seat in the assembly without uttering one word.—I rose up and spoke.—Well, though you were then silent, yet, now, explain your sentiments. Say, what expedient was there, which I should have devised? What favourable juncture was lost to the state, by my means? What alliance, what scheme of conduct was there, to which I should have rather led my fellow-citizens? Not that the time once elapsed is ever made the subject of debate: for that time, no man ever suggests expedients. It is the coming or the present juncture which demands the offices of a counsellor. And in that juncture, when some of our misfortunes, it seems, were coming on, some were already present, consider my intention; do not point your malice at the event. The final issue of all human actions depends on God. Do not then impute it as my offence, that Philip was victorious in the battle. This is an event determined by God, not by me. Let it be proved that I did not take every precaution which human prudence could suggest; that I did not exert myself with integrity, with assiduity, with toil even greater than my strength; that the conduct I pursued was not noble, was not worthy of the state, was not necessary: let this be proved, and then accuse me. But, if a sudden clap of thunder, if a furious tempest, burst at once upon us, and laid prostrate not our state alone, but every state in Greece:—What then? Am I to be accused? With equal justice might the trader, who sends out his vessel equipped and furnished for a voyage, be deemed guilty of her wreck, when she had encountered a storm so violent, as to endamage, nay, to tear down, her tackle. He might plead thus, 'I was not pilot in the voyage.' Nor was I commander of your army; nor I master of Fortune. She it is who commands the world. And let this be duly weighed: if, when the Thebans engaged on our side, we were yet fated to this calamity; what were we to expect if they had not only been detached from us, but united with our enemy in compliance with all his urgent solicitations. If, when the armies fought at a 'distance of three days' march from Attica, such danger and consternation fell on this city, what if the defeat had happened in our own territory? Think ye that we could have stood? That we could have assembled here? That we could have breathed? The respite of one day (at least of two or three) is oftentimes of signal moment to the preservation of a people. In the other case—But I cannot bear to mention what we must have suffered, if this state had not been protected by the favour of some god, and the interposition of this alliance, the perpetual subject (Æschines!) of your clamorous malice.

All this particular discussion is addressed to you, ye Judges, and to those auditors who stand round the tribunal. As to this miscreant, he needs but one short and plain reply. If you, Æschines, were the only man among us who foresaw the issue; it was your duty to have foretold it to your countrymen: if you did not foresee it, you are as accountable for such ignorance as any other citizen. What better right then have you to urge this as a crime against me, than I to accuse you upon the same occasion? When, at this juncture, not to mention others, I approved myself so far a better citizen than you, as I was entirely devoted to what appeared the true interest of my country; not nicely weighing, not once considering my private danger; while you never proposed any better measures; else we had adopted these: nor, in the prosecution of these, were we assisted by any service of yours. No; the event discovered, that your conduct had been such as the basest, the most inveterate enemy to this state must have pursued. And observable indeed it is, that at the very time when Aristratus at Naxus, and Aristolaus at Thassus, equally the avowed foes of Athens, are harassing the Athenian partisans by prosecutions; here, Æschines hath brought his accusation against Demosthenes. But the man

who derives his consequence from the calamities of Greece, should rather meet his own punishment than stand up to prosecute another: the man whose interests are advanced by conjunctures most favourable to those of our public enemies, can never, surely, be a friend to our country. And, that this is your case, your life, your actions, the measures you have pursued, the measures you have declined, all demonstrate. Is there any thing effected, which promises advantage to the state? Æschines is mute. Are we crossed by an untoward accident? Æschines arises. Just as our old sprains and fractures again become sensible, when any malady hath attacked our bodies.

But since he hath insisted so much upon the event, I shall hazard a bold assertion. But, in the name of Heaven, let it not be deemed extravagant: let it be weighed with candour. I say then, that had we all known what fortune was to attend our efforts; had we all foreseen the final issue; had you foretold it, Æschines; had you bellowed out your terrible denunciations (you, whose voice was never heard;) yet, even in such a case, must this city have pursued the very same conduct, if she had retained a thought of glory, of her ancestors, or of future times. For, thus, she could only have been deemed unfortunate in her attempts: and misfortunes are the lot of all men, whenever it may please Heaven to inflict them. But if that state which once claimed the first rank in Greece had resigned this rank, in time of danger, she had incurred the censure of betraying the whole nation to the enemy.—If we had indeed given up those points without one blow, for which our fathers encountered every peril, who would not have spurned you with scorn? 'you, the author of such conduct,' not the state, or me? In the name of Heaven, say with what face could we have met those foreigners who sometimes visit us, if such scandalous supineness on our part had brought affairs to their present situation? If Philip had been chosen general of the Grecian army, and some other state had drawn the sword against this insidious nomination; and fought the battle, unassisted by the Athenians, that people, who in ancient times, never preferred inglorious security to honourable danger; what part of Greece, what part of the barbarian world, has not heard, that the Thebans, in their period of success; that the Lacedemonians, whose power was older and more extensive; that the king of Persia, would have cheerfully and joyfully consented that this state should enjoy her own dominions, together with an accession of territory ample as her wishes, upon this condition, that she should receive law, and suffer another state to preside in Greece? But, to Athenians, this was a condition unbecoming their descent, intolerable to their spirit, repugnant to their nature. Athens never was once known to live in a slavish, though a secure, obedience to unjust and arbitrary power. No: our whole history is one series of noble contests for pre-eminence: the whole period of our existence hath been spent in braving dangers, for the sake of glory and renown. And so highly do you esteem such conduct, so consonant to the Athenian character, that those of your ancestors who were most distinguished in the pursuit of it, are ever the most favourite objects of your praise. And with reason. For who can reflect without astonishment upon the magnanimity of those men, who resigned their lands, gave up their city, and embarked in their ships, to avoid the odious state of subjection? Who chose Themistocles, the adviser of this conduct, to command their forces; and, when Cryailus proposed that they should yield to the terms prescribed, stoned him to death? Nay, the public indignation was not yet allayed. Your very wives inflicted the same vengeance on his wife. For the Athenians of that day looked out for no speaker, no general, to procure them a state of prosperous slavery. They had the spirit to reject even life, unless they were allowed to enjoy that life in freedom. For it was a principle fixed deeply in every breast, that man was not born to his parents only, but to his country. And mark the distinction. He who regards himself as born only to his parents, waits in passive submission for the hour of his natural dissolution. He who considers that he is the child of his country also, is prepared to meet his fate freely, rather than behold that country reduced to vassalage: and thinks those insults and disgraces which he must meet, in a state enslaved, much more terrible than death. Should I then attempt to assert, that it was I who inspired you with sentiments worthy of your ancestors, I should meet the just resentment of every hearer. No: it is my point to show, that such sentiments are properly your own; that they were the sentiments of my country, long before my days. I claim but my share of merit, in having acted on such principles, in every part of my administration. He, then, who condemns every part of my administration, he who directs you to treat me with severity, as one who hath involved the state in terrors and dangers, while he labours to deprive me of present honour, robs you of the applause of all posterity. For if you now pronounce, that, as my public conduct hath not been right, Ctesiphon must stand condemned, it must be thought that you yourselves have acted wrong, not that you owe your present state to the caprice of fortune.—But it cannot be! No, my countrymen! it cannot be, that you have acted wrong, in encountering danger bravely, for the liberty and the safety of all Greece. No! by those generous souls of ancient times, who were exposed at Marathon! By those who stood arrayed at Platæa! By those who encountered the Persian fleet at Salamis, who fought at Artemisium! By all those illustrious sons of Athens, whose remains lie deposited in the public monuments! All of whom received the same honourable interment from their country: not those only who prevailed, not those only who were victorious.—And with reason. What

was the part of gallant men, they all performed! their success was such as the Supreme Director of the world dispensed to each.

—Well then, thou miscreant, thou abject scrivener; thou who, to rob me of the honours and the affections of these my countrymen, talkest of battles, of trophies, of brave deeds of old: and what are these, or any of these, to the present cause? Say, thou vile player, when I assumed the character of a public counsellor, and on an object so important as the natural pre-eminence of my country, with what principles should I have arisen to speak? Those of suggesting measures unworthy of my countrymen? Then must I have met that death I merited. And when the interests of the state come before you, your minds, my fellow-citizens, should be possessed with an extraordinary degree of elevation, beyond what is necessary in private causes. When these are to be decided, you have only to consider the ordinary transactions of the world, the tenor of your laws, and the nature of private facts. But in questions of state, you are to look up to your illustrious ancestors; and every judge is to suppose, that, with the symbols of his authority, he is also invested with the high character of his country. Thus, and thus only, shall he determine on such questions, in a manner worthy of these his ancestors.

But I have been so transported by mentioning the acts of your predecessors, that there are some decrees and some transactions that have escaped me. I return, then, to the points from whence I thus digressed. Upon our arrival at Thebes, we there found the ambassadors of Philip, those of the Thessalians, and the other confederates, all assembled; our friends in terror, his party elevated. That this is not asserted merely to serve my present purpose, I appeal to that letter which we, the ambassadors, instantly despatched on this occasion. Yet, so transcendent is the virulence of this man, that, if in any instance our designs have been effectual, he ascribes it to the juncture of affairs, not to me; in every instance where they have been defeated, he charges all to me, and to my evil genius. It seems, then, that I, the speaker and counsellor, can claim no share of merit in such advantages as have been gained by speaking and by counsel; but where our arms have been unsuccessful, where the conduct of a war hath been unfortunate, I am loaded with the whole blame. Can we conceive a temper more cruel, more execrable in its malice?—Read the letter.

The letter is here read.

The assembly was now convened. The deputies of Macedon were first admitted to an audience, as they appeared in the character of allies. They rose up and addressed themselves to the people: lavishing their praises upon Philip, urging many articles of accusation against you, and dwelling upon every act of opposition which you had ever made to Thebes. This was the sum of all; they called upon the Thebans to make the due return to the benefits conferred by Philip, and to inflict due vengeance for the injuries received from you: and for this they had their option, either to allow the Macedonian a free passage through their territory, or to unite with him in the invasion of Attica. It was clearly proved, as they affected to suppose, that if their counsels were embraced, the cattle, slaves, and all the wealth of Attica, must be transferred to Bœotia; but that our overtures tended to expose Bœotia to all the havoc of the war. To these they added many other particulars, all tending to the same purpose. And, now, I should esteem it my greatest happiness to lay before you the whole detail of what we urged in reply. But you, I fear, are too sensible, that these things are past, that the torrent hath since broken in, and, as it were, overwhelmed all our affairs; and therefore must think it useless and odious to speak of these things at all. I shall therefore confine myself to the resolutions we obtained, and the answer returned to you. Take them: read.

The Answer of the Thebans is here read.

In consequence of these their resolutions, they called you forth: they invited you in due form. You marched, you came to their support: and, with such affectionate confidence were you recived, (for I pass over the intermediate transactions,) that, while their army, both infantry and cavalry, were stationed without the walls, your forces were admitted into their city, were received into their houses, amidst their children, their wives, all that they held most dear. And thus, in one day, did the Thebans give three the most public and most honourable testimonies to your merit; one to your valour, another to your justice, and a third to your continence. For, by determining to unite their arms with yours, rather than to fight against you, they declared their sense of your superior valour, as well as the superior justice of your cause; and, by entrusting to your disposal what they and all mankind are most solicitous to protect, their children and their wives, they demonstrated an absolute reliance on your strict continence: and your conduct confirmed these their sentiments in every particular; for, from the moment that our army appeared within their walls, no man ever could complain of any one instance of your injurious demeanour; such purity of manners did you display. And, in the two first engagements, [1.] that of the river, and that fought in winter, you approved yourselves not blameless only, but worthy of admiration, in discipline, in judgment, in alacrity. Hence, other states were engaged in praises

of your conduct, ours in sacrifices and religious processions.—And here I would gladly ask Æschines this question, Whether, in the course of these events, when the city was one scene of unbounded joy and acclamation, he took his part in our religious rites, and shared in the general festivity; or shut himself in his chamber, grieved, afflicted,and provoked at the successes of his country? If he appeared, if he was then found among his fellow-citizens, what injustice, nay, what impiety, is this, when he had solemnly called Heaven to witness that he approved these measures, to desire that you should condemn them by your present sentence; you who, by your oath, have made as solemn an appeal to Heaven? If he did not appear, is not that man worthy of a thousand deaths, who looks with grief on those events which fill his countrymen with joy?—Read these decrees!

The Decrees relative to the Sacrifices are here read.

Thus were we, then, engaged in sacrificing to the gods; the Thebans, in acknowledging that we had been their deliverers. Thus, the people who had been reduced, by the machinations of my adversary and his faction, to the condition of seeking assistance, were raised, by my counsels, to that of granting it to others. And what the style was which Philip then adopted, what his confusion at these events, you may learn from his own letters sent to Peloponnesus. Take them: read: thus shall you see, that my perseverance, my journeys, my fatigues, as well as my various decrees, now the object of his malice, were by no means ineffectual. And permit me to observe, that this state afforded numbers of able and illustrious speakers before my time. Such were Callistratus, Aristophon, Cephalus, Thrasybulus, and a thousand others. And yet, of all these, not one ever devoted his whole powers, upon all occasions, to the service of his country. He who moved the decree, did not charge himself with the embassy; he who went ambassador, was not author of the decree. Each reserved to himself a respite from business, and, in case of accident, a resource. But I may be asked, 'What! are you so superior to other men in powers and confidence, that you can do all yourself?' I say not so. But such and so alarming was my sense of the danger then impending over us, that I thought it no time for private considerations, for entertaining any thought of personal security, for conceiving any better hopes than that all the powers of every citizen might possibly effect the necessary service. As to myself, I was persuaded, not perhaps on solid grounds,—yet I was persuaded, that no mover of decrees

---

[1.] And in the two first engagements. These, wherever fought, have been considered by historians as of too little consequence to be recorded. And the extrav agance of joy with which the accounts of them were received, strongly mark the levity of the Athenian character.

could frame more useful decrees than I; no agent in the execution of them could execute them more effectually; no ambassador could proceed on his embassy with greater vigour and integrity. And hence did I assume all these functions. Read Philip's letters.

The Letters are read.

To such condescension did I reduce this prince. Yes, Æschines, by me was he obliged to use such language: he, who, on all former occasions, treated this state with so much insolence and arrogance. And my fellow-citizens repaid these my services with the honour of a crown. You were present, yet acquiesced. Diondas, who traversed this grant, could not obtain a fifth of the suffrages. Read the decrees.

The Decrees are read.

Here are the decrees framed literally in the same terms with those which Aristonicus had before proposed, and that which Ctesiphon hath now moved; Decrees which Æschines hath neither impeached, nor united in the impeachment brought against their author. And surely, if this his present accusation be justly founded, he might have prosecuted Dememoles who proposed them, and Hyperides, with much more reason than Ctesiphon. And why? Because Ctesiphon can appeal to these men, and the decisions of your courts in their case. He can plead that Æschines never attempted to accuse them, though their decrees were conceived in the same terms with his. He can urge the illegality of commencing a prosecution on a case already decided. Not to mention other reasons. Whereas, in the former suit, the cause was to be supported only by its merits, without any previous considerations in its favour. But he could not then have pursued his present method. He could not have searched old chronicles, to support his malicious charge: he could not have ransacked our archives, for scraps of obsolete decrees, never once thought of, never once conceived as in any degree applicable to the present case: he could not have made up a plausible harangue, by confounding dates, and disguising facts, with all the arts of falsehood, instead of stating them fairly. No: he must have deduced all his arguments from truths recent, from facts well remembered; all lying, as it were, before you. Hence did he decline the immediate discussion of these transactions; but brings his charge now, after so long an interval: as if this were a contest in a school of rhetoric, not a real inquiry into public affairs. Yes; he must suppose that you are now to judge of speeches, not of political transactions. Then observe his sophistical craft. He tells you, that whatever opinions you had formed of us both, on coming hither they must be forgotten; that you are to judge of what appears on this examination, like men settling an account of money. You may have con-ceived that a balance is yet due; but when you find the accounts cleared, and that nothing remains, you must acquiesce. And here you may observe how dangerous it is to rely on any argument not founded on truth: for by this subtle similitude he hath confessed, that you came hither firmly persuaded that I have ever spoken for my country; he, for Philip. For he could not have attempted to alter your persuasion, unless you had been thus persuaded, with respect to each. And, that he is not justly warranted to demand such alteration, I shall now demonstrate; not by the help of figures, (for we are not counting money,) but by a short summary of my services, which I shall submit to you, my hearers, both as examiners and as vouchers of my account.

By my conduct, then, which he treats with such severity, the Thebans, instead of joining with the Macedonian in an invasion of our territory, as we all expected, united with us, and prevented that invasion. The war, instead of raging here in Attica, was confined to the district of Bœotia, at a distance of seventy stadia from the city. Our coast, instead of being exposed to all the rapine of the Eubœan corsairs, was preserved in tranquillity during the whole war. Instead of Philip's becoming master of the Hellespont, by the possession of Byzantium, the Byzantines joined with us, and turned their arms against him. Are we then to use figures and accounts in examining transactions, and shall these articles be erased from the account? Shall we not rather labour to perpetuate their remembrance?—I do not set it down as an additional article, that the cruelty which Philip was known to exercise toward those he had reduced, was all felt by other states, while we happily reaped all the fruit of that humaneness which he well knew how to assume, when some future schemes were to be advanced. I do not insist on this. —But one thing I shall assert with less reserve: That he who enters on a fair inquiry into the conduct of any minister, without descending to a malicious prosecution, must scorn the mean arts which you have practised, of inventing metaphors, and mimicking phrases and gestures. It essentially concerns the interests of Greece, no doubt, that I use this, and reject that, phrase; that I should move my arm this way, and not to that side. No; the fair inquirer would consider the state of facts: would examine what resources, what powers we possessed, when I first entered on affairs; what accessions I procured to these; and what were the circumstances of our enemies. If I had really weakened the powers of my country, such iniquitous conduct should be detected: if I had considerably increased them, your malice should not have pursued me. But as you have avoided this method, I shall adopt it. And to you, my hearers, I appeal for the truth of what I now deliver.

First, then, as to our powers at this juncture: we commanded but the islands: and not all of these; only the weakest of them. Neither Chios, nor Rhodes, nor Corcyra were then eurs. Of our finances, the amount was forty-five talents : and even this sum had been anticipated. Of infantry and cavalry, except those within our walls, we had not any : and what was the circumstance most alarming, and most favourable to our enemies, their artifices had been so effectual, that the adjacent states, Megara, Thebes, Euboea, were all inclined to hostilities, rather than an alliance with us. Such was the situation of our affairs. It cannot be denied ; it cannot be at all controverted. And now consider those of Philip, our antagonist. In the first place, his power over all his followers was absolute and uncontrolled ; the first great necessary article in war. Then, their arms were ever in their hands. Again, his finances were in the most flourishing condition. In all his motions, he consulted only with himself : he did not announce them by decrees ; he did not concert them in a public assembly ; he was not exposed to false accusers ; he was not to guard against impeachments ; he was not to submit his conduct to examination : but was in all things absolutely lord, leader, and governor. To this man was I opposed. It is but just that you consider my circumstances. What did I command ? Nothing. I had but the right of audience in our assemblies : a right which you granted to his hirelings equally with me. And, as often as they prevailed against my remonstrances, (and oftentimes did they thus prevail, on various pretences,) were you driven to resolutions highly favourable to the enemy. Loaded with all these difficulties, I yet brought over to your alliance the Euboeans, Achaeans, Corinthians, Thebans, Megareans, Leucadians, Corcyreans. And thus did we collect fifteen hundred foot and two thousand horse, exclusive of our own citizens. And thus were our finances enlarged, by as ample subsidies as I could raise.

If you insist on what contingents should strictly have been required from the Thebans, or from the Byzantines, or from the Euboeans ; if you talk of dividing the burden of the war in exact proportion ; I must, in the first place inform you, that, when the united fleet was drawn out to defend the interests of Greece, the whole number of ships amounted to three hundred ; and of these two hundred were supplied by Athens : nor did we think ourselves aggrieved ; nor did we prosecute those who had advised it ; nor did we discover any marks of discontent. That would have been shameful. No : we thanked the gods, that when all Greece was threatened with imminent danger, we were enabled to give twice as much assistance to the common cause, as any other state. And then—little is the public favour which your malicious invectives against me can gain. For why do you not now tell us what we should have done ? Were you not then in the city ? Were you not in the assembly ? Why did you not propose your scheme, if it suited the circumstances of affairs ? For here was the point to be considered ; what these circumstances admitted, not what our wishes might

suggest. Had we once rejected the alliance of any people, there was one ready to purchase them, to bid much higher for them, to receive them with open arms. And, if my conduct is now questioned, what if, by any exact and scrupulous demands, in my stipulations with the several states, they had withdrawn their forces, and united with our enemy ; and thus, Philip had been master of Euboea, Thebes, and Byzantium ? How busy would these impious men have then been, how violent in their clamours ! Must they not have cried out, that we had rejected these states ? That we had driven them from us, when they were courting our alliance ? That Philip was confirmed sovereign of the Hellespont by the Byzantines ? That the whole corn-trade of Greece was at his disposal ? That Thebes had enabled him to push the war to our very confines ? That it had fallen with all its weight on Attica ? That the sea was impassable, for that corsairs were perpetually issuing from Euboea ?— Should we not have heard all this, and more ? —A false accuser (my countrymen !) is a monster, a dangerous monster, querulous, and industrious in seeking pretences of complaint. And such is the very nature of this fox in human shape, a stranger to every thing good and liberal ; this theatrical ape, this strolling player, this blundering haranguer ! For, of what use is this your vehemence to the public ?—do you waste it on transactions long since past ?— Just as if a physician should visit his infirm and distempered patients, should never speak, never prescribe the means of expelling their disorders ; but when one of them had died, and the last offices were performing to his remains, to march after to the grave, and there pronounce with all solemnity, 'If this man had proceeded thus, and thus, he would not have died.' Infatuated wretch ! and dost thou vouchsafe to speak at last ?

As to the defeat, that incident in which you so exult ! (accursed wretch ! who should rather mourn for it.) Look through my whole conduct, and ye shall find nothing there that brought down this calamity upon my country. Let it be considered, that there is no one instance in which the ambassadors of Macedon ever prevailed against me, in any of those states where I appeared as the ambassador of Athens : not in Thessaly, nor in Ambracia, nor in Illyria, nor among the Thracian princes, nor in Byzantium ; in no one place ; no, nor in the last debate at Thebes. But, whatever was thus acquired by my superiority over the ambassadors of Philip, their master soon recovered by force of arms. And this is urged as my offence. My adversary, even at the very time that he affects to ridicule my weakness, is so shameless as to require, that I in my single person should conquer all the powers of the Macedonian, and conquer them by words. What else could I command ? I had no power over the life of any one citizen, over the fortune of our soldiers, or the conduct of our armies, for which thou art so absurd as to call me to account. In every particular where a minister is accountable, there let your scrutiny be strict and severe. I never shall decline it. And what are the duties of a minister? To watch the first rise of every incident, to forewarn his fellow-citizens. And this did I perform. To confine those evils within the narrowest bounds, which are natural and necessary to be encountered in every state; to restrain the fatal influence of irresolution, supineness, prejudice, and animosity; and, on the other hand, to dispose the minds of men to concord and unanimity, to rouse them to a vigorous defence of their just rights. All this did I perform: nor can an instance be produced, in which I proved deficient. If a man were asked, what were the means by which Philip effected most of his designs? the answer is obvious: It was by his armies, by his bribes, by corrupting those who were at the head of affairs. As to his armies, I neither commanded nor directed them. I am not therefore to account for any of their motions. As to his bribes, I rejected them. And in this I conquered Philip: for, as the purchaser conquers, when a man accepts his price, and sells himself; so, the man who will not be sold, who disdains to be corrupted, conquers the purchaser. Well, then! with respect to me, this state remains still unconquered.

Thus have I produced such instances of my conduct, as (not to mention many others) justly authorize this decree of Ctesiphon in my favour. And now I proceed to facts, well known to all who hear me. No sooner had the battle been decided, than the people, (and they had known and seen all my actions,) in the midst of public consternation and distress, when it could not be surprising if the multitude had made me feel some marks of their resentment, were directed by my counsels in every measures taken for the defence of the city. Whatever was done to guard against a siege, the disposition of our garrison, our works, the repair of our walls, the money to be raised for this purpose, all was determined by decrees framed by me. Then, when they were to appoint a commissioner for providing corn, the people elected me from their whole body. Again, when persons, bent on my destruction, had conspired against me; when they had commenced prosecutions, inquiries, impeachments, and I know not what, at first not in their own names, but by such agents as they thought best fitted to conceal the real authors; —yes, you all know, you all remember that, at the beginning of this period, I was every day exposed to some judicial process; nor was the despair of Sosicles, nor the malice of Philocrates, nor the madness of Diondas and Melanus, nor any other engine left untried for my destruction:—I say then, that, at the time when I was thus exposed to various assaults, next to the gods, my first and great defenders, I owed my deliverance to you, and all my countrymen. And justice required that you should support my cause; for it was the cause of truth, a cause which could never fail of due regard from judges bound by solemn oaths, and sensible of their sacred obligation. As you then gave sentence in my favour, on all occasions where I had been impeached, as my prosecutor could not obtain a fifth part of the voices, you, in effect, pronounced that my actions had been excellent; as I was acquitted upon every trial for an infringement of the laws, it was evident that my counsels and decrees had ever been consonant to law; and, as you ever passed and approved my accounts, you declared authentically, that I had transacted all your affairs with strict and uncorrupted integrity. In what terms, then, could Ctesiphon have described my conduct, agreeably to decency and justice? Was he not to use those which he found his country had employed, which the sworn judges had employed, which truth itself had warranted upon all occasions?—Yes! but I am told that it is the glory of Cephalus, that he never had occasion to be acquitted on a public trial. True! and it is his good fortune also. But where is the justice of regarding that man as a mere exceptionable character, who was oftentimes brought to trial, and as often was acquitted; never once condemned?—Yet let it be observed (Athenians!) that with respect to Æschines, I stand in the very same point of glory with Cephalus: for he never accused, never prosecuted me. Here, then, is a confession of your own, that I am a citizen of no less worth than Cephalus.

Among the various instances in which he hath displayed his absurdity and malice, that part of his harangue which contains his sentiments on Fortune, is not the least glaring. That a mortal should insult his fellow-mortal, on account of fortune, is, in my opinion, an absurdity the most extravagant. He, whose condition is most prosperous, whose fortune seems most favourable, knows not whether it is to remain unchanged even for a day. How then can he mention this subject? How can he urge it against any man as his reproach? But, since my adversary hath, on this occasion, as on many others, given a free scope to his insolence, hear what I shall offer upon the same subject; and judge whether it be not more consonant to truth, as well as to that moderation which becomes humanity.

As to the fortune of this state, I must pronounce it good. And this, I find, hath been the sentence, both of the Dodonæan Jove, and of the Pythian Apollo. As to that of individuals, such as all experience at this day, it is grievous and distressful. Look through all Greece, through all the barbarian world; and where can we find the man who doth not feel many calamities in this present juncture? But this I take to be the happiness of our fortune as a state, that we have pursued such measures as are most honourable; that we have been more prosperous than those states of Greece who vainly hoped to secure their own happiness by deserting us. That we have encountered difficulties, that events have not always corresponded with our wishes, in this we have but shared that common lot which other mortals have equally experienced. As to the fortune of an individual, mine, and that of any other, must be determined, I presume, by the particular incidents of our lives. Such are my sentiments upon this subject. And I think you must agree with me, that they are founded upon truth and equity. But my adversary declares, that my fortune hath been greater than that of the whole community. What! a poor and humble fortune, superior to one of excellence and elevation! How can this be? No, Æschines, if you are determined to examine into my fortune, compare it with your own: and if you find mine superior, let it be no longer the subject of your reproach. Let us trace this matter fully. And here, in the name of all the gods, let me not be censured, as betraying any indication of a low mind. No man can be more sensible than I, that he who insults poverty, and he who, because he hath been bred in affluence, assumes an air of pride and consequence, are equally devoid of understanding. But the virulence and restless malice of an inveterate adversary hath forced me upon this topic, where I shall study to confine myself within as strict bounds as the case can possibly admit.

Know then, Æschines, it was my fortune, when a youth, to be trained up in a liberal course of education, supplied in such a manner as to place me above the base temptations of poverty: when a man, to act suitably to such an education, to contribute, in my full proportion, to all the exigencies of the state; never to be wanting in any honourable conduct, either in private or in public life; but, on all occasions, to approve myself useful to my country, and to my friends. When I came into the administration of public affairs, I determined upon such a course of conduct, as frequently gained me the honour of a crown, both from this and other states of Greece. Nor, could you, my enemies, attempt to say that I had determined on a dishonourable course. Such hath been the fortune of my life: a subject on which I might enlarge: but I must restrain myself, lest I should give offence, by an affectation of importance.

Come, then, thou man of dignity, thou who spurnest at all others with contempt; examine thy own life; say, of what kind hath thy fortune been?—She placed thee, when a youth, in a state of abject poverty; an assistant to thy father in his school, employed in the menial services of preparing his ink, washing down his benches and sweeping his room; like a slave rather than the child of a citizen. When arrived at manhood we find thee dictating the forms of initiation to thy mother, assisting in her trade, every night employed with thy fawn skin and lustral bowls, purifying the noviciates, and modelling their little figures of clay and bran, then rousing them, and teaching them to pronounce "I have escaped the bad; I have found the better;" glorying in this noble accomplishment of howling out such jargon louder than the rest. And it is an honour we must allow him. For, as he pleads

with so much vehemence, ye may conclude that in his howlings he was equally piercing and clamorous. In the day-time, he led his noble Bacchanals though the highways, crowned with fennel and poplar, grasping his serpents, and waving them above his head, with his yell of *Evoe, Saboe!* then bounding, and roaring out *Hyes, Attes, Attes, Hyes!*—Leader!—Conductor!—Ivy-bearer!—Vanbearer! These were his felicitations from the old women: and his wages were tart, biscuit, and new-baked crusts. In such circumstances, surely we must congratulate him on his fortune.

When you had obtained your enrolment among our citizens, by what means I shall not mention, but when you had obtained it, you instantly chose out the most honourable of employments, that of under-scrivener and assistant to the lowest of our public officers. And, when you retired from this station, where you had been guilty of all those practices you charge on others, you were careful not to disgrace any of the past actions of your life. No, by the powers! You hired yourself to Simmichus and Socrates, those deep groaning tragedies, as they were called, and acted third characters. You pillaged the grounds of other men for figs, grapes, and olives, like a fruiterer: which cost you more blows than even your playing, which was in effect playing for your life; for there was an implacable, irreconcileable war declared between you and the spectators; whose stripes you felt so often and so severely, that you may well deride those as cowards who are unexperienced in such perils. But I shall not dwell on such particulars as may be imputed to his poverty. My objections shall be confined to his principles.—Such were the measures you adopted in your public conduct (for you at last conceived the bold design of engaging in affairs of state,) that, while your country prospered, you led a life of trepidation and dismay, expecting every moment the stroke due to those iniquities which stung your conscience: when your fellow-citizens were unfortunate, then were you distinguished by a peculiar confidence. And the man who assumes this confidence, when thousands of his countrymen have perished,—what should he justly suffer from those who are left alive?—And here I might produce many other particulars of his character. But I suppress them. For I am not to exhaust the odious subject of his scandalous actions. I am confined to those which it may not be indecent to repeat.

Take then the whole course of your life, Æschines, and of mine; compare them without heat or acrimony. You attended on your scholars: I was myself a scholar. You served in the initiations: I was initiated. You were a performer in the public entertainments: I was the director. You took notes of speeches: I was a speaker. You were an under-player: I was spectator. You failed in your part: I hissed you. Your public conduct was devoted to our enemies: mine to my country. I shall only add, that on this day I appear to be approved worthy of a crown : the question is not whether I have been merely blameless; this is a point confessed. You appear as false accuser: and the question is, whether you are ever to appear again in such a character? You are in danger of being effectually prevented, by feeling the consequences of a malicious prosecution.—The fortune of your life, then, hath been truly excellent; you see it. Mine hath been mean : and you have reason to reproach it.—Come then! hear me while I read the several attestations of those public offices which I have discharged. And, in return, do you repeat those verses which you spoiled in the delivery.

" Forth from the deep abyss, behold I come! And the dread portal of the dusky gloom."

And,

" Know then, howe'er reluctant, I must speak Those evils—"

O, may the gods inflict ' those evils' upon thee! May these thy countrymen inflict them to thy utter destruction! thou enemy to Athens, thou traitor, thou vile player! Read the attestations.

The attestations are read.

' Such hath been my public character. As to my private conduct, if you be not all satisfied that I have approved myself benevolent and humane; ever ready to assist those who needed; I shall be silent; I shall not plead; I shall not produce testimony of these points : no, nor of the numbers of my fellow-citizens I have redeemed from captivity; nor the sums I have contributed to portioning their daughters; nor of any like actions. For my principles are such as lead me naturally to suppose, that he who receives a benefit, must remember it for ever if he would approve his honesty; but that he who confers the benefit, should instantly forget it, unless he would betray a sordid and illiberal spirit. To remind men of his bounty, to make it the subject of his discourse, is very little different from a direct reproach : a fault which I am studious to avoid; and therefore shall proceed no farther ; content to acquiesce in your opinion of my actions, whatever this may be. But while I practise this reserve, with respect to my private life, indulge me in enlarging somewhat farther on my public conduct.

Of all the men beneath the sun, point out the single person (Æschines!) Greek or Barbarian, who hath not fallen under the power, first of Philip, and now of Alexander; and I submit; let every thing be imputed to my fortune (shall I call it ?) or if you please, my evil genius. But if numbers who never saw me, who never heard my voice, have laboured under a variety of the most afflicting calamities, I mean not only individuals, but whole states and nations; how much more consonant to truth and justice must it be to ascribe the whole to that common fate of mankind, that torrent of unhappy events which bore down upon us with an irresistible violence? But you turn your eyes from the real cause, and lay the entire blame on my administration; although you know, that, if not the whole, a part at least of your virulent abuse must thus fall upon your country, and chiefly upon yourself. Had I, when speaking in the assembly, been absolute and independent master of affairs, then your other speakers might call me to account. But if ye were ever present, if ye were all in general invited to propose your sentiments, if ye were all agreed that the measures then suggested were really the best; if you, Æschines, in particular, were thus persuaded (and it was no partial affection for me, that prompted you to give me up the hopes, the applause, the honours, which attended that course I then advised, but the superior force of truth, and your own utter inability to point out any more eligible course ;)—If this was the case, I say, is it not highly cruel and unjust to arraign those measures now, when you could not then propose any better? In all other cases, we find mankind in general perfectly agreed, and determining in every particular with exact precision. Hath a wilful injury been committed? It is followed with resentment and punishment. Hath a man erred unwillingly? He meets with pardon instead of punishment. Is there a man who hath neither willingly nor inadvertently offended; who hath devoted himself to what appeared the true interest of his country, but in some instances hath shared in the general disappointment? Justice requires, that, instead of reproaching and reviling such a man, we should condole with him. These points are all manifest; they need not the decision of laws; they are determined by nature, by the unwritten precepts of humanity. Mark then the extravagance of that cruelty and malice which Æschines hath discovered. The very events, which he himself quotes as so many instances of unhappy fortune, he would impute to me as crimes.

Add to all this, that, as if he himself had ever spoken the plain dictates of an honest and ingenuous mind, he directs you to guard against me, to be careful that I may not deceive you, that I may not practise my arts with too much success.—The vehement declaimer, the subtle impostor, the artful manager,—these are the appellations he bestows upon me. Thus hath he persuaded himself that the man who is first to charge his own qualities on others, must effectually impose upon his hearers; and that they can never once discover who he is that urges this charge.—But you are no strangers to his character, and must be sensible, I presume, that all this is much more applicable to him than me.—As to my own abilities in speaking (for I shall admit this charge, although experience hath convinced me, that what is called the power of eloquence depends for the most part upon the hearers, and that the characters of public speakers are determined by that degree of favour and attention which you vouchsafe to each;)—if long practice, I say, hath given me any proficiency in speaking, you have ever found it devoted to my country; not to her enemies, not to my private interest. His abilities, on the contrary, have not only been employed in pleading for our adversaries, but in malicious attacks upon those his fellow-citizens who have ever in any degree offended or obstructed him. The cause of justice, the cause of Athens, he hath never once supported. And surely the ingenuous and honest citizen never could expect that his private quarrels, his particular animosities, should be gratified by judges who are to determine for the public; never could be prompted by such motives to commence his prosecution. No; they are passions, which, if possible, never should find a place in his nature; at least should be restrained within the strictest bounds.—On what occasion then is the minister and public speaker to exert his vehemence? When the general welfare of the state is in danger; when his fellow-citizens are engaged in some contest with a foreign enemy. These are the proper occasions; for these are the proper subjects of a truly generous and faithful zeal. But never to have demanded justice against me, either in the name of his country, or of his own; never to have impeached any part of my public, or even of my private conduct: yet now, when I am to be crowned, when I am to receive public honours, to commence a prosecution, to exhaust his whole fund of virulence in the attack;—this surely is an indication of private pique, of an envious soul, of a depraved spirit; not of generous and honest principles. And, to point this attack not directly against me, but Ctesiphon, to make him the culprit, is surely the very consummation of all baseness.

When I consider that profusion of words which you have lavished on this prosecution, I am tempted to believe that you engaged in it to display the skilful management of your voice, not to bring me to justice. But it is not language, Æschines, it is not the tone of voice, which reflects honour upon a public speaker; but such a conformity with his fellow-citizens in sentiment and interest; that both his enemies and friends are the same with those of his country. He who is thus affected, he it is who must ever speak the genuine dictates of a truly loyal zeal. But the man who pays his adulation to those who threaten danger to the state, is not embarked in the same bottom with his countrymen, and therefore hath a different dependance for his security.——Mark me, Æschines, I ever determined to share the same fate with these our fellow-citizens. I had no separate interest, no private resource: and has this been your case? Impossible! Yours! who, when the battle was once decided, instantly repaired as ambassador to Philip, the author of all the calamities your country at that time experi-

enced; and this, when, on former occasions, you had declared loudly against engaging in any such commission; as all these citizens can testify.

—Whom are we to charge as the deceiver of the state? Is it not the man whose words are inconsistent with his actions? On whom do the maledictions fall, usually pronounced in our assemblies? Is it not on this man? Can we point out a more enormous instance of iniquity in any speaker, than this inconsistency between his words and actions? And in this have you been detected. Can you then presume to speak; to meet the looks of these citizens? Can you persuade yourself, that they are strangers to your character; all so profoundly sunk in sleep and oblivion, as to forget those harangues, in which, with horrid oaths and imprecations, you disclaimed all connexion with Philip? You called it an imputation forged by me, and urged from private pique, without the least regard to truth. And yet no sooner was the advice received of that fatal battle, than your declarations were forgotten, your connexion publicly avowed. You affected to declare, that you were engaged to this prince in the strictest bonds of friendship. Such was the title by which you sought to dignify your prostitution. Was the son of Glaucothea the minstrel, the intimate, or friend, or acquaintance of Philip? I profess myself unable to discover any just and reasonable ground for such pretensions. No: you were his hireling, indeed, bribed to betray the interest of Athens; and, although you have been so clearly detected in this traitorous correspondence; although you have not scrupled, when the battle was once decided, to give evidence of it against yourself; yet have you presumed to attack me with all your virulence; to reproach me with crimes, for which, of all mankind, I am least to be reproached.

Many noble and important schemes hath my country formed, and happily effected by my means: and, that these are retained in memory, take this proof, Æschines. When the people came to elect a person to make the funeral oration over the slain, immediately after the battle, they would not elect you, although you were proposed, although you are so eminent in speaking; they would not elect Demades, who had just concluded the peace, nor Hegemon, no, nor any other of your faction. They elected me. And when you and Pythocles rose up, (let Heaven bear witness, with what abandoned impudence!) when you charged me with the same crimes as now, when you pursued me with the same virulence and scurrility; all this served but to confirm the people in their resolution of electing me. You know too well the reason of this preference; yet hear it from me.—They were perfectly convinced, both of that faithful zeal and alacrity with which I had conducted their affairs, and of that iniquity which you and your party had discovered, by publicly avowing, at a time when your country was unfortunate, what you had denied with solemn oaths while her interests flourished. And it was a natural conclusion, that the men whom our public calamities imboldened to disclose their sentiments, had ever been our enemies, and now were our declared enemies. Besides, they rightly judged, that he who was to speak in praise of the deceased, to grace their noble actions, could not, in decency, be the man who had lived and conversed in strict connexion with those who had fought against them; that they who, at Macedon, had shared in the feast, and joined in the triumph over the misfortunes of Greece, with those by whose hands the slaughter had been committed, should not receive a mark of honour on their return to Athens. Nor did our fellow-citizens look for men who could act the part of mourners, but for one deeply and sincerely affected. And such sincerity they found in themselves and me; not the least degree of it in you. I was then appointed: you and your associates were rejected. Nor was this the determination of the people only; those parents also, and brethren of the deceased, who were appointed to attend the funeral rites, expressed the same sentiments. For, as they were to give the banquet, which, agreeably to ancient usage, was to be held at his house who had been most strictly connected with the deceased, they gave it at my house; and with reason; for, in point of kindred, each had his connexions with some among the slain, much nearer than mine; but with the whole body none was more intimately connected; for he, who was most concerned in their safety and success, must surely feel the deepest sorrow at their unhappy and unmerited misfortune ——Read the epitaph inscribed upon their monument by public authority. In this, Æschines, you will find a proof of your absurdity, your malice, your abandoned baseness.—Read!

The Epitaph.

1.

These, for their country's sacred cause, array'd
　In arms tremendous, sought the fatal plain:
Brav'd the proud foe with courage undismay'd,
　And greatly scorn'd dishonour's abject stain.

2.

Fair virtue led them to the arduous strife;
　Avenging terror menac'd in their eyes:
For freedom nobly prodigal of life,
　Death they propos'd their common glorious prize.

3.

For never to tyrannic vile domain
　Could they their generous necks ignobly bend,
Nor see Greece drag the odious servile chain,
　And mourn her ancient glories at an end.

4.

In the kind bosom of their parent-land,
　Ceas'd are their toils, and peaceful is their grave:—
So Jove decreed; (and Jove's supreme command
　Acts unresisted, to destroy, or save.)

5.

Chance to despise, and fortune to control,
　Doth to th' immortal gods alone pertain:
Their joys, unchang'd, in endless currents roll:
　But mortals combat with their fate in vain.

Æschines! hearest thou this? it pertains only to the gods to control fortune, and to command success. Here, the power of assuring victory is ascribed, not to the minister, but to Heaven. Why then, accursed wretch! hast thou so licentiously reproached me upon this head? Why hast thou denounced against me, what I entreat the just gods to discharge on thee and thy vile associates!

Of all the various instances of falsehood, in this his prosecution, one there is which most surprises me. In recalling the misfortunes of that fatal period to our minds, he hath felt no part of that sensibility, which bespeaks a zealous or an honest citizen. He never dropped one tear; never discovered the least tender emotion. No! his voice was elevated, he exulted, he strained and swelled, with all the triumph of a man who had convicted me of some notorious offence. But, in this, he hath given evidence against himself, that he is not affected by our public calamities in the same manner with his fellow-citizens. And surely the man who, like Æschines, affects an attachment to the laws and constitution, should approve his sincerity, if by no other means, at least by this, by feeling joy and sorrow on the same occasions with his countrymen; not take part with their enemies in his public conduct. And this part you have most evidently taken; you, who point at me as the cause of all; me, as the author of all our present difficulties.—But was it my administration, were they my instances which first taught my country to rise in defence of Greece? If you grant me this, if you make me the author of our vigorous opposition to that power which threatened the liberties of our nation, you do me greater honour than ever was conferred upon an Athenian. But it is an honour I cannot claim: I should injure my country: it is an honour, I well know, ye would not resign. And surely, if he had the least regard to justice, his private enmity to me never could have driven him to this base attempt to disgrace, to deny you, the most illustrious part of your character.

But why should I dwell on this, when there are so many more enormous instances of his baseness and falsehood?—He who accuses me of favouring Philip!—Heavens and earth! what would not this man assert? But let us, in the name of all the gods, attend to truth, to facts; let us lay aside all private animosity;—and who are really the men on whom we can fairly and justly lay the guilt of all misfortunes? The men who, in their several states, pursued his course (it is easy to point them out,) not those who acted like me: the men who, while the power of Philip was yet in its weak and infant state, when we frequently warned them, when we alarmed them with the danger, when we pointed out their best and safest course; yet sacrificed the interest of their country to their own infamous gain, deceived and corrupted the leading citizens in each state, until they had enslaved them all. Thus were the Thessalians treated by Daochus, Cineas, and Thrasydæas; the Arcadians, by Cersidas, Hieronymus, Eucalpidas: the Argians, by Myrtes, Telademus, Mnaseas; Elio, by Euxitheus, Cleotimus, Aristæchmus; Messene, by the sons of Philiades, that abomination of the gods, by Neon, and Thrasylochus; Sicyon, by Aristratus and Epichares; Corinth, by Dinarchus, Demaratus; Megara, by Elixus, Ptedorus, Perilaüs; Thebes, by Timolaüs, Theogiton, Anemætas; Eubœa, by Hipparchus, Clitarchus, Sosicrates, ——The whole day would be too short for the names only of the traitors. And these were the men who, in their several states, adopted the same measures which this man pursued at Athens. Wretches! flatterers! miscreants! tearing the vitals of their country, and tendering its liberties, with a wanton indifference, first to Philip, now to Alexander! confined to the objects of a sordid and infamous sensuality, as their only blessings! subverters of that freedom and independence which the Greeks of old regarded as the test and standard of true happiness!—Amidst all this shamefully avowed corruption, this confederacy, or (shall I call it by its true name?) this traitorous conspiracy against the liberty of Greece, my conduct preserved the reputation of this state unimpeached by the world; while my character (Athenians!) stood equally unimpeached by you. Do you ask me then on what merits I claim this honour? Hear my answer. When all the popular leaders through Greece had been taught by your example; and accepted the wages of corruption, from Philip first, and now from Alexander; no favorable moment was found to conquer my integrity; no insinuation of address, no magnificence of promises, no hopes, no fears, no favors, nothing could prevail upon me to resign the least part of what I deemed the just rights and interests of my country: nor when my counsels were demanded, was I ever known, like you and your associates to lean to that side, where a bribe had been, as it were, cast into the scale. No: my whole conduct was influenced by a spirit of rectitude, a spirit of justice and integrity; and engaged as I was in affairs of greater moment than any statesmen of my time, I administered them all with a most exact and uncorrupted faith.—These are the merits on which I claim this honour.

As to those public works so much the object of your ridicule, they undoubtedly demand a due share of honour and applause: but I rate them far beneath the great merits of my administration. It is not with stones nor bricks that I have fortified the city. It is not from works like these that I derive my reputation. Would you know my methods of fortifying? Examine, and you will find them, in the arms, the towns, the territories, the harbours, I have secured; the navies, the troops, the armies, I

have raised. These are the works by which I defended Attica, as far as human foresight could defend it; these are the fortifications I drew round our whole territory, and not the circuit of our harbour, or of our city only. In these acts of policy, in these provisions for a war, I never yielded to Philip. No; it was our generals and our confederate forces who yielded to fortune. Would you know the proofs of this? They are plain and evident. Consider: what was the part of a faithful citizen? of a prudent, an active, and an honest minister? Was he not to secure Eubœa, as our defence against all attacks by sea? Was he not to make Bœotia our barrier on the mid-land side? The cities bordering on Peloponnesus our bulwark, on that quarter? Was he not to attend with due precaution to the importation of corn, that this trade might be protected, through all its progress, up to our own harbour? Was he not to cover those districts which we commanded, by seasonable detachments, as the Proconesus, the Chersonesus, and Tenedos? to exert himself in the assembly for this purpose? while with equal zeal he laboured to gain others to our interest and alliance, as Byzantium, Abydos, and Eubœa? Was he not to cut off the best and most important resources of our enemies, and to supply those in which our country was defective?—And all this you gained by my counsels, and my administration. Such counsels and such an administration, as must appear, upon a fair and equitable view, the result of strict integrity; such as left no favourable juncture unimproved, through ignorance or treachery; such as ever had their due effect, as far as the judgment and abilities of one man could prove effectual. But, if some superior being, if the power of fortune, if the misconduct of generals, if the iniquity of our traitors, or if all these together broke in upon us, and at length involved us in one general devastation, how is Demosthenes to be blamed? Had there been a single man in each Grecian state, to act the same part which I supported in this city; nay, had but one such man been found in Thessaly, and one in Arcadia, actuated by my principles, not a single Greek, either beyond or on this side Thermopylæ, could have experienced the misfortunes of this day. All had then been free and independent, in perfect tranquillity, security, and happiness, uncontrolled, in their several communities, by any foreign power, and filled with gratitude to you and to your state, the authors of these blessings so extensive and so precious. And all this by my means.—To convince you that I have spoken much less than I could justify by facts, that, in this detail, I have studiously guarded against envy, take—read the lists of our confederates, as they were procured by my decrees.

The Lists—The Decrees—are here read.

These, and such as these, Æschines, are the actions which become a noble-minded honest citizen. Had they succeeded, heavens and earth! to what a pitch of glory must they have raised you, and with justice raised you! yet, unsuccessful as they proved, still they were attended with applause, and prevented the least impeachment of this state, or of her conduct. The whole blame was charged on fortune, which determined the event with such fatal cruelty. Thus, I say, is the faithful citizen to act; not to desert his country, not to hire himself to her enemies, and labour to improve their favourable exigencies, instead of those of his own state; not to malign his fellow-citizen, who, with a steady and persevering zeal, recommends and supports such measures as are worthy of his country; not to cherish malice and private animosity against him; not to live in that dishonest and insidious retirement which you have often chosen.—For there is, yes, there is a state of retirement, honest, and advantageous to the public. Such have you, my countrymen, frequently enjoyed in artless integrity. But his retirement is not of this kind. Far from it! he retires, that he may desert the public service when he pleases, (and he too often pleases to desert it.) Thus he lies watching the moment when you grow tired of a constant speaker, or when fortune hath traversed your designs, and involved you in some of those various misfortunes incident to humanity. This is his time. He at once becomes a speaker in the assembly: he rushes, like a sudden gust of wind, from his retreat: his voice is already exercised; his words and periods are prepared; he delivers them with force and volubility, but to no useful purpose, with no effect of any real importance.

They serve but to involve some fellow-citizen in distress; and, to his country, they are a disgrace.—But all this preparation, (Æschines!) all this anxiety of attention, if the genuine dictates of loyal zeal, of true patriot principles, must have produced fruits of real worth and excellence, of general emolument:—alliances, subsidies, extension of commerce, useful laws for our internal security, effectual defence against our foreign enemies. Such were the services which the late times required; such were the services which a man of real worth and excellence had various opportunities of performing. But in all these you never took a part; not the first, not the second, not the third, not the fourth, not the fifth nor sixth, no, not any part whatever; for it would have served your country. Say, what alliance did the state gain by your management? What additional forces? What regard or reverence? What embassy of yours? What instance of your ministerial conduct ever exalted the reputation of your country? What domestic interests, what national affairs, what concerns of foreign-

ers have prospered under your direction? What arms, what arsenals, what fortifications, what forces, what advantages of any kind have we received from you? What generous and public-spirited effects have either rich or poor experienced from your fortune? None.

—But, here he replies, 'Though I have not performed those services, I have been. well-disposed, and ready to perform them.'—How? When? Abandoned wretch! who, when the being of his country was at stake, when every speaker, who had ever appeared in the assembly, made some voluntary contribution to the state; when even Aristonicus gave up that money which he had saved to qualify him for public offices, [1.]—never appeared, never once contributed the smallest sum: and not from poverty: no, he had just received a bequest of five talents from his kinsman Philon; besides the two talents collected for his services in traversing the law relative to trierarchs.—But I am in danger of being led off from one point to another, so as to forget my subject.—I say then, that it was not from poverty that you refused your contribution, but from the fear of opposing their interests, who influenced all your public conduct. On what occasion, then, are you spirited and shining? When you are to speak against your country. Then are we struck with the brilliancy of your eloquence, the power of your memory, the excellence with which you act your part;—the excellence of a true dramatic Theocrines. [2.]

We have heard his encomiums on the great characters of former times: and they are worthy of them. Yet it is by no means just (Athenians!) to take advantage of your predilection to the deceased, and to draw the parallel between them and me who live amongst you. Who knows not that all men, while they yet live, must endure some share of envy, more or less? But the dead are not hated even by their enemies. And, if this be the usual and natural course of things, shall I be tried, shall I be judged by a comparison with my predecessors? No, Æschines, this would be neither just nor equitable. Compare me with yourself, with any, the very best, of your party, and our contemporaries. Consider, whether it be nobler and better for the state to make the benefits received from our ancestors, great and exalted as they are, beyond all expression great, a pretence for treating present benefactors with ingratitude and contempt; or to grant a due share of honour and regard to every man, who, at any time, approves his attachment to the public.—And yet, if I may hazard the assertion, the whole tenor of my conduct must appear, upon a fair inquiry, similar to that which

[1.] For public offices.] Such as that of general, trierarch, ambassador, and director of the theatre, which could not be discharged without advancing considerable sums.

[2.] Theocrines.] A man of notorious calumny. He had composed some pieces for the theatre, but soon exchanged this profession for that of an informer; in which his virulence and malice rendered his name proverbial. We learn from St. Jerome, that the Pagans frequently gave this name to the first Christians. Demosthenes adds an epithet to it, calculated to keep the original profession of his rival in view, to which he indeed is particularly attentive through his whole speech. *Tourreil.*

the famed characters of old times pursued; and founded on the same principles : while you have as exactly imitated the malicious accusers of these great men. For it is well known, that, in those times, men were found to malign all living excellence, and to lavish their insidious praises on the dead, with the same base artifice which you have practised.—You say, then, that I do not in the least resemble those great characters. And do you resemble them? Or your brother? Do any of the present speakers? I name none among them : I urge but this : let the living, thou man of candour, be compared with the living, and with those of the same department. Thus we judge, in every case, of poets, of dancers, of wrestlers. Philammon doth not depart from the Olympian games uncrowned, because he hath not equal powers with Glaucus, or Karistius, or any other wrestler of former times. No : as he approves himself superior to those who enter the lists with him, he receives his crown, and is proclaimed victor. So do you oppose me to the speakers of these times, to yourself, to any, take your most favourite character : still I assert my superiority. At that period, when the state was free to choose the measures best approved, when we were all invited to engage in the great contest of patriotism, then did I display the superior excellence of my counsels, then were affairs all conducted by my decrees, my laws, my embassies ; while not a man of your party ever appeared, unless to vent his insolence. But when we had once experienced this unmerited reverse of fortune ; when this became the place, not for patriot ministers, but for the slaves of power, for those who stood prepared to sell their country for a bribe, for those who could descend to certain [1.] prostituted compliments ; then, indeed, were you and your associates exalted ; then did you display your magnificence, your state, your splendour, your equipage, while I was depressed, I confess it : yet still superior to you all, in an affectionate attachment to my country.

There are two distinguishing qualities (Athenians!) which the virtuous citizen should ever possess, (I speak in general terms, as the least invidious method of doing justice to myself ;) a zeal for the honour and pre-eminence of the state, in his official conduct; on all occasions, and in all transactions, an affection for his country. This nature can bestow. Abilities and success depend upon another power. And in this affection you find me firm and invariable. Not the solemn demand of my person, not the vengeance of the Amphictyonic council which they denounced against me, not the terror of their threatenings, not the flattery of their promises, no, nor the fury of those accursed wretches whom they roused like wild beasts against me, could ever tear this affection from my breast. From first to last, I have uniformly pursued the just and virtuous course of conduct ; assertor of the honours, of the prerogatives, of the glory of my country; studious to support them, zealous to advance them, my whole being is devoted to this glorious cause. I was never known to march through the city, with a face of joy and exultation, at the success of a foreign power ; embracing and announcing the joyful tidings to those who, I supposed, would transmit it to the proper place. I was never known to receive the successes of my own country, with tremblings, with sighings, with eyes bending to the earth, like those impious men, who are the defamers of the state, as if by such conduct they were not defamers of themselves : who look abroad ; and, when a foreign potentate hath established his power on the calamities of Greece, applaud the event, and tell us we should take every means to perpetuate his power.

Hear me, ye immortal gods ! and let not these their desires be ratified in heaven ! Infuse a better spirit into these men ! inspire even their minds with pure sentiments ! This is my first prayer. Or, if their natures are not to be reformed; on them, on them only discharge your vengeance ! Pursue them even to destruction ! But, to us, display your goodness in a speedy deliverance from impending evils, and all the blessings of protection and tranquillity ! [2]

(1.) To certain, &c.] He alludes to the complimentary addresses sent to Alexander, which he insinuates were procured by Æschines and his party.

[2.] The event of this contest was such as might be expected from the superior abilities of Demosthenes. His rival was condemned, and involved in the consequences of a groundless and malicious prosecution. Unable to pay the penalty, he was obliged to submit to exile, and determined to take up his residence at Rhodes; where he opened a school of eloquence. Here he read to his hearers these two orations. His was received with approbation, that of Demosthenes with an extravagance of applause. 'And how must you have been affected,' said Æschines, with a generous acknowledgment of his rival's merit, 'had you heard him deliver it.'

It is said, that, as Æschines was retiring from the city, Demosthenes followed him, and obliged him to accept of a large present of money in his distress.

THE END.

Lightning Source UK Ltd.
Milton Keynes UK
UKHW010030231122
412679UK00005B/45